LESSONS FROM THE LEGE

BEYOND THE
X'S AND O'S

FEATURING
COACHING INSIGHTS
FROM

40

NAISMITH
HALL OF FAME COACHES

JERRY KRAUSE AND RALPH PIM

TRIUMPH
BOOKS

CHICAGO

COACHES CHOICE
P.O. BOX 1828
Monterey, CA 93942
www.coacheschoice.com

Library of Congress Control Number: 2004104662

Book Design: Diana Michelotti, Artistic Enterprises, Cary, North Carolina; Jeanne Hamilton
Diagrams and Production: Artistic Enterprises, Cary, North Carolina
Cover Design: Preston Pisellini

All logos contained herein are the trademarks and copyrights of the school or organization represented.

Cover photos courtesy of AP/Wide World Photos. Photos of coaches Auerbach, Blood, Cann, Carril, Case, Chaney, Daly, Diaz-Miguel, Gardner, Gomelsky, Hannum, Holman, Julian, Keogan, Krzyzewski, McGuire, Naismith, Nikolic, Ramsay, Rubini, Sachs, Summitt, Teague, Thompson, Wade, Wilkens, and Wootten are courtesy of the Naismith Memorial Basketball Hall of Fame. All other photographs provided by the Sports Information Departments of the college or university of the particular coach in the image.

Authors' note: In the early days of the game, "basket ball" was spelled as two words and occasionally appears as such in this book in articles that were written before "basketball" became one word.

This book is available in quantity at special discounts for your group or organization. For further information, contact:

Triumph Books
542 South Dearborn Street
Suite 750
Chicago, IL 60605
(312) 939-3330
Fax (312) 663-3557

Printed in U.S.A.

ISBN-13: 978-1-57243-726-5
ISBN-10: 1-57243-726-X

The Naismith Lessons from the Legends series is dedicated to:

The Zag players, coaches, and fans who have made
this part of my basketball life so very special.

— JERRY KRAUSE

My wife, Linda. You have brought peace and
happiness into my life. I love you with all my heart.

My parents, Lorin and Alice Pim.
Thank you for instilling in me the
principles that I try to live by everyday.

To Coach Jack Greynolds. You taught me very early in life
the value of teamwork and the importance of never giving up.
You are deeply missed, but I will carry the memories
and lessons forever.

— RALPH PIM

CONTENTS

Foreword by Jay Bilas . . . .*vi*

Acknowledgments . . . .*vii*

Preface . . . .*viii*

Diagram Legend 1

Allen, Dr. Forrest "Phog" 2
    Phog Allen's Recommendations for the Game of Basketball 6
    Inspirational Coaching 9

Auerbach, Arnold "Red" 10
    Winning Is a Matter of Execution 14

Berenson-Abbott, Senda 16
    Basket Ball for Women 20

Blood, Ernest A. 22
    Tips for Success 26

Bunn, John 28
    The Value of Basketball 32
    Dedication Address for the Naismith Basketball Hall of Fame 34
    Analysis of Basketball Technique 36

Cann, Howard 42
    Basketball—It's Now a Game of Speed and Conditioning 46

Carlson, H.C. "Doc" 48
    The Spiritual Side of Basketball 52

Carrill, Peter J. "Pete" 56
    Pete's Principles: The Princeton Way of Winning 60

Case, Everett 64
    Stand Up and Face the Issue 68

Chaney, John 70
    Winning Is an Attitude 74

Daly, Charles "Chuck" 76
    Winning in the NBA 80

Dean, Everett 82
    Coaching Philosophy 86
    Advice from a Master 88

Diaz-Miguel, Antonio 90
    Dreams Do Come True 95

Gaines, Clarence "Big House" 98
    What I Learned from Coaching 102

Gardner, James "Jack" 106
    Building a Championship Basketball Team 110
    Factors Determining Coaching Success 112

Gomelsky, Aleksandr 114
    Building the Big Player for the USSR 118

Hannum, Alexander "Alex" 122
    Coaching Thoughts 126

Hobson, Howard "Hobby" **128**
   The Shot Clock 132
   The Three-Point Shot 133

Holman, Nat **136**
   How We Can Save Basketball 140

Julian, Alvin F. "Doggy" **144**
   26 Winning Basketball Principles 148

Keogan, George **152**
   The Requisites of a Good Basketball Player 156

Knight, Bob **158**
   Basketball Cornerstones and Credos 162

Krzyzewski, Mike "Coach K" **166**
   The Core of Character 170
   Random Thoughts 172

McCracken, Branch **174**
   The Coach and His Players 178

McCutchan, Arad "Mac" **182**
   Jump Balls 186
   Coaching Thoughts 187

McGuire, Al **190**
   Basketball and Life 194

Naismith, James **198**
   The Origin of Basket Ball 202

Newton, Charles Martin "C.M." **206**
   Building a Basketball Program 210
   Motivating Younger Players 212

Nikolic, Aleksandar "Aza" **214**
   The Nikolic Method of Coaching 218

Ramsay, Jack **220**
   "Absolutes" in Basketball Coaching 224
   Communicate, Communicate, Communicate 226

Rubini, Cesare **228**
   Team Fundamentals 231

Sachs, Leonard "Lenny" **234**
   The Modern Adaptation of the Pro Game 238

Smith, Dean **240**
   Play Hard; Play Together; Play Smart .244
   Building Confidence 246

Summitt, Pat Head **248**
   The Definite Dozen System for Success 252

Teague, Bertha Frank **254**
   Basketball Success 258

Thompson, John Robert **260**
   Motivation and Communication 264

Wade, Lily Margaret **268**
   A Formula for Success 272

Wilkens, Leonard "Lenny" **278**
   Life Lessons 282

Wooden, John **286**
   The Pyramid of Success 290
   Reflective Thinking 293

Wootten, Morgan **296**
   Developing a Basketball Coaching Philosophy 300
   My Favorite Coaching Concepts 304

Lessons from the Legends Trivia Quiz **306**
About the Authors **308**

FOREWORD

In my time in and around the game of basketball, I have been truly fortunate to have spent time with and learned from some of the true giants of the game. Mike Krzyzewski, Bob Knight, and Pete Newell are not only among the finest coaches in basketball, but are also among its greatest teachers and guardians. I have witnessed their respect and admiration for the coaches who were the innovators and strategists of their day. To be a truly great teacher of the game, one must have an understanding of its evolution and an appreciation for its history and those who advanced it to where it is today. To best grasp where basketball is and should be going, it is vital to understand where it has been and how it got to this point.

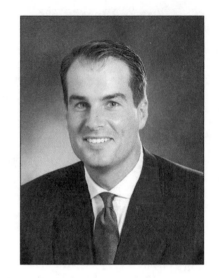

The future of the game lies with its teachers, the bona fide guardians of the game's history and its future. Two fine basketball minds and outstanding coaches, Jerry Krause and Ralph Pim, have provided us with a wonderful and comprehensive reference book full of lessons from these Hall of Fame coaches, who are distinguished teachers. This book should serve as a useful guide and fascinating retrospective of the thoughts and ideas of the game's finest minds. Jerry and Ralph have done the game a fine service with this work; basketball coaches and fans alike will enjoy and benefit from the Legends series.

—Jay Bilas
ESPN College Basketball Analyst

ACKNOWLEDGMENTS

From start to finish, this book has been a team effort. Our deepest thanks go to:

John Doleva, president and CEO, Matt Zeysing, historian and archivist, Dean O'Keefe, vice president, marketing and sales, and Alison Niemyski, marketing manager, of the Naismith Memorial Basketball Hall of Fame for their great support of our project and their warm hospitality on our many trips to Springfield, Massachusetts. Robin Jonathan Deutsch, Michael Brooslin, and Jim Mullins for their friendship and assistance in making the Hall of Fame library materials available to us.

The following Naismith Basketball Hall-of-Famers who were kind enough to speak with us on selected subjects over the years: Leon Barmore, Larry Brown, John Bunn, Lou Carnesecca, Ben Carnevale, John Chaney, Denny Crum, Clarence Gaines, Cliff Hagen, Marv Harshman, Bailey Howell, K.C. Jones, Bob Knight, Mike Krzyzewski, John Kundla, Bob Kurland, Earl Lloyd, Ed Macauley, Arad McCutchan, John McLendon, Ray Meyer, Ralph Miller, Pete Newell, C.M. Newton, Lute Olson, Bob Pettit, Arnie Risen, Adolph Rupp, Dolph Schayes, Bill Sharman, Dean Smith, Pat Summitt, Fred Taylor, Bob Wanzer, Stan Watts, John Wooden, Morgan Wootten, James Worthy, George Yardley, and Kay Yow.

Mr. Pedro Ferrandiz of the International Center of Documentation and Research of Basketball in Madrid, Spain. Hank Raymonds, Ellen Anderson, Les Robinson, Dave Gavitt, Mike Brey, Tom Crean, Dean Lockwood, Jay Carter Biggs, Michael Broeker, Denny Kuiper, Greg Fortier, Jeff Peterson, Rian Oliver, and Lisa Mispley for providing valuable information that helped in our research.

Colonel William Held, lieutenant Jude Frank, and lieutenant Andy Lalinde from the United States Military Academy at West Point for their assistance in translating the articles from the Hall of Fame international coaches. Penny Rose, Rita Hewell, and Nicole Blanchard for their hard work, dedication, and attention to detail.

Special thanks to a basketball scholar from the international basketball world, Dr. Damir Knjaz of the University of Zagreb, Croatia, for his perseverance in helping us locate technical materials from the legacies of the international Hall of Fame coaches.

Finally, sincere appreciation and gratitude to Diana Michelotti of Artistic Enterprises and Jim Peterson of Coaches Choice for their belief in and vision for the Legends series—to provide basketball fans and coaches with these valuable lessons about life and basketball.

**DR. JAMES NAISMITH,
INVENTOR OF BASKETBALL**

PREFACE

The information contained in this book is the authors' best attempt to preserve the legacy of the game's greatest coaches. We spent over three years researching the material that is included in the first edition of the three-volume set of *Lessons from the Legends*. We utilized many resources, including the archives at the Naismith Basketball Hall of Fame in Springfield, Massachusetts. We studied technical books written by Hall of Fame coaches, as well as articles that were published in professional journals. We read newspaper accounts describing their coaching exploits. In addition, we interviewed Hall of Fame coaches and their players, assistant coaches, family members, and school administrators in order to capture the essence of each coach's personal and professional legacy.

Every attempt was made to sort through all the material and present the most accurate description of each coach. We may not have succeeded in every case, but we are confidant that you will enjoy reading this one-of-a-kind book, which features the coaches who have made basketball the world's greatest game. We believe it truly is a close look at the "best from the best"—the best ideas about basketball and life from the best people in this area, the Naismith Basketball Hall of Fame inductees.

Now it is your turn to help the authors improve and "make the next game" better in our second edition. If you have additional information, articles/clinics (technical basketball or just human interest), stories, or pictures that could be included in this book, we encourage you to contact the authors so we can share them with our readers in future editions. Please send materials or contact the authors/publisher at:

The Basketball Legends Series
Attn: Krause/Pim
Coaches Choice
P.O. Box 1828
Monterey, CA 93942
1-888-229-5745
www.coacheschoice.com

DIAGRAM LEGEND	
PLAYERS	① ② ③ ④ ⑤
MOVE DIRECTION	———————➤
MOVE to SCREEN	————————┤
DRIBBLE	⌐〰〰〰〰〰➤
PASS DIRECTION	– – – – – – – ►
PASS SEQUENCE	**1st, 2nd, 3rd Pass**
COACH	**C**
DEFENDER POSITION	**X₁**
DEFENSIVE PLAYERS	**X₁, X₂, X₃, X₄, X₅**

To create consistency throughout the book, the diagrams illustrating the Lessons from the Legends by the Hall of Fame coaches have been redrawn using the diagram legend above.

LEGACY OF
Dr. Forrest "Phog" Allen

- Called the "Father of Basketball Coaching."

- Had a degree in osteopathy and was thought of as a "miracle man" for his ability to quickly rehabilitate athletes.

- Introduced a half-court man-to-man defense in 1952 that overplayed all passing lanes and revolutionized pressure defense.

- Known as a spellbinding motivator.

- Was charismatic, flamboyant, opinionated, and loved being on center stage.

- Became one of college sports' first entrepreneurs.

- Continually campaigned for a 12-foot basket.

DR. FORREST "PHOG" ALLEN

*"Give to the world the best you've got,
and the best will come back to you."*
—Phog Allen

BIOGRAPHY

Born: November 18, 1885 in Jamesport, Missouri

Died: September 16, 1974

Inducted into the Naismith Basketball Hall of Fame in 1959

Forrest "Phog" Allen played basketball at the University of Kansas from 1905 to 1907 for the game's founder Dr. James Naismith. Allen began his coaching career in 1908 and coached at Baker University, Haskell Institute, Warrensburg Teachers College, and the University of Kansas. His innovative tactics and coaching prowess earned him the title "The Father of Basketball Coaching." Allen coached forty-eight seasons and compiled a 746-264 won-lost record. At the time of his retirement, Allen was the all-time winningest coach in collegiate basketball history. During thirty-nine years at the University of Kansas, his teams won or shared thirty championships in the Missouri Valley, Big Seven, and Big Eight Conferences. Allen's 1952 squad won the NCAA championship and his 1923 and 1924 teams were selected national champions by the Helms Athletic Foundation. He was instrumental in establishing basketball as an Olympic sport and was an assistant coach for the USA team that won the gold medal in the 1952 Olympics. Allen was so proud of his Olympic experience that he requested to be buried in his Olympic USA sweatshirt. Allen was co-founder of the National Association of Basketball Coaches (NABC) and its first president. In 1953, the University of Kansas named their new basketball facility the Forrest C. Allen Field House.

Dr. Forrest "Phog" Allen...

"Phog" Allen and James Naismith became basketball's first "odd couple." Even though Allen played for Naismith at the University of Kansas and they became lifelong friends, their views on basketball were as different as night and day. Naismith invented basketball as a leisure-time activity to promote healthy exercise and saw no need for someone to coach the game. Allen, on the other hand, envisioned universities competing against each other for national championships, large arenas built to accommodate masses of spectators, and coaches who were compensated for their coaching ability. Allen reputedly was hired as one of the first basketball coaches in the country at nearby Baker University (KS). He rushed back to Lawrence and excitedly told the news to his mentor Naismith. Naismith was less than enthusiastic with his response, "You don't coach basketball, you just play basketball."

During the 1909 season, Allen accomplished a feat never replicated again in college basketball. He simultaneously coached three different teams to a combined 74-10 record. He directed Kansas to a 25-3 record; Baker University to a 22-2 mark; and the Haskell Institute Indian School to a 27-5 record.

To most everyone, Allen was known as "Phog." He acquired the nickname as a young man when he umpired baseball games and people thought his voice sounded like a foghorn. Allen's friends initially called him "Foghorn" and then a sportswriter shortened it to just "Phog." To keep his throat clear during basketball games, Allen kept

quart bottles filled with water under his seat and it wasn't uncommon for him to drink six quarts during the course of a contest. At practice or in the office, "Phog" devoured horehound candies which he bought in 60-pound boxes.

To his players, Allen was known as "Doc," as in doctor of osteopathy. He completed osteopathy school in 1912 and was often thought of as a "miracle man" for his ability to quickly rehabilitate athletes. The medical profession criticized Allen for treating just about anything less serious than a broken bone, but that did not keep well-known athletes such as Casey Stengel, Ralph Houk, George Halas, Johnny Mize, and Mickey Mantle from seeking his services. Allen spent hours pushing, pulling, rubbing, and cracking the bones of his athletes and the players were convinced his medical attention helped them win games. Rubdown tables were kept in "Phog's" office, home, and were taken with the team on every road trip.

Allen was one of college sports' first entrepreneurs. He marketed items such as basketball shoes, basketballs, rulebooks, and medicine kits that all carried the "Phog" Allen name. In 1939, Allen invented a game similar to basketball that he called Goal-Hi. It was played with one goal that was positioned in the center of a circular playing court. Unlike basketball, the goal was not attached to a backboard. The height of the goal was adjusted depending on the age of the participants (8 foot for elementary; 9 foot for junior high; and 10 foot for high school and college). A successful field goal was returned through a chute in one of three directions and shots made from beyond 15 feet counted three points. Allen thought it was perfect for women's teams and elementary-aged children because it was less strenuous than basketball. Unfortunately for

Allen, the manufacturer of Goal-Hi ceased production in 1942 due to World War II.

Allen's insights into the medical profession helped in the formation of his basketball philosophy. He believed natural body movements must be incorporated in the daily practice routine. Allen preached the importance of the "ape man" theory. "Look at any animal," explained Allen. "Whether attacking or defending, he assumes a semi-crouching position. How can you react otherwise? The knees are the only springs in the body. Bend them slightly and you can make any move rapidly required in basketball." (Padwe, 1970, p. 65)

Allen believed defense was the key to success. During the 1920s and 1930s, Allen made famous a defense that he called the "stratified transitional man-to-man defense with zone principles." It was a fancy name for a defense that combined man-to-man and zone techniques. In the 1950s, Allen implemented a pressure man-to-man defense that cut off the passing lanes and made it difficult to complete even the simplest of passes. It carried his Kansas Jayhawks to the 1952 national championship and stands as Allen's tactical legacy in college basketball. Legendary coach John Wooden referred to Allen's pressure defense as a defensive turning point in the game of basketball. His 1953 Kansas team, using this pressure defense, returned to the Final Four after graduating a majority of players. During the summer of 1953, future Hall of Fame coach Phil Woolpert visited the University of Kansas to study Allen's pressure defense. Woolpert incorporated many of Allen's defensive concepts and his San Francisco teams went on to win back-to-back national championships in 1955 and 1956.

One of Allen's greatest attributes was his motivational skill. He was charismatic and moved people to action through his inspirational speeches. After Kansas lost consecutive games during the 1951-52 season, Allen read to his team the story, Casey at the Bat. At the end of the story Allen wept and implied that the Jayhawks, like Casey, had hit bottom. With his players listening to every word, the master psychologist picked up and read the lesser-known sequel to the story called Casey's Revenge, written by Grantland Rice. Allen dramatically revealed how the washed-up Casey returned to the jeers of the fans to hit the game-winning home run. The poem ends, "He came through hell to scramble back—and prove a champ belongs." (Kerkoff, 1996, p. 171) Allen's speech made an impact on his players because Kansas came charging back to win not only the Big Seven Conference but also the NCAA championship.

Allen was sharp-tongued and opinionated. In his own words he stated, "I've never been accused of being a shrinking violet." (Kerkoff, 1996, p. xv) Unfortunately, his accomplishments were often overshadowed by his feisty and provocative comments. He battled with rival coaches, the AAU, the NCAA, and at times his own administration. Allen angrily declared that the letters AAU stood for "Asinine and Unfair" and the NCAA meant "Nationally Confused Athletic Absurdity." He further stated, "I like the AAU like a fellow likes garlic for dessert." (Kerkoff, 1996, p. 198)

In basketball's infancy, there probably was no more passionate a supporter than Forrest "Phog" Allen. In 1951, future Hall of Fame coach Hank Iba expressed his thoughts about Allen in these words, "Since 1908, no man has contributed as much to the game." (Kerkoff, 1996, p. 158)

Adolph Rupp, legendary Kentucky coach and Hall of Famer, proclaimed in 1974 that Allen was "the greatest basketball coach of all time." (Kerkoff, 1996, p. 204)

SOURCE

Allen, Forrest. Vertical Files, Archives. Naismith Memorial Basketball Hall of Fame. Springfield, MA.

Kerkhoff, Blair. (1996). *Phog Allen The Father of Basketball Coaching.*, Indianapolis: Masters Press.

Padwe, Sandy. (1970). *Basketball's Hall of Fame.* Englewood Cliffs, N.J.: Prentice-Hall, Inc.

Smith, Dean. (2002). *A Coach's Life: My 40 Years in College Basketball.* New York: Random House, Inc.

LESSONS FROM THIS LEGEND...

PHOG ALLEN'S RECOMMENDATIONS FOR THE GAME OF BASKETBALL

Authors' Note: This article was written by the authors.

"Phog" Allen was extremely creative and often assumed the role as a champion of innovation. He voiced his opinions outwardly and never missed an opportunity to verbally oppose those whom he thought were wrong. There was no institution sacred to Allen, and he was always embroiled in some type of controversy. He openly attacked the Eastern basketball establishment and was adamant regarding various rule changes.

Allen proposed establishing a commissioner's position that would oversee and rule college basketball. He believed this would free the basketball world from undesirable people and ideas. Allen, of course, had the perfect individual to assume this position: himself.

The game of basketball, as we know it today, would look a lot different if Allen had his wishes. Many of his recommendations were radical and controversial, but some of his visions proved to be quite perceptive.

RECOMMENDATIONS

1. RAISE THE HEIGHT OF THE BASKET TO 12-FOOT

- In Allen's opinion, basketball discriminated against shorter players, and he wanted the basket to be out of reach for all participants. Allen concluded that the increase in the number of tall players had reduced basketball to a "freakish demonstration" and severely handicapped athletes of a normal

height. Allen said, "We have seen tall players in many team lineups born without any special gift in basketball, but who were on the team solely on the accident of extreme height." He went on to describe tall players as "mezzanine peeping toms" and "goons." Later in his coaching career, Allen witnessed the domination of George Mikan and Bob Kurland and had a change of heart regarding tall players. In fact, two of his prize recruits were 6' 9" Clyde Lovellette (who still remains as the only player to lead the nation in scoring and simultaneously lead his team to the NCAA championship) and 7'1" "Wilt the Stilt" Chamberlain.

- By raising the basket two feet higher, goaltending by the defense would be eliminated.
  Authors' Note: Defensive goaltending was legal until 1944, and tall players would stand under the basket and swat away shots from the opponent.

- The 12-foot basket would reduce the number of personal fouls, because there would be less congestion in the free throw-lane area. Allen calculated that 80 percent of fouls occurred in the lane, as shorter players attempted to stop taller players from catching the ball or scoring close-in shots.
  Authors' Note: Until 1944, a player was allowed only four fouls.

- Allen believed the three-second lane violation would not be necessary because tall players would

move out from under the basket. Using a 12-foot basket, a higher-percentage shot would be an 8-foot bank shot, rather than a shot from under the basket.

- Allen also knew the 10-foot height of the goal was accidental. It was determined solely by the height of the balcony of the indoor running track in the YMCA where the first game was played.

- Allen never stopped campaigning for the 12-foot basket and proclaimed in 1949 that, "the 12-foot basket is coming as sure as death and taxes." (Kerkhoff, 1996, p. 99) One of Allen's greatest disappointments was the fact that he did not prove to the basketball world that he was right about the higher basket. Allen voiced his disappointment in these words, "Frankly, I wanted my last chance to show the Basketball Rules Committee that their continued stubbornness in holding to the rule for the ten-foot height was silly and ineffectual. Wilt Chamberlain can jump and reach 24 inches above a ten-foot basket. And I wanted him to throw that ball right through the Rules Committee's collective ten-foot teeth." (Kerkhoff, 1996, p. 190) Allen was forced to retire at the age of 70 and did not have the opportunity to coach Wilt Chamberlain. Chamberlain was a freshman at Kansas during Allen's last season, when NCAA rules did not allow freshmen to compete on the varsity level.

LESSONS FROM THIS LEGEND...

2. INCREASE THE POINT VALUE OF FIELD GOALS TO THREE POINTS

- With the 12-foot basket, Allen wanted field goals to be worth three points. He gave credit for this idea to the game's founder, Dr. James Naismith.

3. REINSTATE THE CENTER JUMP AFTER EVERY BASKET

- During almost all of the game's first fifty years, the ball was brought to center court for a jump ball after every score. Allen vehemently opposed the elimination of the center jump in 1937. Without the center jump, Allen believed the game had become too hectic. He accused the proponents of the new rule of trying to "hockey-ize basketball to attract attention." Allen went on to state, "by eliminating the center-jump, they made it the rambling, scrambling, fire-wagon game, sans finesse and adroit playing. They've substituted speed for skill in ballhandling." (Kerkhoff, 1996, p. 96)
- Allen believed the elimination of the center-jump put undue strain on both fans and players. "Spectators, I'm sure, wish for a few lulls in the game. Continuous excitement is too much for those with weak hearts. To put the ball in play immediately after a successful field goal would continue the strenuous exertion giving the players no moment for relaxation," stated Allen. (Kerkhoff, 1996, p. 96)
- Allen urged the Basketball Rules Committee to reinstate the center jump and install a jumping order (similar to a batting order in baseball) that dictated which players participated in the jump ball.

4. MODIFY THE WIDTH OF THE COURT

- Allen was convinced the width of the playing court should be enlarged because of the increasing physical size of the game's participants. He wanted the width of the court to be changed from 50 to 56 feet.

5. INCREASE THE FLOOR AREA BETWEEN THE BASKET AND THE END LINE

- Allen felt the area between the basket and baseline was too small. He believed the game would be improved if the basket were positioned further away from the end line. This would allow coaches opportunities to devise offensive strategies to attack the basket from behind (similar to lacrosse).
- Allen recommended the baskets be positioned six feet from the end line. *Authors' Note: In 1940, the Basketball Rules Committee moved the end line from two feet behind the basket to four feet.*

6. REPLACE RECTANGULAR BACKBOARDS WITH FAN-SHAPED BACKBOARDS

- Allen created a fan-shaped backboard with a white background that he felt was better than the rectangular glass backboard. He believed the white background improved shooting accuracy. Allen also felt the fan-shaped boards, because they were narrower and shorter, allowed opportunities for players positioned behind the basket to pass over the top to a teammate.
- The NCAA approved Allen's fan-shaped board in 1940 and schools were permitted to use either the rectangular or fan-shaped backboard. Unfortunately for Allen,

the fan-shaped backboards were short lived in college basketball. In 1946, the NCAA authorized the rectangular transparent backboard.

7. INSTALL BASK-O-LITES

- Allen endorsed a product called the Bask-O-Lite. When the ball went through the net, this device triggered a red light that indicated that the basket had been made. *Authors' Note: Allen's idea was similar to what is used in hockey today.*
- Allen thought this light helped spectators who were located in poor seats the opportunity to know when goals were scored.

8. CREATE A "SAFETY ZONE"

- Allen came up with the idea of implementing a "safety zone" in the game of basketball.
- The "safety zone" was a 16-foot radius around the basket. A player could dribble in and out of the "safety zone" but was only allowed to drive in and shoot the ball if no other teammate was in the "safety zone."

9. PAY COLLEGE ATHLETES

- Allen wanted players to be paid a monthly stipend of $80.
- The driving force behind Allen's desire to pay players was his fear of gambling ruining the game of basketball. He believed poor players were vulnerable to accepting bribes from gamblers and felt this could be stopped if colleges provided a monthly stipend to players.
- Allen repeatedly warned people about the rampant gambling in college basketball, but few listened. NCAA leaders even criticized Allen for creating unfavorable publicity. Allen adamantly stated, "Judge Landis is fighting

LESSONS FROM THIS LEGEND...

betting on professional baseball in his vigorous manner, but the colleges are doing nothing about it, and as sure as you live, the thing is going to crack wide open sometime when they lay bare a scandal that will rock the college world." (Kerkhoff, 1996, p. 142)

- Allen was correct in his accusations, and college basketball was rocked with a gambling scandal during the 1950-51 season. As many as 86 games had been fixed in 23 cities between 1947 and 1950, and seven colleges were cited as the greatest offenders.

Allen was angry that Kentucky and CCNY were allowed to keep their NCAA championships in spite of their convictions and called their teams the "Black Wildcats" and the "Black Beavers." Even after the 1951 scandal, Allen remained unconvinced that gambling had stopped and continued to speak out. His accusations again proved to be correct. In 1961, officials uncovered a point-shaving scandal that included 50 players from 27 colleges.

- To protect basketball from the perils of gambling, Allen wanted

all college games played on campus and removed from big city arenas and professional promoters. He even went as far as stating that the NCAA tournament should be kept out of lucrative places like New York and Kansas City.

SOURCE

Kerkhoff, Blair. (1996). *Phog Allen -The Father of Basketball Coachin*g. Indianapolis: Masters Press.

INSPIRATIONAL COACHING

By Forrest "Phog" Allen

Perfect technique, perfect teamwork, and good conditioning are not enough. The truly successful coach must go with his players beyond the field of conditioning and the field of play. He must get into their hearts; he must know their families; he must find what interests them most; he must study their temperaments, as he would study the temperaments of his own children. In short, he must "get under their skin," feel their sorrows, and help to find remedies for them.

SQUAD SIZE

I believe in squads of twenty-five to thirty players because of the morale factor. A large squad touches more lives and creates keener interest. It also gives the players who may later make the team valuable experience. It is spirit that pulls teams to victories, and large squads produce it. Large squads, like large families, grow to be more unselfish.

COACHING RESPONSIBILITIES

A coach should not only direct; he should lead. Where he leads, his players will follow. Never lose sight of your opportunity to direct by personal example. Always strive to be worthy of the trust imposed upon you. In the mind of a youngster, if a coach does a thing, it is all right, and if a star player does the same thing, it is better still.

Let no night be too dark; no task too forbidding; and no hour too late; for you who are out to make good, to go to your players if they need you. Willing and whole-hearted service will bring to you some of the best in compensations.

Give to the world the best you've got, and the best will come back to you. This is the truest message I can leave with you who are young in the game as coaches.

A coach must persevere during the difficult times. Your vision must abide in rough going; else you cannot be an inspiration to your players. You must, time and time again, meet the knocker and hand him a knockout wallop. Be always "up and at 'em" with the vision more in command. Your vision should be a sacrifice of love for your profession and for the opportunities that it offers in dealing with young people.

If your team is beaten some times, as all teams are, and you know that they have given their all, be kinder to them than usual. In every way, show them that you are satisfied. It is not only their victory that you want, it is their respect and their best.

Great athletes have great imaginations. Imagination and initiative and the will to win must be woven into the very fabric of the player's makeup to enable him to say "No" a thousand times to temptation before he can say "Yes" once to victory. It certainly is the coach's duty to outline a successful path of discipline for the ambitious and maturing boy and to assist him in adhering to its denials.

THE FRUITS OF COACHING

To have a former player tell you, years after you thought that he had forgotten, that he would have quit many times if there had not flashed through his mind some of the never-quit athletic "pep" talks of other years, brings more comfort than does gold. To have been able to aid a person in forcing his will to obey makes the game worthwhile

Education teaches us not to measure the best things in life by the standard of gold. At each commencement time, you will watch your players, people you have learned to love, graduate from your institution. Never get callused or indifferent toward the passing of these men who stand at this time, happy because life's mysterious adventure is before them, and sad because they are leaving something beautiful behind, for they are your concrete results. Out of these associations will grow deep and tender affections.

IN THE AFTER WHILE

After the fretfulness of these zestful years of desire to win and dread to lose have passed away, your experiences as a coach will mellow and will strengthen your philosophy; and you, a veteran in the game, will desire to drift into serene maturity with the fruits of these deep affections that you have fostered along the way, as your truest satisfaction. These will be your compensations. The rest, the games you have played—the games you have lost, and the games you have won—will be as a dream.

ESPRIT DE CORPS

Every worthy organization is built upon an ideal, and the perpetuity of that organization is largely determined by the sincerity with which the ideal is fostered. Likewise, great teams are built around both discipline and tradition.

It is altogether fitting that institutions of learning should keep alive the stories of their greatest games and the exceptional feats of skill and sacrifice of their own heroes. The spoken word and the printed page, the photographic halls of fame and the trophy rooms, all should be employed to preserve the valorous deeds of their passing athletic supermen.

To add dynamic punch to the athletic days ahead and to match the courage of today with that of yesterday, true athletic esprit de corps must march militantly forward with its long procession of sports warriors ever passing in review.

Esprit de corps means simply the spirit of the corps or group. It is French for an association of ideas with effective group effort. A dictionary may define the phrase as "loyalty to one's comrades; spirit of solidarity or group morale." However, with a more universal usage of the phrase this definition has become incomplete. For esprit de corps has come to mean a spirit of sympathy and pride and enthusiasm – a feeling of oneness that makes the whole corps akin. Like the slogan of "The Three Musketeers," athletic esprit de corps means "all for one and one for all."

SOURCE

Allen, Forrest C. (1924). *My Basketball Bible*. Kansas City: Smith-Grieves Co.

Allen, Forrest C. (1937). *Better Basketball*. New York: McGraw-Hill Book Co.

LEGACY OF
Arnold "Red" Auerbach

- Considered a basketball genius for his ability to maximize the talents of his players within a team-oriented system.

- Developed the concept of the "sixth man" in basketball.

- Directed the Boston Celtics to eight straight NBA championships.

- Possessed a keen ability to identify and acquire players that fit perfectly into his system.

- Established the fast break as the trademark of the Celtics.

- Smoked a "victory cigar" in the closing minutes of a game he knew he would win.

ARNOLD "RED" AUERBACH

*"Strategy is something anyone can learn.
But not all coaches take the time
to understand a man's personality."*
— Arnold "Red" Auerbach

BIOGRAPHY

Born: September 20, 1917 in Brooklyn, NY

Inducted into the Naismith Basketball Hall of Fame in 1969

Arnold "Red" Auerbach was the architect behind one of the most dominating franchises in professional sports history, the Boston Celtics. He was named head coach of the Celtics in 1950 and led Boston to ten Eastern Division titles in sixteen years. From 1959 to 1966, the Celtics won eight straight NBA championships, a streak unmatched in professional basketball history. Auerbach began his professional coaching career with the Washington Capitals in the BAA in 1946 and also coached the NBA's Tri-Cities Blackhawks before joining the Celtics. He compiled an overall coaching record of 1037-548 and was selected by the Professional Basketball Writers Association of America as the greatest coach in the history of the NBA. Auerbach coached eleven Hall of Famers and was the first coach in history to win 1,000 games. After retiring from coaching in 1966, Auerbach joined the Celtics' front office and was named NBA Executive of the Year in 1980.

Arnold "Red" Auerbach...

As a youngster growing up in the Williamsburg section of Brooklyn, "Red" Auerbach pressed pants in his father's dry-cleaning store and also earned nickels washing taxicabs. He spent hours playing basketball on the local playgrounds and the rooftop court of Public School 122. Auerbach realized that he lacked speed and quickness, but he was not going to let that stand in his way. "Hour after hour, I worked on starts and stops, ran sideways, and backwards, and drove at full speed from one end of the court to the other until I was ready to fall down," said Auerbach. "I kept at it day after day, every day, because I was convinced that through proper application, you could make your body do a good deal more than it seemed capable of doing. I took this conviction all through my career, both as an athlete and a coach." (Padwe, 1970, p. 137)

After earning All-Brooklyn honors at Eastern District H.S. in 1935, Auerbach attended Seth Low Junior College for one year and then received a scholarship to George Washington University. Upon arriving at GW, Auerbach found himself competing against five players for the one guard spot that was open. Auerbach had four fistfights during the first two weeks of practice and emerged as the starting guard. Under coach Bill Reinhart, Auerbach learned the running game that would later become the Celtic's trademark.

With Reinhart's recommendation, Auerbach received his first coaching position at prestigious St. Albans Prep in 1940. Auerbach earned his master's degree and then spent three years at Roosevelt H.S. in Washington D.C.

During World War II, Auerbach was an officer in the United States Navy and also served as an assistant basketball coach at the Norfolk Naval Base. In 1946, while still in the Navy, Auerbach learned that a group of men planned to form a professional basketball league. He convinced the owners of the Washington franchise that he knew a lot of outstanding players at the Norfolk Naval Base who would be interested in playing professionally after their military duty was over. Washington hired Auerbach and he led the Capitals to two division titles in 1947 and 1949.

Auerbach joined the Tri-Cities Blackhawks franchise in 1949, but quit when his owner did not consult him before trading the team's best player. The irate Auerbach returned home to Washington D.C. Walter Brown, the owner of the Boston Celtics, was desperately looking for a head coach and offered Auerbach a one-year contract at $10,000, which he accepted.

"Red" Auerbach built championship teams in Boston for over four decades. He won nine NBA championships as a head coach, six as a general manager, and one as the team president. The ingenious Auerbach had three unique talents that separated him from his counterparts. First, he possessed a keen ability to identify players who would fit perfectly into the Celtic's system. Second, he had a precise plan on how to acquire these players. Third, Auerbach was masterful at getting his players to play as a team.

Boston's acquisition of Bill Russell and Larry Bird were prime examples of Auerbach's organizational genius. Auerbach saw the potential in Russell and knew the shot-blocking, defensive star would transform the Celtics into a fast-breaking powerhouse. But the entire world knew about Russell's exploits at the 1956 Olympics and the University of San Francisco, where his team won fifty-five straight games and back-to-back NCAA championships. Boston had the 3rd pick in the NBA draft, behind Rochester and St. Louis, and it seemed highly unlikely that Russell would still be available at that time. Auerbach immediately went to work and did some swift maneuvering to get his coveted star. Rochester had a strong frontline and indicated they would select guard Sihugo Green, but Auerbach did not leave anything to chance. He offered Rochester the touring Ice Capades as additional incentive not to draft Russell. Auerbach then directed his attention to St. Louis and traded NBA All-Star Ed McCauley and hot prospect Cliff Hagen for the rights to the 2nd pick. The Celtics proceeded to sign Russell, and in his first year, he led the team in rebounding, and Boston won the NBA championship. The following year, Russell injured his ankle in the finals against St. Louis, and the Hawks won the 1958 title. That year was pivotal in NBA basketball, because it was the last time that anyone besides the Celtics would win the NBA championship for eight straight years.

Auerbach drafted Larry Bird in the 1978 draft, even though the Indiana State star was only a junior and would not join Boston for another year. Five NBA teams passed on drafting Bird in the first round. When Bird joined the Celtics, he made an immediate impact, averaging 21 points and 10 rebounds, and Boston doubled their number of wins from the previous year. The move that brought Bird to Boston was followed by the acquisition of Robert Parrish and Kevin McHale and formed what many people believe was the greatest frontline in the history of the NBA.

The dictatorial Auerbach ruled with an iron fist. He liked to describe himself as "a dictator with compassion."

(Padwe, 1970, p.136) Auerbach preached team play and demanded maximum effort from his players. He taught players not to accept losing. Bill Russell described Auerbach in these words, "Auerbach cannot stand the thought of losing. If you don't play to win, Auerbach has no place for you." (Deutsch, 1996, p. 21)

Auerbach didn't care who his starting five was because he believed victory belonged to the team and not the individual. He instilled team pride in his players. Russell answered the question "Why were the Celtics so good?" in these words, "Because we were a team. That's it. We were a team. We all recognized that and understood it, and when you do, you find that all the other things just aren't that important. My concern was the Celtics. Period. We were a family. Maybe I could have made another million dollars playing someplace else, but I couldn't imagine wanting to play anywhere else. I was a Celtic." (Auerbach, 1977, p. 178)

He was the first coach to develop the concept of the "sixth man." Every player had a well-defined role that fit into the team's mission. The 1960-61 squad, which may have been Boston's best under Auerbach, had six players average between 15 and 21 points per game, yet no Celtic was in the Top Ten in scoring in the NBA. An Auerbach-coached team never had a league-scoring champion.

Auerbach's approach to the game was simple. He believed in conditioning, discipline, and execution. His offense consisted of only six basic plays. The Celtics always displayed unselfishness and were known for their relentless fast break, precision plays, and pressure defense. "One thing I've learned is never allow a player to get himself in shape," said Auerbach. "They all have a tendency not to work hard enough, and they always tell you they're ready before they actually are. You have to have strong legs to play basketball, which is why so much of our training revolves around the running game." (Padwe, 1970, p. 141)

Auerbach was a firm believer that arm length was often as important as height in evaluating talent. To prove his theory, he used Jerry West as an example and stated that West had the arms of a man 6' 7". "West used those long arms to poke away your dribble," said Auerbach. "Jerry's talents are legendary. What people don't realize is that he was one of the greatest defensive guards ever." (Goldaper, 1996, p. 18)

An important attribute of Auerbach was his ability to listen. He insisted that players tell him exactly what was on their mind. Russell stated, "When I think of Red Auerbach and the leadership he provided, I think of someone who not only had a supreme basketball mind, but a great set of ears.

Red's greatest talent was that he was a listener who translated what he heard into effective action." (Russell, 2001, p. 63)

Another Auerbach trademark, which stirred the anger of opposing fans, coaches, and players, was his "victory cigar." Auerbach would often light a cigar on the bench in the closing minutes of a game he knew he would win. He claimed that it was not meant to "show-up" an opponent, but it did create hostility. Through the years, the cigar-lighting ceremony became a symbol that constantly reminded opposing teams that they were not good enough —they were second best. Paul Seymour of the Syracuse Nationals said it was his ambition in life to have Auerbach light up prematurely and lose, so that he could stuff the "victory cigar" in his face. The management in Cincinnati had a special promotional night and gave out 5,000 cigars in anticipation of a victory over the Celtics. Cincinnati fans were instructed to "light up" during the closing minutes to celebrate their victory. The promotion backfired as the Celtics soundly defeated their Royals.

Besides his love for cigars, Auerbach had a passion for Chinese food and was considered the league's leading expert on Chinese restaurants in NBA cities.

Hall of Fame coach Jack Ramsay named "Red" Auerbach the top NBA coach of all time because he was smart enough to see that Bill Russell would change the game, shrewd enough to acquire him, and knowledgeable enough to build the game around him.

SOURCE

Auerbach, Arnold. Vertical Files, Archives. Naismith Memorial Basketball Hall of Fame Library.

Auerbach, Arnold and Joe Fitzgerald. (1977). *Red Auerbach: An Autobiography*. New York: G.P. Putnam's Sons.

Deutsch, Robin Jonathan. (Ed.). (1996). *Basketball Hall of Fame Class of 1996 Yearbook*. Springfield, MA: Naismith Basketball Hall of Fame.

Goldaper, Sam. (1996). Fond Memories. *Basketball Hall of Fame Class of 1996 Yearbook*. Springfield, MA: Naismith Basketball Hall of Fame.

Padwe, Sandy. (1970). *Basketball's Hall of Fame*. Englewood Cliffs, NJ: Prentice-Hall, Inc.

Russell, Bill and David Falkner. (2001) *Russell Rules*. New York: Dutton Published by the Penguin Group.

WINNING IS A MATTER OF EXECUTION

By Arnold "Red" Auerbach

I've never been much for Xs and Os and all kinds of fancy diagrams. Throughout my whole career, I believed proper execution of the fundamentals separated the great teams from the also-rans.

KEEP IT SIMPLE

My basic rule was to keep things simple. I believed that if you had too many sets, too many plays, and too many intricacies in each play, then your execution suffered. It took too long to teach all of that, and the players often forgot half of what you taught them anyway. Always remember to keep things as simple as possible.

SET PLAYS

In all my years of coaching the Celtics, we had just six plays, six basic setups, and every one of them involved the center. The "1" and "3" had the center in a high post; the "2" had the center on a pick; the "4" made the center into a passer; the "5" involved him more indirectly; and the "6" play went directly to him. The big man was important either as a shooter, a passer, or a screener. I did this to keep my center motivated and to reward him for his rebounding efforts at the defensive end. We had options off of each setup, so altogether there were 26 plays that we could run. But the basic six setups never changed.

We never forced plays. I told my team that a play did not have to succeed to be good. A play might be good just because it opened up something else. A play was merely the beginning of a multitude of scoring opportunities. My players were trained to keep moving and never panic when a play did not work.

THE CELTIC FAST BREAK

The fast break was a trademark of my Celtic teams. It was ingrained into my players' thinking and became a way of life. Our fast break was built on fundamentals, discipline, hustle, conditioning, and teamwork.

We were ready to fast break at all times. Anytime our team got possession of the ball, whether it was on a rebound, interception, or whatever, we immediately knew where to head on the floor. We practiced for hours and hours on executing the fast break correctly.

The ideal fast break occurred after a rebound. Everyone knew exactly what to do when the shot was taken. Players were taught to turn toward the outside as they secured the rebound and always look before making a pass. We tried to get the outlet pass as far down the court as possible on the side.

When a player received the outlet pass, he immediately looked downcourt. If a teammate was open, he passed the ball ahead. The thumbs were pushed down to ensure that the ball was thrown straight. Many teams did not work on the fundamentals of passing, and they wasted fast-break opportunities because the passer curved the throw and the ball sailed out of bounds. I wanted the ball in the hands of my best ballhandler and the passer in the middle of the court as often as possible.

Opponents feared our fast break. They did not crash the offensive boards because they were afraid we would beat them downcourt. When a shot was taken, they stepped backwards, instead of forward.

NEVER REST ON DEFENSE

It was much harder to teach offense than defense. Defense meant hard work. You played defense until you got the ball. It was very basic. Your defensive responsibilities were not complete until you got the ball.

Defense depended on superior conditioning. Your opponent eventually tired and began to miss shots and make mistakes. Regardless of how powerful our players were offensively, there was no substitute for hard-nosed, tenacious defense.

I watched our opponents closely, and any time I saw someone loafing on defense, I instructed my players to run the ball right at him. A lot of big scorers gave false hustle on defense and tried to save their energy for the spectacular offensive moves they liked to make. When we identified someone like that, we embarrassed him. You can't rest on defense.

PLAY SMART

There were certain things I expected my ballplayers to know. During the last five minutes of play, they had to know the score, how many time-outs were left, and how many fouls had been called against the other team and against their own team, too. They must be aware of what's happening at all times on the court.

AVOID OVERCOACHING

In all of these areas—setting up plays, running a fast break, playing defense—the biggest danger is overcoaching. Don't give your players too much. Don't confuse them. This is a mistake so many young coaches make today. They want to be great strategic leaders and miss out on what is really important. The coach's biggest job is to get his players in shape and then keep them hustling. Forget the fanciness. I have said it a million times. You've got a basket over there. You've got to put this ball into that basket, and then stop the other team from putting it into the other basket. And the easier you do that, the better off you are. Keep it simple!

THE TEAM CONCEPT

I was very concerned with the way my players got along—both on and off the court. If they had a card game going, for instance, I'd make sure that nobody lost too much money. I never allowed anybody to be hurt by a teammate. That's very bad for a ball club. Another thing that I was determined to avoid was cliques. Cliques killed teams quicker than anything else.

Another area that was very important to the team concept was convincing players that their contributions were appreciated. I attempted to make everyone on the team feel special. Take the bench, for instance. On most teams, they made a big deal out of the "starting five." If you don't start, it implied you were not as good or as valuable as the next player. That was not the way that we looked at the men on our bench in Boston. Our "starting lineup" in the minds of every one of our players was the lineup that finished the game, not necessarily the one that began it. This was where my idea of the "sixth man" originated.

RESPECT AND DISCIPLINE

From the first day a player joined the Celtics, he understood that discipline was a very big thing with us. There were no loudmouths, no complainers, no dissenters, and no clubhouse lawyers on the Celtics.

When I told someone to do something, I wanted it done, and I wanted it done

immediately. We live in a democracy, and I believe in a democracy. But in sports, you can't have a democracy because there just isn't time for one. So my word was law. If you had to call a meeting every time you wanted to make a decision, you'd never get anything done.

I told my players right away that I wasn't worried about keeping them happy. There were twelve of them and only one of me, so it was a lot easier for them to study me and find ways to keep me happy than for me to satisfy all of them.

What is discipline? Discipline is just a proper response to authority. To be successful, there must be discipline. You can have discipline without having one hundred rules. The way to get it is through respect; respect for the team, respect for one another, and respect for the coach. I never expected my players to love me. I just wanted them to respect me and obey me. If you can win their respect, then everything else comes rather easily. But you don't get respect by demanding it. You can get obedience that way, but not respect. When I was thinking of a new play, I'd discuss it with them at practice. And when a player had a suggestion, I'd always listen and consider it. I never kidded myself into believing that I had all the answers. I respected their knowledge of the game. But when the time came to make a decision, everyone knew the responsibility belonged to me and nobody else.

COMMUNICATION

My strongest attribute as a coach was my ability to communicate with my players. That was the thing that I took the most pride in. There are a lot of coaches who know their Xs and Os, but what they say doesn't translate once the player gets out on the court. The player gets out there and forgets what was just said. I prided myself

in my ability to communicate, to get my point across in a way that the player could understand.

It is important to remember that you cannot communicate with all your players in the same way. You can't be successful doing that. It just doesn't work. There were some players who could take getting bawled out, and responded to that type of communication. I never bawled out Bob Cousy or K.C. Jones because that didn't work with them. I could scream at Bill Russell or Frank Ramsy. I could get on Tom Heinsohn and Jim Loscutoff. Those players were able to take that type of approach.

SUCCESS IN LIFE

I do not have one piece of advice for success in life. There are many factors involved in success. I'd say that you've got to be willing to pay the price, that's the most important thing. And then there are the other things that count – integrity, honesty, respect, and promptness. Those things are all part of the package.

SOURCE

Auerbach, Arnold and Joe Fitzgerald. (1977). *Red Auerbach: An Autobiography*. New York: G.P. Putnam's Sons.

McClellan, Michael D. (2002, August 28). *The Godfather*. Website: http: Celtic-Nation.com

LEGACY OF
Senda Berenson-Abbott

- Organized the first basketball game for women in 1893 at Smith College.

- Called the "Mother of Women's Basketball."

- Pioneered basketball rules development for women.

- Emphasized the development of the "whole person" through sport; stressed social, intellectual, emotional, and physical skills.

- Divided the court into three equal sections and restricted player movement to their assigned areas.

- Advocated the development of intramurals for women's basketball, rather than intercollegiate play.

SENDA BERENSON-ABBOTT

"The greatest emphasis should be made from the very beginning on the importance of team play. A team that plays harmoniously will be stronger than a team composed of brilliant individual players who are each eager to do all the playing."
— Senda Berenson

BIOGRAPHY

Born: March 19, 1868 in Vilna, Lithuania

Died: February 16, 1954

Inducted into the Naismith Basketball Hall of Fame in 1985

Senda Berenson became a teacher at Smith College and Northampton High School at the age of 23. She was initially selected to fill a vacant gymnastic instructor position as a three-week substitute. This short stint stretched into a nineteen-year physical education career at Smith College. Senda became a missionary, preaching the values of good health for all women at the college. Her basic program featured traditional Swedish gymnastics, but she introduced many sports as a supplement in the hope of developing character through participation. When notified about a new sport invented at the YMCA Training School, Berenson introduced it in her exercise classes. She modified the rules and adopted basketball as an intramural sport for the Smith College women in 1893. She thus became known as the "Mother of Women's Basketball," even though she never coached the sport. She organized the first game for women, which was held at Smith College on March 22, 1893. Berenson became editor of the *Women's Basketball Guide for Women* and eventually held the position as chair of the National Women's Basketball Committee. She died in 1954 and despite many efforts to induct her into the Hall of Fame over the years, she was denied acceptance until 1985.

Senda Berenson Abbott...

Senda Berenson was born in Lithuania in 1875, several years before the birth of basketball in 1891. She migrated to the Boston area with her family at the age of seven. Senda's early years were filled with invalidism on the one side and enthusiasm for many diversified interests, among them art, music, and literature, on the other side. The slightest amount of exercise had always been a painful experience for her. She even had to give up playing the piano because practicing made her back ache.

Berenson was encouraged by a friend to enroll in the Boston Normal School of Gymnastics, which featured the early form of physical education called Swedish Gymnastics. She thrived in the program and, even though immersed in the arts, became a lifelong devotee of health exercise and sports for women.

Senda began her teaching career at the age of 23 at Smith College. In her second year at the school, she was persuaded to substitute for the director of physical education. Thus began her career as a physical educator. Berenson was more than a teacher. She was a missionary, preaching the values of and showing the way to good health. Swedish Gymnastics was her Bible. She planned an effective program, required for freshmen and sophomores, which encompassed the Swedish system. As a supplement to the program, she introduced athletic activities such as basketball, fencing, field hockey, and volleyball. Berenson believed that participation in all physical activities should enhance the development of character.

Throughout her career, Senda believed in strict and careful supervision of all activities. A girl exercising on her own could easily use the wrong positions or methods, and thus, do herself more harm than good. She also believed in offering "the most for the most." Instead of spending her time with a small group of highly skilled girls, she preferred to include girls of all levels of skill in a variety of activities.

The origin of basketball for women is an unusual tale. In the spring of her first year at Smith College, Berenson read in *The Triangle*, a physical education magazine published by the YMCA Training School in Springfield, Massachusetts, about a new game called "Basket Ball". James Naismith invented the game as a physical activity for boys, but Berenson immediately saw the game as a possibility for girls. She traveled to Springfield College to watch the new game and meet with its inventor Dr. Naismith. Her instant appreciation of the possibilities of the game gave tremendous impetus to the development of basketball.

Berenson took the same concepts developed by Dr. Naismith and integrated them into her female classes. She adapted the game to meet the needs of her young women. Berenson stressed socialization and cooperation, rather than competition. On March 22, 1893, she organized the first game. It featured a contest between the Class of 1895 and the Class of 1896, and no males were allowed to attend. To Senda's surprise, nothing like it had ever happened before on the Smith College campus.

"We thought that just a few students would to watch, but the whole college with class colors and banners turned out, " said Berenson. "They filled the broad balcony, the early ones sitting on the edge dangling their legs. They stood along the walls. As I threw the ball for the beginning of the game, it struck the uplifted hand of the center player, the captain of the freshman team, in a particular way so that it put her shoulder joint out of place – a joint dislocated earlier but of which she had forgotten to tell us when she had her physical examination. The onlookers, already excited, became more so. We took the girl into the office and pulled the joint into place, another center took her place, and the game went on. Except for the fact that we had nine on a side, we played the men's rules. The cheering of the spectators was a high-pitched sound that had never been heard before. At times it was deafening."

The day after the first women's game, the local newspaper appeared with the flaming headline: "The Gladiators Appear, One Dying." The article gave a shocking description of the event and had many local residents wondering whether the founder of Smith College, Sophia Smith, had been wise to start a college in which young women might receive an education equal to that given to young men. It must be remembered that up to this time, women had never played anything that required teamwork. Unfortunately, they had little or no opportunities through sport to develop their sense of good sportsmanship, fair play, and teamwork.

Berenson misinterpreted Naismith's diagram showing three equal court sections, and she required players to stay in their assigned sections. Since vigorous exercise for women was frowned upon at the time, she permitted each team to have only three players per section (see Diagram 1.0). This misinterpretation resulted because Naismith's diagram had dotted lines to describe player positions at the start of the game.

The misinterpretation by Berenson, plus the Victorian notions for women at that time, seriously handicapped the development of competitive women's basketball until the early 1970s. Play in women's basketball was often described as "dull, uninspired, unathletic, and unartistic."

.....SCOUTING REPORT.....SCOUTING REPORT...

In the authors' opinions, the women's game was underdeveloped more for societal reasons than anything else, and a great deal of gratitude is owed to basketball pioneers such as Senda Berenson.

Senda organized the U.S. Women's Basketball Committee in 1905 for the purpose of modifying the rules to meet the needs of women and served as its chair until 1917. She edited the *Basket Ball Guide for Women* from 1901 to 1907. The purpose of the guide was to provide the same rules for everyone. Until 1899, so many different sets of rules were followed that it was difficult for one school to play another. A similar type of guide for men's basketball was not published until 1915.

She strongly believed the purpose of the game was to develop the "whole person." Berenson believed that basketball could enhance characteristics that were necessary to the modern woman, such as "self-reliance, quickness of mind, quickness of body, self-control, and the sacrifice of the individual to the team." She never let the girls forget that they were women, even during the most exciting basketball games. Senda insisted on: 1) no chewing gum; 2) tidy appearance; and 3) hair in ribbons and braids.

Berenson supported a strong intramural program. She disapproved of intercollegiate games and declined all invitations to play other colleges. She thought intercollegiate games were unnecessary and hinted of professionalism. "I do not believe in intercollegiate or interscholastic games," said Berenson. "The great desire to win and the hard grind of practice in order to develop a winning team often bring about nervous excitement, worry, sleeplessness, and all the evils of athletics. Mild competition is good and indeed necessary, and in most cases can be brought about through inter-class contests."

Berenson was also against men coaching women players. "Men are ignorant of woman's physiological organism and are interested only in developing a winning team and are apt to leave out all ethical and recreation elements of the game."

She emphasized the concept of play, rather than competition, and believed the aim of women's athletics was to promote both mental and physical health. To avoid the bad influences of competition, Berenson established the following rules: 1) no interschool games if possible; 2) no fees; 3) limited audience; and 4) a social event after the games for the players.

Senda wanted participation in basketball to be an educational experience. She often consulted with her students and used their suggestions to improve the way the game was played. Berenson also used her captains as student coaches – a revolutionary idea at the time.

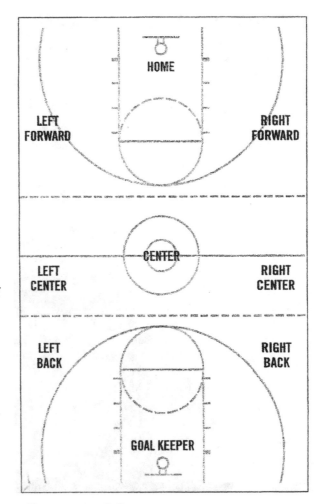

BERENSON 1.0

Senda Berenson deserves a very special place in the history of the game of basketball. Her decision to allow girls to play a "boy's game" opened the door for young women and changed the face of women's sports forever.

SOURCE

Benoit, Amy. (1999). Risk Taker. *Naismith Memorial Hall of Fame Enshrinement Program.*

Berenson, Senda. Vertical Files. Archives. Naismith Memorial Basketball Hall of Fame. Springfield, MA.

"Senda Berenson: Director of Physical Education at Smith College 1892-1911." (1941) In: "Pioneer Women in Physical Education." *Supplement to The Research Quarterly.* (American Association for Health, Physical Education, and Recreation)

Smith College Archives, Senda Berenson Papers, Series 6, Speeches, "Athletics for Women." URL: http://clio.fivecolleges.edu/smith/berenson/6speeches/

BASKET BALL FOR WOMEN

By
Senda Berenson

When one considers the natural growth of most of the standard games now in existence – hockey, football, and golf having a history of hundreds of years – one is the more astonished at the phenomenal popularity of basketball, a game which not even in its teens is yet, in this country at least, already is rivaling football among men and with no peer among women.

One of the strongest reasons for its remarkable success as a game for women is that it was introduced at the right psychological moment in the development of the American girl. It is not so long ago when the mere word athletics applied to women seemed rather out of place. It had a disagreeable sound and brought up visions of maidens in padded trousers and nose protectors.

Not long after this, however, educators began to appreciate the value of physical training. When its propaganda reached out so far and wide that even the masses came to realize that a certain amount of exercise was necessary, the necessity for games was also made manifest. And so games even for girls became more and more common. Anxious mothers who at first feared their daughters would become tomboys if they wore loose clothing and played games gradually allowed them to become more natural children. It began to be considered quite in keeping with womanly qualities to play tennis, to ride, and to swim. This very enthusiasm for game, this natural outlet of the play instinct created a need for a game that

should require teamwork, organization, and scientific development. And out of the clear sky came basketball.

Mr. Naismith, the originator of the game invented it merely, we are told, to quicken the interest in the daily gymnastic work of the Young Men's Christian Training School men. He probably had no ideas that women would even take it up. Yet a month after it came into existence in January, 1892, Smith College introduced it—as a dubious experiment, it must be confessed—and from that day to this, it has been by far the most popular game in that college. The different colleges and physical training schools took it up, and their pupils made it an integral part of their scheme of work. They thus introduced it into many schools. Society girls formed basketball clubs and today it is played by thousands of young women all over the country.

And well does it deserve this wide recognition. One needs only to try the game once to become an enthusiast. As has already been suggested, it came at the right moment in the history of the development of games for women. Women needed a game that exercises as many muscles as any one game can, and also develops endurance and physical courage. Basketball also develops enthusiasm and love of fun.

One of the strong arguments in the economic world against giving women as high salaries as men for similar work is that women are more prone to illness than men. They need, therefore, all the more to devel-

op health and endurance if they desire to become candidates for equal wages. Basketball provides splendid motor training. It develops simultaneous quickness of thought and action. And how valuable a training it is which enables a woman to meet an unexpected situation, perhaps of danger, with alacrity and success. Many of our young women are lazy, listless, and lack vitality. Let such a person try this game, she will forget herself at the first throw of the ball, will take deep draughts of air with unaccustomed exercise, and "tingle and throb with the joy of the game."

Above all, it provides the opportunity for teamwork. The willingness to surrender the individual to the common good will is brought out in her if she gives her best to it. The more she mixes in the affairs of the world, the more does she have to live by the unspoken code of the people she mingles with. Many a woman would get much more out of life if she could make herself realize that not all shafts are directed to her, that she is one individual among many, and that her world should go beyond her own pleasures and sorrows and opinions.

How much basketball has already done can be seen at our colleges for women today. The game has helped women redirect feelings into a natural channel. It has made the college woman stronger and thus saner. It has put a deeper meaning into the idea of loyalty—loyalty to one's team, class, and college.

One of the greatest moral benefits the game can offer is self-control. The girl who helps

LESSONS FROM THIS LEGEND...

the team is the one who is always on the alert, yet is outwardly calm and collected.

The greatest emphasis should be made from the very beginning on the importance of team play. A team that plays harmoniously, in which each member is in perfect sympathy and accord with the others, will be more stronger than a team composed of brilliant individual players who are each eager to do all the playing. A game in which all members of the team play for each other is exciting and delightful to watch.

The most important factor in bringing about clean basketball is the captain. The captain should be the one who embodies the noblest spirit of the team. She should be a leader; she should have tact, intelligence, and above all, character. Her spirit should be such that clean playing and good feeling can be the only outcome of her leadership. Coaches, too, should be chosen as much for the right spirit they will instill into the team as for their knowledge of the game.

Although the rules seem simple, they continually offer possibilities. Basketball gives so much pleasure from the first that it is very tempting to just get together and "play." One can get much fun and exercise out of a few games played in this manner, but it leads to roughness and bad playing in the end. It should be worked up scientifically from the start. Each player should learn how to throw and catch a ball with quickness and precision, at first without a guard and then under different ways of correct guarding. Few basketball girls are expert in both catching and throwing the ball. Each team should be made to realize the importance of practicing. One play or combination should be played over and over again until it becomes almost automatic.

One should remember that one's umpire is a self-sacrificing individual who has been chosen because of her sense of fairness and honesty. Someone will always have cause to find fault, but "put yourself in her place" and be generous. It is also well to remember to play according to the spirit of the game. Whatever is conducive to a clean game should be encouraged. Whatever is conducive to rough or underhanded playing is wrong, even if it is within the letter of the rules.

SOURCE

Smith College Archives, Senda Berenson Papers, Series 6, Speeches, "Basket Ball for Women."
URL: http://clio.fivecolleges.edu/smith/berenson/6speeches/

LEGACY OF
Ernest A. Blood

- Became the first coach in the history of the game.

- Possessed exceptional athletic skills and was the first coach to be able to demonstrate all fundamental skills.

- Led Passaic (NJ) H.S. to a 159-game winning streak, the longest in basketball history.

- Believed the best defense is a strong offense.

- Was the first high school coach elected to the Naismith Basketball Hall of Fame.

- Fostered sportsmanship and believed basketball participation prepared players for success in life.

- Entertained fans by wrestling a black bear during the halftime of games.

ERNEST A. BLOOD

"The best defense is a powerful offense."
—Ernest Blood

BIOGRAPHY

Born: October 4, 1872 in Manchester, NH

Died: February 5, 1955

Inducted into the Naismith Basketball Hall of Fame in 1960

Ernest "Prof" Blood coached fifty-one years and compiled a 1,268-165 record. He coached the Passaic (NJ) High School "Wonder Teams" to a 200-1 mark, squads whose 159-game winning streak is believed to be the longest in basketball history. Blood coached at Passaic from 1915 to 1924, and his teams won seven state championships. Prior to his arrival at Passaic, Blood coached at Potsdam State Normal and Training High School (now Potsdam State University). He also later coached at the United State Military Academy and Clarkson University. Blood finished his spectacular coaching career at St. Benedicts Prep (NJ), where he led his teams to five prep state championships. His teams used a full-court press and liked to fast break. Blood was one of the first coaches to emphasize conditioning, which he believed was a key ingredient to success.

Ernest Blood...

Ernest Blood started playing basketball in 1891, just a few months after the game's invention by Dr. James Naismith. He was twenty years old at the time and played his first game with a soccer ball and a peach basket for a goal. Blood said that he immediately took to the game of basketball "like a duck to water."

Blood never finished high school but attended the Harvard Summer School of Physical Education. This program, established by Dudley Sargent, was the most significant source of professional education in the United States during physical education's early years. He was called "Professor" Blood because of his extraordinary athletic abilities and expertise in the gymnasium.

Blood was a great promoter of the game of basketball. He introduced and taught the game to young people in public schools, recreation departments, and YMCAs. "Prof" Blood possessed a "noble, manly Christian spirit" and believed that participation in basketball "developed healthier and stronger bodies." (Hess, 2003) Blood's basketball philosophy fostered sportsmanship and prepared players for success in life. He stated, "I train boys for the game of life, not to win basketball games. To play one game clean is better than winning one hundred." (Hess, 2003)

Between 1896 and 1906, "Prof" was the physical director at several YMCAs and coached his basketball teams to a 310-24 record. He left the YMCA to coach at the Potsdam State Normal and Training High School, where his teams never lost to another high school team. Blood left Potsdam because the school temporarily closed its gymnasium for renovations, and he did not want to be away from the game that he loved. He accepted the Director of Physical Education position at Passaic (NJ) High School and immediately announced to prospective players that "anyone who plays for me must sacrifice individual honors for teamwork."

As a token of their appreciation, basketball supporters in Potsdam later gave Blood a black bear cub. Professor Blood named the bear Zep and kept him in his home in New Jersey along with a pet rattlesnake and an alligator.

Blood was a basketball visionary, and his teams featured a host of innovations that seemed radical for coaches of his era. Blood went against the widely accepted theory of the deliberate offense and preached that the best defense is a strong offense. He instructed all his players in the art of shooting and designed offensive plays that created high-percentage shooting opportunities. Blood's offense was predicated on passing, and he told his players "to shelve the old dribble game and pass, pass, pass." One of his key teaching phrases was "short pass, short shot."

Blood developed his players to take advantage of the center-jump rule, and his team once scored nine straight field goals with the ball never touching the floor. Bill Mokray, a team manager at Passaic, who later went on to compile *"Mokray's Averages,"* a statistical book used by the NBA, once estimated that Blood's teams controlled the ball 70 percent of the time. (Benagh, 1937, p. 48)

His teams used a full-court pressing defense and always looked to fast break. Blood was a proponent of conditioning, a revolutionary idea at the time, and believed it was a prerequisite for winning. Blood's innovative style of play did not become widely used by other coaches until the 1930s and 1940s. His system of play was founded on common sense and teamwork. Blood believed that "perfection in small things lead to the complete accomplishment of greater ones." (Hess, 2003)

The Passaic "Wonder Teams" of 1919 through 1925 were the greatest high school teams of all time. They set the national record of 159 consecutive victories and rolled over the state champions of New York and an all-star team from Philadelphia. During their streak, the "Wonders" were 11-0 against junior colleges, college freshmen, business colleges, and what were then called "normal schools." They averaged sixty points per game while allowing only twenty-one points per game during the winning streak. During a time when basketball was not known for its big scores, they scored 100 or more points twelve times and 70 or more points thirty-four times.

Transportation was a difficult problem for Blood's teams. The school didn't supply buses; both cars and roads in post-World War I days often proved to be unreliable. After one game, a bus driver denied permission for Blood's pet and team mascot, Zep, to board the bus. Blood simply took his black bear and walked five miles home. The next day the headline in the Passaic Daily News stated, "Prof. Blood Walks from Paterson to Passaic with Bear Behind." (Campbell, 1988, p. 167)

Blood often entertained the fans at halftime by wrestling his black bear and claimed that he never lost a single match.

Blood was an outstanding athlete and would suit up and practice with his players even when he was in his fifties. One day, John Roosma, who later won ten letters in four sports at the United States Military Academy at West Point and was inducted into the Naismith Basketball Hall of Fame, made 89 straight free throws. Not to be out-done, Blood, matched him shot for shot and eventually made 105 shots in a row. (Benagh, 1937, p. 49)

Blood coached basketball for almost his entire life. He ended his coaching career in 1949 and died six years later at the age of 83.

SOURCE

Blood, Ernest. Vertical Files, Archives. Naismith Memorial Basketball Hall of Fame Library.

Benagh, Jim. (1937). *Basketball: Startling Stories Behind the Records*. New York: Sterling Publishing Co.

Campbell, Nelson. (1988). *Grass Roots & Schoolyards*. Lexington, MA: The Stephen Greene Press.

Hess, Charles. (2003, April 5). Prof Blood and the Wonder Teams. Presentation at AAHPERD.

Hess, Charles (2003). *Prof Blood and The Wonder Teams*. Newark: Newark Abbey Press.

TIPS FOR SUCCESS

By Ernest Blood

Our high school's official mascot is a husky black bear named Zep. I wrestle Zep quite often, and I always win. I don't mean to say that the bear is not determined, quick-witted, or strong. He's all of those. If you promise not to tell Zep, I'll let you in on my secret. It's this: By watching Zep's eyes, I can tell exactly what he intends to do. Consequently, I am prepared, and I win.

Many times I have seen a basketball team that reminds me of Zep. It is alert, in fine condition, and eager. But somehow the opposing team solves its offense, detects each forthcoming play, and smothers it. The losing team, like Zep, fails because it can't cover up its offense. This is one of the points that I want to talk to you about.

I'm not going to be technical. I'm not going to describe specific plays. I'll simply pass on some tips, some basketball common sense, that more than thirty years' experience has taught me.

BASKETBALL IS A BUILDER OF MEN

Basketball is a great game. It is a builder of men. If I want a boy to turn out, I don't have to appeal to his love of the school; I point out what basketball is capable of doing for him. Nearly anyone can play basketball, and he need not stop when his high school days are over. I first played basketball the year it was invented, in 1891. Last year, I played against our first team in every practice.

In nearly every other sport, there is a comparatively long lapse to every instant of action. Football is an example of this kind of sport. Basketball keeps everybody on the move all the time. Basketball also permits quick, individual thinking on the part of every player, besides an endless variety of plays. I explain all this to prospective candidates for the team.

The success of my coaching methods naturally has given me a feeling of deep satisfaction, but there's a reward far greater than team victories. Life has no greater kick for me than to see a grinning young man return a few years after his graduation to tell me of his success, and they do come back, year after year. Hardly a season goes by without a dozen or more boys dropping in to see me.

The more I see of these returning young men, the more convinced I am of my coaching theories. For, after all, my primary interest is not basketball victories, but the development of clean, wholesome young men. Every boy who comes under my jurisdiction for basketball education understands from the start that the game is only a means to an end. He is taught that the activity and concentration on his job will give him an effective weapon against worldly obstacles. If any boy of mine cannot think beyond the game he is playing, he must leave the squad and find something else to do.

SQUAD SIZE

Last season I used twenty-six players. Once a boy turns out I make every effort to get him in the "big" games. We schedule doubleheaders early in the season, and I can play as many as twenty boys in a single evening. Many people maintain that large squads are harder to coach but I believe they're an economy in the long run. They eliminate dependence on a few individual stars and also lay the foundation for next season's team.

THE BEST DEFENSE IS A STRONG OFFENSE

Passaic High School has often been complimented on its splendid defense, but the secret of our defense is the lack of it. I believe that the best defense is a strong offense. I tell my players that basketball is a trinity—get the ball, keep the ball, and cage the ball (make the basket). The soul of the trinity is offense.

The success of all my basketball teams has been due chiefly to one thing: possession of the ball. All my offenses are built around constant possession of the ball. I have never paid much attention to defense, comparatively speaking.

Possession of the ball is useless, however, if the team's pass work is poor and spotty. The secret of good passing lies in sending the ball in the proper direction and to the proper teammate. My boys are trained to detect openings and opportunities at first glance. Their eyes have been trained to gauge a moving target so that a teammate in full motion will receive a perfect pass. Accurate passes create greater opportunities for scoring.

THREE-IN-ONE MACHINE

We must have a well-oiled, three-in-one machine. I impress on my players these three things. First, we must block and intercept enemy passes and thereby capture the ball. Second, we must pierce any kind of defense that our enemy puts up. Third, we must score. Every player must learn how to shoot effectively. It's no use to get the ball if you can't put it through the hoop. Shoot in practice as though the game depended on every shot. Every miss is a personal defeat, and it ought to hurt you. You've got to score points to win. That's where the appeal of the game lies from the spectators' standpoint. They want to see action and as much of it as possible. The best defensive tactics to use, according to my way of thinking, is to go after the ball.

Now and then a team comes up against us with the avowed intention of playing a defensive game. This is a bad attitude; it amounts to a quitter's attitude. Instead of two forwards, we in effect have five. We are able to devote all our attention to shooting. Our guards play an offensive defense; they press the opposition forwards so strongly that we are constantly in possession of the ball. Our opponents get little or no chance at our basket; they are too busy following us around. Consequently, we win by a lopsided score. The team that deliberately chooses a defensive game severely handicaps itself and at the same time lowers its own scoring effectiveness.

TEAMWORK IS TEAM UNSELFISHNESS

Anyone would guess that a team that has won ninety consecutive games, as Passaic High has, must have developed excellent teamwork. We try to subordinate individual play to the play of the team as a whole. Teamwork is nothing more or less than team unselfishness, curbing of one's desire to shine individually. Therefore, it's an important lesson for every player to learn.

Our large-squad system encourages unselfishness. We are constantly making changes to develop new material and speed up the offense. The player who wants to "hog the ball" soon finds himself a misfit. True teamwork requires each player to understand his teammates' style of play and to work with them so as to help them play their strongest game.

LEARN YOUR OPPONENTS' STYLE OF PLAY

Now let's think back to our friend Zep and his style of wrestling. The more you learn about your opponents' style of play, the easier it is to stop. Conversely, the easier your

plays are to solve, the nearer the opposition is to victory. It's ridiculously simple, yet how many games Passaic has won because of it!

Nearly every opponent has used the three-lane crisscross offense, or variations of it that we quickly solved. The "lanes" are imaginary paths down the center and each side of the basketball court. To execute the three-lane crisscross, three players invade the opposition territory, passing the ball back and forth between them. Naturally, when we defend against this play, we block or intercept the ball before it has gone very far.

Passaic, on the other hand, avoids cut-and-dried plays. We do not confine our plays to specific lanes or spots. Try and go where your opponents don't want you and try to draw your opponents where you want them. That's our working plan.

TIMING

Timing is the keystone of a strong offense. As in the case of the automobile, smooth running and maximum power are impossible without it. If one player is too fast, there is a backfire; if he is too slow, the play is spoiled. If all players are moving at once, timing is likely to be bad. A quick starting, fast-moving team with some of its players at a standstill, however, is the most formidable of all. A moving player is easy to follow. A standing and starting player, on the other hand, can't be closely checked. Remember that all plays are bad plays unless correctly timed.

STUDY THE GAME

I believe a key to success, whether you are a player, coach, or spectator, is to learn new things about basketball every season.

SOURCE

Benagh, Jim. (1937). *Basketball: Startling Stories Behind the Records*. New York: Sterling Publishing Co.

Blood, Ernest A. (1931, November 25). How I Teach Basketball. *Street & Smith's Sport Story Magazine*.

Blood, Ernest A. (1923, January). Tips for Victory in Basketball. *The American Boy*.

LEGACY OF
John Bunn

- Was the driving force behind the development of the Naismith Memorial Basketball Hall of Fame.

- Applied the laws of physics to sports in his landmark book, *Scientific Principles of Coaching*.

- Conducted clinics throughout the world and was dubbed the "American Ambassador of Basketball."

- His Stanford team, with Hank Luisetti, was best known for making the one-handed shot a powerful offensive weapon.

- Led Stanford to the 1937 Helms Foundation National Championship.

- Played for "Phog" Allen and was the first athlete to win 10 letters at the University of Kansas.

JOHN BUNN

"A coach should change positions every ten years—
good for them, their family, and the school."
—John Bunn

BIOGRAPHY

Born: September 26, 1898 in Wellston, Ohio

Died: August 13, 1979

Inducted into the Naismith Basketball Hall of Fame in 1964

John Bunn was the first athlete to win 10 letters at the University of Kansas. He graduated in 1921 with a degree in Mechanical Engineering and served as an assistant coach for "Phog" Allen for nine years. In 1930, Bunn became the head coach at Stanford and led the Cardinal to national prominence. Stanford won the 1937 Helms Foundation National Championship. In 1938, Bunn was appointed Professor of Physical Education and Dean of Men at Stanford. During World War II, Bunn took an extended leave of absence to establish facilities and programs for the U.S. Armed Forces in Europe. He was the basketball coach and athletic director at Springfield College from 1946 to 1956 and concluded his teaching and coaching career at Colorado State College (now called the University of Northern Colorado) in 1963. Bunn served as editor of the *NCAA Basketball Guide* and authored six books on coaching, officiating, and team basketball. He conducted clinics throughout the world and was given the title "American Ambassador of Basketball." In 1948, Bunn urged the NABC to form a committee to study the idea of a basketball hall of fame. For his efforts, the Hall of Fame annually presents the John Bunn Award, the highest single honor the Basketball Hall of Fame awards outside of actual Enshrinement.

John Bunn...

The basketball world was blessed when little Johnny Bunn grew up and went to school in the Great Plains town of Humboldt, Kansas. There, he would star as an athlete in four sports and be recruited by and attend the University of Kansas. That coincidence would put Bunn squarely in the path of the legendary "Father of Basketball Coaching" Phog Allen, the first college basketball coach, and even under the tutelage of basketball's inventor, Dr. James Naismith. Thus, John Bunn would form a part of the main branch of the basketball family tree with a direct line to the sports roots of Naismith and Allen, plus his later employment at Springfield College (MA), the birthplace of basketball. This really set the stage for the person who would become a legendary contributor to basketball's development.

What a contributor he was! John Bunn made these lifelong contributions:

Athlete—12 high school letters and 10 college letters, considered the best ever in the state of Kansas (along with Ralph Miller of Chanute, Kansas). His record of 10 letter awards has never been topped.

Engineer—He earned a B.S. and M.S. in Engineering from the University of Kansas, where he taught engineering classes and eventually applied his knowledge of engineering to sports and coaching. His landmark book, *Scientific Principles of Coaching*, was one of the first books in physical education on the mechanics (physics) of movement applied to sports. His ideas were the forerunner of the proven scientific way to teach fundamental skills.

Professor—Bunn was the consummate teacher and coach; he taught engineering at Kansas, physical education at Stanford, Springfield and Colorado State. Dr. William Ross, President of Colorado State College (now called the University of Northern Colorado) when Bunn retired in 1963 said, "Colorado State College was highly rewarded in utilizing the abilities of a great coach and educator to train future teachers of tomorrow. There is no doubt that John Bunn has made some of the greatest contributions of all-time in the fields of physical education and basketball."

Administrator—He became assistant Athletic Director of Kansas in 1926 at the age of 28. Assumed the Dean of Men's position at Stanford in 1938, highly unusual for a physical educator or basketball coach. As Director of Athletics at Springfield, he reinvigorated and reorganized the Athletic Department after World War II, until it was considered the equal of all other academic departments.

Coach—At Kansas, he coached three sports (and was a basketball assistant under the legendary Phog Allen and studied under the inventor of the game, James Naismith). At Stanford, he led his teams to three Pacific Coast Conference titles and coached Hank Luisetti, who was one of the several college players to develop and popularize the one-hand shot in basketball. His Stanford teams were the most colorful of the "thirties." In three years, they lost one game on the road (to the famous Long Island University team coached by future Hall of Famer Clair Bee). Under Bunn, Stanford was one of the college teams to popularize basketball as a national sport through play in the famed Madison Square Garden (NY) doubleheaders. Stanford, traveling from one end of the continent to the other to play basketball, never lost a game in "The Garden". Luisetti and his one-handed set shot startled the East Coast basketball world. John Bunn also coached at the small-college level (by choice) where he finished his career at Springfield and Colorado State as a teacher/coach. Bunn was truly a coaching educator who took his teaching/coaching skills worldwide through fundamental skill coaching clinics in Europe, United States, and Asia/Australia. He earned the title "American Ambassador of Basketball". He wrote six books on coaching and officiating, and received an honorary doctorate degree from Springfield in 1955 for contributions to man's well-being through physical education and sport.

Service—Bunn believed in giving back to the sport and did so in a multitude of ways:

1. *Professional organizations*—He was an early member of the national coaching

organization, joining the NABC in 1931. Over the years, he served on nearly every NABC committee. He was elected NABC President in 1949-50.

2. *Rules and officiating*—He authored two books on officiating and served as national rules editor/interpreter for nine years. Gave officiating clinics around the world—very insistent on playing/coaching by letter and intent of rules. Bunn was rules editor for many major changes in basketball, the most notable being the elimination of the center jump.

3. *Hall of Fame*—Bunn was a leader in starting the Naismith Memorial Basketball Hall of Fame. He served for fifteen years on the NABC Hall of Fame Committee and spoke at the dedication of the first Hall of Fame building on the Springfield College campus in 1968. The Hall of Fame annually presents an award in his name for outstanding lifetime achievement to basketball. It is the highest single honor the Basketball Hall of Fame awards outside of actual enshrinement.

4. *American Ambassador of Basketball*—He spread the game throughout the country, as well as Europe, Asia and Australia, through coaching and officiating clinics. Served as

Executive Director of the umbrella organization for basketball in the United States, the National Basketball Federation—one of very few basketball people who carried that much respect.

Bunn acknowledged the Stanford teams he coached, and Luisetti, as his greatest coaching experiences. Luisetti opened the eyes of the nation with his one-handed shot and became the first man to score 50 points in a game. He was applauded by the opposing team, California, when he set a national scoring record in his final game of the 1937-38 season. Bunn considered Luisetti as "the greatest all-around athlete who ever lived. And he had the perfect temperament and attitude to be great."

How ironic is it that Bunn considered Luisetti the greatest athlete ever, when many considered his own athletic accomplishments more than worthy of that distinction—another tribute to his selfless service and professional approach

John Bunn was selected by the NABC as the 1960 Metropolitan Award winner for outstanding contributions to basketball.

SOURCE

Bunn, John. Vertical File Archives. Noismith Memorial Basketball Hall of Fame. Springfield, MA.

THE VALUE OF BASKETBALL

By John Bunn

Authors' Note: This article was written for the 50th anniversary of basketball in 1941. The poem by Hall of Famer H.V. Porter was also developed for the occasion. Porter published the first high school rulebook in 1936 and developed the molded ball. Both authors depict their perception of what they hoped the game could and would become as it continued on after its first 50 years. It also gives a clear insight into how Bunn viewed the game of basketball during its formative years.

The occasion of The Golden Jubilee of Basketball suggests that an evaluation of the sport is in order. Future trends can best be directed by an intelligent review of the past.

The far-sightedness and modesty of Dr. Naismith, as he tackled the problem submitted to him by Dr. Gulick back in 1891, augured well for the future growth of the sport. First, he set up the limitation incident to an indoor game and then established the principles under which it should be played. These same five principles—throwing the ball in any direction, prohibition of running with the ball, elimination of blocking and tackling (personal contact), an elevated longitudinal goal, and the element of continuous contest for possession of the ball—have been maintained inviolate throughout the life of the game.

These factors and the comparative simplicity of the game have permitted and encouraged a worldwide spread and continuous growth. It is doubtful if any other game is played by as many people in as many countries and by as many different groups. Herein lies it greatest value. The game fits a recreational and physical education program. Youngsters of all ages, the high school, college, club, YMCA, industrial groups, and girls enjoy it with equal enthusiasm and play it with comparable vigor. There seems to be equal fun for the dub and the expert, for the gym class, the intramural group and the highly organized teams.

A second value lies in its test of self-control. The challenge to get the ball from the other fellow, and to score a goal, but with the requirement to avoid personal contact under the most intense situation, tests the caliber of every red-blooded individual.

While some specialization is possible, the game emphasizes team play first of all. Cooperation, or the lack of it, can be easily observed. As I look back on my coaching experiences with one of the game's greatest, Hank Luisetti, I remember not that he was a great scorer, passer, dribbler or guard. I see him rather as a boy who was an unselfish part of a team and who insisted upon being considered as one of a team. Any game that can develop this trait or can bring it out in a player is of inestimable value in our society today. How we do need to teach more cooperation so that we can get along with each other on friendly, unselfish terms!

Finally, the game has value for me for sentimental reasons. I knew the man who developed the idea. I had the privilege of working under him for fifteen years. How pleased he was to see his brainchild give pleasure to so many. How modest he was to refrain from assuming any great amount of credit. Dr. Naismith would not permit the game to be named after him.

The objectives of the game, as indicated by the values listed above, represent the ideals of the man himself. It was fortunate that he should receive recognition for it all while he lived and how fitting now that we should commemorate fifty years of growth and perpetuate by a memorial at the birthplace of the game, the memory of the noble man and the game he created.

SOURCE

Bunn, John. (1941). The Value of Basketball. *NABC Basketball Bulletin.*

BASKETBALL
IDES OF MARCH
BY
H.V. PORTER

(1)
The gym lights gleam like a beacon beam
And a million motors hum
In a good will flight on a Friday night;
For basketball beckons, "Come!"
A sharp-shooting mite is king tonight.
The Madness of March is running.
The winged feet fly, the ball sails high
And field goal hunters are gunning.

(2)
The colors clash as silk suits flash
And race on a shimmering floor.
Repressions die, and partisans vie
In a goal acclaiming roar.
On Championship Trail toward a holy grail,
All fans are birds of a feather.
It's fiesta night and cares lie light
When the air is full of leather.

(3)
Since time began, the instincts of man
Prove cave and current men kin.
On tournament night the sage and the wight
Are relatives under the skin.
It's festival time - sans reason or rhyme
But with nation-wide appeal.
It's a cyclone of hate, our ship of state
Rides high on an even keel.

(4)
With war nerves tense, the final defense
Is the courage, strength and will
In a million lives where freedom thrives
And liberty lingers still.
Let dictators clash and empires crash
"Neath a bloody victory arch!
Let our boys tread where hate is dead,
In this happy Madness of March!

DEDICATION ADDRESS FOR THE NAISMITH BASKETBALL HALL OF FAME

By John Bunn

APRIL 16, 1968

President Fagan, distinguished guests, ladies and gentlemen: I consider it a distinct honor and privilege to be accorded this opportunity to speak to you on this occasion.

As this edifice was contemplated and as the contents it was to house were envisioned, it was never thought of as a cold structure of brick and mortar or concrete and steel. From the beginning, it has the soul of a man and his game. It glowed with the warmth of human kindness that epitomized the man and characterized his life.

This Basketball Hall of Fame, unlike similar edifices, has been raised through sentiment and love for and dedication to a man and his game. One should not conclude, however, that the trip from the idea to a tangible material reality was without incidents — detours and obstructions. It was a long, tortuous effort. But, like the meandering stream, headed for the sea as its goal, the delays and setbacks, such as World War II, differences concerning the site, interrupted constructions, personality and personnel problems, withdrawal of support, were detours which caused delays, but which never detracted from the ultimate goal — this beautiful building with all that it holds and represents.

All of these experiences are comparable to the experiences in the life of the man himself — a man who seemed destined to find his ultimate niche in life where his influence for good could be most effectively exerted. Dr. Naismith planned to be a doctor and worked toward that end, but he never had a medical practice of his own. He studied to become a minister, but never occupied a pulpit of his own. These noble walks of life were sidetracked because of an incident which was the turning point in Jim Naismith's career.

He was always a lover of sports and was a talented performer. During a football game in Canada, a teammate became enraged and automatically swore vulgarly. Then, turning, he saw Jim Naismith near him. This teammate was embarrassed and apologized immediately for his violent, thoughtless outburst by saying, "I am sorry, Jim, I didn't realize you were near." Naismith had always been a clean-living and clean-speaking individual and was held in high esteem by his teammates. At the moment of this experience, Jim Naismith knew that his contribution and service to mankind was through the influence which the right kind of leadership in sports could exert. This realization brought him to Springfield College, where he invented his game.

Is it any wonder that his colleagues would be inflated by the spirit of this man? Is it not inevitable that they would think of a fitting manner in which to recognize and perpetuate the memory and contributions of this noble servant?

It all began when Dr. Forrest C. Allen, the first president of the National Association of Basketball Coaches, initiated the move to raise funds through the NABC to send Dr. and Mrs. Naismith to Berlin in 1936 to witness basketball played for the first time as an Olympic sport. This undertaking was so successful that the suggestion of a Basketball Hall of Fame grew out of it.

The idea was presented to Dr. Naismith who begged in his usual humble manner that no memorial be built to honor him. He requested, however, that if there was interest in building a museum for the memorabilia of basketball, it be located on the campus of Springfield College where the game was invented.

At this point, Springfield College took the initiative and, through a fund-raising agency, launched a campaign in 1941 for a memorial to Dr. Naismith, who had died in 1939, as a part of a program for a Fieldhouse for the college. This effort had just begun to gain momentum when the entrance of the United States into World War II on December 7, 1941 caused the collapse of the campaign with only enough funds raised to cover the expenses involved.

However, Springfield College alumni, in a separate effort, had raised approximately $10,000.00 which was held in readiness should a new attempt be made after the war.

True love and gratitude never fade. Immediately after the war, the National Association of Basketball Coaches revived the subject of a Basketball Hall of Fame as a memorial to Dr. Naismith. In 1948, Buck Reed, president of NABC, appointed a committee to study the idea and to bring its recommendations to the next convention.

This committee, under the chairmanship of Bill Chandler of Marquette University, recommended the creation of a Hall of Fame Committee as a standing committee of the NABC. The responsibility of this committee, as stated in the by-laws of the NABC, was to: "formulate and execute plans and policies for establishing a Basketball Hall of Fame. This assignment shall include the selection of a site, development of plans for a structure, collection and choice of items to be stored and displayed, organizing for collecting and handling funds, creating a permanent organization for the purpose of getting contracts, expending funds and managing and operating the completed structure."

The first significant action of this Committee was to secure Ed Hickox, a past president of NABC and retired basketball coach of Springfield College, as Executive Director. Lovable Ed, reflecting the spirit of Dr. Naismith, devoted 15 years of his life to planning and carrying out the fund-raising program and collecting memorabilia which would depict the history and development of the game when displayed in the building to be erected. He refused to accept any remuneration for this valuable service, which he considered a labor of love. He had the able assistance of his devoted wife and Mrs. Ruth Silvia, his secretary, during the whole period of his service. Springfield College furnished office space.

Next, the Committee decided that all fund-raising should be carried on by the committee; that every individual or organization anywhere in the world interested in or associated with basketball should be invited to contribute, and that the whole effort should be a personal family approach. The success of this policy is best attested by the enthusiastic response of coaches, officials, players, institutions, schools, colleges, clubs, friends of basketball, and grateful admirers of Dr. Naismith throughout the world.

The NABC, to demonstrate its debt of gratitude to the man who provided its members with a profession, voted to underwrite all promotional expenses so that the committee could guarantee that 100 percent of every contribution would go into the building and its furnishings. The total expenditure by the NABC from 1949 to

1963 (the period during which Ed Hickox served as Executive Director) for this purpose was approximately $45,000.00

As funds accumulated and as plans for the building progressed, it became necessary to create a permanent organization which could arrange for a lease for the site with Springfield College, get contracts for construction, expand funds, and transact all other business incident to the management and operation of an undertaking of this kind. Thus, the Naismith Memorial Basketball Hall of Fame was incorporated in 1959.

Ground-breaking ceremonies took place on November 6, 1961. Construction began shortly thereafter. Unforeseen sub-soil conditions required unanticipated expenditures, which forced a delay until additional funds were available.

At this stage, the Joint Civic Agencies of Springfield, Massachusetts came to the rescue of the project by organizing and conducting a fund-raising campaign in the greater Springfield area in 1963. The stimulus from this local interest and support gave the needed impetus to revive activity in every direction.

Under the able and untiring leadership of Bob Cowls of Springfield, a retired lumberman and building contractor who was named chairman of the building committee, the architect, Munson and Mallis, graciously cancelled outstanding indebtedness to them and revised the plans to meet anticipated funds and at the same time provide adequate facilities. A new contract, most favorable to the Hall of Fame thanks to the generosity of the contractor, A.R. Green & Son, was negotiated, and construction was completed, and the building formally opened on February 17, 1968, after a total expenditure of approximately $650,000.00.

Now, under the able, imaginative, and enthusiastic leadership of the present Executive Director, Lee Williams, this proj-

ect will continue to grow and prosper. It will perpetuate, through the various displays, the records, the events, the developments of the game, and the memory of the individuals who have shared in the growth of this great game.

Today, April 16, 1968, we who are here have the pleasure of viewing and enjoying this beautiful structure and dedicating it to the memory of that kindly, gracious been a labor of love in which a tremendously large and generous family has participated. To all, we extend a warm and grateful thank you.

SOURCE

Notes from the address delivered by John W. Bunn, Chairman of the Hall of Fame Committee of the National Association of Basketball Coaches from 1949 to 1963, at the dedication ceremonies for the Hall of Fame on April 16, 1968 on the campus of Springfield College, Massachusetts.

ANALYSIS OF
BASKETBALL TECHNIQUE

By John Bunn

Authors' Note: This is a chapter taken from Bunn's book, Scientific Principles of Coaching, *which was one of the first publications to apply the laws on mechanics/physics to sport.*

While there are many theories about basketball and many techniques practiced, the principles of dynamics, which govern the actions of the body, are invariable. Therefore, whatever the theory may be, it should be in harmony with these principles.

FOOTWORK

Quick starting and stopping, changes of direction, feinting, maneuvering, and change of pace form the basis of successful basketball. These tactics are all problems in the control of the center of gravity and application of force. The analysis is not unlike many aspects of the presentation of the tactics of the ball carrier in football. At least, the objective is the same—to out-maneuver an opponent.

For quick starting, the foot position should be such that push may be exerted most effectively by both feet. The sprinter's start position cannot be taken because action is required in all directions. But the feet should not be too widely spread. It is better to have one foot slightly ahead of the other. Thus, no matter which way the player turns; he has an assimilated track position, which study has demonstrated gives the fastest start. The base need not be wide, nor does the center of gravity need to be low (starting is faster with the center of gravity unstable) as in the football stance, since the contact and charging feature is absent. The position, however, must not deviate too widely from the stopping position, or too much valuable time will be lost in recovery.

BUNN 1.0

Some adjustment is, however, possible in the recoil from the stop.

Quick stopping, on the other hand, requires a low position for the center of gravity to reduce or eliminate the turning moment forward. It requires that one foot be placed ahead of the center of gravity for the same reason. A scoot or low hop with the bend of the knees (which drops the center of gravity) provides better body control and places the player in a position to start off in another direction by pushing from both feet, which is faster. The speed with which a player is moving may require a very low stop from which a recoil is necessary for quick starting. The low crouch in stopping also relieves the force on the feet because here force is traded for distance. If

there were no give in the knees and at the hips, the feet would be subjected to a terrific pounding (see **Diagram 1.0**).

Feinting, which consists of head, body, arm and/or foot moves, is designed to deceive an opponent and cause him to act to his disadvantage. These are not likely to be effective if the center of gravity is thrown outside the base or too near the edge of the base in the direction of the feint. The time required to recover equilibrium and start in another direction will offset the advantage otherwise gained by the feint. Therefore, there must always be a compensating move which maintains equilibrium. For example, if a player who has the ball steps back with the hope, as the result of a previous maneuver, of causing his opponent to move toward him to attack the ball so that he, the player with the ball, may dribble by, he must compensate for this move. This is done by bending forward at the waist as the foot drops back. In this way, the center of gravity is kept toward the forward edge of his base and permits him to move in that direction more quickly.

A head-and-shoulder feint in one direction is compensated by a dip of the opposite knee. This permits a quick push in the opposite direction of the feint. The center of gravity, by reason of the dip of the knee, is prevented from moving in the direction of the feint. One compensates for a thrust at the ball, a stop by one foot, and an arm reach by a bend of the opposite knee, which presents the center of gravity from moving forward. If, as a result of this maneuver, it is necessary for the defensive player to turn and move in the opposite direction from that of his thrust, he should throw his center of gravity outside his base and directly backward by a deep knee bend of the back leg, as the forward leg pushes in that direction.

Change of pace consists of an alternation of slowing down and speeding up. To slow down, one foot is put down ahead of the center of gravity and the body straightens, but the knees may bend slightly. To speed up, the body is inclined forward, the center of gravity is thrown ahead of the forward foot, and the legs extend as they push off for speed.

If the dribbler indulges in the change of a pace, the speed of advance of the ball is controlled by the angle at which the ball is pushed to the floor. For speed, the angle of the line of movement of the ball with the floor is reduced. To slow up, the angle of the line of the ball with the floor is more nearly a right angle.

JUMPING

Several principles govern the jump. In the first place, a player will jump higher if he steps or hops before he takes off. Such a maneuver overcomes the inertia of the body and starts it in motion (Newton's first law). It also permits him to push off of the floor with greater force which in turn will give greater height (Newton's third law). The stamp of the foot by means of the hop before the jump not only increases the force of reaction between the foot and the floor, but the stamp stretches the muscles if the foot. This gives a more forceful elastic rebound. A muscle will contract faster and with greater force immediately after being stretched.

By the same token, a slight crouch of the knee and hip permits a more forceful action of the muscles which control these joints. The amount of the crouch will depend upon the strength of the muscles. Boys with weak leg muscles should not take as deep a crouch as those with strong leg muscles.

At the take-off, the arms should swing up hard to give momentum to the jump. If the take-off is from one foot, the thigh of the free leg should swing up hard for the same reason. Just before the maximum height is reached, the leg should be extended downward sharply. The arm not used in reaching or tipping should be swung down in the same manner. This raises the position of the center of gravity in the body and thus gives more reach to the tipping hand.

All force and movement should be directed as nearly vertical as possible. The more nearly vertical all forces are directed, the greater will be the effective force for the jump. Any sideward swing of the free arm, for example, will waste a part of the force which is exerted.

All these principles should be followed whether the jump is after a held ball or whether the player is jumping to tip the ball at the basket. These principles suggest that a player at the basket should stay back far enough to be able to take a step before jumping. Maneuvering to get a position from which this can be done is quite important.

The movement of the jumper is confined when he is in the jumping circle. However, by standing at the very edge of the circle, the player will have sufficient space to take a short quick step before jumping. Few, if any, players have developed this technique. Most, because of the universally bad practice of officials in tossing a ball, jump from a stationary position and attempt to "steal" the ball. Actually, as the ball is thrown up (if the official throws it high enough), the player should take his preliminary step so that he can develop maximum force for his jump.

Jumping is of great importance in basketball and merits the special attention of players and coaches alike. The ability to outjump an opponent is the difference between ball control and the lack of it on many occasions. A fraction of an inch increase in the jump can be the difference. When it is realized that as much as three inches may be added to the jump by the position of the center of gravity in the body, the importance of concentration on all the principles which govern the technique of the jump can be understood.

PASSING

A few points need special emphasis because of the size of the ball and the peculiar characteristics of the game.

Because of the large cross-sectional area of the basketball, the effect of air resistance is quite pronounced. As a consequence, the spin of the ball must be carefully controlled to prevent wide divergence from the intended direction. For long passes, passes of 40 feet or more, the ball should be thrown with backspin directly opposite to the direction of flight. If spin across the direction of flight is imparted to the ball, it will often times curve so far out of its direct line as to be out of reach of the receiver. This, of course, depends upon the speed of spin in proportion to the forward speed of the ball and the distance of the pass.

Quickness in the movement of the ball is an important factor in basketball. Except for long passes, great force is not necessary. As a consequence, the problem of imparting maximum force is not significant with the exception noted. Attention, therefore, should be given to those factors which contribute to speed of movement of body members.

Two points are important. The wrist snap is the primary sources of force for passing the basketball. The other body movements which are used in throwing are relatively slower. Film studies of the shot put and baseball throw show that the wrist snap is the fastest movement in the sequence of body movements.

In order to eliminate or reduce the other and slower body movements to a minimum in passing the ball short distances, the ball is held with the wrists cocked and ready for the release of the ball. In the two-hand pass, for example, the ball should be held back against the chest with the elbows bent. Only the quick partial forward extension of the forearm and the wrists is necessary to develop sufficient force for the pass. For the one-hand pass, only a slight amount of upper-arm rotation is necessary, and no body rotation. Therefore, the upper arm is held almost at right angles to the body, and the forearm is in a position slightly back of vertical with the wrist cocked. These are the positions for the forearm and wrist when they start their movements in the normal throwing movement. Thus, for the purpose of quickness that portion of the throwing movement which contributes the greatest speed but the least force is emphasized for the short pass.

In the case of the hook pass, a new element is introduced. The hook pass, in addition to other movements, involves a circular movement of the arm in a plane which is perpendicular to a sagittal section of the body. In order to offset the centrifugal force developed from this movement, the hand is laid around the ball, with the ball rolled back on the forearm. In this way, the ball can be controlled better and prevented from flying off at a tangent before the desired release point.

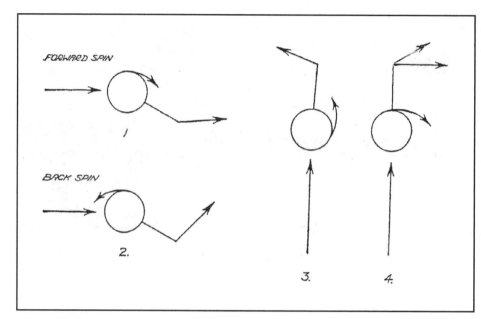

BUNN 1.1

The bounce pass is used to get the ball by an opponent by means of deflecting the ball off the floor. In the pass, the principle of spin plays an important part. If one desires that the ball gain speed after hitting the floor, forward spin is imparted to it. If he desires that the speed be retarded and the ball bounce high, backspin is put on the ball. Backspin is used when bouncing the ball in front of a fast-moving player. The forward speed of the ball is retarded, and it bounces higher so that the receiver is able to catch the ball and still maintain his speed. *Authors' Note: Backspin is usually preferred to produce a "catchable" ball.*

Spin across the direction of flight of the ball is also used in bounce passes. This is done when it is desired to pass to a teammate who is directly behind an opponent. The ball can be bounced to the side of the opponent and by means of the spin be deflected directly to the teammate (see **Diagram 1.1**).

Because of the fact that bounce passes travel a greater distance (not on a direct line between passer and receiver) and because of the bounce element, more bad bounce passes are made. Raws (1939) discovered this

fact in a study of Big Ten Conference games. He also found that direct passes were used 84.3 percent of the time and that of these, 72 percent were short passes.

Authors' Note: Bounce passes are slower than direct air passes because of this distance factor.

SHOOTING

The amount of arch with which to shoot, whether to shoot direct or to bank the shot, and whether to impart spin to the ball, has long been matters of controversy. All these can be answered by a consideration of same if the trigonometric factors involved. In addition, the dynamics need some attention.

The amount of arch to put on the ball is a problem of accuracy, strength, and defense. If a player was absolute in his accuracy, then the amount of arch would be that necessary to clear the upraised hand of the opponent and the near edge of the rim of the basket. If the opponent were close, more arch would be necessary than if he were some distance away from the shooter. The arch in this case would be inversely proportional to the distance of the defensive player from the shooter (see **Diagram 1.2**).

Few, if any, players are accurate enough to fit into this category. Therefore, the problem becomes one of trigonometry that involves strength. The basket is 18 inches in diameter. If the ball is dropped from directly above the center of the basket, the full area and diameter of the basket is projected at a right angle to the line of flight of the ball. If the ball is shot at an angle of 60° with the plane of the rim, only .8661 of the diameter is projected at a right angle to the line of flight. If it is shot at an angle of 45°, then .7071 is available as a target. If the angle is dropped to 30°, the margin is reduced to .5. This ratio is actually the sine of the angle, which the line of flight of the ball makes with the horizontal plane of the basket, multiplied by 18 inches, the diameter of the basket. Thus, as the angle is reduced, it becomes evident that the chances of the ball hitting either the front or back edge of the rim and bouncing away from the basket increases proportionally. Therefore, the lower the angle of flight of the ball, the greater must be the accuracy of direction. All this emphasizes a rather high arch of the ball. A study of film in the underhand free throw of a group of Springfield College varsity players shows that the ball leaves the hand at an angle of about 30 degrees from the vertical or 60 degrees from the horizontal. The ball travels in a parabola. The basket is above the point of release of the ball. The angle at which the ball would enter the basket would thus be something less than 60 degrees with the plane of the basket. Mortimer (1951) studied basketball shooting and found that an angle of 58° with the horizontal, with the ball traveling at a speed of 24 +feet/second, would probably produce the greatest accuracy.

The horizontal distance of the ball from the basket is the same from any one spot, regardless of the arch. The deviation of the

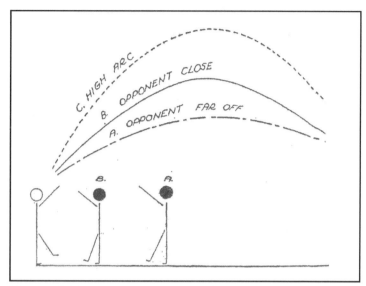

BUNN 1.2

ball to the right or left, therefore, would be the same regardless of the arch.

However, the higher the ball is arched, the longer its parabolic path. More power is necessary to project the ball through the high arch. A player who is not strong in the wrists will find it necessary to press beyond the realm of accuracy for him when shooting long distances, 20 feet or more, if he arches the ball too high. Not only will his shot deviate more from the right to left because of varying force in the right and left hand in an effort to cause the ball to reach the basket, but his accuracy, with respect to long and short shots, will decrease also.

Therefore, the amount of arch for each individual will vary with the strength of the individual. Each should emphasize as much arch as possible, consistent with his own strength.

The degree of accuracy which is necessary in shooting may not be apparent to all coaches and players. The following example will serve to emphasize its importance. A player whose shot deviates 4 degrees to the right or left from a distance of 20 feet from the basket will miss the rim entirely. The ball will be 16-3/4 inches off line when it reaches the basket. The ball will miss the edge of the basket by almost three inches. If his shot deviates 3 degrees, he will just hit the rim on the outside without any chance of making the basket. A shot which deviates 2 degrees will probably score a goal but his shot can be neither long nor short. If the reader will use the trigonometric functions, he may check these statements. **Diagram 1.3** illustrates this situation. If a player shoots from farther than 20 feet, the margin of error allowed becomes increasingly less. **Diagram 1.4** shows the degree of accuracy in shooting from different distances.

The ball should be shot with backspin. Such spin serves two primary purposes: 1) it helps the ball to maintain its direction by

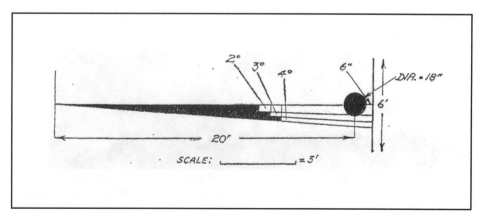

BUNN 1.3

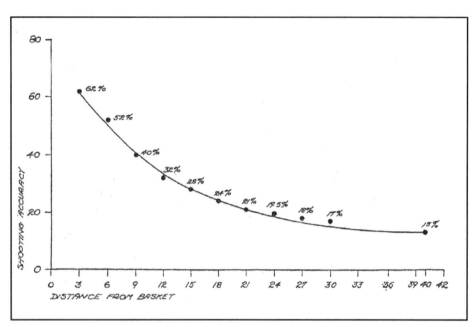

BUNN 1.4

preventing it from drifting; and 2) it retards the ball's rebound from the board and causes it to drop more sharply (that is, the angle of rebound is less than the angle of approach), which draws the ball down to the basket and lessens the chances of its rebounding too forcefully. In addition, 3) backspin retards the speed of the ball when it hits the rim, thus adding to the possibility of its dropping through the basket, rather than bounding away. In general, backspin tends to compensate for too much speed on the ball in shooting.

The speed with which a ball rebounds is dependent upon the co-efficient of restitution of the ball, its mass and the speed with which it is traveling. All these are constant, except the speed. It follows, therefore, that in order to prevent a fast rebound, the ball should be shot as softly as possible, that is, with as little velocity as necessary.

From the foregoing, it would appear that from the point of view of dynamics, all shots should be banked shots. This fact is enforced somewhat by two other facts. A tabulation of shots indicates that more shots fall short than long. This is probably caused by the fact that most players are taught to use the nearest point on the rim

as a target. With this as the focus, the distribution of shots will be short of and beyond this point. As players tire, they begin to fall short of their target. It would appear, therefore, that one should emphasize overshooting with the use of the backboard. Thus, short shots would fall in the basket and long ones, particularly with the help of backspin, would drop in from the backboard. Certainly, the target should not be the front edge. A study on shooting at a target in the center of the basket showed that scores improved 20 percent over the aim at the front of the rim.

Note: A study which placed spots on the backboard six inches apart and one foot above the rim of the basket showed that players who used the spots as targets improved faster than those who shot at an unmarked aboard. Those who used spots improved 10.8 percent after four weeks practice. Those who shot without spots improved 4.4 percent. Removing the spots later did not affect accuracy. The image had been set. Surprisingly, little improvement was shown after four weeks of practice. This tends to indicate that a four-week practice period was sufficient for optimum results.

Much of the shooting is muscle control. Thus shooting with eyes closed will test muscle control. All factors of a mechanical nature which can be applied to assist shooting should be utilized.

ENERGY

Much has been written about the strenuousness of basketball. A study of the recovery from various activities showed that players recovered from playing a basketball game sooner than swimmers after swimming 100 yards or runners after running a 400-yard dash. One of the reasons for this fact is that basketball is a discontinuous activity with as many as 150 interruptions per game. Swimming and running are continuous activities with much greater intensity but less duration.

A study of movement on defense tends to reflect the strenuousness of various defenses. By means of a pursuit apparatus, Blake (1939) found that players in a zone defense traveled less distance than those playing a man-to-man defense. He further found that a 2-1-2 defense was the most economical from the standpoint of distance traveled. Forwards traveled the least distance of all and guards the greatest.

SOURCE

Raws, Raymond S. (1939). A Comparative Study of the Bounce Pass and the Direct Pass in Basketball. Master's thesis, University of Iowa.

Mortimer, Elizabeth M. (1951, May). Basketball Shooting. *Research Quarterly.*

Bunn, J.W., (1936). Recovery from Fatigue after Exercise. Master's thesis, University of Kansas.

Blake, Raymond, (1939). Distance Traversed by Basketball Players in Different Types of Defense. Master's thesis, University of Iowa.

LEGACY OF
Howard Cann

- Selected the "Greatest Basketball Player in the World" in 1920.

- Participated in the 1920 Olympic Games and finished seventh in the shot put.

- Coached 35 years at NYU and led teams to both the NCAA championship game and the NIT finals.

- Led NYU to a victory over Notre Dame in the inaugural college basketball game at Madison Square Garden.

- Believed physical conditioning was a prerequisite to basketball success, and his style of play was built on speed, and quickness.

- Instructed his players in fair play and sportsmanship, and his teams were among the most fundamentally sound in the country.

HOWARD CANN

*"Speed is the goading theme of the court wars.
It takes courage, loyalty, and iron legs to score
in this speed-burning sport."*
—Howard Cann

BIOGRAPHY

Born: October 11, 1895 in Bridgeport, CT

Died: December 18, 1992

Inducted into the Naismith Basketball Hall of Fame in 1968

Howard Cann coached thirty-five years at New York University and compiled a 409-232 record. During the 1933-34 campaign, Cann directed NYU to an undefeated season. He led his teams to the NCAA championship game in 1945 and to the NIT final game in 1948. During his playing career at NYU, Cann excelled in basketball, football, and track, and was considered the greatest athlete ever to have performed at the school. In 1920, Cann was selected as the Helm's Athletic Foundation Basketball Player of the Year, led NYU to the AAU national basketball championship, and was a member of the U.S. Olympic team as a shot-putter. Howard's brother, Ted, was an Olympic swimmer, and they were the first members of the same family ever chosen for the U.S. Olympic Team.

Howard Cann...

Basketball was still a rather obscure sport when Howard Cann attended the High School of Commerce in New York City. Cann was a three-sport standout in high school and won the Public School Athletic League (P.S.A.L.) low and high hurdles, and shot-put championships, all on the same day.

After high school graduation, Cann spent one year at Dartmouth College and then enrolled at New York University (NYU) in 1915. He studied industrial engineering and starred on the varsity football, basketball, and track teams. Cann's excellence in sports came as no surprise to most people. His father, Frank Cann, was a famous athlete in his day and served as director of athletics and head of the physical training department at NYU for forty years. Upon his arrival at NYU in 1895, Cann's father instituted mandatory physical education requirements that included periodic assessments so students could appreciate how the regimen improved their appearance and their health. His emphasis on physical fitness provided strong performers for NYU's newly formed varsity baseball, football, and gymnastic teams.

Howard's brother, Ted, was an Olympic swimmer, held the world record for 220 yards, and later received the Congressional Medal of Honor in World War I. Howard and Ted Cann were the first members of the same family ever chosen for the U.S. Olympic team.

Cann attended NYU for three years and then enlisted in the U.S. Navy during World War I. He was promoted to the rank of lieutenant and served on the U.S.S. New Mexico. Cann returned to NYU in 1919 and was captain of the football team. He was one of the leading runners and kickers in the East and was selected on the All-Eastern Eleven.

Cann's basketball exploits in the National AAU tournament in 1920 led NYU to the national championship and earned him the *Atlanta Constitution's* award as the "Greatest Basketball Player in the World." One Atlanta journalist suggested that if Cann and an opponent rebounded a missed shot at the same time, Cann would throw both the ball and the opposing player through the basket.

Paul Mooney, Cann's teammate on the national championship team, said, "I scored 78 points in four games in the AAU tournament. That's an awful lot of points, but Howard was awarded the trophy for the world's best basketball player, so you can imagine what he did." (Frank, 1936)

Standing 6 feet and 4 inches and weighing 220 pounds, Cann's athletic skills captured the attention of New York City basketball enthusiasts. In 1920, a landmark game took place that demonstrated basketball's enormous potential for spectator appeal. Cross-town rivals NYU and the City College of New York (CCNY) were both in the midst of outstanding seasons. NYU did not have its own gymnasium and played some of its games on a barge located on the Hudson River and others in available dance halls. Since a large crowd was expected, it was decided that the game between the two schools would be played at the 168th Street Regimental Armory. Nearly 10,000 basketball fans crowded into the Armory and watched Cann and his teammates defeat CCNY.

Cann averaged seven field goals a game during his NYU career and was described as being "fast, utterly fearless, and a grand competitor." Cann attempted almost every shot inside the foul line and was considered by most people to be unstoppable.

A few months after being selected the Helm's Athletic Foundation Basketball Player of the Year, Cann was commanding attention for his exploits in track and field. At the Penn Relays, Cann won the shot and the discus, and was one of the leaders in the pentathlon. He ran the last event, the 1500 meter-run, in baseball shoes because he had only one pair of track shoes and they were for the field events. Cann was a member of the USA Olympic team and finished seventh in the shot-put in the 1920 Olympic Games.

Cann played professional basketball for the New York League Mohawk Indians for one season before accepting a coaching position at NYU. He worked for his college mentor, Ed Thorp, for one season and then became NYU's head coach in 1923. Cann coached basketball at NYU for the next thirty-five years. He also assumed the position of director of physical training that was previously held by his father. Cann was universally respected for his warmth, modesty, and exemplary leadership qualities.

During basketball's first fifty years, each geographic area had its own distinct style of play. Rarely did teams from different regions have the opportunity to test their different coaching styles. One such game occurred in 1935, when Adolph Rupp brought his Kentucky Wildcats for the first time to New York City to meet Cann's NYU

squad. In a game marked by contrasting playing styles and controversial officiating, NYU prevailed 23-22. In December of 1934, Cann's NYU team inaugurated Madison Square Garden with a historic victory over Notre Dame. It was contests such as these that broke down the game's regionalism and brought basketball into its modern era.

As a coach, Cann was a patient and thorough teacher. His pleasant and gentlemanly demeanor instilled confidence and enthusiasm in his players. His belief in physical conditioning made his teams aggressive, fast-breaking, and high scoring.

Players remembered Cann as being very big, very strict, and very kind-hearted. "He had a warmth and a relationship with the players that was special," stated Ray Lumpp, who played for Cann in the late 1940s and later coached with him at NYU. "He was demanding of you, but he got results. You learned from him things that you carried out later in life." (Steele, 1992) Cann's most famous motivational phrase was "fire and desire." "I'll never forget that phrase," said Mike Muzio, a senior on Cann's last team who later coached NYU when the program was revived in 1983. "It was the stuff you use in the game that carried over after you were through playing. He helped me become a man at NYU. He really made you tow the mark." (Steele, 1992)

Cann's teams were among the most fundamentally sound in the country. The Violets were undefeated in 1934 and won 36 out of 37 games from 1933 to 1935. In 1945, NYU were finalists in the NCAA tournament, losing the title game to Oklahoma A&M 49-45.

Cann was named national Coach of the Year in 1947 and received the NABC Merit Award in 1967. Two of his former players, Dolph Schayes and Ben Carnevale, were also enshrined in the Naismith Memorial Basketball Hall of Fame.

Cann died in 1992 at the age of 97.

SOURCE

Deutsch. Robin Jonathan (1986) *Basketball Hall of Fame Class of 1996 Yearbook.*: Bordeaux Co.: West Springfield, MA.

Frank, Stanley. (December 14, 1936) Coaches Now, but Glamour Boys Then: King Cann. *New York Post.*

Steele, David. (December 21, 1992). NYU's Cann Left Imposing Legacy Long Island, NY: *Newsday.*

BASKETBALL—IT'S NOW A GAME OF SPEED AND CONDITIONING

By Howard Cann

Speed is the goading theme of the court wars. It takes courage, loyalty, and iron legs to score in this speed-burning sport. Speed is necessary in shooting goals, in passing and retrieving the ball, in moving about the court, and even in thinking. There must be no lost motion, and a team in order to win must go at a fast clip the full forty minutes.

PHYSICAL FITNESS

Physical fitness is now as never before the factor that a player needs most to be ready to engage in this sport today. It is true that players must have courage, determination, and a proper spirit of team loyalty, mental alertness, and experience. But over and above all, physical conditioning means nine-tenths of the game. With the new collegiate rules, it's of paramount importance as there are no rest periods afforded by center taps as formerly. The game is now go, go, go!

Just as a chain is as strong as its weakest link, so a basketball team is as strong as its individual players. One weak link will prove the chain's undoing, and one poorly conditioned player will ruin a team's efficiency. There is no team sport like basketball for demanding so much of its contestants. Successful coaches the world over attest to the absolute necessity of physical fitness over and above other qualifications.

DETERMINATION AND COURAGE

Determination and courage are equally important attributes for basketball players. A member of any team ought to remind himself at every turn that no matter how hard he has to work at mastering the sport,

he'll make of himself a better player. As for courage, the contestant needs it more than he does his shoes. There is no place on a court for a player who hesitates or shrinks from heated combat. A team of true championship caliber always drives harder and faster in the face of hardship and seemingly insurmountable obstacles.

MASTERING THE FUNDAMENTALS

The mastering of the fundamentals of the game plays an important role in our system at NYU. A team will not fail as quickly and as easily if the players are equipped with a thorough knowledge of the fundamentals of individual and team play. A first-hand acquaintance with the game's fundamental principles will eliminate the possibility of costly error in missing passes, handling the receiving of passes, and in shooting.

OUR SYSTEM

I am not a disciple of any complicated system of play. We have certain set formations, especially on jump balls and on outside balls, but we keep things simple. Our system is based on physical conditioning, thorough training in the fundamentals, a love of the sport and the school, and fellowship among teammates. The good of the team must be the underlying rule, rather than the good of the individual in our basketball set-up. I have no time for players who are selfish and who are seeking personal glory at the expense of their teammates. Basketball is first and always a team game and must be played as a unit. Occasionally, a player strays from the fold, and then a coach has a real educational problem on his hands.

SCOUTING

Scouting of rivals has become almost as prevalent in the court rivalries as on the gridiron. When we look over the opponents' games, we watch for defects in their style of play and peculiar characteristics of the players. We model our attack and defense accordingly.

TRAINING

The training season—or lack of it—can give a coach plenty of worry. Basketball is normally a winter game, but some colleges begin their preparations with the opening of fall semester. In a few cases, coaches are forced to wait until the end of the football season in order to get some of their players. As a rule, it takes a football player two or three weeks to get used to the court routine, and it has been my experience that no football player was able to last more than six minutes when the going got tough in a speedy basketball game. The pace generally has been too fast and is a great contrast over the gridiron game. I have also introduced spring workouts for my squad. Considerable work is spent on brushing up on fundamentals and in developing speed.

BASKETBALL TODAY

Basketball has added many attractive trimmings. The game is far different than the one originated by Dr. James Naismith. The original rules, thirteen in number, called for a couple of baskets or boxes about fifteen inches diameter across the opening and about fifteen inches deep, suspended one at each end of the grounds or court, about ten feet from the floor. The number comprising a team depended upon the size of the court area, but it was permissible to have from three on a side to forty.

Today, fifteen rules with many subdivisions and added notes covering fifteen pages control the sport, and the rules specify definitely that two teams of five men each play the game of basketball. But outside of these structural changes in the conduct of the sport, there are changes in the uniforms of the players, the size and type of gymnasiums, the introduction of various systems of coaching, special types of flooring, glass backboards, a new ball, boards of approved officials, committees of regulation, and each season an attempt to codify the sectional interpretation of the rules.

Today, thousands play the sport in every corner of the world. College, club, and military organizations have carried the sport to distant lands, and the game earned international recognition with its inclusion on recent Olympic Games programs in Berlin.

Thousands upon thousands are sitting in attendance at basketball games today. Midwest and Eastern college games have attracted anywhere up to 18,000 for a single game in recent seasons. Last winter, 150,000 attended the twelve nights of double-headers in basketball arranged at Madison Square Garden in New York City.

The sport has made great strides. It is up to the coaches and players to keep abreast of the changes. It is fatal for a coach or team to remain behind the times in regard to styles of play and systems. The youngsters who make up our squads demand the best type of instruction and coaching, and we coaches have a real duty to perform in seeing that this is available at all times. We hope to do our duty to a grand sport and the fine lads who follow it.

SOURCE

Cann, Howard G. (1937) Basketball—It's a Game Guy's Game! *Basketball Stories*. Volume 1, No. 1

LEGACY OF
H.C. "Doc" Carlson

- Designed the figure 8 continuity offense.

- Practiced medicine as a registered physician, as well as coached basketball.

- Led Pittsburgh to the Helms Foundation national championship in 1928 and 1930.

- Produced teams that were highly conditioned.

- Conducted landmark research in the area of fatigue and basketball.

- Was the first coach to take an eastern collegiate team across the country to play western universities.

- Was the originator of the first college basketball clinic in 1930.

H. C. "Doc" Carlson

"Learning the value of team play is to learn one of life's lessons."
—H.C. "Doc" Carlson

BIOGRAPHY

Born: July 4, 1894 in Murray City, OH

Died: November 1, 1964

Inducted into the Naismith Basketball Hall of Fame in 1959

H.C. "Doc" Carlson was the basketball coach at the University of Pittsburgh from 1922 through 1953 where he and compiled a record of 369-247. The charismatic Carlson also doubled as a practicing physician. Known for his invention of the figure 8 offense, Carlson led Pittsburgh to Helms Foundation national championship in both 1928 (with a record of 21-0) and 1930. The figure 8 offense was a continuity offense that broke down an opponent's defense and created lay-up opportunities. In 1931, Carlson was the first coach to take an eastern collegiate team across the country to play western universities. He served as president of the NABC Coaches Association in 1937 and was elected to the Helms Foundation Basketball Hall of Fame. Carlson was the main speaker for the dedication of the Basketball Hall of Fame in 1961.

H.C. "Doc" Carlson...

H.C. Carlson spent his boyhood years in Pennsylvania and graduated from Fayette City H.S. (PA) in 1912. Both his father and stepfather died in mining accidents, and his family could not afford to provide him with a college education. Carlson attended the University of Pittsburgh on an athletic scholarship. During his collegiate years, Carlson was much better known as a football star than as a basketball player. During his football career, Pittsburgh lost only one game. Carlson was captain of the undefeated 1917 team and earned All-American honors. He also starred in basketball and baseball. While attending medical school, Carlson financed his education by playing professional football for Cleveland.

In 1920, the University of Pittsburgh Medical School granted Carlson his M.D. degree. As a young doctor, Carlson found it difficult to face the potential death of a patient nearly everyday. To take his mind off the problems of his vocation, Carlson turned to coaching. In 1923, he became the head basketball coach at Pittsburgh. During sleepless nights, he diagramed plays in his prescription book and tried to create new plans of attack. It was from this setting that Carlson designed what many basketball historians called the first true continuity offense, a system that he called the figure 8 offense. (Bjarkman, 1996, p. 12)

Carlson's continuity offense revolutionized offensive thinking because the initial pass was made to a player moving away from the basket, rather than toward the basket. The passer then cut toward the basket looking for a return pass. The figure 8 offense originally had three players moving and two players stationary. Carlson eventually developed a four-player and a five-player continuity. Joe Lapchick, legendary Hall of Fame coach, claimed that every modern offensive scheme evolved from the innovations of "Doc" Carlson.

Carlson believed basketball was an important endeavor because of its carryover into life. He regarded it as a lesson in discipline, sportsmanship, honesty, cooperation, companionship, and, most of all, a lesson in the competitive democratic system. Basketball was never an end in itself, but was the means for building upon the formal education of the classroom, with the practical experiences of life. Carlson emphasized that it was impossible to always score more points than your opponent, but "everybody can win all the time in the synthesis of enduring healthy and happy patterns of life." (Carlson, 1962, p. 19)

Carlson wanted his students and players to see the good in everyone. He was a special person who generated sunshine and made life pleasant for everyone around him. Carlson was called a healer. "He could seize your heart without a scalpel and sutures,... and he could ease your pain. His smile was more quieting than a sedative. 'Doc' gave out gaiety and he felt it coming back at him. It was like a boomerang—a blessed boomerang." (O'Brien, 1982, p. 11)

Students remembered how Carlson wrote encouraging notes and urged them to be more compassionate and focus on the good, rather than the bad. "Doc" felt his daily duty was doling out happiness. He loved to buy students ice cream cones, and his office was always well stocked with candy and chocolate bars. (O'Brien, 1982, p. 11)

Carlson believed "offense is the highlight in any sport" and that a good offense was the best defense (Carlson, 1928, p. 75). He always wanted his team to control possession of the ball, because it eliminated scoring opportunities for the opposition. At the end of games in which his Pittsburgh team had a big lead, they would put on a passing exhibition. Spectators counted every pass and watched the clock to see if they could really make 70 passes in one minute as Carlson claimed they could. This group came to be known as the "runners" and did nothing but move the ball without any intention of taking a shot.

Carlson was a strict man-to-man defensive strategist. He despised zone defenses and thought they ruined the action of the game. He often instructed his team to hold the ball for much of the game in order to counter "tactless" zone play. When his team stalled on the road, Carlson was known to throw candy and peanuts into the stands to the hostile home crowds. (Bjarkman, 2000, p. 7)

Carlson was a colorful showman on the sidelines and often received the wrath of opposing fans. A fan at Washington and Jefferson hit Carlson on the head with an umbrella. West Virginia fans tried to cool him off by pouring a bucket of ice water on his head after Carlson continually complained of bad officiating by saying, "This burns me up." (Bjarkman, 1996, p. 14)

During Carlson's long and distinguished career, he was one of the most outspoken critics of officiating that basketball has ever known. He was very disturbed over what he considered were "home calls" and advocated officiating that was consistent and fair to both teams. On one occasion, Carlson offered his glasses to the referee. Another time, he took the water bucket and other supplies from the bench and set them at the referee's feet announcing, "You might as well have these, you've taken everything else from us!"

"Doc" Carlson was the originator of the college basketball clinic, the first being held at the University of Pittsburgh in 1930. Originally, he devoted most of his effort to teaching his system of offense, but as the clinic developed over the years, he included coaches from all of the local colleges as clinicians.

Many critics said the removal of the center jump after each basket would make the game so fast that it would kill or seriously injure many players. To counter such criticism, Carlson undertook extensive research in fatigue. Carlson's "Basketball Research in Fatigue" provided concrete evidence that the new faster version of basketball did not have any adverse side effects on the players. Carlson's research was one of the greatest contributions to this phase of basketball coaching.

A Carlson-coached team was always in superb physical condition. Hall of Fame coach "Phog" Allen said that he had never seen better trained teams than Pittsburgh.

Carlson died at the age of seventy, just two months after retiring as director of the student health services at Pittsburgh. The famed and beloved Carlson had been associated with the University for half a century.

SOURCE

Bjarkman, Peter C. (1996). *Hoopla: A Century of College Basketball.* Indianapolis: Masters Press.

Bjarkman, Peter C. (2000). *The Biographical History of Basketball.* Chicago: Masters Press.

Carlson, H.C. (1928). *You and Basketball.* Braddock, PA: Brown Publishing.

Jones, Tommy Ray. (1964). *Henry Clifford Carlson M.D.: His Contributions to Intercollegiate Basketball Coaching.* Unpublished Master's Thesis. University of Pittsburgh.

O'Brien, Jim. (1982). *Hail to Pitt: A Sports History of the University of Pittsburgh.* Pittsburgh: Wolfson Publishing.

LESSONS FROM THIS LEGEND...

THE SPIRITUAL SIDE OF BASKETBALL

By
H.C. "Doc" Carlson

Everybody has the urge to contribute to the general welfare of mankind in one way or another, even though the urge varies as to intensity and consistency. The author, with a feeling of gratefulness to a kindly world, has the idea that you can have anything worthwhile if your desire is intense and persistent enough, and if you will back up this desire by an unfaltering faith in eventual accomplishment.

The desire of everybody is happiness, although its manifestations may be as different as the number of individuals. Ralph Waldo Emerson has defined happiness as "congenial occupation with a sense of progress." Everyone has some occupation, work, or play; but this is insufficient without progress, which means success. To some, money is synonymous with success and happiness; and while it is necessary to have some money to be happy, financial security is no assurance of happiness.

The factors entering into the more universal forms of happiness prove that the best things in life are free. Health, air, sunshine, friends, good will, love, and vision of beautiful things are within possession of all who make even gestures in their direction.

In order to achieve success or happiness, anyone must have an intense and specific desire accompanied by faith in its achievement. There are fundamentals, including health, effort, honesty, and personality, common to all lasting and full success; and further, to each occupation, there belongs certain fundamentals that, if followed, surely lead to our goal.

Each of us knows the formula or the common fundamentals of every success, together with the fundamentals of his particular occupation. In this manner, we can find why we are not progressing; or having once been near the top and finding ourselves going back, we can trace the cause to its source and attempt correction.

While the principles of this formula – desire of a specific goal and faith in the ability to reach it – control all successes in life, we want to apply them particularly to the game of basketball. Any man with reasonable study can master the technique of the game. The spiritual will to win is far more important, however. A team perfect in technique can be beaten; the same team with a burning desire to win and an absolute faith in its ability to win cannot be beaten.

I believe that any boy who applies the spiritual principles on the basketball floor will live a happier and more successful life by applying them to his career. If the boy gets the right ideas in basketball and then applies himself equally as enthusiastically and systematically in his life's work, then he is bound to succeed.

As for basketball itself, there has been an effort to develop it from the beginning. The hope is that the individual can improve his technique, and that the coach will find the germ of an unbeatable system.

It is my attempt to put forth in concrete form a guiding beacon in the formation of happier, more useful careers. It is my attempt to express gratitude to the innumerable friends who have made life's journey sweeter by their friendship and encouragement. To succeed in doing this, even in a small way, and thereby increase the sum total of the world's happiness, would amply compensate for all efforts.

FUNDAMENTALS COMMON TO ALL SUCCESSES

You build as you go. You know your desire and have faith in its achievement. Since the foundation of all success has the same fundamentals, it is well for us to know them in name and in practice, and have them a part of our mental equipment.

There are certain habits that help form our makeup as we go along. They are our second nature. Certain ones are constructive and common to any career leading toward success. Just to keep their names before us, even passively, is to stimulate us in the right direction and possibly lead to a more consistent practice of them.

We should get the habit of health, cheerfulness, enthusiasm, courage, honesty, promptness, accuracy, economy or thrift, right thinking, courtesy, expression, efficiency, cooperation, tact, tolerance, sympathy, and common sense. The result is a gentleman, and a sportsman, and a success.

In this day of efficiency, we should exercise the greatest care in formation of habits, since they are savers of energy and are, therefore, efficient. They are more easily formed in plastic youth and are harder to break with increasing age. To do the simplest of tasks may be difficult the first time, but practice makes it easier. Our habits are always with us. As we choose our friends, so we should choose our habits – carefully. It is just as easy to form winning habits as it is to form losing ones. Winning habits stimulate success. If you get the habit of winning, you don't lose. Try also to improve your assets of self-control, observation, attention, imagination, and foresight. Get the habit of visualizing your desire for good and the faith in accomplishment of the desire.

LESSONS FROM THIS LEGEND...

In the formation of constructive habits or in the elimination of destructive habits, realize that though the proper course may be more difficult at first, with continued application it becomes easier. You should never break from the right habits. If no one ever took his first drink, there would be no drunkards; if there was no little cheating at first, there would be no eternal triangles. It's the first little leak that starts the wide-open breach.

Proper habits can lead only to success. As physical habits bring physical dexterity, so can proper habits of thinking lead to mental dexterity. Map out your habits in line with your worthy desire and faith. Do not depart from your ideal the first or second day, the first week or month, or year, and your desires will be accomplished.

GET THE HABIT OF HEALTH

The prime requisite of success and happiness is health. The state of your health may actually decide your whole course of life. Get the habit and vision of good health, for that is essential to achievement, and is, in itself, a stimulus to faith and courage. Regular, moderate eating, exercise, and rest, pay big dividends. Cleanliness is next to Godliness. Recreation, as a term, is often-times misused as a guise for dissipation. It should be what it really is – re-create, to renew your image and its details of success and health, or to re-create dormant desires or ambitions.

A healthy mind can come only in a healthy body, and both are equally important and interrelated. Anything that poisons the body poisons the mind, and the reverse is practically true. You need money in the bank for a rainy day. It is just as important and essential to have an abundance of health and a heart reserve to meet possible strains that are greater than the usual demand. Health is your first wealth, and to feel the joy of living is a step towards your goal. Never allow your habits of health to be compromised to the slightest degree.

GET THE HABIT OF EFFORT

Next to health comes effort, since activity is the law of growth. With a clearly defined desire backed up by unfaltering faith, effort will surely bring you to your goal. Intelligent effort will be more efficient and cut down the time requirement. Avoiding procrastination can minimize expenditure of time. Get the most out of today; strive to intensify your desire, and let each day end on further advances to your goal. Take care of the first part of the day, and the momentum may carry your efforts through to happiness and success for the remainder of it. You get what you give, a smile for a smile.

Start out in the morning with the winning spirit and bring it home enhanced at night with advances physically, materially, moral-ly, and intellectually. Figure you are going ahead today, and that it may be your day of destiny. Act as if snapshots of your daily activities are to form your record, rather than the unnatural poses of rare occasions.

Enthusiasm is synonymous with pep, and the amount of enthusiasm determines the amount of pleasure derived from effort. Enthusiastic effort means preparedness, and is essential to success. Failure comes with partial preparation. Preparation through training and attention to details leads to lasting successes. In this process, time can-not be considered. Jesus made His first pub-lic appearance at twelve, and He did not begin His life's work until thirty. In three years though, He made a lasting impression upon the world. The building of a good foundation led to the world's greatest mira-cle. Such building you should do. Start at the bottom and work up through the details of your job. Then you will know its possibil-ities, for halfway knowledge brings only halfway success. Knowledge is power and it is well to have plenty in reserve. There is only about two-percent difference between accomplishment and failure. You should work up to the limit of your capabilities, and then do two-percent more.

Real effort results in concentration. This process is aided by a definite desire. In this age of specialists, concentration on one thing is the only path. Try something, take the initiative, be persistent, and you'll suc-ceed in it, because concentration on one idea may generate one hundred supplemen-tary ideas. An apparent drawback may prove an asset. Feel that you can win as others have. For you to go ahead, however, the force must come from within. You must drive yourself ahead. The more you strive, the greater your capabilities. Aim to gener-ate more energy, applying your effort to your desire to win. It is the extra inch that makes the hero. To work means to win. To be thorough is to have your standards rise and approach perfection. Your efforts and faith in the accomplishment of your desires should breed patience and tact; for you know that ultimately you will win. He, who knows he will win, does not grow impa-tient.

GET THE HABIT OF HONESTY

To be honest is to have character; to suc-ceed without being honest is only a tempo-rary success. To lose everything material and retain honesty is to retain credit and power to rise again. To have everything but honesty is to have nothing, while to have honesty is to compensate for other deficien-cies and inspire confidence, which cannot be bought. With conscience as an alley, you will not make the first break that may later cost you dearly.

Honesty generates courage to go ahead, as well as does faith. The combination of hon-esty and faith is a good substitute for genius. American history is filled with sto-ries of poor boys carried to the greatest heights by that combination. Only such a combination can bring you through the critical dangers of life. Without it, you will be always waiting for an ideally easy propo-sition to come along. While you wait, the fellow who has it will have jumped into success, perhaps into your job.

If you are honest, there is no reason why you should not bring yourself to the atten-tion of others, passively if not actively. Think well of yourself, because the world takes you at your face value. Your faith in yourself should be evident to others. They will respect you for it, if you are honest in it. Respect of others increases self-respect.

LESSONS FROM THIS LEGEND...

GET THE HABIT OF PERSONAL MAGNETISM

Personality is the sum total of health, effort, and honesty, plus the ability to meet and to like men. Cheerfulness in an individual is always an attractive trait. Often your chance will come because men like cheerfulness. There is no place for a grouch, and a smile will disarm an opponent quicker than a sneer or a curse. Just so far as you are boss of your job and not your job of you, you can smile. Many a game has been won because the master of the situation could smile. Broadcasting your troubles will increase them and wreck team play. If you form the habit of a lovable disposition, although you may not be a millionaire, you can be a bigger philanthropist by dispensing good cheer and encouragement. The man who can smile is the healthy man, and he lives a longer life than the grouch.

True sportsmanship demands courtesy as a habit. Courtesy wins friends and keeps them; rudeness, thoughtlessness, and snobbishness repel. "Thank you" and "I beg your pardon" compensate for many deficiencies. The boor never gets far in amateur sports or anywhere else. Great winners have generally been gentlemen. A boy with good manners stands out in the crowd; he wins respect and confidence – two essentials of good team play. Just as society makes courtesy an obligation, so does team play make it an essentially social thing. Rude criticism not only shows lack of home training, but it spoils teamwork. Remember that even though you may have a heart of pure gold, you will be judged by your external signs of good breeding. To get along with your fellow men, you must develop the art of expressing what you should feel. That is better than excusing yourself for saying what you did not mean. The golden rule is the first fundamental of politeness.

The habit of courteous expression includes the virtues of brevity and directness without abruptness. It is a matter of common experience that those people long on words are generally short on ideas. Above all, never offend by being careless in speech or writing. Remember that a crab generally goes backward. You can always express optimism better than pessimism. Intolerance will smash any team or social group, no matter how well built it may be.

GET THE HABIT OF PERMANENCE

Oftentimes, people who have reached great heights forget the cause of their ascendancy. With a temporary lull in progress, or even a little slide backwards, a rout or complete defeat can be avoided by checking over the concrete points of success. Do you still have a clear image of your desire? Do you still have an unfaltering faith in achievement? Are you maintaining your habits of health, effort, honesty, and personality?

Perseverance is holding on when things seem their worst. Remember that it is the putting in of that extra two-percent which brings victory. To have that "never-be-beaten attitude" is never to lose. The help of your teammates is as necessary as the contribution of your best. Give all that you have, but work with others. Exert that grit which insists on a solution for every problem. Never allow your thoughts to defeat you. Hold on, and your second wind may allow you to fight a little longer and a little harder. The end result will be ultimate victory. To have played a bad hand well is better than to have played a good hand poorly.

The habit of thrift will help you win and will give you the feeling of permanence. To live within your income is a real test of strength. At the same time, spending to best advantage helps to improve self and community. To save a little strengthens will and foresight. Both of these attributes a winner must have. Thrift is efficiency and builds faith, because the possession of a reserve makes you feel prepared for opportunity. To be able to seize the opportunity is oftentimes the difference between success and failure.

Happiness should be permanent. Success generally brings happiness. Because happiness creates more energy and determination, and increases faith, it brings success.

To be a winner is to be happy. To be a loser is to be unhappy. Races of winners have been healthy races; nations of losers have been sick nations. Sick nations have died.

Your good reputation should be as permanent as the mountains. To have good standing with your neighbors and your teammates is to help yourself visualize and reach your goal. To have poor standing is to impede your progress. Aim to go up in public opinion and to influence that opinion righteously. Remember that one bad deed or associate may tear down years of careful building.

With the years and proper habits come experience, good judgment, and common sense, leading to the achievement of your goal.

GET THE HABIT OF AVOIDING DESTRUCTIVE ELEMENTS

To ignore fear is to ignore one of the greatest impediments to progress. To have faith is it's greatest antidote. The next great evil to fear is worry. Worry never did anything but make a good picture look bad and cause the patient to die a thousand times before his last breath. It destroys sleep and rest, with accompanying loss of mental and physical energies. It is to put defeat foremost, and to make victory an accident. And victories are never accidents. To live with your troubles is to associate with the worst possible company. Realize that most of your troubles never occurred and thereby avoid dissipating your mental assets.

Beside fear and worry, there are other negative attributes to be avoided. Neither anger, hate, envy, distrust, nor pessimism should be a part of anybody's makeup. Banish the negative attributes and give play only to constructive forces. This is the way to success and happiness in any pursuit.

SOURCE

Carlson, H.C. (1928). *You and Basketball*. Braddock, PA: Brown Publishing.

LEGACY OF
Peter J. "Pete" Carril

- Designed a methodically patient, team-oriented offense that featured exceptional passing, shooting, and backdoor cuts.

- Taught his players how to beat teams comprised of superior athletes.

- Considered to be one of the top coaches of all time in teaching players how to read and react to a defense.

- Believed the objective of coaching is winning with integrity.

- Became the first coach in Division I basketball history to win 500 games without athletic scholarships.

- Led Princeton to the 1975 NIT Championship.

PETER J. "PETE" CARRIL

"I believe the objective of coaching is winning with integrity."
—Pete Carril

BIOGRAPHY

Born: July 10, 1930 in Bethlehem, PA

Inducted into the Naismith Basketball Hall of Fame in 1997

Pete Carril took over the Princeton program in 1967, after serving thirteen years as a high school coach and one year as the head coach at Lehigh University. In twenty-nine years at Princeton, his teams registered ten seasons with twenty or more wins, led the nation in fewest points allowed fourteen times, and suffered only one losing season. Carril's thirty years of college coaching brought an overall record of 525-273, thirteen Ivy League championships, thirteen postseason tournament appearances, and the NIT championship in 1975. His offensive system featured exceptional passing, shooting, and backdoor cuts and was known as the Princeton offense. Carril was an assistant coach with the NBA Sacramento Kings for six years and helped lead the Kings to the 2002 Western Division finals. He is currently the Special Assistant to the President of Basketball Operations for the Sacramento Kings.

Peter "Pete" Carril...

Pete Carril's legacy in basketball was his pressing-style defense and methodically patient offense. Carril described his system this way, "I wanted my teams to behave like the old Boston Celtics. We pass, we cut, we shoot the ball well, and we look for good shots. The main thing is to get a good shot every time down the floor." (Price, 1977, p. 13)

"The basic difference between this system and others is that there's a greater use of cutting, and not much picking. It's supposed to take tension out of a game, so five guys aren't complaining about getting enough touches. You know the ball's going to come to you at the right time. If you're not skillful, you can't play in this offense, because everyone is the point guard. The minute you have the ball in your hand, you're expected to see what to do, to read the defense," explained Carril. (Wahl, 2003, p. 60)

Carril's offensive system was known as the Princeton offense and became popular on all levels of the game. In 2002, the New Jersey Nets reached the NBA Finals using Carril's concepts. The Princeton offense is not for everyone. It requires selfless players who can read the defense. The offense makes no distinction between its four nonpost players. Jim Burson, head basketball coach at Muskingum College, called Carril's offense "absolute genius." He studied the offense for several years and identified the following key principles: (Wahl, 2003, p. 62)
1. Unselfishness is more important than brains.
2. Five players must work together.
3. No traditionally numbered players are allowed. Instead, there is one post and four players. Very few plays are called.
4. Keep the center high and keep the area below the free throw line empty.
5. The offense is about cutting, not screening. Always cut with credibility. When you screen, screen and read.
6. It is about hypnotic cuts, passes, and handoffs. Do not run to the ball.
7. There is a counter for everything the defense does.
8. Think change of direction.
9. On any denial, go backdoor.
10. Hit the cutter with a bounce pass.
11. If there is no answer at the back door, knock on the front.

12. If the defender lays off, shoot the three-point shot. If the defender overplays you, cut backdoor.

Carril's well-drilled Princeton teams frequently frustrated and occasionally upset some of the nation's top teams. In 1989, Princeton was paired against Georgetown, the number one-ranked team in the country, in the first round of the NCAA tournament. Instead of a blowout, Princeton used their backdoor-oriented offense to combat Georgetown's pressure defense and led most of the game. Georgetown finally prevailed 50-49, but it took two blocked shots by Alonzo Mourning in the final six seconds to preserve the victory. Many observers questioned whether Mourning cleanly blocked the shots and thought there should have been a foul called on one or even both of the attempts. Regarding Mourning's fouls, Carril stated after the game, "I'll take that up with God when I get there." (Price, 1997, p. 15)

In Carril's last season at Princeton, the Tigers were matched against UCLA, the defending national champion, in the first round of the NCAA tournament. UCLA looked like they were in control with a 41-34 lead with six minutes to play, but Princeton came charging back with a three-point basket and two lay-ups. With the score tied and only 3.8 seconds remaining, Princeton executed their patented backdoor lay-up for a stunning 43 - 41 victory. The win was Carril's 525th and last victory of his illustrious college career. It was a victory that Carril said brought him "unparalleled happiness."

Few coaches have ever achieved more with less than Pete Carril. He was the first Division I coach to win over 500 games with no athletic scholarships. Carril's approach to recruiting was simple. First, he selected players who could pass, shoot, and play defense. Second, he spoke the truth. Instead of telling high school seniors that Princeton's basketball program would be built around them, Carril discussed their weaknesses and things they needed to do in order to improve their game. Very rarely did Carril make a home visit to a prospect during the recruiting process. Bill Carmody, who succeeded Carril as head coach and led the Tigers to a 24-4 record and another Ivy League title in his first season, said, "In my fifteen years with him, I think he made three home visits, and I don't think we got any of those kids." (Price, 1997, p. 13).

Carril, basketball's look alike to Yoda from "Star Wars," was one of the most revered figures on the Princeton campus. Tiger fans loved to watch their animated coach with the wispy white hair march up and down the sidelines. Carril wore his emotions on his sleeve and seemed to be in anguish during every minute of the game. His great success at Princeton caught the attention of high-profile basketball programs nationwide, but Carril rejected every offer because he did not want to compromise his principles. He explained it in these words, "It's a different life. I don't think I'd be good at that kind of life. Too many times, big-time schools are involved in defending things that are indefensible." (Atkins, 1997, p. 1)

Although Carril enjoyed being in a highly academic environment, he claimed that it didn't make his coaching any easier. Carril joked that his players aspired to an M.B.A., not the NBA. "I don't think there's a correlation between high grades and high board scores and smart playing. When I coached in high school, I had some special-education students who were at the bottom in the classroom but were star players. At Princeton, I had guys who scored well on their board exams, yet were not very smart basketball players. They were in the library all the time, but culturally deprived on the court," said Carril. (Atkins, 1977, p. 2)

Carril was a master teacher. Hall of Fame coach Bob Knight claimed that no coach did a better job of teaching players how to read a defense and how to react to it than Pete Carril. He taught his teams how to compete against players with superior athleticism, size, and power and still win.

Hall of Famer Bill Bradley believed Carril's honesty with his players set him apart from others. "He had a clear idea what he wanted his players to do. He had a philosophy of life that was implemented through his teaching of the game and insistence on how the game should be played," said Bradley.

Pete Carril began his career as a high school coach and never lost touch with his roots. He constantly reminded people of the importance of high school coaches and called them "the salt of the earth." Carril described his high school coach, Joe Preletz, as the best human being that he had ever met.

One of the greatest lessons that Carril learned came from his father, a Spanish immigrant steelworker. Every day on his way to work, he reminded Pete and his sister how important it was to be smart. Carril's father went on to explain that in life, the "big, strong guys are always taking from the smaller, weaker guys but the smart people take from the strong." That message served as Carril's theme for his entire coaching career.

SOURCE

Atkins, Ross. (October 30, 1997). Basketball Coach Pete Carril Comfortable in His "New" Career. *The Christian Science Monitor*.

Price, Jerry. (1997). Pete's Principles. *Naismith Basketball Hall of Fame Enshrinement Program*. Springfield, MA.

Wahl, Grant. (February 17, 2003). It All Starts Here. *Sports Illustrated*.

PETE'S PRINCIPLES:
THE PRINCETON WAY OF WINNING

By Pete Carril

I believe the objective of coaching is winning with integrity. What other reason besides winning with integrity is there for sports in the first place? It is my belief that whenever two players or teams of equal ability play, the one with the greater courage and intelligence will win. If a player will work out his limitations on his own and practice long hours, he will win. Winning brings out the best in people who are good, the worst in people who are not. Losing does not bring out character.

RELATIONSHIP BETWEEN ATHLETICS AND LIFE

I think there is a relationship between athletics and life. Sports do not build character. They reveal character. They can help you realize who you are, what your potential is, and maybe what it is you have to change about your habits to realize your full potential. The fans and the sports world make the mistake of acclaiming a player's success without noticing his work habits, which are a reflection of his character.

MY DEFINITION OF SUCCESS

I define success as having a chance to win every game. It's my job to give my players the chance to have their character, their drive to win, determine the outcome. I believe an athlete who is fundamentally sound and plays intelligently and hard will generally come out on top. The strength of my Princeton teams has always been attitude, intelligence, and discipline.

KNOWING WHAT TO COACH

It's in the best interests of a coach to make sure he is not spending three hours a day practicing things that don't happen very much. If you watch what your players are doing when they play, they'll show you what to teach them—which is an important principle in coaching. When a coach picks a style of play, that style cannot be his; it has to come from what his players indicate they can do and can't do.

When I first came to Princeton, we had fast teams and averaged close to 80 points a game. I like to remind people who criticized us recently for playing a deliberate style of offense, or a slowdown game, of that little bit of history. Our later offense wasn't slow; it was judicious. As the players got slower afoot here, they dictated to me that it was time to change our style of play. If a coach has a fast team and he wants to play a control game because that's his style, he'll have a revolution on his hands—the players will naturally want to run. On the other hand, if you have a slow team and it's your style to run and the other team beats you down the court, you had better change that, too. Your team will dictate the things you can teach them—and you find out by watching them carefully.

WHAT I LOOK FOR IN A PLAYER

What qualities do I look for in a player? Les Yellin, former coach at St. Francis College in Brooklyn, and I would often talk about qualities that we value, and he summarized the main virtues in the form of acronyms that I liked. He referred to them as IQ, EQ, and RQ.

1. INTELLIGENT QUOTIENT (IQ)

IQ means knowing what to do. A smart player will not take a shot he knows that he can't make. He will know things about himself that enhances the way that he plays.

2. ENERGY QUOTIENT (EQ)

EQ means having the energy to work at what you're doing. There is a Spanish saying that goes like this: "When the legs go, the heart and the head follow quickly behind." When your EQ is good, you practice harder, play the game harder, and when it looks as though you cannot move anymore, you find a way to move some more.

3. RESPONSIBILITY QUOTIENT (RQ)

RQ means that you know what to do, and that you will do whatever it takes to get it done.

Regarding basketball skills, the first thing I look for in a high school player is his passing ability. If he can pass, he's the same person who can cut and can defend. He's also the player who can see everything, the man he is passing too, the players around him, and the opportunities for creativity. Excellent passers set up the shots that their teammates can make. People told my players that if they wanted to go to Princeton, they had to be able to pass to play. That was essentially correct. Passing was the single greatest attribute of my teams over the years.

My ideal player loves to play, constantly learns, has good character, and does not give in to defeat. He uses all the parts of his abilities, not just one particular thing. I want a player who goes ahead and does what he knows has to be done, who doesn't give himself an excuse to fail. All I ever wanted as a coach was to get the best from every player I had. I will never be able to understand why someone doesn't play his best all the time. A player who gives you less than what he can give is, one, telling you what he thinks of you, and two, telling you what he thinks of himself. In both cases, it's bad.

DEFENSE IS THE HEART OF THE GAME

When I talk about basketball and strategy, about my way of playing the game, I begin with defense, because defense is the heart of the game. Good defense is recognizable even when you're losing.

The object of my defensive strategy is to contest every pass and shot, to force the opponent to move under continuous pressure. I want the other team to play offense longer than they're used too. Most teams can't pass well, or be patient for very long, so they'll eventually rush a shot, and then we have won the battle.

Defense is not a variable. It's a constant. Defense has to be deeply embedded in your attitude. It is something you can do well every time—both individually and as a team. There are three things that are very prominent in good defense: courage, intelligence, and energy.

I've heard some coaches say they have to "sell" their team on defense before they can teach it. I resent the word "sell," and I've never used it in my life. You must SHOW a

player how important defense is. You educate him.

PRINCIPLES OF TEACHING DEFENSE

The first principle of teaching defense is to recognize what your players can do defensively. Not all players are equally good in all phases of defense, and a coach has to see what the differences are. I used to rely exclusively on man-to-man defense, because I thought playing zone was an admission of weakness and that I was saying I couldn't play man-to-man, which requires speed and character. I started getting players who weren't able to keep their bodies in front of shooters, weren't able to contest shots, and had a knack for running into screens. It's hard to play man-to-man defense under those circumstances.

The second principle is that there is no single absolute. The result counts no matter how you do it. Any type of defense is good if it's effective.

The third principle is for the coach to recognize that the faster a team is, the more pressure it can apply defensively. Speed narrows the court and makes it less long. The court is larger to a slower team.

The fourth principle states that whatever you emphasize, and to the degree that you do, determines your success, up to the level of your ability. Let's say you develop a defense that prevents easy, unrestricted movement of the ball. You will be better at it than somebody who doesn't emphasize it—up to the level of your ability.

The fifth principle declares that the force of the coach determines the quality and intensity of the defense. Principles alone do not get the job done. Some coaches might know more defense but don't have the same strength of personality. Knowledge alone is not enough.

Not many coaches understand or appreciate these principles of defense. Their willingness even to listen to them is low. I feel sorry for them, young coaches especially, because they have the propensity to spend too much time tinkering with the offense. What's missing on defense is some clear thinking. I knew that I was rarely going to get good physical specimens at Princeton, so I stressed attitude and thinking. Always remember, it's mostly attitude and effort that make a defense successful.

LESSON NUMBER ONE ON OFFENSE

There is only one ball. Basketball is a series of one-, two-, and three-man plays; if all five players were trying to get into the action at the same time, they would run into each other. There cannot be competition for the ball. If you have five players competing for the ball, it makes it a lot easier for the defense to guard them.

I love the movement of the ball and all that it entails for the game. When there's movement of the ball, then there's movement of the defense and things start happening, such as open shots, driving opportunities, backdoor cuts, and open passing lanes. The epitome of great basketball is five players passing, cutting, moving the ball, doing what is natural, and not fighting for possession of the ball.

PRINCIPLES OF TEACHING OFFENSE

There are six key principles for teaching offensive basketball. They are geared on simplicity. We try to get the point across to our players that every little thing they do on offense counts. That means that every pass, every cut, every screen, and every dribble is part of the end result and therefore requires care and concern. Our disciplined offense is based on the great Boston Celtic teams of

LESSONS FROM THIS LEGEND...

the 1950s and 1960s and is built on timing and execution.

1. GET A GOOD SHOT

The main goal of the offense is to get a shot you can make, a good shot, every time you have the ball. The quality of your passing determines the quality of your shots. Our offense at Princeton always tried to make effective use of a center that likes to pass the ball. Bad passing is a limitation on the number of things that you can do. My approach on offense is to do something and create options so you have alternatives when the opposing team stops you from doing one thing. We try to create a flow or movement to cover all possibilities. We learn how to react to various defenses and to take what the defense gives us.

2. SHORTEN THE GAME AND CLOSE THE TALENT GAP

Against a run-and-shoot team with more talent and speed than your team, you want to make the game a shorter contest in order to close the gap between their talent and yours. You don't want to take the first good shot you get, but wait for the third or fourth good shot. We played North Carolina A&T in the preliminary round of the NCAA in 1983, were out rebounded 67 to 25, and won 53-41. We played deliberately, waiting for good shots, and then making them. You are never in trouble as long as you have the ball.

3. LEARN HOW TO PLAY WITHOUT THE BALL

We do have some set plays, but we try to teach all the possibilities that can come from any one play. The fundamental teaching point here is to watch your teammate in front of you. It's a fundamental tenet that applies to every offense that I know of. The player in front of you will tell you what you

should do by what he does. He might cut to get open, or cut to free an area—to make it open for someone else to go in there, or he might go to help someone else by setting a screen. Every player must learn how to play without the ball—keep their defensive men moving, divert them, get them to turn their head. Two further points: I do not like to have my players cut and go behind the man with the ball. It leads to trouble. I like them to go away from the ball. Secondly, if you watch your teammate with the ball pass it and then cut to the basket, you must know that you cannot cut in the same way he did. If you do, then the man who now has the ball has no one left to play with.

4. CUT WITH CREDIBILITY

What I like my players to do on offense to start a game is pass and cut through the defense. The minute you do, you start to move the defense, a main goal. The primary reason to cut, of course, is to get open to receive a pass, or to clear an area, and help set up something for a teammate. It also helps to identify the defense, whether it's a zone, a combo, or a man-to-man. Most of the time, your defender will tell you which direction to cut by how he moves. If he is contesting your movement, you will probably cut behind him. If he is playing you loosely, you will probably cut in front and toward the ball. You step one way and cut back another. The cut should be crisp and hard. If he tries not to let you cut, he is playing denial defense, or overplaying you, then cut behind him. This cut is called a backdoor, or give-and-go.

5. USE BACK-DOOR CUTS

If you're the dribbler and your teammate is open, throw the ball to him, that starts the offense. But what if you can't throw it to him because he's covered? You start dribbling toward him. He sees you dribbling toward him and reacts to how his defender

is guarding him. We want him to fake a step in one direction, and then turn sharply on an angle that forms a V and cut behind the defender, looking for a pass from his teammate. When you're guarded so closely that you aren't free to catch a pass, it means the defender is playing denial defense. He has turned his back partially to the ball, that's when you want to go back door. The defender can't watch the ball out front and you cutting behind him at the same time. We have made a living out of this play at Princeton. We have had as many as fifty back-doors in a single game. It takes a while to teach the back-door, because instinctively, the player without the ball wants to go toward the ball, rather than make the back-door cut.

We like to throw bounce passes off the dribble on our back-door plays. I tell our players to pass off the dribble, because if you pick up the ball, the defender who's guarding you sees you, thinks pass, and sticks his hands where you're going to throw it. But if you don't pick up the ball, the defender can't tell whether you're going to continue to dribble, or pass. The pass off the dribble is just a little push. You don't have to wind up. We tell the passer to aim for the rear end of the defender so that when the defender turns or opens to the ball, which is what most coaches teach, it's too late, and your player already has the ball. The bounce pass works well in close quarters because it makes the defender have to bend over to stop it. We spend hours perfecting this pass.

We have a back-door off the low post that involves the center. We create the back-door from a dribble screen. The possibilities flow one from the other, and we work on them until they become natural: the player comes around and goes in for a lay-up, or he comes around and stops behind a screen, or he drives the opposite way, or he passes and goes back-door for a return pass—all of these are possibilities when two players come together. We work on these options over and over. First, without a defender, we put a defender in there to guard the dribbler, then to guard the player who is going to get the pass. We work on getting each player to see what he is doing and where he is going, and what the others are doing and where they are going.

6. MAKE A ZONE DEFENSE "RUN"

When attacking a zone defense, you must first recognize the type of zone. You must remember that your decision on how to attack the zone has to be based on the shot you can make. The goal is to get an uncontested shot or a shot with a good opportunity to get fouled. The quality of your passing will determine the quality of your shot. To me, nothing makes attacking a zone more difficult than bad passing. If you aren't going to beat the zone by fast breaking, then develop good patience and put the zone to work for you.

Try to put your man in between any two of theirs. When you throw a pass, there should not be anyone in front of you. When you catch the pass, there should not be anyone in front of you either. Try to make as many cuts as you can from behind the zone. When you cut in front, the defense can see you, and that makes it easier to defend against what you're trying to do.

Move the ball and move yourself so that you make the zone "run," that takes the zone out of its shape, or makes the slides longer and more difficult to do. If you're going to penetrate or drive through a zone, try not to stop in between two of their men, but rather go past them. Teach your players the slides used by the defense in the zone.

SOURCE

Carril, Pete and Dan White. (1997). *The Smart Take from the Strong*. New York: Simon & Schuster.

TWENTY-FIVE LITTLE THINGS TO REMEMBER

1. Every little thing counts. If not, why do it?
2. When closely guarded, do not go toward the ball. Go back-door.
3. Whenever you cut, look for the return pass.
4. Whenever you commit to a cut (or back-door), do not stop and do not come back to the ball.
5. Bad shooters are always open.
6. On offense, move the defense.
7. Putting defensive pressure on the ball makes it harder for the other team to run an offense and gives your team a better chance to defend.
8. In a zone or any defense, when their five players guard your three, look to throw cross-court passes.
9. Watch the player in front of you. He shows you what to do.
10. Keep your dribble. Use it when you're going to do something useful.
11. A pass is not a pass when it is made after you've tried to do everything else.
12. A good player knows what he is good at. He also knows what he is not good at and only does the former.
13. You want to be good at those things that happen a lot.
14. When the legs go, the heart and the head follow quickly behind.
15. Defense involves three things: courage, energy, and intelligence.
16. If your teammate does not pass the ball to you when you're open and he doesn't say anything, then he did not see you. If he says, "I'm sorry," he saw you and did not want to throw you the ball.
17. In trying to learn to do a specific thing, the specific thing is what you must practice. There is little transfer of learning.
18. Whatever you are doing is the most important thing that you're doing while you're doing it.
19. Anyone can be average.
20. Being punctual is good in itself. However, what is more important is that your punctuality tells your teammates what you think of them.
21. Hardly any players play to lose. Only a few players play to win.
22. I like passers. They can see everything.
23. The way you think affects what you see and do.
24. Rarely does a person who competes with his head as well as his body come out second.
25. The ability to rebound is in inverse proportion to the distance your house is from the nearest railroad tracks.

LEGACY OF
Everett Case

- Promoted the growth of basketball in the Southeast and is called the "Father of ACC Basketball."

- Led North Carolina State to a third place finish in the 1950 Final Four.

- Popularized fast-break basketball in the South.

- Turned games into gala events with his spotlight introductions and pep bands.

- Known by his admirers as the "Old Gray Fox" because of his gray hair and his chess player's mind.

- Created the Dixie Classic, the premier holiday tournament of its day.

- Led the Frankfort (IN) High School Hot Dogs to four state championships.

Everett Case

"In the future, you will have many disappointments that you will have to face. I am an optimist and have faith in the future. Do not feel sorry for ourselves, but buck up and fight, and be ready to do the things necessary."
—Everett Case

BIOGRAPHY

Born: June 21, 1900 in Anderson, IN

Died: April 30, 1966

Inducted into the Naismith Basketball Hall of Fame in 1982

Everett Case coached North Carolina State University from 1946 to 1964 and compiled a 376-133 record. He was named ACC Coach of the Year in 1954, 1955, and 1958. During Case's first ten years, the Wolfpack won six consecutive Southern Conference tournaments, three straight Atlantic Coast Conference tournaments, and six of seven Dixie Classics. Case's teams dominated the Southern Conference and won 108 of 119 league games. North Carolina State finished third in the NIT in 1947. Case took the Wolfpack to the NCAA Final Four for the first time in school history and finished third in 1950. Prior to Case's arrival at North Carolina State, he carved a niche as a future Indiana Basketball High School Hall of Fame coach by leading the Frankfort Hot Dogs to four state championships. In twenty-one seasons at four different high schools, Case registered a 467-124 record.

Everett Case...

Throughout basketball's history, few have devoted more to the game than Everett Case. A lifelong bachelor, Case's passion for the sport was ignited during his formative years in Indiana as he experienced the excitement of "Hoosier Hysteria." He never played the sport in high school, yet Case's 1919 Anderson High School yearbook stated his future goal was to become a basketball coach. He was to realize his dream at age eighteen and continued coaching for forty-seven years. The young coach with the engaging smile and dynamic personality immediately proved that he was in the right profession. In 1922, Case arrived in Frankfort, Indiana and changed the way the game of basketball was played.

His 17 year-career as the Frankfort Hot Dog coach resulted in a 385-99-1 record. Case ranks second to Bill Green in Indiana high school state championships with four. The man with an astounding record and innovative coaching tactics is credited with starting such traditions as the announcing of starting lineups before the game, using game films to scout opponents, and cutting down nets after a championship win. ESPN The Magazine recently highlighted the fact that most of his money came from owning a small hot dog stand just blocks from the high school. Frankfurters forever.

The Hot Dogs put it all together in the 1925 season to finish 27-2 and win the state championship. The final game saw Frankfort run past the upstart Kokomo Wildcats 34-20. That year was the first time radio broadcasts were heard and sixty-four sectionals were used. To top off the magical season, Dr. James Naismith watched the game from press row at the State Fair Grounds, and presented the victors their medals. The 15,000 spectators were the largest crowd ever to witness a basketball game.

Current New Castle resident and former Frankfort forward Buck Plunkett still remembers the celebration after the game. "On our way back home, cars lined up along the side of the road to greet us at Lebanon. They lined up for over fifteen miles until we arrived at the courthouse for a celebration."

A classic contest between Frankfort and Logansport in 1927 created much controversy. The Berries were stranded by snowdrifts on their way to the game, had to get picked up by Frankfort officials, and started the varsity game

shortly before midnight. At the time, there was no ten-second rule in high school basketball, and Case held the ball the final eleven minutes of the first half with Logansport leading 7-6. By holding the ball at the opposite end of the court, the Hot Dogs stalled the entire second half, until just under four minutes remained. They rallied for a controversial 10-7 victory, and another chapter was written in the Everett Case file. The game caused post-game fights, cancellation of a rematch, and the creation of a ten-second line.

After collecting another championship in 1929, and dealing with accusations of illegal recruiting, Case left Frankfort to coach at Anderson for the 1932-33 season. He left the state to coach at the University of Southern California during the 1934 season while he earned his master's degree and worked under Coach Sam Barry. One year in the sun led Case to return to the state where basketball is king and the city he loved, Frankfort. One mediocre season was followed by another state championship.

The 1936 team produced two college All-Americans, a high-school coach, and two college coaches. They compiled a record of 29-1-1. According to the Times Weekend Edition, March 6, 1986, "It was and is generally considered the finest basketball team until the Oscar Robertson led Crispus Attucks champs of 1955-1556."

The tie came from two overtime grudge matches between the Hot Dogs and Indianapolis Tech. After nine ties, and fifty-one field goal attempts from each team, Case and Coach Bayne Freeman agreed to end the game.

Ansel Street commented in the Times article, "Nobody knows quite why they decided to leave it at a tie. I guess the coaches just decided that was enough." The IHSAA ruled after the season to prohibit ties, hence that is the only tie in Indiana high school history.

Ralph Montgomery is one of just two members of that team still alive. He still resides in Frankfort, and has fond memories of playing under Coach Case. "He had a lot of confidence in us and used much psychology in his coaching methods. We had confidence in him, and played the way he taught us. We played as a team and not as individuals like many teams today."

Case was one of the first basketball coaches known to film games. He meticulously studied every play and looked for options to maximize the strengths of his team. While pursuing his master's degree and working for Hall of Fame coach Sam Barry at the University of Southern California, Case analyzed various methods for shooting free throws.

His results supported the use of the underhand shot.

At the conclusion of World War II, Case was selected head coach at North Carolina State University. The selection of Case forever changed the game of basketball in the South. A brilliant coach, promoter, and motivator, he became the catalyst that made basketball the number one sport on "Tobacco Road." Jim Weaver, the first commissioner of the Atlantic Coast Conference, believed that Everett Case meant more to basketball in the South Atlantic region of the country than any other person. Case started the tradition carried on by Hall of Fame coaching legends Frank McGuire, Dean Smith, and Mike Krzyzewski.

"Coach Case was a visionary," said Les Robinson, who played for Case and later coached the Wolfpack. "He was a great coach, yes, but he was also a great promoter. Coach was a Madison Avenue type of businessman. He was years ahead of his time. He was marketing the game in an era when 'market,' meant where you go to get groceries." (Robinson, 2002)

Case directed his attention to promoting his team and his sport throughout North Carolina. He crusaded for every youngster to have a basketball hoop in his backyard. He often used his own money to purchase basketball equipment for playgrounds and boys clubs. Case dreamt of creating in North Carolina the same "basketball fever" found in his native state of Indiana.

Case created a tournament called the Dixie Classic. He knew it was the perfect way to bring national attention to basketball in North Carolina. The eight-team, three-day tournament matched the "Big Four" of the area (North Carolina State, North Carolina, Duke, and Wake Forest) against four of the nation's top teams. The Classic became a fixture on the holiday social calendar for North Carolinians and its reputation quickly spread throughout the United States. It became the premier sporting event in the South Atlantic region and was the forerunner of the many popular holiday tournaments that make up basketball today.

Known by his admirers as the "Old Gray Fox," Case was a magnificent showman and turned game night at Reynolds Coliseum into a gala event. By darkening the Coliseum, he heightened the crowd's anticipation and introduced the Wolfpack under a spotlight to the cheers of the fans. This type of pregame ritual had never been seen before in the South. Case also installed a sound meter to supposedly measure the noise level in the Coliseum. In reality, the sound meter was not functional and was controlled with a switch by a man standing courtside. Nevertheless, it was a great way of building excitement and increasing State's

home court advantage. Case was the first coach to authorize a pep band to play at home games. Opposing coaches accused Case of hiring the organist that played "Dixie" and sent the crowd into a frenzy. Cutting down the nets after winning a championship was also brought by Case to North Carolina, a tradition from his days as a high school coach in Indiana.

Another great highlight on game night was watching the silver-haired Case. It appeared that Case spent as much energy on the sidelines as his players did on the court. "I shoot for every one of my boys," stated Case. "If it looks like they're going to miss, I try to lean, or twist or scrooch'em in." (Lowery, 1951)

Case was one of the true innovators during his era. His racehorse style of basketball spread like wildfire across the state of North Carolina. The up-tempo, run and shoot game created excitement for both the players and the fans.

Case and his teams were so dominant that it forced other schools in the conference to revamp and update their basketball programs. North Carolina hired Frank McGuire, Duke brought in Vic Bubas, and Wake Forest chose Bones McKinney in an attempt to catch the Wolfpack. And in the process, the Atlantic Coast Conference (ACC) became one of the most respected leagues in college basketball.

Eight years after Case's death, North Carolina State defeated Marquette to win the 1974 NCAA championship. The Final Four that year was held in Greensboro, North Carolina. On the triumphant trip back to Raleigh, Wolfpack coach Norm Sloan ordered the team bus to stop at the cemetery where Everett Case was buried. It was in the early hours of the morning when Sloan led his players to the gravesite to honor the man who made the NCAA title a possibility. It was a fitting tribute to the "Father of ACC Basketball."

SOURCE

Case, Everett. Vertical Files, Archives. Naismith Memorial Basketball Hall of Fame. Springfield, MA.

Lowery, Raymond. (1951, February 25). Tar Heel of the Week: Everett N. Case. *The News & Observer.*

Morris, Ron. (1988). *ACC Basketball: An Illustrated History.* Chapel Hill, NC: Four Corners Press

Robinson, Les. Interview with Ralph Pim, May 22, 2002.

STAND UP AND FACE THE ISSUE

By Everett Case

Authors' Note: The darkest hour of Case's coaching career occurred when he discovered that three of his players had been involved in the point-shaving scandals of 1960-61. Case called authorities when he suspected something was wrong with the play of his team and was devastated when the investigation confirmed his players' involvement. "His players were his family," stated Les Robinson. "When the point-shaving scandal broke, it was as if one of his own family members had stolen from him. He never recovered from this hurt." The following is a manuscript of Case's first talk to the team after the conspiracy.

As I come before you this afternoon, I know that all of you are sad at heart over the events that have happened during the past two weeks. No one, however, is more disappointed and sadder than my assistant coaches and myself. Sad and disappointed because three of my boys, who were your teammates, conspired with gambling fixers to shave points and lose games.

Evidently, your teammates did not think of the great harm that they would do to all of us, when they succumbed to the temptation of the gamblers and those responsible for all of this. Especially true after all the warning that each of you had been given as to the eventual results of yielding to their sly remarks and approaches.

A BLACK MARK FOR THE GAME OF BASKETBALL

These boys have let down a great many people who had confidence in them, and also are a black mark on the great game of basketball. Very few of you would be here in college at this time if you did not possess some ability in the game of basketball. The great game of basketball has been good to a great many of us, and some of our boys have not stood up and faced the issue.

I really feel sorry for the three boys, that they yielded to the fixers and tinged their reputation and partially ruined the future with such actions. I do realize, however it was a great temptation for young boys, but one that the law enforcement officials and we had warned all of you about.

BE STRONG AND FACE THE ISSUE

This is not the time, however, to run or quit, but to stand up and face the issue. Naturally, this is a disappointment, but it is not the first disappointment you have ever had, nor will it be the last. In the future, you will have many disappointments that you will have to face. I am an optimist and have faith in the future. Do not feel sorry for ourselves, but buck up and fight, and be ready to do the things necessary. If you cannot meet the challenge now, you will not be able to do so in later life when you will face more vital issues and disappointments.

WE MUST TAKE THE LEAD IN HAVING A SAFER AND SANER PROGRAM

In the basketball scandals of 1951, many of the schools involved terminated intercollegiate basketball, and some of them cut to a limited schedule. I feel that the latter action is the sanest and soundest option of the two. I have hopes that our actions and conduct in the near future will bring a return of the Dixie Classic and some increase in our schedule. I have reason to believe that this investigation is just getting underway nationally, and may strike many other schools in all sections of the country. There seems to be a trend now by the NCAA to make a further cutback on schedules, so we may be the first of a long line to take the lead in having a safer and saner program.

WE HAVE NOT LIVED UP TO THE BASIC VIRTUES

I think we must take a good look at society and ourselves in general. There clearly has been deterioration in moral values; we certainly have not lived up to the basic virtues of loyalty, honesty, and integrity. Instead, there has been a sharply intensified self-indulgence typified in "What is in it for me" attitude.

LOOK AT THE BRIGHT SIDE

There are always two sides to any issue. On one side, we have the disappointment of a very reduced basketball schedule and loss of the Dixie Classic Tournament. On the bright side of the picture, however, we will have some advantages.

Your first objective here is to secure a good sound education, and to earn a degree so that you can obtain a creditable position out in life upon graduation. That certainly should remain your number one objective. Under the present program you will have:
1. More time for studying.
2. Less distraction from the classroom.
3. Less traveling and less class absences.
4. Longer holiday vacation at home, or chance to work during that period.
5. More time for individual work with each player.

6. Each game will mean a great deal more.
7. A closer team relationship that should develop in a better team effort.

More time to prepare for your games and more time for individual work. We should have ample opportunity to be ready for every game, and every boy should be a far better basketball player individually.

In the past, once the season had started, games came so fast that there was very little time to get ready or to work on individual faults. If you have ambitions to go ahead with basketball after graduation here, you should be a far tougher player under the present setup.

We will be allowed to participate in the annual ACC Tournament, of which the winner will represent the conference in the NCAA, and this has always been our main goal of achievement—to win the tournament.

WE ARE FACED WITH THE BIGGEST CHALLENGE IN THE HISTORY OF OUR SCHOOL

You boys are faced with the biggest challenge of any group in the history of our school, and we're confident you can overcome it. We'll be in the national spotlight more in the next two or three years than ever before. We'll need a strong spirit and unified effort from every man to do our utmost in erasing the black mark that has been brought upon us. Everyone will be watching you closely, not only in your athletic achievements but also as individuals. They'll judge you on your character, honesty, and integrity more than they ever have before. I think the student body will rally behind you if you give them an opportunity to do so. Take part in student activities and become more closely involved in the functions of your school. We have many true and loyal fans all over this and other states who want us to meet this challenge successfully.

YOU ARE THE FUTURE OF OUR PROGRAM

I want to assure you that your scholarship status is the same as always. As long as you continue to make progress towards a degree and do the right thing, your scholarships will be protected. We will be operating a full scholarship program in the future. You'll be the core of this program, and we will have to build around you. When all this dies down, we will continue to attract outstanding athletes to our school, but the future of our program depends on you.

There will be absolutely no summer league participation at all in basketball. This means that you cannot play any organized basketball anywhere, under any circumstances, during the summer months. Your basketball play is limited to informal play, such as schoolyard participation. If you violate this rule, you'll lose a year's eligibility and your scholarship. This is an NCAA rule.

I want you to concentrate on your exams and put in the necessary hours of study needed to do the best job possible. Don't be talking around town or on campus about any of the recent happenings. If you have something to say or would like to discuss any of this with the staff, come by the office. We'll be happy to chat with you about it.

WE WILL ACHIEVE

This has certainly been an unfortunate situation for all of us, but we intend to fight back and achieve the best results. I trust that none of you will do anything erratic or on the spur of the moment; you owe allegiance and honest effort to a great deal of people. Your integrity and your loyalty are at stake. It goes back to the old slogan, "A winner never quits, and a quitter never wins."

SOURCE

Case. Everett. (November 1961). Text of Talk to the Varsity Basketball Squad. *The Basketball Bulletin.*

Robinson, Les. Interview with Ralph Pim, May 22, 2002.

LEGACY OF
John Chaney

- Prepared players for success in life through his disciplined system and emphasis on character development and teamwork.

- Scheduled the toughest teams in the nation to prepare his players for conference play.

- Conducted daily practice sessions during the early morning hours to help instill discipline in his players.

- Became the all-time winningest coach at Temple University in 1999.

- Led Cheney State to the Division II national championship in 1978.

- Earned a reputation as one of the top defensive coaches in the nation because of his match-up zone defense.

JOHN CHANEY

"The only thing that can save a poor person's life is education."
— John Chaney

BIOGRAPHY

Born: January 21, 1932 in Jacksonville, FL

Inducted into the Naismith Basketball Hall of Fame in 2001

John Chaney began his collegiate coaching career at Cheney State University in 1972. In ten seasons at Cheney State, his teams compiled a 225-59 record, won the 1978 NCAA Division II national championship, finished third in the nation in 1979, and participated in eight NCAA tournaments. Chaney was named the Division II National Coach of the Year in 1978. He accepted the head coaching position at Temple University in 1982 and led the Owls to twenty consecutive post-season tournaments. During a remarkable five-year stretch between 1983 and 1988, Temple won twenty-five or more games each season. The USBWA, AP, UPI, NABC, and CNN/USA named Chaney the National Coach of the Year in 1988. Chaney became Temple's all-time winningest basketball coach in 1999, surpassing the legendary Harry Litwack, also a Hall of Fame coach.

John Chaney...

"Be...the dream," was John Chaney's motto. He had it written on the walls in the locker room and coaches' offices. Chaney's players were walking examples of his philosophy. He taught young men how to be successful in life.

Chaney was a dedicated and strong-willed teacher who molded the character of his players with positive values of discipline, teamwork, and common decency. Chaney did not think of discipline as a form of punishment. "Discipline is an order, an orderly situation," stated Chaney. "It's a well thought-out plan to direct somebody. It's another form of higher intellect. When you get a team that wants to play together, combines their skills together, and goes out and plays well together, that to me is one of the higher forms of intellect." (Cornfield, 2001)

According to many of his players, Chaney was the father figure that they never had. He taught players how to become better-rounded individuals and how to become successful members of society. "The winning or losing of basketball games should not be the thing that gives me access to having an influence on someone's life or to be viewed as a good coach or a good person," said Chaney. "The thing that should give me access is the fact that my major concern is to try and develop good character in the people I have under my wing. What is truly important is the growth of another human being and knowing you had something to do with it." (Wartenberg, 1991, p. 65)

It bothered Chaney that many people equated winning with being a successful coach. "The most bothersome and misunderstood aspect of this business, as I see it, is that people who win are looked at as people who are good coaches," said Chaney. "That disturbs me. I don't think you can measure a good coach based just on winning. A coach must be judged on some of the altruistic things that sports are all about—developing character, good sportsmanlike conduct, developing confidence, good will, good competitive spirit, the will to win, and the knowledge to know and distinguish that winning has nothing to do with the score. A coach with a lesser record or from a less prestigious program could have a greater impact on the lives of people." (Wartenberg, 1991, p. 144).

Chaney did not want his players focused on the opposition. His theme was "winning is within you."Chaney said, "The strength of a great team is they are effective in what they do and force the other team to surrender. You make the other team deal with who you are. If you move toward what the other team is about and worry about stopping what they do, you're moving toward their side of the court." (Wartenberg, 1991, p. 171)

Chaney believed in making the toughest non-conference schedule possible for his teams. He scheduled the nation's top opponents in the most hostile basketball environments, knowing his teams might suffer some losses. Chaney believed this helped his players mature and learn how to handle adversity. He wanted his players to know that on the road to any goal worth striving for, there would always be obstacles. "We've always made the schedule so my teams can experience playing the best teams early. That's not going to be a successful adventure. You're going to go out, you're going to get beat, and you're going to get scraped. That's why they are great teams. But somewhere along the line, in the first part of January, latter part of January, or the beginning of February, a light comes on, and they begin to play well." (Cornfield, 2001)

Chaney's disciplined system required players to begin practice at 5:30 a.m. He began this routine when he was a substitute teacher and coach of the cadet team (one step below the junior varsity) at Overbrook High School (PA), and it was the only time that he could get the gymnasium. Chaney believed it helped create self-discipline and incorporated the early morning practice sessions at every school he coached. "I've always worked with youngsters who very often are from tough situations in the inner city," stated Chaney. "It's always been my contention that you have to start somewhere, by raising the bar for young people and making sure they understand that it's not an easy trip that they're on."

Chaney was a high school basketball legend at Benjamin Franklin HS in Philadelphia and earned the Public League's MVP honors in 1951. His specialty was dribbling and scoring, and he was one of the first high school players in Philadelphia to shoot a jump shot. Chaney was an All-American at Bethune-Cookman College and was

named MVP of the 1953 NAIA championship. Chaney played professionally in the Eastern Basketball League for ten seasons and was the league's MVP in 1959 and 1960.

One of the tenets of Chaney's basketball philosophy was to protect the ball at all times. He detested turnovers and wanted his team to average less than ten turnovers per game. He preached that ball possession created scoring opportunities, while turnovers were nothing more than wasted opportunities. Chaney believed that nothing in life was worse than wasting an opportunity. "In basketball, you try to avoid as many mistakes as you can when you have possession," said Chaney. "A great team—every time they come down the floor something good happens. You cannot play basketball here if you're going to commit turnovers." (Wartenberg, 1991, p. 36)

Chaney was very superstitious and believed the clothes that he wore could affect the outcome of a game. If he felt a particular article of clothing was unlucky, he discarded it immediately. After one game, Chaney gave his assistant coach a pair of Italian leather shoes because he felt they were cursed. Conversely, once an article of clothing proved itself to be a good luck charm, he wore it repeatedly. Other superstitions included a fear of black cats, no open umbrellas in the house, and no hats on the bed.

Chaney was a fighter who always believed in standing up for what was right. He battled the NCAA because he thought that Propositions 48 and 42 were unfair to disadvantaged youngsters and poor inner-city children. "There should be more emphasis on helping children in the primary grades," said Chaney. "You have to spend more time with the kids from K through 12. The NCAA makes a lot of money. If they could give some of the money to the schools and communities where most of the players come from, that would make a big difference." (Hunt, 2003, p. 14)

John Chaney rose from poverty and overcame prejudice and lack of opportunity to become one of the most respected and successful coaches in the country. His mission in life was to help others become winners—both on and off the court. He helped his players understand that success has a narrow door and only through hard work was someone able to step through. Chaney believed fear and anger were prerequisites to success. "Fear says I will not leave any stone unturned," explained Chaney. "I will remember all of the things that I have to remember. Fear opens your eyes to what you must overcome. Anger says I'm going to play the game tough and mean, so fear and anger work together."

"As a coach, I've had plenty of players go to the NBA, but that's not important to me. I'm just happy we were able to give them a chance to improve their lives. Now they can go out and help others who didn't have the same opportunities they did." (Hunt, 2003, p. xiii)

SOURCE

Chaney, John, Vertical files, Archives. Naismith Memorial Basketball Hall of Fame. Springfield, MA.

Cornfield, Josh. (2001). Interview with John Chaney. *The Temple News.*

Hunt, Donald. (2003). Chaney: *Playing for a Legend.* Chicago: Triumph Books.

Wartenberg, Steve. (1991). *Winning Is An Attitude.* New York: St. Martin's Press.

WINNING IS AN ATTITUDE

By John Chaney

I adopted the slogan "Winning is an Attitude" when I was coaching at Cheyney State University and have used it ever since. It has nothing to do with the winning of basketball games. It is about winning at the game of life. "Winning is an Attitude" means that if something around you is bad, is negative, is evil, then there must be something inside of you that says flip that record over because there is something better on the other side of the record. When things are bad, real bad, you have to flip it over and make things better. This is the attitude I teach. I want to teach someone to say no to something that is negative and yes to something that is positive and right. If my players accept this, then they are winners before they ever step out onto the floor. They'll be winners in life. I have a specific way the slogan must be written. "Winning is an" is written across the top line in small letters, and underneath in big, bold letters is the word "Attitude." The key word is attitude, not winning. Attitude is everything.

HOW YOU START IS HOW YOU FINISH

The first day of practice is an extremely important day. The first day of anything is important. Anytime it's a first experience, it's very important. There are rules, and there are roles that we must involve ourselves in and understand. It's almost like formulating a contract. How you start is how you finish. If you start off being a family, that's the way you're going to end up. If players cannot live with the contract I spell out, then I must know that. As we move on, and the ship goes out to sea, a player can't jump ship. If a player does something that is contrary to what we discussed on the first day, then the ship is not going very far out to sea. We are not going to be successful as a team.

THE OPENING SPEECH

I begin every year with "The Speech." My players hear it four straight years and could probably come in and recite it. It goes something like this.

We're charged as a coaching staff to teach you something; that you're in college to learn about life. If we can't convince you of that, you have no reason to be here. You have a responsibility to recognize that you have something here. You have to look at the fact that this is a four-year investment in yourself that will last a lifetime. College is the fountain of life. You have to drink from it. You can't sit around for a whole semester and hope something will happen. You have to work at it.

The greatest assurance of success is that each and every one of you must agree that you are in a family setting. There are different rules that exist when you try to live together as a family. You can do certain things as an individual and get away with it because you only have responsibility for yourself. But, when you're on a team, when you're in a family, you have to always think about if what you're doing is going to create a problem for someone else. This might be the only time in your life that you will be part of something so strong and a part of something so meaningful. You can't be successful, no matter how talented you think you are, if you decide to go in another direction than the one we agree on today.

This basketball bounces a certain way every time it hits the floor. It's not like a football. A football bounces a different way every time. Your behavior must be like bouncing a basketball. I have to be able to predict success based on your behavior, and your behavior must be the same every time I call on you.

If you don't go to class, if you don't function in the classroom, we can't function as a team. They are one in the same. They're no different. They're equal. When you fail in the classroom, you fail out here on the basketball court. You just don't die in one place and live in another. If you're having a problem with one of your classes, you must let us know. We'll get somebody to help you—not somebody to do your work, but someone to help engage your mind. I don't care how good a player you are; if you are not balanced, I have to cut you off. It's that simple.

What I am selling, you must buy. You have to buy it. If you don't buy it, we can't live together. The contract says you go to class, and function in class, and then you can play basketball. One hand washes the other. It's very difficult to talk to somebody about life on the basketball court when he's not functioning in the classroom. The team can't be successful with players that don't think well or don't respond.

LESSONS FROM THIS LEGEND...

I want to put good human beings out on the floor. People who are playing sports for the right reasons. Sports are a vehicle. It's a car that takes you from one point to another. You use sports to get your degree. That's the main reason you're here. Always remember the value and importance of your education.

One of the things we can't involve ourselves with is someone with a weak mind who can be swayed in a negative direction. I don't care how poor economically you are, you cannot be the kind of person that will lean toward another value system. Just because you see someone walk around in expensive clothes and have gold chains around their neck and money in their pocket doesn't mean you can be swayed and forced to move in a direction that will mean loss of our structure as a family. If you're going to let yourself down, you're going to let all of us down.

You have to put things in the right priority. You have a lot of long days ahead of you consisting of practice, classes, and study hall.

Character is very important for us. Make sure I understand what you are and whom you are. I want gentlemen. I don't want people who are heathens. You can't teach someone who is dumb. You just can't. Stupidity is something that is very difficult to deal with because it is forever.

You're at a stage now where you are responsible for the decisions you make. Mom and Pop are not here with you. You've got to make the right decisions. It's very simple. If I'm walking the down the street and there's a dark alley and I see twenty-five or thirty guys walking out of that alley with baseball bats, I know that they are not going to a baseball game. I get out of there as quickly as I can. I don't go up and say, "Hey fellas, what's up? How you doing?" You have to make a good decision. You have to clearly read what's right and wrong. If something or someone will drag you down, stay away. You may have to elevate yourself from the people that you used to hang with. If you want to remain in the same spot the rest of your life, there's something wrong.

College is something that moves people in a positive direction. It cultivates and develops, and if you allow it to, it will nurture your development. Having a good attitude, a responsible attitude, is the only way that you can be successful. College is for responsible people. If you're looking for a shortcut, an excuse to lose, you'll always be able to find one.

The people who are very successful are the people who think well and make the right decisions. When you're on the basketball court and looking at the opposition, you have to take into consideration what is there. Do I shoot? Do I pass? That kind of reading is very important, and that is the same kind of reading you must have throughout life.

If I am yelling at you on the basketball court because you're not functioning and you're not doing what you're supposed to be doing—after we have taught you and worked with you—you must realize it's not you I'm yelling at, it's your behavior. You have to be able to separate the two.

I don't want a team that escapes from reality and escapes from the truth. I don't want people who are always escaping, who always have a story and are always conniving. People like that will not face trouble when it comes. They become immersed in failure. They learn how to fail. They get good at being bad. Nobody wants to take the last shot in a game. No one wants to try because there is a comfort zone in failure. I don't want a team that can't negotiate life, that won't take a chance at life. I don't want a team that avoids responsibility.

SOURCE

Wartenberg, Steve.(1991). *Winning Is an Attitude*. New York: St. Martin's Press.

LEGACY OF
Charles "Chuck" Daly

- Excelled at uniting players with diverse personalities into championship teams.

- Led the Detroit Pistons to back-to-back NBA championships in 1989 and 1990.

- Believed defense and aggressive rebounding were the keys to winning.

- Became the first Hall of Fame coach to win both an NBA championship and an Olympic Gold Medal.

- Received worldwide notoriety as coach of the Olympic "Dream Team" in 1992.

- Regarded as one of the best-dressed coaches in the game of basketball.

Charles "Chuck" Daly

"A pessimist is an optimist with experience."
—Chuck Daly

BIOGRAPHY

Born: July 20, 1930 in St. Mary's, PA

Inducted into the Naismith Basketball Hall of Fame in 1994

Charles "Chuck" Daly began his coaching career at Punxsutawney High School (PA) where he coached from 1955 to 1963. He was an assistant at Duke University from 1963 to 1969 and then became the head coach at Boston College. In 1971, Daly became the head coach at the University of Pennsylvania. He led Penn to four straight Ivy League championships and NCAA tournament appearances from 1972 to 1975. In the NBA, Daly coached at Philadelphia, Cleveland, Detroit, New Jersey, and Orlando. He was the first Hall of Fame coach to win both an NBA championship and an Olympic gold medal. Daly coached the Detroit Pistons to back-to-back world championships in 1989 and 1990. He led Detroit to three Central Division titles, five 50-plus win seasons, and nine straight winning seasons. He gained worldwide notoriety as coach of the Olympic gold medal "Dream Team" in 1992.

Charles "Chuck" Daly...

Chuck Daly called himself a basketball "lifer." His passion for the game began as a youth growing up in Kane, Pennsylvania. Daly spent hours in the gymnasium improving his basketball skills. He also discovered that the school library had a subscription to *Scholastic Coach,* and he anxiously awaited each issue so he could learn more about the game he loved. When Daly was in the tenth grade, he told his mother that he was going to be a college basketball coach.

Daly's coaching career started in Punxsutawney, Pennsylvania, a town made famous by its legendary groundhog. Daly nurtured his coaching skills by reading, attending clinics, and visiting with legendary coaches. One of the best clinics that he attended was at Kutsher's Country Club in the Catskill Mountains that featured speakers like Clair Bee, Pete Newell, and Frank McGuire. In the summers, Daly attended basketball camps all over the country, including the Everett Case Camp at North Carolina State.

During his high school career, Daly learned what might have been the most important lesson in his life. After seven successful years, Daly suffered through a disastrous losing season. During the course of that year, Daly discovered that you couldn't win without good players. Daly described the impact of the losing season in these words, "It gave me a deeper understanding of what coaching is all about, of what is possible, and what isn't. How much I knew was not all that mattered. I could know every way to throw a bounce pass, every man-to-man defense, and everything about attacking a zone, but if my players couldn't execute it, the team wasn't going to win."

In 1963, Daly traveled to Louisville to see the NCAA semi-final and championship games. It was the first time that he had attended the Final Four, and he anxiously bought a ticket from a scalper and sat in the last seat of the last row of Freedom Hall. After the game, Daly read in the newspaper that Fred Shabel, an assistant coach, was leaving Duke University. He decided that he would write Duke's head coach, Vic Bubas, concerning the opening on his staff. Daly explained it in these words, "Talk about chutzpah! He (Bubas) was one of the most famous coaches in the country, just back from taking his team to the Final Four, and he gets a letter from an unknown high

school coach in Punxsutawney, Pennsylvania, who wants to be his assistant. Well, I'm here to tell you that miracles do happen." (Daly, 1990, p. 47.) Daly interviewed for the position and was given the job. Ironically, one year after attending the Final Four with a ticket bought from a scalper, Daly was on the bench as an assistant, coaching the Blue Devils in the NCAA semi-final game against UCLA.

Daly accepted his first head coaching collegiate position at Boston College. He then coached six seasons at the University of Pennsylvania and led his teams to four Ivy League championships and four NCAA tournament appearances. Daly left the Quakers for an assistant's position in the NBA with the Philadelphia 76ers.

In December of 1981, Daly accepted the head coaching position with the Cleveland Cavaliers. After just ninety-three days, Daly was fired. It was the most difficult time in his career. Daly described it this way, "I was nearly fifty-two and didn't have a job and didn't know where I could go. Once you've been in the pros, you become a little tainted and there's no going back to the college ranks. I was feeling pretty low, and a lot of people were asking pointed questions about whether my career was over. None of the people I used to know were calling anymore. It was a disaster. My phone never rang, and nobody came around. It was as if I had died." (Daly, 1990, p. 81)

Daly finally received another chance in the NBA and accepted the head coaching position at Detroit in 1983. Jack McCloskey, the Piston's general manager, had watched Daly's teams at Penn and knew that he was an outstanding coach who stressed defense.

Over nine seasons, Daly molded Isiah Thomas, Joe Dumars, Bill Lambeer, Dennis Rodman, John Salley, and Rick Mahorn into one of the toughest and most intimidating defensive units in NBA history. They were called the "Bad Boys" and won back-to-back NBA championships in 1989 and 1990.

The stylish Daly was selected coach of the year by *Gentleman's Quarterly*, and was also called "The Rock Hudson of Coaching" for his beautiful head of hair. His success was built upon his ability to unite diverse personalities into a smooth functioning team. A prime example was Dennis Rodman. Daly saw the potential in Rodman to be an outstanding player because of Rodman's desire to run the floor, rebound, and play defense. Daly described it in these words, "I saw in him a mustang out on the range—a wild colt who wanted to run loose, to be free. He didn't want any restraints on him, so I knew handling him would be a touch-and-go matter. But he loved to play, and he loved to win." (Daly, 1990, p. 152)

Daly was highly competitive and described himself as being on edge all the time. "It's the fear of losing, that's what it is. I've had to live with it my entire life. I am a competitive person, and the fear of failure, the fear of losing, overwhelms me at times." (Daly, 1990, p. 184)

Daly's fear of losing even surfaced when he coached the star-studded Dream Team in the 1992 Olympics. Lenny Wilkens, an assistant coach for the Dream Team, said, "Chuck worries about everything. He worries when he can't find anything to worry about—because he figures he missed something, and something had to be going wrong if only he could find it. No wonder the *Boston Globe's* Bob Ryan nicknamed him "The Prince of Pessimism." (Wilkens, 2000, p.221)

Daly knew that he was described as a pessimist but responded in these words, "A pessimist is an optimist with experience." (Daly, 1990, p. 192)

Daly believed the most important assets for a coach were "a lot of experience, bad hearing, and a small ego."

Daly stressed to his players that teams win championships, not individuals. "The players must have ability," said Daly, "but it is essential that they perform as a team. They have to be unselfish, and it's hard to find unselfish players."

Daly built his championship teams on defense. "The big step was to get our players to believe in playing defense, which is nothing but hard work," said Daly. "But how do you do it? How do you get guys to play defense when all the glory is on offense?"

Daly (1990) answered his questions with the following answer. "If you study the game by reading, listening, watching, and learning from others, you realize that defense is the only common denominator to winning. I've read a lot about successful basketball coaches, and I've learned that if a team's defense is consistent, the team will win more than it loses, even if it has only average players. I believe that 90 percent of the coaches in our profession want to be known as defensive-minded coaches. The problem is convincing the players. A player's mentality is always geared toward scoring. That's what the game is all about. Scoring produces victories and makes the crowd cheer. When the ball goes through the hoop, the player is the hero. Every eye is on him, and every cheer is for him. It can be a hard sell."

Daly continued his emphasis on defense by stating, "Probably the most important factor in playing defense is defensive rebounding. There's a basic philosophy that goes back to the invention of the game that all coaches spout, but don't necessarily believe. I probably say it a thousand times a year. 'If you don't give them a second shot, you'll never lose a game.' Boxing out and not letting your man get a second shot is the single most difficult thing to sell to your players. Defense isn't very entertaining, but if you want to succeed, it is the only way to go. If I have any phrase that sums it all up it is 'Defense wins championships.' It's not very colorful, but it works for us."

A key component in Daly's coaching style was his communication with his players. He involved them in the decision-making process and listened to their opinions. He also tried to keep them fresh throughout the season. Daly cautioned coaches not to take the fun out of the game for players. "Be careful not to make the game too complex," Daly said. "Players love to play this game, and we can't take that joy away from them."

SOURCE

Daly, Chuck and Joe Falls. (1990). *Daly Life.* Grand Rapids, MI: Masters Press.

Daly, Chuck. Vertical Files, Archives. Naismith Memorial Basketball Hall of Fame. Springfield, MA.

Wilkens, Lenny and Terry Pluto. (2000). *Unguarded.* New York: Simon and Schuster.

LESSONS FROM THIS LEGEND...

WINNING IN THE NBA

By Chuck Daly

To be a successful coach in the NBA, it's essential to have a good relationship with the superstars on the team. Paul Westhead learned this lesson the hard way. He coached the Los Angeles Lakers to a championship, and a year later he was fired. He had an alleged disagreement with Magic Johnson about how the game should be played, and Magic won. This should not detract from Westhead's ability as a coach. He's been successful throughout his career, and went from the Lakers to little-known Loyola Marymount, which he turned into a national power.

If you don't get along with your best player, you don't survive. You have to give up some self-esteem, and maybe some ego, to pacify him, but it must be done or your chances for success are zero. I knew immediately I could never win in Detroit unless Isiah Thomas was in my camp. It has nothing to do with him or me—just the way things are in the NBA. It happens on all teams. Coaches handle it in different ways.

I've never been good at holding onto my anger, but Vic Bubas at Duke taught me to bite my tongue. There are a lot of things I'd love to say at times, but it's better to be quiet. I'd get hot and want to tell my players a thing or two on the bench, but instead, I put my hands in my mouth or lower my head or simply turn away and look at something else. This form of self-discipline is very hard to acquire, but it's necessary if you're going to win in the NBA.

Some coaches try to be dictatorial, but I avoid that approach. You might get away with it in high school, and sometimes in college, but as you move up the ladder, you've got to let the players have some say in running the show. The players must be involved in the decision-making process, because you will get more out of them, and you'll be more successful. This isn't always easy to do because it goes against the grain of coaching. We all want to be authoritarian; we all want to dominate. It takes great discipline to go the other way.

I look at the other coaches in our league. The older ones seem to have the most success lately, with some exceptions, and I think that's because they've learned to listen to the players. They've learned they can't have two-hour film sessions every day, because it will bore players to death and take away their desire to play. The freshness of the mind, the desire to play—these are the important things. We play a kids' game. We can't make it too simple, but we can make it so complex that the fun goes out of it. Players love to play this game, and we can't take that joy away from them.

I guess I'm a so-called "player's coach." That doesn't mean I'm easy on them -just that I try to understand them. I try to understand their mentality, and I try to understand them on and off the floor. I don't have a doghouse. If a player has a bad game, it's over at midnight. Then it's a new day, and we go on from there.

In coaching, you go with the players you can trust—the ones who know all parts of their job and play both ends of the court, the ones who know how to rotate, how to box out, how to get to the free-throw line. That's how you're going to win, and that's whom you trust. But you can also get too

comfortable trusting the same players; you have to keep reevaluating yourself and everyone on the roster.

Defense wins championships. Every team, from high school to the pros, tries to play good defense. But how do you do it? How do you get guys to play defense when all the glory is on offense?

If you study the game by reading, listening, watching, and learning from others, you realize that defense is the only common denominator to winning. I've learned that if a team's defense is consistent, the team will win more than it loses, even if it has only average players.

I believe that 90 percent of the coaches in our profession want to be known as defensive-minded coaches. The problem is convincing the players. Even though they know the best way to become a macho player is to play tough defense, it's still a hard sell. A player's mentality is always geared toward scoring. When you score a basket, you are a success, and players who want to be basketball players develop an appreciation for offense long before they know anything else about the game. As these young players develop, their coaches have to battle them constantly to work on the more difficult parts of the game. They have to teach them to chase their man around a screen, be in position to rebound, and dive for loose balls.

When you go into coaching, you must decide what philosophy to follow. There are successful coaches who are defensive-minded, some who are offensive-minded, and some who balance both. In my own case, I believed from the start that defense was the answer to winning. My conclusion seemed logical because defense was the one thing that could be consistent every night.

Maybe the most important factor in playing defense is defensive rebounding. There's a basic philosophy that goes back to the invention of the game that all coaches spout but don't necessarily believe. I probably say it a thousand times a year: "If you don't give them a second shot, you'll never lose a game." You can't possibly lose if you hold them to one shot on every possession. They can't shoot well enough to score enough points to win.

Boxing out and not letting your man get a second shot is the single most difficult thing to sell your players. It drives you insane as a coach. I never stop saying it, even though I know they hate to hear it. I hate to say it, but in the biggest games of the year, I say it even more.... and a lot louder than during the season.

After we won our second consecutive NBA title, Detroit held a celebration at The Palace. As I sat on the stage, I thought of all the things I wanted to say about this team. I wanted to tell the fans about the sacrifices these players had made to win. They gave up personal glory, points, assists, rebounds, minutes played. All the things most players live for. Our players gave up these things so we could develop other players and become a team. We won because our players were secure enough within themselves and unselfish enough to give up their personal stats and glory.

We also won because we were willing to change. I see our team as a kind of an amoeba, a form that has a nucleus but is always changing. We have twelve players on our roster, and we keep trying to improve each position.

Having coached at all the levels, I know one thing: teams win championships, not individuals. The players must have ability, but it's essential that they perform as a team. They have to be unselfish, and it's hard to find unselfish players.

SOURCE

Daly, Chuck and Joe Falls. (1990). *Daly Life*. Grand Rapids, MI: Masters Press.

LEGACY OF
Everett Dean

- Led Stanford to the 1942 NCAA National Championship.

- Designed a free-lance offense, called the "Stanford weave" that featured a four-man continuity combined with strong pivot play.

- Called the "Gentleman from Indiana" by his coaching colleagues.

- Authored two popular basketball textbooks.

- Led Stanford's baseball team to a fifth-place finish in the 1953 College World Series.

- Enshrined into both the Naismith Basketball Hall of Fame and the College Baseball Hall of Fame.

EVERETT DEAN

*"I believe that most coaches consider themselves
as educators of boys, and not just sports technicians.
The individual comes first. I've tried to develop
boys through educational experiences.
The goal is to give the players
more than just a sports education."*
—Everett Dean

BIOGRAPHY

Born: March 18, 1898 in Livonia, IN

Died: October 26, 1993

Inducted into the Naismith Basketball Hall of Fame in 1966

Everett Dean began his coaching career at Carleton College in 1921 and compiled a three-year record of 48-4. He became the head coach at Indiana University in 1924 and helped established Indiana's rich basketball heritage. Dean led the Hoosiers to Big Ten titles in 1926, 1928, and 1936. He left IU in 1938 and became a legendary coach at Stanford. Stanford won the 1942 NCAA National Championship. He is the only unbeaten coach in NCAA Final Four history, compiling a 3-0 record in the 1942 tournament. Dean's career collegiate record was 374-217. He served on the All-American Selection Committee and the National Sports Committee. Dean received the Metropolitan Intercollegiate Award in 1958. As an undergraduate at Indiana, Dean became Indiana's first All-Big Ten basketball performer, as well as their first basketball All-American.

Everett Dean...

Everett Dean was an all-around athlete at Salem (IN) High School. from 1913-1917 and won ten letters in football, basketball, and baseball. He attended Indiana University and was a three-year starter in both basketball and baseball. Dean became the first All-American basketball player at Indiana University in 1921, when he was selected to the Helms Athletic Foundation All-American team. He was also an exceptional student and received the highest honor in Big Ten athletics, the Western Conference Medal for Proficiency in Scholarship and Athletics.

When Dean graduated from Indiana, he turned down several professional baseball contracts in order to embark on a coaching career. His first job was at Carleton College (MN) where his basketball teams compiled a 48-4 record. Dean returned to coach his alma mater in 1924. In fourteen years at Indiana, Dean had an impressive record of 162-93 and led the Hoosiers to three Big Ten Conference championships. Dean also coached the baseball team to three Big Ten titles.

Hall of Fame coach Bob Knight recognized Dean's contributions to Indiana University in these words, "Everett Dean has almost as much of a claim to being considered the Father of Indiana University basketball as George Washington has for our country. In 1921, Everett was selected Indiana's first basketball All-American; before his arrival, Indiana's basketball record was 19-67. In 1925, he

coached the first Indiana basketball team that won a Big Ten title. He recruited Branch McCracken, who became an All-American and Hall of Famer. McCracken then succeeded Everett as coach and won two national championships. Everett had a role in Branch's 1940 national championship. He brought in the players who, after he left for Stanford, Branch coached to not just that championship, but three great seasons. Everett was an outstanding athlete with an extraordinary astute mind that was geared to the fundamentals of the game. Indiana never had a better or more respected alumnus than Everett Dean, nor did I ever have a nicer friend." (Knight, 2002, p.243)

In 1939, Stanford University selected Dean to replace Hall of Famer John Bunn as their basketball coach. Bunn resigned his coaching position to become the Dean of Men at Stanford. Dean coached the basketball team for eleven seasons and compiled an overall record 167-120. He led Stanford to the 1942 NCAA championship. In 1950, he was named baseball coach and held both jobs for two seasons. Dean's baseball team finished fifth in the 1953 College World Series. Dean was enshrined into both the Naismith Basketball Hall of Fame and the College Baseball Hall of Fame.

The NCAA basketball tournament was only four years old when Stanford claimed the title in 1942. The team was a powerhouse and finished the season with a record of 28-4. In an era when any player taller than 6 foot was considered big, the team's nickname, "The Tall Redwoods of California," said it all. The starters averaged 6-foot 4-inches and were fast as well as tall. Dean said, "They moved very well for big men, and we could easily alternate positions. Remarkably, three of Stanford's starters, Don Burness, Bill Cowden, and Howie Dallmer, attended the same high school (Lowell High School) in San Francisco.

.....SCOUTING REPORT.....SCOUTING REPORT...

Dean utilized a versatile, free-lance style of play that featured a four-man continuity, combined with good pivot play. Dean called the four-man continuity the Stanford Weave. This offense had two or three basic set-ups from which 12 to 15 play options were developed to exploit weaknesses in the defense. Dean stated, "Players like this offense because of its equality of scoring chances and the many free-lance opportunities. All in all, it adds up to an interesting, potent, and practical style of attack." (Dean, 1945, p.36)

The championship game between Stanford and Dartmouth matched teams from the most distant sections of the country for the first time in tournament history. It also had two schools with the same nickname, Indians. Additionally, Dartmouth coach Ozzie Cowles had played for Dean at Carleton College in Minnesota.

Jim Pollard, Stanford's All-American and future Hall of Famer, was stricken with the flu the day before the championship game and could not play. He had scored 43.4 percent of his team's points in its first two tournament games. Pollard was nicknamed "The Kangaroo Kid" because of his extraordinary leaping ability and deadly jump shot. Another starter, co-captain Don Burness, was troubled by an ankle injury and was replaced without ever scoring a point. Stanford played without two All-American performers in the most important game of the season.

The score was tied at 26-26 four minutes into the second half when Stanford raced ahead and won comfortably, 53-38. Stanford shot an impressive 39 percent from the field and showed its depth in front of a capacity crowd of 9,500 in Kansas City. Howie Dallmar, who later coached Stanford for twenty-one years, was the leading scorer and the Tournament MVP. The NCAA tournament was in its

infancy, and the game wasn't even broadcast live back to the San Francisco Bay Area. After expenses, Dean took a meager check for $93.75 back to Stanford.

During World War II, Dean served as director of physical education for both the Army and civilians at Stanford. In the summer of 1945, he served as an associate director of athletics for the War Department in Europe.

Dean's coaching colleagues called him "The Gentleman from Indiana." Dean authored two popular basketball textbooks, *Indiana Basketball* (1933) and *Progressive Basketball* (1949). After Dean retired from coaching, the U.S. State Department sent him to South America to do good will through basketball. He served as an assistant to the President of Indiana University in alumni athletic affairs and was awarded the Indiana University Distinguished Alumni Service Award in 1960.

SOURCE

Dean, Everett. (November 1945). Stanford's Weave. *Scholastic Coach*.

Knight, Bob and Bob Hammel. (2002). *Knight: My Story*. New York: Thomas Dunne Books.

COACHING PHILOSOPHY

By Everett Dean

The first fundamental of coaching is a sound philosophy of athletics. A coach's philosophy of athletics is an important segment of his beliefs. He cannot have one attitude toward life and a different one toward athletics, because his convictions and principles in coaching will carry over into other phases of his life. Each coach has a definite philosophy, whether it is good or bad. Right and wrong thinking and acting constitute two kinds of philosophies. Therefore, the development of sound principles of coaching in our present system of athletics, where winning is often overemphasized, is a real challenge to all coaches of sports.

It is urgently recommended that each young coach start his career with a clearly defined and wholesome sports philosophy. It can serve to crystallize his attitudes and beliefs and to guide him in his thinking, which will result in a consciousness of the worthwhile of coaching.

THE WILL TO WIN

The winning of games has too long been the public yardstick for measuring coaching success. There is more to athletics than winning. The coach must realize the educational aspects and responsibilities of coaching in order to be happy in his work. The coaching of basketball is a medium through which the "educator-coach" functions in his effort to give his boys more than a sports education. One of the important responsibilities of a coach is to develop the will to win. The psychology of a winning spirit is important in the complete development of an athlete.

BASKETBALL COACHES CREED

George R. Edwards of the University of Missouri wrote the "Basketball Coaches Creed" for the National Association of Basketball Coaches. It is difficult to state a philosophy that can improve upon the following creed:

I believe that basketball has an important place in the general educational scheme and pledge myself to cooperate with others in the field of education to administer it so that its value never will be questioned.

I believe that other coaches of this sport are as earnest in its protection as I am, and I will do all in my power to further their endeavors.

I believe that my own actions should be so regulated at all times that I will be a credit to the profession.

I believe that the members of the National Basketball Committee are capably expressing the rules of the game, and I will abide by these rules in both spirit and letter.

I believe in the exercise of all the patience, tolerance, and diplomacy at my command in my relations with all players, co-workers, game officials and spectators.

I believe that the proper administration of this sport offers an effective laboratory method to develop in its adherents high ideals of sportsmanship, qualities of cooperation, courage, unselfishness and self-control; desires for clean, healthful living; and respect for wise discipline and authority.

I believe that these admirable characteristics, properly instilled by me through teaching and demonstration, will have a long carryover, and will aid each one connected with the sport to become a better citizen.

I believe in and will support all reasonable moves to improve athletic conditions, to provide for adequate equipment, and to promote the welfare of an increased number of participants.

BUILDING YOUNG PEOPLE OF CHARACTER

This is now and always will be the first responsibility of the coach. He should coach boys first and basketball second. If this policy is followed, the team will achieve greater success. The coach who develops youth through athletics as an educational experience, and who uses sports as a technique of learning, will find his efforts well rewarded.

Athletics must be an educational experience to boys. As education is to our democracy, so is athletics to education. Some of the educational values that coaches attempt to teach are:

- Social, emotional, personality, mental, and moral adjustments
- Leadership, followership qualities
- Respect for authority
- Development of good health habits
- Good citizenship
- Sportsmanship, or the Golden Rule
- Team play – the ability to work and play with others
- That with right goes responsibility

Sports are a means of expressing a phase of one's preparation for the game of life. General Doglas MacArthur once said, "On the fields of friendly strife are sown the seeds which in other years and on other fields will bear the fruit of victory."

LESSONS FROM THIS LEGEND...

VALUES IN ATHLETICS AND PHYSICAL EDUCATION

The coach is the guiding figure in the successful or unsuccessful athletic program. Athletics can be a constructive or destructive force in a school system, depending greatly on the type of leadership. An athletic program well-conducted is one of the most important departments of any school system. That type of program satisfies the fulfillment of the objectives of education as much or more than any other school program.

The values in athletics lie in what the students learn in the program. The development of health and good citizenship is the broad objective. The development of the complete man is one of the aims of education, and I firmly believe that no department of our educational system can contribute more to the fulfillment of this aim than a sound, properly conducted department of athletics and physical education.

MY FAVORITE MAXIMS

1. As he lives, so will he coach.
2. Know where you are going.
3. You are an educator and a coach.
4. Be prepared when opportunity knocks.
5. Building boys is better than mending men.
6. No price is too high to pay for a good reputation.
7. Rules are made to observe.
8. Ethics is what you do when no one is looking.
9. Have ideals and live them.
10. A man's value is that which he places upon himself.

SOURCE

Dean, Everett. (1950). *Progressive Basketball*. New York: Prentice-Hall.

LESSONS FROM THIS LEGEND...

ADVICE FROM A MASTER

By Everett Dean

Authors' Note:

Everett Dean must rank with the most successful collegiate basketball coaches in the history of the game. Coach Dean retired in 1955 and returned to Salem, Indiana.

Compliments he considers the highest paid him have come from fathers who said, "I wanted my boy to play under Everett Dean."

The tremendous respect that he acquired wherever he coached speaks volumes for his character, and his philosophy strongly reflects it: "I believe that most coaches consider themselves as educators of boys, and not just sports technicians. The individual comes first. I've tried to develop boys through educational experiences. The goals is to give the players more than just a sports education."

After his long career of X's and O's, whistles and clipboards, Coach Dean had the following comments and advice: "If I had it to do over I would be a basketball coach again. But I think I would do a better job."

THINGS I WOULD DO DIFFERENT
IF I COULD START OVER:

1. I'd study up and be an authority on psychology to understand the boys better.
2. I'd try to be absolutely tops in public relations to represent my school better.
3. I'd set up a definite savings and investment plan from the very first to give me independence later in life.
4. I'd educate myself in guidance and counseling services so I could improve my communication with players.
5. I'd try hard to give all my players a better set of values.
6. I'd be a stricter disciplinarian, because all boys need discipline and are grateful for it later.
7. I'd train all my assistants to become head coaches. I might not keep them long, but they would be worth more to me while I had them.
8. I'd put my family above my job. You can always find another job, but never another family.
9. I'd be a better churchman, because the work of a good coach is much like the work of a good churchman.
10. I'd give more time to civic activities and community service, because no man is better equipped for that work than a leader of young men.

SOURCE

Dean, Everett. Interview with Jerry Krause, 1979.

LEGACY OF
Antonio Diaz-Miguel

- Coached the Spanish National Team for 27 years and led Spain to six Olympiads, including winning a silver medal in 1984.

- Was the longest reigning national Olympic coach in the history of world basketball.

- Helped bring American basketball to Spain and Europe.

- Recognized an outstanding teacher whose teams were well prepared, fundamentally sound, and displayed exemplary sportsmanship.

- Named the "Best Spanish Coach" of the 1980s.

- Won two silver medals (1973, 1983) and one bronze medal (1991) in the European Championships.

ANTONIO DIAZ-MIGUEL

*"Keep your faith in a few and
defend them forever."*
—Antonio Diaz-Miguel

BIOGRAPHY

Born: July 6, 1933 in Alcazur de San Juan, Spain

Died: February 23, 2000

Inducted into the Naismith Basketball Hall of Fame in 1997

Antonio Diaz-Miguel graduated from Bilbao University (Spain) with a degree in industrial engineering in 1963. Playing in the club sports system of Europe, he was exposed to basketball at an early age and become a player for the Spanish National team at the age of 18. He played in the Spanish Professional League for 13 years, including a stint with the Real Madrid team from 1958-60. In 1965, at the age of 32, he was named as Spain's National Olympic Coach, a position he held for 27 years (1965-92). In more than 300 games, he guided the team to six Olympiads, including winning a silver medal at the 1984 Olympic Games in Los Angeles. His teams played in 14 European Championships and four World Championships. His best finishes were two silver medals (1973, 1983) and one bronze medal (1991) in the European Championships. Diaz-Miguel coached the European All-Star team six times and was named the "Best Spanish Coach" of the 1980s. He finished his coaching career as head coach of Pool Getafe, a woman's team in the Spanish League.

Antonio Diaz-Miguel...

Antonio Diaz-Miguel was born in Spain in the 1930s, a decade when basketball was maturing as a sport in the United States. Among the notable basketball-related occurrences during this period were the following:

- court divided into halves
- center jump eliminated
- molded ball developed
- jump shot discovered
- basketball first played in Olympics (1936)
- International Amateur Basketball Federation (FIBA) founded in Geneva, Switzerland.

As Antonio grew up in Spain and graduated with a degree in industrial engineering from Bilbao University (Spain) in 1963. At an early age, he became heavily involved in the club basketball system of Europe. At the age of 18, he was selected to play on the Spanish National Team and competed in the Spanish Professional League for 13 years — Estudiantes in 1950 and 1951, Cave 1952, Real Madrid from 1958-60 (league champions in 1959-60), again from 1953-57 and Aguilas in 1961 and 1962. He represented his country 27 times on the National Team.

In November of 1965, after the Spanish National Team played poorly in the European Championships in Moscow, the national coach quit. Anselmo Lopez, President of the Spanish Basketball Federation, appointed Diaz-Miguel as interim Spanish National Coach in order to play an exhibition game. Diaz-Miguel was to lead and train the team until they found an American coach to teach basketball in Spain and coach the Spanish team. Twenty-seven years later, Antonio Diaz-Miguel was still the Spanish National Coach, shedding the interim label to coach the team from 1965-92.

As coach of the Spanish National team, he became the longest reigning national Olympic Coach in the history of world basketball. His teams recorded "best classifications" in world competition nine different times, culminating with a Silver Medal in the 1984 Olympic Games in Los Angeles. The Spanish National Team coached by Antonio played in:

- Six Olympiads (49 games)
- Five World Championships (45 games), with a 4th place in Cali, Colombia (1982)
- Fourteen European Championships (93 games)
- Two Silver Medal finishes (1973, 1983)

He coached the Olympic team in 504 games, with a record of 318-186. Diaz-Miguel coached the European all-star team six times and was named "Best Spanish Coach" of the 1980's. Anselmo Lopez, Director of Olympic Solidarity, said, "Under Antonio's direction and during his tenure, Spanish basketball reached it's highest level ever."

Hall of Fame coach Dean Smith of North Carolina said, "No one has done so much with as little material as Antonio" (Smith, 1993). His teams were well-prepared, fundamentally sound, and displayed outstanding sportsmanship. He became more renowned when, as coach of the European all-stars, they defeated a USA all-star team with Michael Jordan in a game played in Geneva, Switzerland. In 1982, his Spanish team first beat the USA team in Cali, Colombia. Antonio was one of the first non-USA coaches inducted into the Naismith Memorial Basketball Hall of Fame.

Basketball, from its very beginnings, was an international sport due to its quick spread through the worldwide YMCA movement. Diaz-Miguel furthered the globalization of the sport through FIBA, international competition, and the international exchange of coaches and teams between the United States and Spain/Europe, as well as the placement of U.S. players on foreign teams. Recently, foreign players have made it a two-way exchange, with many of them making it to United States colleges and to the National Basketball Association (NBA). Antonio was considered a gracious host and an ambassador of goodwill by being deeply involved in this global movement. Bob Knight, now at Texas Tech University, proclaimed Diaz-Miguel as "far and away the best foreign coach ever involved in the game." Hall of Fame coach Lou Carnesecca of St. John's University, said of Diaz-Miguel, "He was a pioneer in the globalization of basketball and had the greatest history of any international coach."

By all accounts, he was a tireless worker on behalf of basketball in Spain and throughout Europe. Antonio first began his in-depth education in the sport he loved by visiting United States colleges to study the game and inviting renowned coaches, such as John Wooden of UCLA, to Spain for clinics. Wooden stated, "I know of no one more devoted to the game of basketball than Antonio."

Coach Diaz-Miguel devoted his adult lifetime to teaching basketball and promoting the game worldwide (Europe, United States and South America). Furthermore, he promoted mini-basketball throughout Europe. Antonio gave basketball clinics and lectures around the world.

.....SCOUTING REPORT.....SCOUTING REPORT...

Finally, Antonio Diaz-Miguel was a humanitarian who used his basketball fame to further worthwhile causes. As a household name in Spain, he led the Educational Foundation Against Drug Addiction to give clinics for over 10,000 young people. His hometown, Alcazar de San Juan, designated him as "Favorite Son" in 1985, and he has been honored with many humanitarian awards. In 1993, his native country of Spain honored him by selecting him for the Gold Medal for Sporting Merit award, their highest honor.

SPAIN

SOURCE

Diaz-Miguel, Antonio. Vertical Files, Archives. Naismith Memorial Basketball Hall of Fame. Springfield, MA.

CITIUS · ALTIUS · FORTIUS

COMITÉ INTERNATIONAL OLYMPIQUE

CHÂTEAU DE VIDY, 1007 LAUSANNE, SUISSE

THE PRESIDENT

Mr. Joseph O'Brien
Executive Director
Basketball Hall of Fame
1150 West Columbus Avenue
PO Box 179
Springfield

MA 01101-0179 / Etats Unis

Lausanne, 29th September 1994 / pav
4228

Dear Joseph,

The purpose of this letter is to give my wholehearted support to the nomination for entry into the Basketball Hall of Fame, of coach Antonio Diaz-Miguel who, for 27 years, has been the coach and selector for the Spanish National Olympic Team.

I have known coach Diaz-Miguel since he was an international Olympic player (26 representations). He quickly progressed to become a coach and was in charge of the junior and cadet teams. At 32 years old he was named National Olympic Coach and has maintained this position for the last 27 years thus becoming the longest reigning national olympic coach in the history of world basketball.

Coach Diaz-Miguel has contributed much to spreading the practice of American basketball not only in Spain but in many other parts of the world, France, Yugoslavia, China, Argentina, Mexico, El Salvador, Chile, Italy, Morocco , among others.

During the time with the National Team he has contributed a great deal to raising the level of basketball in Spain obtaining two silver and one gold medal at European Championships and a silver medal at the Los Angeles Olympic Games. Furthermore, he has bettered the record of the National Olympic Team some nine times.

In Spain, and I would even say throughout the world, coach Diaz-Miguel is well liked and admired by all and has become a very popular figure whom everyone associates with basketball. Last year, he received the prestigious Spanish award of the Gold Medal for Sporting Merit.

I appreciate that there will be other deserving candidates. However, I sincerely believe that coach Antonio Diaz-Miguel fully merits his place in the Hall of Fame and I would ask you to kindly consider his candidature.

Kind regards,

Yours sincerely

Juan Antonio Samaranch
President

LESSONS FROM THIS LEGEND...

DREAMS DO COME TRUE

By Jose Luis Mateo
Gigantes del Superbasket

It was a cold February morning when Antonio Diaz-Miguel received the call at his home in Spain. The Basketball Hall of Fame had just phoned to inform him that he had been elected to the Hall of Fame's Class of 1997. It was good news indeed. Diaz-Miguel had just become the first Spanish native elected into the world's basketball temple.

For Antonio Diaz-Miguel, election into the Naismith Memorial Basketball Hall of Fame was his personal equivalent of winning an Oscar, a Pulitzer, or a Nobel Award.

"I'd be lying if I said that being elected into the Basketball Hall of Fame wasn't a dream come true," said Diaz-Miguel. "It's like the Oscar of basketball. After a long career, reaching this point is the greatest thing that can happen to anyone in basketball. It means even more to me, since I am such a big fan of American basketball."

These words confirmed the excitement that Diaz-Miguel surely felt in the hours after learning of his election into the Hall of Fame. He had reached the pinnacle of a career that had started some 32 years earlier.

Diaz-Miguel's run as the director of the Spanish National Team began in November of 1965. Pedro Ferrandiz, the director at that time, resigned following an 11th place finish at the European Championships. Ferrandiz fate became a huge opportunity for the 32-year-old Diaz-Miguel. Anselmo Lopez, Executive Director of the Spanish Basketball Federation, suggested that Diaz-Miguel, then the Director of the Spanish Junior Team, assume the responsibility of coaching the Spanish National Team on an interim basis. His first assignment: a tournament in Holland just weeks after his appointment.

Understandably, Diaz-Miguel felt the weight of the assignment. "No, I am sorry, I am not ready yet," Diaz-Miguel offered. Lopez convinced Diaz-Miguel to take the position. He was assured that his tenure as coach was interim, a single week—seven days—until the Federation successfully hired a true replacement for Ferrandiz. Diaz-Miguel was faced with extremely short notice and practically no preparation time. Despite all, Diaz-Miguel led the Spanish National Team to a second-place finish in the Tournament.

That was the beginning, the opening act for this Spanish coaching legend.

Diaz-Miguel coached a group of athletes, many of whom were former teammates or even better, older than him, and led them to an improbable finish in Holland.

April, 1966, (five months later) the Spanish Basketball Federation had yet to find a replacement for Diaz-Miguel, who was the replacement for Ferrandiz. Certainly the longest seven days of Diaz-Miguel's life was when Diaz-Miguel led the team into competition at the World Championships in Chile. The Spanish squad placed sixth, its best-ever finish. The young and still relatively inexperienced Diaz-Miguel had done what no Spanish coach before him was able to accomplish. Suddenly, the words "young" and "inexperienced" no longer applied to Antonio Diaz-Miguel.

In 1968, with the Olympic Games in Mexico just five weeks away, the Federation was still deciding whether or not to keep Diaz-Miguel as coach of the Spanish National Team. Instead of sitting around and waiting to be hired or even fired, Diaz-Miguel sought to improve his basketball

knowledge and improve Spain's chances in the Olympics. Through thorough investigation of U.S. college basketball, Diaz-Miguel sought out the expertise of the best. He sought out a visit to the campus of UCLA, home of the national champion Bruins and legendary coach John Wooden.

"I knew my team only had five weeks before the Olympics" Diaz-Miguel recalls. "UCLA had six weeks before its season began, so I figured I would see how Wooden's team prepared."

The eager Diaz-Miguel wrote to UCLA for permission to visit the school and watch the team train in Pauley Pavilion. It was a landmark trip. Diaz-Miguel became the first coach in Spanish history to travel to the United States to study American basketball.

"I remember sleeping in the dorms with the students," explained Diaz-Miguel. "At first, I didn't have a good time away from my home, but the more I learned, the better I felt. Everybody was nice to me, especially John Wooden. I was on my own for Thanksgiving, living at the residence hall, and Wooden brought me to his home to have dinner with his family. I'll never forget that."

Wooden's influence that day and on the entire trip played an important role in Diaz-Miguel's Hall of Fame career. He had learned valuable lessons about the American style of basketball that he would ultimately bring home to Spain. In fact, Diaz-Miguel became his country's lone authority on the world's best brand of basketball,

"At the time, you couldn't find videos or books," said Diaz-Miguel. "You took notes

LESSONS FROM THIS LEGEND...

using paper and a pencil. You had to travel extensively to see teams and coaches work in order to teach others. At the time I visited UCLA, I also made a visit to West Point. Bob Knight was the coach then and his team played a defense that I had never seen before. Everybody was pressuring, everybody was running, everybody was helping each other out."

With new techniques in hand, Diaz-Miguel returned to Spain and prepared his squad for the Olympic Games in Mexico. The result was a seventh-place finish, Spain's best-ever in Olympic competition. The Federation began to consider the idea of keeping Diaz-Miguel as permanent Director of the Spanish National Team. Diaz-Miguel had won two championships along with two historic finishes. Those results were hard to ignore.

Not only did Diaz-Miguel produce results, but he was very careful in the type of players who would play for the National Team. He decided that past national teams lacked size, but Diaz-Miguel had an innovative solution. He asked Lopez, the Spanish Basketball Federation Executive, to produce a television spot that would encourage tall people to apply for the team. It was the beginning of the Spain's "Operation Height."

The national program was a success. Over 2,000 letters of application were submitted to the Federation,

With "Operation Height" in place, Diaz-Miguel cultivated great Spanish National Team centers, and the team continued to improve and make national history . There were more creative plans on the horizon for Spain's national team.

Diaz-Miguel initiated a competition with an American college on his native soil for the first time ever. The opposition was no lightweight. The University of North Carolina coached by Hall of Famer Dean Smith was secured in December, 1971, for a three-game exhibition set.

"I remember the first time I saw them play," said Diaz-Miguel "They had already played

15 minutes and I had not taken a single note. I was amazed at their speed. I had never seen anybody play the game that fast before."

After seeing North Carolina perform in his own country, Diaz-Miguel decided that he should repay the visit to Chapel Hill. It was during that trip that coach Diaz-Miguel learned new defensive strategies that he would bring to European basketball. The most important revelation: defensive intensity. As Diaz-Miguel recalls from his second U.S. trip: "If the man you were guarding went to the bathroom, you went with him."

Diaz-Miguel's desire to learn new techniques and strategies constantly raised the level of play of the Spanish National Team. Such was the case in the 1973 European Championships in Spain. A year earlier at the 1972 Olympics in Munich, Diaz-Miguel had been impressed by a strong Cuban team. "They played at a higher physical level than we did in Munich," Diaz-Miguel recalls. "I had to find out what they were doing. I asked the Cuban assistant coach Carmel Ortega to let me view their physical training program. I traveled to Cuba, and we had a good exchange of techniques."

Once again, Diaz-Miguel's long distance traveling proved fruitful. At the 1973 European Championships, the Spanish squad captured a Silver Medal, the country's best finish ever.

The years rolled on and so did Spain's impressive finishes. Following a fifth-place finish at the World Championships in Puerto Rico, Diaz-Miguel added a member to the team that generated a great deal of controversy across the country. He decided to place Juan Antonio Corbalan, a 16-year old point guard from the Real Madrid Junior Team, on the National Squad. Spain's national sporting media publicly doubted the great Spanish coach. Headlines read: "He's Crazy," "He won't really let him play in a game," and "What's Diaz-Miguel Doing?" Despite the controversy, Diaz-Miguel put Corbalan into the starting rotation, and the young point guard turned into one of the country's best-ever playmakers.

The high point of Diaz-Miguel's career came at the 1984 Olympics in Los Angeles. For the first time in its history, the Spanish National Team earned a spot in the Gold Medal game. Despite losing to a powerful U.S. team that was coached by Bob Knight and led by Michael Jordan, Diaz-Miguel brought great honor to Spain by capturing an Olympic Silver Medal. The team received a hero's welcome when it returned to the Barajas Airport in Madrid.

To be exact, Diaz-Miguel coached the Spanish National Team for 26 years, nine months and one day. Throughout his career, he did much to develop and improve basketball in his native Spain and throughout Europe. Whatever medals his teams won were an afterthought. Improvement was the key.

As such, Diaz-Miguel was an interpreter between two basketball worlds. He helped bring American basketball to Spain, Europe and beyond. Thanks to his efforts, Spanish basketball employed American techniques long before their European counterparts.

Thanks to Antonio Diaz-Miguel, Spain's name will forever be represented in the world's basketball shrine in Springfield, Massachusetts. For his tireless efforts, his name will now reside among those of Abdul-Jabbar, Auerbach, Carnesecca, Knight, Smith and Wooden. Without a doubt, Diaz-Miguel's career has been a successful journey. He reached this basketball pinnacle by applying a simple rule to his life that he now teaches to young coaches: "Keep your faith in a few and defend them forever."

SOURCE

Mateo, Jose Luis. (1997). Dreams Do Come True. *Naismith Memorial Basketball Hall of Fame Enshrinement Program.*

LEGACY OF
Clarence "Big House" Gaines

- Mentored by John McLendon, the "Father of Black Coaches," and was one of the first coaches to break the color barrier in collegiate basketball.

- Spent 47 years at the same school and is the namesake of the C.E. Gaines Center at Winston-Salem University.

- Retired as the second winningest coach in college basketball history.

- Coached teams that were nationally acclaimed for their up-tempo, fast-breaking style of play.

- Led Winston-Salem to the NCAA College Division national championship in 1967.

- Respected as an outstanding humanitarian who truly cared about his students and players.

- Enshrined in eight Halls of Fame.

CLARENCE "BIG HOUSE" GAINES

"Coaches come and go. Records come and go. But if you touch peoples' lives, they remember you."
—Clarence "Big House" Gaines

BIOGRAPHY

Born: May 21, 1923 in Paducah, KY

Died: April 18, 2005

Inducted into the Naismith Basketball Hall of Fame in 1982

Clarence Edward Gaines was born just before the Great Depression of the 1930s. He attended Lincoln (Paducah, KY) H.S., where he was a star football and basketball player. Gaines then attended Morgan State (MD) College, where he played basketball for four years and excelled as a football tackle. After graduation in 1945, Gaines accepted a job at Winston-Salem College as an assistant coach in three sports: football, basketball, and track and field. In 1947, he was promoted to head coach in all three sports and eventually became athletic director, professor of physical education, and director of the physical education department. Gaines spent his entire career (47 years) at Winston-Salem, where his basketball teams were 828-447. By 1981, Gaines had become the nation's winningest active coach. His teams won 20 or more games 18 times and captured the Central Intercollegiate Athletic Association (CIAA) championship 12 times. In 1967, his team compiled a 31-1 record and became the first historically black school to win a NCAA national basketball championship (College Division). Gaines retired in 1993 with 828 wins, making him the second winningest coach in NCAA history at the time (behind legendary Adolph Rupp). He has been inducted into eight Halls of Fame, served as president of the NABC, and was selected National Coach of the Year in 1967.

Clarence "Big House" Gaines...

Clarence Gaines came from Kentucky bluegrass country with humble beginnings in Paducah. He played a lot of basketball as a youngster, even though he didn't have a real basket or even a ball. Gaines' father nailed a barrel hoop on a coal-house door, and they would shoot baskets with any kind of ball they could find.

Gaines starred in football and excelled in basketball at Lincoln (Paducah, KY) H.S. His inspiration was his mother, Olivia. She was an outstanding athlete and would play against Clarence in basketball, softball, and tennis. "I could never beat her," stated Gaines (2003). "Plus the most important thing was that she insisted that I practice and master the basic fundamentals of basketball."

As a young child, Gaines was taught to adhere to the Golden Rule. "My parents emphasized three key points," said Gaines. "Don't lie, don't cheat, don't steal. I've carried these values with me throughout my entire life."

After graduation from high school, Gaines enrolled at Morgan State (MD) College. He left home with 50 dollars in his pocket, driving an old Ford. Upon his arrival at the campus, Clarence stopped at the administration building to ask for directions from the school's business manager, Jimmy Carter. Upon seeing Gaines, he remarked, "I've never seen anything bigger than you but a house." Thus, the nickname "Big House" was originated, and it stuck. He left with a degree in chemistry and Little All-American status in football.

Following his graduation in 1946, "Big House" packed his bags for Winston-Salem State College in 1946, where he was to be assistant coach in football, basketball, and track and field. He planned to stay one year, just long enough to save money for dental school. Forty-seven years later, he was still at Winston-Salem (now a university). "I don't think I was meant to be a dentist," says Gaines, "Coaching is what the Lord called me to do."

What a fantastic forty-seven years it became. Gaines spent only two years as an assistant coach before being elevated to head coach of all three sports, common in those days. His stated goal became to "succeed not only as an athletic coach but also as a respected and significant asset to the university and community." He did that and more. At the time of his retirement, Gaines was the second winningest coach in college basketball history. He also held the positions of athletic director and chairperson of the physical education department and had attained the academic rank of professor of physical education.

In addition, he became a champion of youth sports, not only in the Winston-Salem area, but also in North Carolina. Clarence became a fixture in local youth sports programs and civic organizations. He was truly an educator who reached out to touch the lives and make a difference in the lives not only of his athletes and students, but also young people and others in his community.

"The greatest pleasure I got out of athletics was to see all the guys we work with, who weren't supposed to make it (by society's standards), grow into successful young men." said Gaines. "I've been around for a long enough time to have coached some of the guys who are now retired, and every time I see one of them, I just smile."

Coach Gaines developed an effective system of play, based on fast-breaking, up-tempo basketball. He emphasized ball movement and wanted his post players to flash toward the ball, rather than standing on the block. Gaines also used the "give-and-go play," one of the first plays ever used in basketball. Gaines said, "We did a lot of practicing with no dribbling allowed. The ball had to be passed, rather than dribbled. Players could not stand and wait for the pass. They had to move toward the ball to meet it."

Gaines also used the "four corners" offense popularized by Dean Smith at North Carolina. Hall of Fame coach John McLendon actually developed the concept and called the strategy "Jack in the Corner." Early in his career, Gaines was befriended and mentored by the legendary McLendon, who is called the "Father of Black Basketball Coaches."

Winston-Salem's star player on their 1967 national championship team was future Hall of Famer Earl "The Pearl" Monroe. Under Gaines' direction, Monroe was allowed to develop, perfect, and popularize the "spin dribble." Gaines said, "Earl was truly a 'pearl'—a coach's player. I never had a more conscientious player, a harder worker, or a player with a better personality."

Consistency and level-headedness were characteristics of "Big House" Gaines. He handled both victory and defeat with a level response. If the team won, he commended his players for good execution. If they lost, stress was placed on the part of their execution that could be improved. It was a very evenhanded approach that was one component that produced a local legend and a national treasure. Big House seemed always to praise his players and show appreciation for their efforts. Perseverance and humility were trademarks of his classy, professional approach. On the occasion of the New Year's Eve day before his team would achieve win number six hundred for him as a head coach, Clarence was asked how he nervously spent the day. He responded that he "scrubbed the kitchen floor," because his lovely wife, Clara, had asked him to do just that. Win number six hundred followed that night before a sparse crowd and honored only by a private party afterwards.

Clarence Gaines also was respected as a humanitarian. He regularly hosted the visiting coach after their game to get a barbecue sandwich or something to eat. Big House stated that he believed it was just the right thing to do. "We are both coaches of basketball, not going to war, but playing a game." He was so revered that he regularly was asked to speak at sports banquets, as are all coaches. But Clarence was asked to speak to rival schools (unheard of in coaching circles). As a humanitarian coach, he was most concerned about players' academic achievement, focusing on hard work. Gaines was especially honored with the prestigious Paul Robeson Award in this area of achievement.

His forty-seven year coaching career was also noteworthy because it occurred in the following challenging eras:

- **1947-57**, the "Dark Years," when the contributions of Black colleges in the United States were unknown and invisible. Black coaches had the added burden of travel, lodging, and board for movement between campuses and competitions in a very hostile social climate— "like a GI plotting a course through a minefield," avoiding and managing hostile racial confrontations and at the same time, maintaining a necessary role of respect, dignity, and leadership." (McLendon, 1982)

- **1960-70**, the period called the social revolution of protest or the "Turbulent Sixties." Victories were difficult in this time period, but a Gaines team reached the pinnacle of success by winning the 1967 College Division Championship.

- **1970-80**, the period of uncertainty and focus on "me" (the drug generation). Through this period of change (times/athletes/students/administrations/rules), the constant factor was Coach Gaines, a "Big House" on the scene—disciplined, adhering to moral coaching principles, unassailable integrity, and a style of gentle, yet firm, authority with class (McLendon, 1982). It was also said that his abilities as a coach were exceeded only by his integrity and his concern for the welfare and education of his athletes. "Gaines has done more to improve the quality of coaching and general conditions of play among predominantly black colleges than any other person" (Fritz, 1980). Big House, in his own way, was responsible for developing higher coaching standards, as well as higher academic and performance standards.

Throughout his career, Gaines was influenced by several future Hall of Fame coaches. The following examples illustrate his thoughts on some of the game's greatest coaches:

- "Coach John McLendon was a great innovator, mentor, and fundamentalist."
- "The most impressive clinician had to be Adolph Rupp. He could teach more basketball in 15 to 20 minutes than a lot of coaches could teach in two days. I learned all about the continuity offense from him."
- "Nobody ever wrote as many books and articles or ran more clinics both in the U.S. and abroad than Clair Bee. He also wrote the greatest series of juvenile sports novels ever published—the Chip Hilton series."
- "Everett Dean was another outstanding clinician. He wrote *Progressive Basketball,* which I consider the first 'scientific' textbook on basketball."
- "Another outstanding coach and person is Bob Knight. I believe he is the greatest humanitarian in basketball. He helps a lot of people and gets involved in a lot of good causes, without attracting attention to himself."

Gaines urges coaches today to teach fundamental skills and stress the importance of education. Gaines (2003) said, "The low graduation rates worry me. Education is the answer. Back in the old days, there was no professional basketball for black youngsters. We worked with everyone and stressed the importance of a college degree. We need to get back to emphasizing the importance of education."

Gaines would like to see two rule changes in the game of basketball. First, the distance of the three-point shot should be lengthened. Gaines would like to push the three-point arc back to the international distance. Second, the number of personal fouls allowed before disqualification should be increased, giving each player an extra foul—six instead of five.

Finally, notice should be made of the universal respect and recognition given to Clarence Gaines for his personal and professional accomplishments. He has been inducted into eight Halls of Fame, including CIAA, North Carolina Sports, Winston-Salem State University, National Association of Intercollegiate (NAIA), and the Naismith Basketball Hall of Fame. Uniquely, his nomination for the Naismith honor was sponsored by a rival institution in the CIAA conference, a real tribute to the respect earned by Clarence.

SOURCE
Fritz, Harry. (1980, May 29). Letter to Naismith Memorial Basketball Hall of Fame.

Gaines, Clarence. Vertical Files, Archives. Naismith Memorial Basketball Hall of Fame. Springfield, MA.

Gaines, Clarence. Interview with Ralph Pim. September 6, 2003.

Gaines, Clarence. (1994, April). Break Out at the Big House. *Scholastic Coach.*

McLendon. John. (1982, May 3). Presentation at the Naismith Hall of Fame.

WHAT I LEARNED FROM COACHING

By Clarence Gaines

I have never run my own business, so I can't give any sports analogies as business advice to help business owners and managers become healthy, wealthy, and wise.

What I have done is spend 47 years working with young, impressionable men, showing them how to work together in teams to achieve goals that individually they could not reach. I have shown mostly poor boys how they could overcome the lack of a stable home life to become successful and financially secure. I have demonstrated that if a coach stays around long enough in one job and recruits enough top players, he will win enough games to attract attention to his college.

MOST IMPORTANT LESSONS LEARNED FROM COACHING

The most important thing I learned from coaching is what Jackie Robinson proved in 1947. By hanging tough and ignoring the catcalls, Jackie proved that the barriers put up between races and social classes can be taken down, when the people on both sides work at understanding each other.

I now know that when that happens, both sides are better off because they both have increased their understanding of the other side.

I did not come by this enlightenment easily. When I started coaching in 1945, I had no real idea what I was supposed to do to motivate players to win ball games. My job as an assistant coach was to pick up the practice footballs and wash the uniforms. That hardly called for any coaching philosophy.

I did possess two key elements that all coaches need. First, I understood that

organization is an essential part of coaching. Second, I wanted to know everything there was to know about the game.

Here are some of the other key points that I learned from all my years in coaching:

1. NEVER JUDGE A YOUNG PERSON'S ABILITY BASED ON THE CIRCUMSTANCES OF HIS SURROUNDINGS

I did not pluck my players out of white middle-class homes with a father going to an office every day, while the mother stayed home baking cookies so the neighborhood boys would have something to eat after they got through shooting hoops in the driveway. I took most of my players out of tenements and slums that no one would categorize as a "home."

My players were poor – the type of kids that society tells us will always be poor. When I found them, they were in a welfare and educational system that treated them as hopeless victims. Though they were not yet 18 years old, many people had already evaluated their future as dismal.

I saw those poor kids differently than the welfare administrators saw them. While some might have dismissed them as playground players, I saw them as athletic young men whose minds had never been challenged.

Their athletic skills were obvious to anyone who watched them wheeling and spinning on the playground. What was less obvious was how well they could think. I trusted my scouts to get inside the heads of those young men by asking them what they wanted out of life and how they would get there.

Sometimes, we did not like what we heard. My scouts and I discarded the fast-buck hustlers who did not want to put in the time in college to learn the life skills to achieve their goals.

I learned from coaching that young men and women could accomplish just about anything, if given the chance and the knowledge that their elders and teachers expect them to succeed. I know this sounds simplistic, but my teams proved it time and time again on the football field, on the basketball court, and in the classroom.

I sincerely believe that kids, assuming there is nothing mentally wrong with them, can learn college-level professions. I do not think it matters how disruptive or poor an environment they came from. Every kid can learn.

I am not saying every person can master every course. What I am saying is that, in college, most kids can discover something they can do. All it takes are adults – parents, guardians, friends, and elementary, junior-high and high school teachers and counselors – to tell those kids that they can achieve whatever they want to achieve.

Dumb jocks should not be the college norm, and standards should not be lowered for athletes. To prove my point that colleges today are not demanding enough academically of their players, one only has to listen to pre- and post-game interviews of college players on television or radio. Those players – white or black – can barely communicate with the person interviewing them. If the phrase "you know" were ever banned from the vocabulary of today's college sports stars, there would be no interviews at all.

LESSONS FROM THIS LEGEND...

I find the slurring of speech and the use of street slang to be beneath the level of what I would expect of young men taking college-level courses. All of my players went to English and vocabulary classes in college, and they passed them. They had to pass them because they were planning to be teachers, not professional basketball players.

It was just that simple in their day, and it is just that simple today. I do not understand why the same standards we expected in the 1940s, 1950s, and 1960s do not apply in today's colleges.

It is not completely the fault of the players that they cannot string sentences together. I blame the public school systems that did not force those young men to learn proper English at an early age. Those college kids sound the way they do because their elementary, junior-high, and high-school teachers, plus their college professors and college coaches, did not believe they could be taught to speak proper English. That is ridiculous. If the kids I plucked from the inner cities could learn proper English, there is no reason why college kids cannot learn it today.

Nothing brings greater satisfaction to me than watching former players, who according to society's standards would never amount to anything, grow into successful members of society.

2. There is a Difference between "Wannabe" and "Gonna Be"

I started my sports career as a wannabe. I wanted to be the best high-school lineman in Kentucky – and I was. I wanted to be the best lineman in college – and I was.

But my life was also filled with role models who taught me what my life was "gonna be" after college, if I applied myself. "Gonna be" was much more realistic than "wannabe." I had parents, grandparents, aunts, uncles, neighbors, schoolteachers, Sunday-school teachers, Boy Scout leaders, high school football coaches, and family

doctors who pointed out to me at an early age that my physical prowess would start to fade once I got out of college.

I learned from coaching that I had to get through to my team members that they were "gonna be" teachers or some other type of professional once they graduated from college. Even if they were lucky and good enough to try out for professional basketball, they may not make it past training camp. Most of them didn't. But when they didn't, they had a profession that would take them as far as they wanted to go.

In only a few instances did I reluctantly agree that a kid should chase his "wannabe" be over the "gonna be" reality of getting a college education. Carl Green was one of the exceptions. Carl followed his dream of playing with the Harlem Globetrotters, but he had retained enough of the "gonna be" talks I had with him while he was in college, that he became a successful businessman once he left the Globetrotters.

3. Never Stop Preparing

I learned from coaching that you never stop preparing. Whenever I realized that my team was not going to be as strong as I would have liked, I would begin for the coming season by going out and recruiting new players. If I already had all my slots filled, I would begin practicing the team. I never coasted at the beginning of a season.

I don't think anyone should ever say, "I've prepared enough" for a meeting, a game, or a profession. I found that the more I learned and the more I prepared, the better I was as a coach and as a person.

4. Don't be a Dummy

One thing that I learned from coaching is so simple that my grandsons say it is the most important piece of advice that I have given them. It is simply – "Don't be a dummy."

There are so many ways that piece of advice can be used. It can be literally applied to the use of one's brain. Stay in school. Get

the best education you possible can and then use that education to make your life better. So many people are given the opportunity to go to high school and then college, and they throw away that opportunity by not going to classes regularly or even dropping out entirely. Once they are out of school, they ask society and the government for help in making a living. They portray themselves as victims of a poor education, when they consciously chose to ignore the educational opportunities given them.

It can be figuratively applied to how people conduct themselves. People who drink too much or who use illegal drugs remove themselves from the reality of life and fit the definition of dummies. If their drug abuse becomes harmful to themselves or others, they might even find themselves removed from society by being put in jail. I saw that happen to one of my best players. I could never understand how he allowed himself to be used by an inanimate substance like alcohol or drugs. He was the strongest player I ever had, but he gave in to his weakness.

5. Never Set Too Many Rules

I learned from coaching – and from being a parent – never to set too many rules. Some coaches had lights-out rules. Some had bed checks. Some demanded this or that. And if you did not live by the coach's law, you were out.

I never did that. The only rules I imposed on my players were to conduct themselves civilly to everyone they met on campus, to report to class, to report to practice, and to report to the games. Other than that, I expected them to use their own judgment as to how to conduct themselves as young men. In one sense, I was not giving them any limits at all, which theoretically would have allowed them to run wild. But in reality, they kept themselves in check because they knew I expected more of them.

If I had one hard-and-fast rule, it was that they treat everyone they met on campus with respect. My players knew from me that the lady in the lunchroom was just as important to me as the chancellor of the university. They had better not give her any "athlete attitude."

I do not understand why coaches tolerate "athlete attitude." Just because an athlete can play a child's game a little bit better than others on campus, there is no reason to let that kid think he has any more privileges than any other student on campus.

I am not saying that athletes should not have egos. That is part of being good. What I am saying is that athletes should keep those egos under control until they get on the court or the field. When they are not playing the game, they are no better than anyone else on campus.

In reality, by keeping my rules to a minimum, I was being more restrictive on my players. I was making them think how they should comport themselves. Part of the way I did that was to give them every opportunity to see how my family acted. Many of them had never experienced an intact family with a father, mother, and children sitting down to eat at the same table. Many of them never had a mother asking them about homework and a father imposing discipline when it was necessary. For most of those kids, this simple exposure to family life was instructive in how they should raise their own families.

6. EVERY STUDENT IS MOTIVATED BY SOMETHING DIFFERENT

I learned from coaching that every student is motivated by something different, and that all kids will not respond to the same stimulus.

Some kids came to my teams already finished players. I never had to tell them a word as to how to play their position. Some kids were like clay and had to be molded into the kind of players I needed at that particular time.

Some kids wanted me to talk softly to them. Others wanted me to yell at them. Some wanted to fear me. Other wanted to love me. I think all of them wanted to respect me. They all knew I wanted to help them get through college and to become better basketball players along the way.

I think all my work with those players helped me to be a better parent. My son, Clarence Jr., remembers that one of his most important early jobs was being a ball boy for my team. Whenever anyone fell on the court, Clarence was out there in a flash, wiping up the sweat with a towel. He knew the sweat on the court could make another player fall in the same place, possibly hurting himself. Clarence took great pride in drying off that spot. I had given him a job of great responsibility. He knew it and

appreciated it as the ball boy and as my trusted son. Today, Clarence Jr. laughs when he sees the sometimes-casual way sweat is mopped up from a court. He swears no one was as efficient as making that court dry again as he was.

That may sound funny coming from an adult, but Clarence Jr. knew I depended on him for that job. That job was important to me and critical to the safety of all the players on the court. I think my trusting him with that job made him respect me just a bit more as a dad.

Clarence Jr. sometimes reminds me that both Clara and I demonstrated to him and Lisa and all my players how much we valued a college education by displaying our diplomas on the walls of our home. He has a point. We were teachers trying to convince young men that they should also be teachers. What better way to show our pride than to display the diplomas from our universities?

SOURCE

Gaines, Clarence E. (2004). *They Call Me Big House*. Winston-Salem: John F. Blair, Publisher.

Gaines, Clarence. Interview with Ralph Pim, September 11, 2004

Gaines, Clarence. Interview with Ralph Pim, September 6, 2003.

LEGACY OF
James "Jack" Gardner

- Only coach in basketball history to direct two different schools to the Final Four at least twice.

- Built his teams on speed, quickness, and fast break basketball.

- Nicknamed "The Fox" for his clever tactical abilities.

- Believed "details win games" and utilized statisticians to compile precise charts on every phase of the game.

- Revolutionized recruiting and was one of the first coaches to make home visits with recruits.

- Was the driving force behind the construction of new arenas at Kansas State and Utah.

JAMES "JACK" GARDNER

"Most players want to be winners, but it is the degree of commitment that determines the extent they will exceed."
—James "Jack" Gardner

BIOGRAPHY

Born: March 29, 1910 in Texico, NM

Died: April 10, 2000

Inducted into the Naismith Basketball Hall of Fame in 1984

Jack Gardner coached 36 years, and his teams registered an overall 649-278 record. He coached at Alhambra H.S. (CA), Modesto Junior College (CA), Kansas State University, and the University of Utah. Gardner spent twenty-eight years at the major-college level, and his teams compiled a 486-235 record. He was the first coach to direct two different schools to the Final Four at least twice (Kansas State in 1948 and 1951 and Utah in 1961 and 1966). Gardner coached at Kansas State from 1939-1942 and 1946-1953, won three Big Seven titles, and led K-State to the 1951 NCAA championship game against Kentucky. During World War II, Gardner was a Lt. Commander in the Navy and coached some of the finest service teams in the country. During his 18-year tenure at Utah (1953-1971), Gardner's teams won seven conference titles and posted a record of 339-154. He coached ten teams to the NCAA or NIT tournaments. At the time of his retirement in 1971, Gardner ranked behind only Adolph Rupp and John Wooden as the winningest active coach in college basketball. During his retirement, Gardner served as a consultant for the Utah Jazz.

James "Jack" Gardner...

If you listened to pop music during the early 1960s, you will remember the lyrics of Barry Mann's hit song, *Who Put the Bomp*, asking the question,

> "Who put the bop
> In the bop shoo bop shoo bop?
> Who put the ram
> In the rama lama ding dong?
> Who put the dip
> In the dip da dip da dip?
> Who was that man?"

For basketball fans during this period of time, there was no question who put the "run" in the "Running Utes." That man was James "Jack" Gardner.

Gardner's revolutionary fast-break style propelled Utah to two Final Four appearances and a record of 339-154 during his 18-year tenure (1953-71). From 1959 to 1962, Utah won 51 out of 56 games. His philosophy was built on speed, running, and hard-nosed basketball. In his words, he wanted to keep things "sound and simple." Gardner believed that the modern game required speed and quickness. He demanded that his players got up and down the court quickly.

"We plan on breaking every time we get the ball," said Gardner. "Keeping constant pressure on our opponents by fast breaking as soon as one of our players secures the ball is the rule. Psychologically, the threat of a fast break forces opponents to throttle their offense by constantly thinking of defensive balance and the necessity of speed in assembling their defensive formation."

Jack is the only coach to direct two different schools to the Final Four at least twice. Prior to his arrival at Utah, Gardner coached at Kansas State from 1939-42 and 1946-53 and led the Wildcats to the Final Four in 1948 and 1951. Kansas State was beaten in the 1951 NCAA championship game by Adolph Rupp's Kentucky Wildcats.

"I don't think there is any question that he was an outstanding coach," said Ernie Barrett, an All-American guard on the 1951 K-State team. "In those days, you had to fight for anything you could get, and he was pretty tenacious in that regard. One of the fun things with Coach Gardner was the rivalry that he had with the University of Kansas. He and "Phog" Allen totally hated each other."

The intense rivalry between K-State and KU led Allen to mockingly call Gardner a "wonder boy." Undaunted by Allen's importance, the feisty Gardner won nine of 11 meetings from 1947 to 1951.

Gardner's engaging personality charmed prospects and parents, and he was nationally recognized as a great recruiter. He was one of the first coaches to make home visits with recruits. "His recruiting style was definitely years ahead of other coaches," said Barrett.

Gardner's recruiting success awakened Allen to the importance of hitting the recruiting trail. Phog hated the idea of recruiting. He normally sent a form letter back to prospects who contacted him, stating that he had never contacted a young man for his basketball playing ability. For years Allen's philosophy was that young men in Kansas who wanted to play basketball should attend their state university and be pleased with their jobs working in the towel room for 35 cents an hour. Former Kansas assistant Dick Harp said, "Jack Gardner's teams ultimately changed Doc Allen's perspective. K-State had become more than a worthy competitor. Doc realized Jack Gardner was a real threat to the future, the first real threat he had ever faced. Before that, Doc had gotten most of the good players out of Kansas, and his coaching ability allowed him to dominate."

Gardner's players and peers affectionately knew the affable coach as "The Fox" because of his clever tactical abilities. *Sports Illustrated* claimed that Gardner was capable of winning with "an old maid in the post and four midgets."

An apostle of preparation, Gardner coached basketball as if it were a science. Jack believed that "details win games." His theory was "if it moves, chart it." During games and practices he utilized statisticians to compile precise charts on every phase of the game. Gardner's office was referred to as a "Basketball Library of Congress," because there were neatly bound files containing game-by-game, minute-by-minute analysis of everything that had happened during Gardner's coaching career. He believed that keeping accurate records took a lot of the guesswork out of coaching

Gardner considered rebounding as the most important single phase of the game. He told his players, "Your height doesn't mean everything. Your reach, your arm spread, jumping ability (explosive power), and timing are more important. Timing can be developed through practice. Rope-jumping and weight lifting will improve your spring, as well as teach good footwork and coordination."

During games, Gardner called time-outs by waving a white handkerchief. Gardner remembered, "Over the years, this attracted some attention. Quite often fans would wave back at me. But the most comical experience I encountered with the hanky-waving took place when Dick Shores was playing for me. Dick stuffed a handkerchief in his basketball pants and when I waved for a time-out, he pulled it out, waved back, and continued on with the game."

Another memorable incident occurred when Gardner was coaching at Utah, and his team was playing at the University of Wyoming. Jack always kept a bottle of milk under his seat and would frequently take swigs during the course of the game. On this night, some of the Utah players spiked his milk with a laxative resulting in Gardner missing some of the second-half action.

Gardner was the driving force behind the construction of Ahearn Field House at Kansas State and the building of the Huntsman Center at the University of Utah. At K-State, Gardner invited members of the Legislature to attend a game at the tiny 2,800-seat Nichols Gym and then encouraged students to drop ketchup-soaked dummies from the rafters. His efforts, despite opposition from some university administrators and legislators, eventually led to the building of the 14,500-seat Ahearn Field House in 1950.

At Utah, the Huntsman Center was a "state-of-the-art" arena that included a spacious locker room for the home team. But for the visiting team, there was a room so small that the opposing players had to squeeze into the shower area or meet in the adjoining hallway for the pre-game talk. Rival coaches complained that it was just another way "The Fox" was trying to gain a home-court advantage.

Jack was a master at molding players into winning teams. "Most players want to be winners," said Gardner, "but it is the degree of commitment that determines the extent they will exceed. It is my job to enhance the qualities that will make athletes successful. Players must learn that only a maximum effort and positive attitude can bring winning results. But they must also know that while winning is not everything, striving to is. And you cannot profit by losing, unless you have extended yourself to the utmost to win. If you have done these things, you have won regardless of the score."

Gardner did not believe in many rules or regulations. "I never try to impose my will on a player," stated Gardner.

"You can't get a player to play at the top of his natural ability if you try to rule him with an iron hand. I try to show the reason for doing certain things to the boy, and in that way, create the will to accomplish in him."

Gardner took great pride in preparing his players for life after basketball. "The mark of a coach is the men his players become," said Gardner.

Jack was born in New Mexico but spent much of his youth in southern California. Gardner credits Dick Lee, principal and basketball coach at Lincoln H.S. (CA), for fostering his love for the game of basketball. Lee opened the gym and provided Gardner with a ball so he could practice the sport whenever he desired. Gardner became an outstanding athlete and won 16 letters in four sports at Redlands H.S. (CA). He set the pole vault record that remained in place for 30 years.

Gardner attended USC and played for future Hall of Fame coach Sam Barry. At USC, he captained the 1932 basketball team and won the MVP award. Gardner began his coaching career as an assistant to Barry while attending graduate school at USC. "Coach Barry," said Gardner (1961), "was one of the great minds of basketball and my inspiration and close friend."

Gardner then coached at Alhambra H.S. (CA) and Modesto Junior College. From 1935 to 1939, Gardner led his teams at Modesto to three state championships in basketball and three in baseball.

Gardner spent his entire life devoted to the game of basketball. He attended every Final Four for 58 years, starting with the first NCAA tournament in 1939. After his retirement from college coaching, Jack served as a consultant for the Utah Jazz.

At the time of Gardner's death in 2000, Kansas State president Jon Wefald said, "Coach Gardner will go down as one of the greatest coaches of all time. He's a legend, there's no question about it."

SOURCE

Gardner, Jack. (1961). *Championship Basketball with Jack Gardner.* Englewood Cliffs, NJ: Prentice-Hall, Inc.

Gardner, Jack. Vertical Files, Archives. Naismith Memorial Basketball Hall of Fame. Springfield, MA.

Kerkhoff, Blair (1996). Phog Allen: *The Father of Basketball Coaching.* Indianapolis, IN: Masters Press.

BUILDING A CHAMPIONSHIP BASKETBALL TEAM

By Jack Gardner

A coach's duties are not limited to the floor. To build winners, a coach must be an organizer and administrator. Forms, charts, and checklists are an essential part of the job. These would include such things as coaching and game plans, schedule analysis, game management, trip information, player and staff meetings, equipment check, game charting, clinic outlines, and many more. A coach should break down in writing practice sessions, offenses, defenses, tactics, strategy, scouting, and tournament play. Remember, a project left unattended goes to the dogs.

Here are the things that we do at the University of Utah. I believe they have been invaluable in helping us achieve our record. I recommend them to all coaches. Is it a lot of work? It sure is. Nobody ever won without work.

BASIC COACHING PRINCIPLES

You've got to be clear in your own mind on how you are going to operate.

1. We make our drills and practices fun. Driving players through a monotonous drill is drudgery. We coach through friendly play-inspiring games.
2. We give fundamentals top priority. Before we teach any style of play, we teach the skills: footwork, cutting, screening, passing, dribbling, shooting, guarding, and rebounding.
3. We permit discussion of fundamentals, offenses, and defenses—so long as it is not at the expense of diligent practice and development of team play.

4. We teach driving, aggressive play — with the realization that it will lead to more mistakes and more fouling than in cautious play.

DRILLS

1. A drill that does not develop a game skill is of little value and may be harmful.
2. We reverse the usual procedure of teaching. We start with a game offensive or defensive maneuver and then break it down so that it will constitute a drill. These breakdown drills make up virtually all of our drill work.

SCRIMMAGES

1. You can't develop team play without scrimmages.
2. We get game experience by running scrimmages on a formal basis: regular officials, time-outs, between-halves procedures, and statisticians. We make it as similar to a regular game as possible.

STYLE OF PLAY

1. I have studied, and continue to study, the different systems of leading coaches and evaluate them on the basis of my own experience.
2. The result is that I have used practically the same offense and defense since the first day I started coaching.

THE PLAYERS

1. This is the big job. I feel that selecting superior players and

welding them into a team is much more important than a style of play.
2. I feel strongly that a coach will be more successful if he or she picks the player who gives his or her all. The player who fights all the way is the one who will win the tough games for you and put your team in the championship class.
3. Stay away from the player who is intent on personal glory and may loaf in practices and games. This type is usually important in winning games that you probably would have won anyways.

EQUIPMENT

1. It goes without saying, that at Utah we try to select the best player equipment available: uniforms, warm-up suits, shoes, balls, and other items.
2. Comfort, attractiveness, and durability are the most important factors—in that order.
3. Don't underestimate attractiveness. You all know the warm, comfortable feeling that you get when you wear a new, good-looking suit of clothes. This lift is no different from that a player gets in a colorful, well-fitting uniform.

FACILITIES

1. Make sure that all facilities are well lighted and spotless—dressing rooms, spectator seats, benches, and playing courts.
2. I know not all coaches are blessed with the best and most modern

place to play, but everyone should do the best with what they have to work with. This is part of building championship teams and is a responsibility of the coach.

RULES

1. All coaches must know the rules inside out. This is a must!
2. We are very sure that the players know all of the rules that govern their play.
3. We devote an early practice session to the rules and the changes in the rules.
4. During practices and scrimmages, we explain the application of the rules to the situations that develop.

OFFENSE, DEFENSE, GAME STRATEGY

1. We prepare a complete outline of all offenses and defenses that we will use during the year. Before the first practice session, we check it over thoroughly.
2. Much of this comes out of pre-season meetings with my assistants. We go over, time and time again, offenses, defenses, game tactics, and strategies that we expect to use.

PRACTICE OUTLINES

1. We prepare outlines for practice sessions. This helps assure that nothing is overlooked in preparing our teams.
2. The outlines are divided into four periods: preseason; in-season; post-season; and tournament.
3. When preparing our outlines, we use the records of the preceding season to help us determine the frequency and time allotments for the things we do in practice.

CLINICS

1. I feel it is the duty of every coach to subscribe to the basketball development of youngsters and to assist them in getting started right. They are the varsity players of the future.
2. This responsibility falls on my assistants and myself. We conduct a great number of clinics and use the youngsters who attend as demonstrators.

SCOUTING

1. Before the season starts, we get together all the charts and records we have for each opponent and work out a complete scouting program.
2. We review all scouting forms and objectives and make any changes we feel will help us get better information.

TRIPS AND TOURNAMENTS

1. Except for post-season tournaments, we try to complete all trip and tournament information before the first practice session.
2. Utah plays a national schedule. This means that the players are forced to give up many student pleasures and vacations. We like to give them complete information on travel, hotel accommodations, and length of stay in various cities.

CHARTS AND STATISTICS

1. "If it moves, we chart it." This is not a figure of speech at Utah; we mean it. We place great importance on our "look-a-the-record" program.
2. We study and analyze the preceding season's findings to see where we can improve.
3. All charts and forms used to get information are discussed and new ones prepared.

My closing advice is to remember: Coaching a champion is a full-time job, every day of the year. When the coach leaves the practice floor, his job is just beginning.

SOURCE

Gardner, Jack. (1966). Building a Championship College Basketball Team. *Best of Basketball From the Coaching Clinic*. West Nyack, NY: Parker Publishing.

FACTORS DETERMINING COACHING SUCCESS

By Jack Gardner

Herbert Hoover has said that next to religion, athletics provides the greatest opportunity for the teaching of morals. Based upon this premise, it is obvious that the coach is one the most influential persons in a boy's life. This presents a serious challenge, since the coach is faced with a big share of the responsibility of guiding youngsters during their growing-up years. His stature as a coach is measured by his success in helping them firm up their personality traits; intelligently face their personal and emotional problems; develop self-discipline; and recognize the importance of good citizenship.

What greater reward is there for a coach than to have a former player return years later as a successful and distinguished man and say, "Coach, I'll never be able to repay you for what you did for me when I was in school."

Now, before I go any further, I want to state that I have no illusions concerning my coaching ability or my knowledge of the game. The age of the miracle man in the coaching field is as dead as the center jump. No coach has a corner on basketball, although some coaches do seem to have a corner on good players. However, when it comes to coaching, there are almost as many systems and ways of doing things, as there are coaches.

There are few secrets left in the game, and I make no claim that my way of coaching is the only one or the best. However, my methods have proven successful in coaching high school, junior college, and college teams, and they are the only ones I know.

REQUIREMENTS FOR COACHING SUCCESS

Everything else being equal, a coach's success depends largely on his: 1) material; 2) philosophy; 3) knowledge of the game; 4) methods of imparting information to his players; 5) organization; 6) practice outlines; 7) practice rules; 8) team record; 9) ability to evaluate results; and 10) luck.

1. MATERIAL

In college, the coach has a chance to select his material. In high school, the coach develops it. There are a few things coaches can do to help develop their material. First, they can encourage summer practice. It is difficult for a growing youngster to get too much basketball. It would be wise to encourage players to put up hoops at home and to see that they have a ball with which to practice. It has been my observation that the big, tall, awkward boy is sometimes overlooked by the high school coach simply because he cannot execute the skills of the game. If you will work with him for a couple of years, he may be the one to carry you to the championship in his senior year. Give him a chance to develop. It will pay off!

2. PHILOSOPHY

Whether you realize it or not, your philosophy has already been formed. It constitutes your general attitude, thinking, and actions. Your coaching methods must work hand-in-hand with your philosophy.

It is wise that a coach be himself and refrain from trying to be somebody else! A case in point relates to Frank Keaney, former

Rhode Island coach, and Frank McGuire, former University of North Carolina coach.

Keaney was a dramatic and colorful coach, who used to inspire his players with poetry just before they took the floor. It must have worked, because his teams average 80 points per game, and that was years ago.

Well, Frank McGuire, who was coaching at St. John's University at the time, decided that Keaney's flair for poetry must be the answer, and he decided to try it just before an important game. The result was reflected by a remark made by one of Frank's players as the team filed out of the locker room: "Gosh, fellows," he said worriedly, "we've got to win this one for Frank…He's gone nuts!"

3. KNOWLEDGE OF THE GAME

Coaching schools, books, coaching publications, movies, and other sources all add to a person's knowledge of the game. It's what a coach learns *after* he thinks he knows it all that really counts. When you think you have all the answers, you are kidding only yourself.

4. COACHING METHODS

It is not enough that a coach has developed a good philosophy and unlimited knowledge of the game. He must acquire good teaching and coaching methods. It is not what the coach knows, but what his players know that counts.

5. ORGANIZATION

Organizing ability is vital to coaching success. At Utah, we feel that planning the season, organizing the duties of the coaching staff, the managers and trainers, outlining our coaching techniques and strategies, charting player and team progress, and summarizing results are as essential to good coaching as to good business.

During the season, we measure and summarize the results of individual and team performances. We feel that only through these means can we determine the factors that contribute to victory or defeat.

In addition to detailed practice plans, I also like to stress a daily saying, which the players recognize as our "Thought for the Day." This saying may be slanted toward basketball techniques or to life in general.

6. PRACTICE OUTLINES

Practices are planned in advance for each week, day, hour, and minute. They are planned so that every phase of the game is covered before the first game of the season. Practice at Utah begins each year on October 15. This gives us between 30 and 35 practice sessions prior to the first game. Then, after the game season gets underway, we start reviewing and working on weaknesses that have shown up in competition.

7. PRACTICE RULES

Utah players are expected to observe a number of practice rules so that our practice sessions will run smoothly. Several of our rules are:

- Check the bulletin board each day.
- Report promptly for practices and meetings.
- Hustle at all times on the court.
- Stop immediately on the whistle.

8. STATISTICS AND RECORD BOOK

As each season progresses, we compile a book that contains daily and weekly outlines and statistics. The practice outline and record book provides a permanent and complete picture of the season and is vital to our intelligent planning for future years.

9. MEASURING AND ANALYZING RESULTS

All coaches know who won or lost the game, and most coaches are familiar with the details of the box score. But how many know precisely from what phase of the offense the points were made, and from what place on the floor and at what stage of the game? Is this too much to remember? Of course it is, unless you have a detailed statistic program. At Utah, we have a saying: "If it moves – chart it." I believe statistics speak for themselves and measure the effectiveness of player and team performances.

The day after each game we have a "look-at-the-record" session to analyze the game. The record provides an exact analysis of the mistakes and the good and bad plays of both teams.

The only figures withheld from the players are the shooting statistics. However, we occasionally make an exception and point out high percentages in order to boost the confidence of the team or an individual. We do not approve of our players worrying about the number of shots or points scored by themselves or teammates. Basketball is a team game, and it is unnecessary to emphasize individual scoring.

10. LUCK

Lady Luck seems always to be around when preparation meets opportunity. Time after time, we have been lucky enough to win crucial games simply because we had a special play ready to go when the opportunity presented itself. Nothing, but nothing, gives a coach and his players more of a thrill than to win a hard-fought contest by means of a special play at a crucial time in the game.

Not infrequently, however, the breaks desert us even when we are prepared. All of us can cite games in which the breaks turned against us and cost us victory. But that's the way the ball bounces and what makes the game interesting. The big objective is to be prepared – and to try to *help* the ball bounce in your direction.

SOURCE

Gardner, Jack. (1961). *Championship Basketball with Jack Gardner*. Englewood Cliffs, NJ: Prentice-Hall, Inc.

LEGACY OF
Aleksandr Gomelsky

- Known as the "Father of Soviet Men's Basketball."

- Regarded as having one of the most shrewd basketball minds in the world.

- Made the Soviet Union a dominant world power.

- Led the Soviet Union to the gold medal in the 1988 Olympics and ended the Olympic domination of the United States.

- Compiled a 490-177 record with the Soviet Union's National Team, including seven European Championships and two World Championships.

- Authored 10 books on basketball coaching and conducted clinics around the world.

ALEKSANDR GOMELSKY

*"It is easier to play with hungry players
than with those who are satisfied"*
—Aleksandr Gomelsky

BIOGRAPHY

Born: January 18, 1928 in Leningrad, Russia

Inducted into the Naismith Basketball Hall of Fame in 1995

Aleksandr Gomelsky is regarded as having one of the shrewdest basketball coaching minds in the world. Born and reared in Leningrad, Russia, he became involved in basketball in the club system of Europe. He graduated from #79 Leningrad, Russia schools in 1945. During that time period, he played basketball for the Leningrad club team, was considered an all-star, and served as team captain. The team became Leningrad region champions. He was selected and attended the elite coaching school in Leningrad, where he continued to play basketball and graduated in 1948. Gomelsky began his coaching career in 1945, while attending the Leningrad Coaching School. He coached the Soveit Union national team for over 29 years. His teams won 85 percent of the 2,600 games that he coached in a career that spanned over 50 years. He compiled a 490-177 record with the Soviet Union's national team and won seven European Championships, two World Championships and the 1988 Olympic Gold Medal that ended the United States National Team's winning streak at 21 consecutive victories. Gomelsky also coached Soviet Union national teams to Olympic bronze medals (1968, 1980) and the silver medal (1964). He made the Soviet Union a dominant world power in basketball. Gomelsky conducted clinics around the world and authored ten basketball-coaching books.

Aleksandr Gomelsky...

Aleksandr Gomelsky is the father of modern basketball in the Soviet Union. The success of Soviet (now Russian) basketball in the international arena is directly attributable to the coaching talents of this man.

Gomelsky coached four Soviet Olympic teams—1964, 1968, 1980, 1988—winning a silver medal in Tokyo at his first Olympiad, the gold medal in his final assignment in Seoul, and a pair of bronze medals in 1968 and 1980. He was a Soviet assistant coach for the 1956 Olympic Games. Had the Soviets not boycotted the 1984 Olympics, he would have coached that year's Soviet Olympic team.

Gomelsky's teams won World Championships in 1967 and 1982, was runner-up in 1978, and finished third in 1963 and 1970. They were also victorious at eight European Championships—1959, 1961, 1963, 1965, 1967, 1969, 1979, 1981, and winners of 15 Soviet Union national titles.

In the 1988 Olympics, the Soviet Union opened play with a loss to Yugoslavia. When asked whether this meant an end to their quest for the gold medal, Gomelsky retorted, "We didn't come here for the first game, but for the championship game," which they eventually won. After the Olympic title, he left as coach of the Soviet national team to coach in Spain with a nondescript club, Tenerife, on the Canary Islands. Alexsandr gave the reason that he wanted to "step sideways" for a bit. "After 40 years of compulsory victory in our drive to the top, I am worn out." Gomelsky returned to Russia in 1990 as Chairman of the Basketball Federation.

Gomelsky was raised in Leningrad, Russia, when the former Soviet Union was prominent as a Communist nation. He was educated and exposed to a strong nationalistic sports program and club system. The 5'5" Russian basketball mentor attended the Russian National Coaching School from 1948 to 1953. He excelled in the national program, both in coaching and education. He eventually attained the rank of Professor and Doctor of Pedagogy in the Moscow Physical Education Institute, the pinnacle of sport expertise.

Gomelsky began coaching in 1945 at the age of 17, following two years as an all-star player at Leningrad's High School #79. He was an all-star three years running at the Coaches College in Leningrad.

Gomelsky coached SKA Leningrad 1948-52, ASK Riga 1953-66, CSKA Moscow 1966-88, and the Sbornaya (the Soviet National Team) 1958-60, 1962-70, and 1976-88. He also coached Spain's Tenerife 1988-89, the European All-Star Team 1989-90, and Limoges CSP (France) 1990-91.

He is probably best remembered in the West as coach of a Soviet Olympic basketball team that he did not coach. Gomelsky calls the 1972 Soviet team "my boys," but the KGB (Russia's secret police), fearing that the outspoken Jewish coach would defect to Israel, took away his visa, preventing him from traveling to the Munich Games.

Nevertheless, it was Gomelsky's Central Army Sports Club (CSKA) team, the 1972 Russian National Champions, that represented the Soviet Union in Munich, under a different coach. The gold medal match-up that year against the United States—that had never lost an Olympic basketball game—ended in the most publicly controversial result in the history of the quadrennial games.

When time ran out, stadium spectators and an international television audience watched the U.S. team celebrate its 50-49 gold medal victory. But, one of the floor referees claimed that seconds were still left on the clock. The time clock was backed up several ticks, and the Soviets were given the ball out of bounds. However, they had no success, and the game ended a second time. Then, once again, a floor referee made another judgment call, and again the Soviets were handed the ball with several new seconds on the clock. This extra life proved golden for the Russians. A length-of-the-court, "Hail Mary" pass was converted into the winning basket. Gomelsky calls the moment the most exciting and most disappointing of his life.

Although he was relieved of his duties on five occasions when his international teams failed to win a gold medal, bringing home 'only' silvers and bronzes, Gomelsky was always recalled and enjoyed great popularity in and out of the former Soviet Union.

When asked how he accomplished so much during his career, Gomelsky provided some interesting insight. He said, "First, our players were hungry for success. Next, the Soviet National Team was sacred. Nothing was left undone, and we had everything needed for success."

.....SCOUTING REPORT.....SCOUTING REPORT...

Another key component was Gomelsky's drive and unrelentless pursuit of victory. He never comprised his high standards and demanded the maximum effort from all his players. Through the years, he had many nicknames such as, "Aleksandr the Great," "Napoleon of Basketball," "Iron Fist of the Iron Curtain," and "The Silver Fox."

Interestingly, Gomelsky was also very active in international basketball in a variety of roles. He was a member of Coaches Technical Commission (rules responsibility), Central Bureau member, Member of Honor, and a certified FIBA official. At the age of 28, Aleksandr was a referee in the 1956 Olympic Games in Australia.

Gomelsky authored ten books on basketball that have been published in Russian and other international languages. He commitment to basketball lifted Soviet basketball to unparalleled heights.

SOURCE

Gomelsky, Aleksandr. Vertical Files, Archives. Naismith Memorial Basketball Hall of Fame. Springfield, MA.

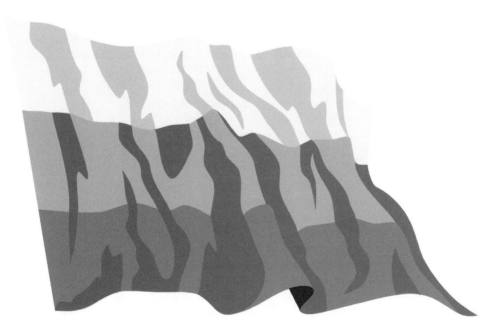

RUSSIA

LESSONS FROM THIS LEGEND...

BUILDING THE BIG PLAYER
FOR THE USSR

By Aleksandr Gomelsky

Authors' Note: Gomelsky was one of the most prolific authors of non-USA coaches, probably due to his academic training and Professor and Doctor of Pedagogy. These clinics notes, from a Gomelsky coaching clinic in 1990, reflect his scientific training, coaching expertise, and dramatic effect on basketball in the Union of Soviet Socialist Republics (USSR).

INTRODUCTION

In today's clinic I will first cover the theoretical side of the topic and then show the practical side with a demonstration on the basketball court.

I have worked as a coach for more than 30 years with the national team and the best players in the Soviet Union. During that time, I have coached more than 40 of our outstanding centers and big basketball players. Not only did I teach them, but they also taught me something new every time I worked with them. I think a coach remains a coach only as long as he is ready to learn and keep learning. When he stops learning from others, his destiny as a coach has been determined.

Nature is full of contrasts. I am short, and that is probably why I have always liked working with big players. My belief is that tall players have always been needed for a good team, and that it is practically impossible to develop a great team without tall players. There are many examples of the truth in that statement:

- 1988 Seoul Olympics – Sabonis/Blostenjin/Goborov of the Gold Medal Soviet team, the Silver Medal Yugoslavian team with Divac/(Vrarkovio)/Rada and the American team

- Bill Russell and the professional Boston Celtics dynasty
- Los Angeles with Kareem Abdul-Jabbar

Even after FIBA introduced the three-point field goal rule to help shorter players, the role of big players has not diminished. Talented shorter players are important, but team success is impossible without true centers or big men. The best example might be Brazil with the great shooter Oscar Schmidt not being able to win a Gold Medal in the absence of a true center. In addition, big players have added to their importance with more defensive rebounds from the increase of three-point field goal attempts. Thus, it is seen that, in spite of rules change to favor small players, the value and skill of big players in modern basketball has only increased.

SELECTING BIG PLAYERS

For a long time, selection of "giants" has been left to coaches of adult club teams. They found them in the streets, in the underground, and in club tournaments. However, these big players were already 14 or 15 years of age or older. At this age, learning to play basketball at a high level presents many difficulties. The development consequences were noted in their training and play – it was too late and took too long for them to reach their full potential.

This contrasts with the American system where big players might begin selection as early as 6 or 7 years old, which gives them a considerable advantage in training and experience.

Therefore, the Soviet system changed, and we looked at our ballet schools as a model.

Youngsters are selected early on according to scientific criteria and then given extensive training. Learning from their experience, we consulted scientists, psychologists, pedagogists (experts in teaching methods), and psychologists to develop a series of tests to determine if a tall boy or girl at age six or seven would likely become a good basketball player. Examples of big players selected early are Aleksander Belov (age 6) and Sabonis (age 7), who were selected and began early training. They had a more complete preparation and developed much better techniques. Sabonis was a good defender—forward. Eventually, he finally became a center, where he developed into one of the best big man passers of all time.

So we now test and select players from age 4 to age 12. If a ten-year-old boy's shoe size is 38-40, we know he will almost certainly grow to be a big player up to 2.05 to 2.10 m. tall. We also use x-rays of the spine to detect distortion or an anomaly of bone structure. The coach and physician can then determine the natural movement abilities of the child and the proper development of the trunk core area.

NUTRITION & EARLY DEVELOPMENT

With the parents' permission, we then focus on proper nutrition for the child to enhance his full development. We give vitamins A and C to encourage growth, plus a diet that includes large quantities of vegetables (carrots, onion, celery, dill, cod-liver oil) and fruits rich in Vitamin C (such as sour cherries and peaches). We focus on all that encourage growth, especially as it affects the thyroid gland. In our work with parents, we focus on the social development of children to convince them to enter our early specialization program. We also include high jumping and swimming to encourage growth and light weight training from 10 years of age on (weights of no more than 20% of their body weight).

DEVELOPING THE BASKETBALL STAR

Another aspect of big-player development also applies to basketball players in general. From early selection on, we find ways and techniques to make him a top player.

Most coaches focus solely on correcting weaknesses of young players, as we do also. However, we think the main purpose of individual work is to choose a proper technique suitable for each player's physical and psychological abilities, which will help him reach virtuosity and perfection. There are three or four optimal techniques that we use all the time when working with players in order to educate them to become sports stars. This goes far beyond just correcting their weaknesses.

PSYCHOLOGICAL PREPARATION

Psychological preparation must play an important part from the earliest stages of training, with a special orientation for big players/centers. Their height is a special mental challenge. It not only presents high expectations as a basketball player, but it presents many difficulties in ordinary life. Tall people tend to be more vulnerable, sensitive to their height, and less protected/adopted to life. Their appearance arouses interest as an oddity—in shopping, getting clothing, and living. They need basketball to become "real people,"—where they are developed and valued.

The coaching role is especially critical; coaches must establish a true human relationship with their giants of the court. Deceiving that tall player, even once, may mean losing his confidence in you, and that can be devastating. Coaches need to develop all the good human qualities, such as

honesty, humanity, and kindness. However, we should also encourage players' ambition and passion as fighters on the court. Start from the player's point of view but develop that aggressiveness.

Pay special attention to these giants and build around their unique mental makeup. Every great player has one basic characteristic and training must center on that. For example, Sabonis was a true center and a passer, and we worked around that.

PHYSICAL DEVELOPMENT

No other player in basketball must be as physical fit and skillful as the center, because he is constantly in contact with one or two opponents. The big player seldom receives a free ball under the hoop. He always has to fight for the ball. So we want big players to be strong and physically fit.

We improve the physical fitness of centers by doing other sports compatible with basketball, like track and field plus acrobatics. Our focus is on functional physical fitness needed for basketball skills and movements common for all basketball players. Functional fitness is first achieved through running, especially in the preseason. Running is done for 15-60 minutes with a pulse rate of 170 to 180 beats per minute. Centers continue this training throughout the year.

In addition, big players always practice with their arms up. His moves must be effectual, and he is expected to think about it constantly. When running, he uses basketball stances with forward/backward/left/right moves, with both arms up. This is necessary for games (arms up all the time), so he can catch the ball and be effective. We want arms up while passing and catching, and we develop assigned tasks for players to use while running (use your imagination).

Speed improvement and power development are constant emphases for big players through the use of exercises with weights. Speed drills should be combined with ball drills, whenever possible, to develop the

physical and skill components. Exercises with weights are done at 15-20% of a player's weight in order to focus on speed. But weights of up to 70-80% of a player's weight are also used to develop explosive strength and speed. In addition, we increase the strength of muscles around joints with the use of isometric exercises (no more than 5-7% of the total program). We also emphasize speed development in our court skill and drill work.

Some of the specific speed oriented exercises are:

- Sitting, squatting, and jumping with weights on one or both feet
- Quick basketball steps with weights of 20-30 kg – forward, back, right, left (2-3 steps for 30-60 seconds). We report this without weights and with one or two balls.
- High and low starts – for 10-15 m on the coach's signal. We do these in pairs and may also go 50 m. This is also done forward and backward (10 m), with and without the ball.
- Hopping and jumping – for knee joint strengthening (with the ball)
- Ball juggling with speed running (1 or 2 balls) – pass/catch or taking ball around waist or knees
- Hurdle jumping with the ball – one or both legs over 10 hurdles while dribbling the ball
- Jump from a defensive stance – (focus on slight knee bend and jumps from calf/achilles tendon/ankle)
- Hand speed exercise – pass/catch, juggling, starts/stops dribbling (1, 2, 3 balls)

RELAXATION & FLEXIBILITY

Our training also centers on deep relaxation (autogenic training) and flexibility. One method used after each practice is two minutes of deep relaxation with players lying on the court. We believe it is important to cool down from hard work (pulse of 200-220 beats per minute) to a normal resting pulse rate in this relaxation time in order to begin the regeneration process before the next practice. Otherwise, it may take 2-3 hours.

To enhance flexibility, we use acrobatic training as a permanent exercise for bigger players for 15-20 minutes. They are taught to fall properly, with and without a ball, and with and without a spring board. We also use front-roll exercises, with and without a ball, and carrying and catching the ball. Ball pickups in running are used as well as stair jumping (while dribbling). Acrobatic turnover drills are also used to strengthen ankles and shins (wall lean with one foot against wall and squats/jumps). Players can work in pairs with one partner jumping, while the other partner applies resistance by placing his hands on the shoulders of his partner for two minutes.

GENERAL STRENGTH

The Soviet program focuses on basic strength development three times a week. This is a must for all big players. We have a special focus on the trunk core, with spine muscles and abdominal muscles developed in special station work in pairs:

- Lift maximum weight (3-4 reps) while in prone position
- 30 seconds – use 20-30 Kg weights while moving forwards/backwards/right/left (3-4 reps)
- Squats with weights and jumping out of squat position with 70-80% of body weight (3-4 reps)
- Jumping to full leg extension with weight of 25-30 Kg on back of neck (one minute)
- Push-ups on fingertips (one minute)

- Jerking weight overhead with 70-80% of player weight
- Medicine ball throws – sitting or lying, one or two hands for 15-20 m. (behind back/forward/left/right)

SOURCE

Gomelsky, Aleksandr. (1990). Clinic Notes.

LEGACY OF
Alexander "Alex" Hannum

- Known as "Sarge" for his no-nonsense approach with players.

- Excelled at blending the talents of his players and turning them into a championship team.

- Exhibited his moods on the bench — harshness, urgency, and concentration — that reflected qualities that drove his teams to success.

- Became the first coach to win championships in both the NBA and the ABA.

- Coached the 1967 Philadelphia 76ers to a record for regular season wins (68) — a squad that was selected the best team in the NBA's first 35 years.

- Coached 13 future Naismith Hall of Fame inductees.

ALEXANDER "ALEX" HANNUM

*"A player is supposed to perform
to the best of his ability.
It's the coach's job to see
that this gets done."*
—Alexander "Alex" Hannum

BIOGRAPHY

Born: July 19, 1923 in Los Angeles, CA

Died: January 18, 2002

Inducted into the Naismith Basketball Hall of Fame in 1998

Alex Hannum began his coaching career as a player-coach with the St. Louis Hawks during the 1956-57 season. He coached 16 years and compiled a 471-412 NBA record and a 178-152 ABA record. Hannum was the first coach in professional basketball history to win an NBA and ABA championship. He also coached the Wichita Vickers to the National Industrial League title in 1959. His 1967 Philadelphia 76ers set an NBA record for regular season wins (68) and were later voted the best team in the NBA's first 35 years. Hannum coached 13 Hall of Famers and was selected Coach of the Year in both the NBA (1964) and the ABA (1969). He played professional basketball for nine years. Hannum went to the University of Southern California to play for future Hall of Fame coach Sam Barry in 1941. He left school and served in the Army from 1943 to 1946. He returned to USC after World War II, received All-Conference honors in 1947 and 1948, and was the team's Most Valuable Player in 1948.

Alexander "Alex" Hannum...

Alex Hannum was an All-City performer at Hamilton High School (CA) and went to the University of Southern California on a basketball scholarship in 1941. After serving in the Army from 1943 to 1946, he returned to USC and graduated in 1948. Hannum played for Hall of Fame coach Sam Barry and was USC's MVP in 1948. He also earned All-Conference honors in 1947 and 1948. Among his other USC teammates were Bill Sharman and Tex Winter.

Hannum played three seasons with the Los Angeles Shamrocks, an AAU team, and then joined the Oshkosh All-Stars in the NBL. During his NBA playing career, Hannum played for Syracuse, Baltimore, Milwaukee, Fort Wayne, and St. Louis. "I was a journeyman player in the truest sense of the word," said Hannum. "But I think it has made me a better coach because I got to play with so many different players with different styles." (1969)

During his nine-year professional playing career, the 6-foot 7-inches, 220-pound forward was regarded as a hard-nosed defender and tenacious rebounder. "Alex was a tough, quality team player who gave his all," said Hall of Fame player Tom Gola. "Any team trying to overpower Alex was in for a tough night." (Gola, 2002)

Hannum began his professional coaching career with the St. Louis Hawks during the 1956-57 season. Coach Red Holzman was fired at mid-season, and star guard Slater Martin grudgingly accepted the coaching job. A week later Martin persuaded Hawks owner, Ben Kerner, to appoint Hannum as player-coach. The Hawks went on to win the Western Division title and were defeated by the Boston Celtics in the seventh game of the NBA Finals. The next year, Hannum began his first full season as head coach and guided St. Louis to the 1958 NBA championship. Hannum left St. Louis after the championship season because of Kerner's reputation as a compulsive trader and his impatience with his coaches. Kerner had released seven coaches during a seven-year period.

Hannum accepted a position at Wichita, where he coached the Vickers to the 1959 National Industrial League title. Hannum returned to the NBA in 1960 and directed the Syracuse Nationals to the play-offs three consecutive years.

Hannum possessed the ability to take floundering teams and turn them into champions. In 1963, Hannum

became head coach of the San Francisco Warriors, a team that had finished in fourth place the previous year, and led them to the Western Division championship. Under Hannum's guidance in San Francisco, Wilt Chamberlain altered his offensive-oriented game to one of defense, rebounding, and team play. Hannum convinced Wilt to concentrate less on shooting and look for open teammates when the defense converged on him.

Both Hannum and Chamberlain left San Francisco, but were reunited in Philadelphia in 1966. Soon, the Philadelphia attack became the most potent in the NBA. Although Chamberlain's scoring average dropped to only 24 points per game, the lowest of his career, he was credited with 630 assists, a career-high and the third-best in the NBA in 1967. Largely as a result of Chamberlain's unselfish play, Philadelphia won the 1967 NBA championship and compiled a 68-13 regular season record.

It has been said that one of Hannum's greatest coaching accomplishments was his "psychological conquest" of Chamberlain. Hannum disagreed (1968). "I do not subscribe to the theory that I was the only coach who could ever "handle" Wilt. Wilt will accept coaching, and he has tried, in his way, to cooperate with every coach he has ever had. Wilt has a fine mind and is quick to grasp ideas and offer his own suggestions."

The relationship between Hannum and Chamberlain was not without conflict and healthy debate, but since it was based on respect, mutual understanding, and common goals, it worked. Chamberlain called Hannum the best coach he had played for and presented Alex with a special trophy thanking him for his emphasis on team play.

Even though the 1967 Philadelphis 76ers were selected as the best team during the NBA's first 35 years, Hannum refused to take credit for the team's success. "I like to think I've added something," said Hannum, "but it hasn't been much. I keep the players hustling and enthusiastic about winning. That's the essence of a coach's job. The technical aspects of basketball can be gained from a textbook—it's the coach's job to make sure the players are always in the proper frame of mind."

In 1968, Hannum became the head coach of the Oakland Oaks in the upstart American Basketball Association. The year before Hannum's arrival, the Oaks finished in last place with a 22-56 record. With the addition of Rick Barry, Hannum led Oakland to a 60-18 mark and the ABA championship.

As a professional coach, Hannum (1969) believed that you "don't foul up the talent you've working with." He stated, "Over-coaching has ruined too many players. When we get a player in this league, he already is a polished performer. The only basic fundamental we have to deal with is defense. A coach is no more important than that of any player. I'm the 13th man on this team and the only difference is that I have veto power over the other twelve."

Hannum earned the reputation as a tough-guy, but he also demonstrated qualities of softness and understanding. The keystone of Hannum's coaching success was his matter-of-fact- honesty. He was a take-charge type of coach who possessed excellent, up-front rapport with his players.

"You must be honest with your players in this league," said Hannum. "Let them be perfectly aware of your motives and then be dedicated and firm in accomplishing them. How else can you gain their respect? "Hannum blended the talents of his players into powerful teams. "He was a player's coach who, while making strong demands on each individual, got them to accept their roles and play together as a team," stated Hall of Fame coach Jack Ramsay (1996).

Hall of Fame player Nate Thurmond said, "I love Alex Hannum. He was so much a builder of men. I played with a lot of pain in my back. I did it for myself, for the Warriors, and for my teammates. Mostly, I did it for Alex. With the pain, I'm not sure that I could have done it for anybody else."

John Kerr, former coach of the Chicago Bulls, described Hannum in these words, "He's a man's man. If you could pick a father, you'd pick Alex Hannum."

SOURCE

Hannum, Alex. Vertical Files, Archives. Naismith Memorial Basketball Hall of Fame. Springfield, MA.

Hannum, Alex and Frank Deford. (1968, November 25). Old Days and Changed Ways. *Sports Illustrated.*

Hannum, Alex. (1969). An Interview with Rockets' New Coach, Alex Hannum. *San Diego Rockets Game Program.*

Ramsay, Jack. (1996, May 15). Letter to Joseph O'Brien.

COACHING THOUGHTS

By Alex Hannum

COACH-PLAYER RELATIONSHIPS

Unlike most professional coaches who try to remain aloof from their players, I want to stay friendly and sociable with mine. I want to go out with my players after a game and laugh, eat, and argue with them.

I acknowledge that a coach must maintain stature and respect, and certainly it is easier to manage this if you isolate yourself and don't get personally involved with your players. But I could never do it this way. I think it is a greater challenge and a deeper reward if you can mix with your players and still retain your stature.

If anything, this closeness of coach and player has become even more important since race entered the picture. It is my feeling that bigotry is founded on a lack of understanding and knowledge of the other race. If you know about something or someone, then you are not liable to be afraid. I think that I have very little fear, and, therefore very little prejudice.

My main concern in basketball is that my players know each other and know me. You must be honest with players. I want them to understand exactly what I am like, how dedicated I am, what my motives are, what I am out to accomplish. If I can help my players know that, then I don't have to waste a lot of our time trying to baloney them into thinking I am some kind of genius. It comes to this: if they can understand me, then they can trust and like me.

My only criterion for any player is the following question: Can he help the team and can he get along with his teammates? Basketball is a team game, the finest team

game ever devised. You have to work together to win. You'll never have a good team if you are top-heavy with grunts. A grunt is a word we use in the construction business in California to describe a man who will do exactly what he is told and no more. He either waits for new orders or makes the one job last all day.

Grunts don't make suggestions. In fact, I never coached a good player who was a grunt. The good ones are forever involved, forever thinking, even if you don't agree with their schemes—and I demand that the coach retain a veto power. Still, the interest that players show in a game or practice can never replace the all-day commitment that we had to the game in the old days. There was no aspect of the game we did not discuss.

Coaching is almost always a bewildering experience, never precise or predictable. Sometimes, you make one little remark, and you get the most amazing results. Other times, you can talk yourself blue in the face to no avail. You see your whole team get cold, you try everything and everybody, and they're still cold. All right, coach, what now? Well, I'll tell you, the first thing a professional coach should be is the glue. You must hold things all together, or you just can't do anything else.

COACHING STYLE

In my career, there was never anyplace like Syracuse. Syracuse in the 1950's was like the Athens of basketball, so many good coaches came out of there: Al Cervi, Paul Seymour, Johnny Kerr, Larry Costello, Dolph Schayes, and Al Bianchi in the pros; George King and Bobby Harrison in col-

lege, and Earl Lloyd, who may be the best of us all, but who never really had a chance. If I ever decide to stop coaching at Oakland, I think I'd like to have Earl replace me. All these men learned under Danny Biasone. It was as if you were taking a master's degree when you worked under him.

The two years I had previously played at Syracuse, 1949-51, Cervi was the coach. I learned an entirely different game from him. At Southern Cal, under Sam Barry, and in high school I had been taught to play slowdown, deliberate basketball. Syracuse played the Eastern style, which also placed a premium on possession, but had a broader definition of what constituted a good shot. Eastern shooters were so much better than those from any other section of the country that a 25-foot set shot was considered good. It was a whole new world to me.

Boston originally played a game much like that at Syracuse, although under Auerbach — and with Russell—it evolved into something different. The Rochester Royals worked pretty much in the Syracuse manner, too, but they had such a great group of guards—Bobby Davies, Bobby Wanzer, Jack McMahon, Red Holzman, Fuzzy Levane, Pep Saul—that more play was directed to the backcourt. When I played at Rochester, I really learned to set screens for those long set shots, and I learned to move without the ball, because if you got open, you knew those guards would get the ball to you.

When I came back to coach Syracuse myself, I added some of the Rochester guard play and some of the deliberate Sam Barry principles to the pure give-and-go

Eastern game. The old Syracuse style was basically a continuity offense. There were really no patterns or set plays at all. You tried something, and if it didn't work, there were several options you moved to naturally. The point was to keep going off whatever you started with originally. Barry at USC had what I would call an offensive thrust. You set something definite up—like a double screen (which I used with great success with the 76ers)—but if it didn't work, you abandoned the idea altogether and started with something new.

Anyway, I like to combine thrust and continuity offenses, and I always want my team to run. Every team I've ever had, I have instructed my players to try and run. Always look for the fast break.

Syracuse was a great team to coach because it was a running, freewheeling group and everybody got in the act. The Nationals had more talent among them than any team I ever coached. I don't suppose I could ever find more satisfaction than I had with them. But I disagree when people suggest I must have enjoyed coaching the Nationals more than I did the 76ers, dominated as they were by Chamberlain, and a team, they said, wasn't my type.

Well, I'll tell you, I haven't really got a type. Each team, depending on its personnel, has its own best style, and that is the one I want to find. I've never yet read a coaching book, and I've got a bunch sitting around the house that people sent me.

The real answer is that I coached Syracuse for three years, and it was great, and I loved that style, but we never had a champion. I was with Wilt Chamberlain three full seasons, and maybe it was a little less inspiring always working that ball into the middle, but in those three years we won three divisional titles, one world championship and we should have won another. And I have to say, that is my style.

SOURCE

Hannum, Alex and Frank Deford. (November 18, 1968). "I've Barely Begun To Fight." *Sports Illustrated*

Hannum, Alex and Frank Deford. (November 25, 1968). "Old Days and Changed Ways." *Sports Illustrated*

LEGACY OF
Howard "Hobby" Hobson

- Coached the University of Oregon to the first NCAA national championship in 1939.

- Became one of the first coaches to analyze and evaluate the game of basketball statistically.

- Reported the results of his basketball analysis in the acclaimed book, *Scientific Basketball*.

- Lobbied for the adoption of the three-point field goal, 12-foot widened lane, and shot clock.

- Organized an experimental game, played with the three-point line, in 1945 between Fordham and Columbia.

- Pioneered intersectional play at Oregon, making the Ducks the first Western team to travel to the East Coast for games.

HOWARD "HOBBY" HOBSON

"The three-point field goal will act like a good cough syrup and break up congestion around the lane."
—Howard "Hobby" Hobson

BIOGRAPHY

Born: July 4, 1903 in Portland, Oregon

Died: June 9, 1991

Inducted into the Naismith Basketball Hall of Fame in 1965

Howard "Hobby" Hobson's 27-year coaching career included stints at Southern Oregon College, University of Oregon, and Yale University. His overall coaching record was 495-291. Hobson led Oregon to the first-ever NCAA championship in 1939. His teams at Yale won or shared five Big Three titles. He also pioneered intersectional play while at Oregon, making the Ducks the first western team to travel east for games. Hobson was an outstanding coach, administrator, author, and clinician. He was president of the NABC and served on the U.S. Olympic Basketball Committee for 12 years. Hobson was one of the first coaches to analyze and evaluate the game of basketball statistically. He contributed heavily as a distinguished member of the National Basketball Rules Committee and lobbied for the three-point field goal, the 12-foot lane, and the shot clock.

Howard "Hobby" Hobson...

Reared in Portland (OR), Howard Hobson became one of basketball's influential pioneers after becoming first exposed to the game in 1915 at the age of 12. As Hobson states, "the game was played in an old elementary school gymnasium, and there was no coach." The Portland Athletic Club had received permission to use the court, and the boys played the best they could with little knowledge of the game. "Our opponents had an outstanding player who was scoring most of their points, and I tried to stop him. I recall that I left my feet and dived for him with the result that I lost my two front teeth." He was severely reprimanded at home and, from that time on, became very interested in learning the fundamentals of the game. "Hobby" went on to become one of the true basketball scholars of the game; also publishing the results of his basketball analysis in a book entitled *Basketball Illustrated*.

He became a star basketball and baseball athlete at University of Oregon, later returning to coach there for 11 years, starting in 1935-36. At Southern Oregon Normal, his basketball teams were 57-14 (.803) from 1932-35, including three straight wins over his Alma Mater. The 1934-35 season, which ended with a loss to Hutchinson, KS in the national AAU tournament, was also the college's first 20-win campaign. Hobson's 1938-39 Oregon team was called the Tall Timbers due to their size. They were led by "Slim" Wintermute, one of the game's first big men. Oregon was crowned as the first NCAA I

champion in 1939, when the team won the eight-team championship at Northwestern University in Evanston, Illinois. This first tourney was organized and directed by the coaches' organization (NABC). His Oregon Ducks also pioneered college intersectional play, being one of the first teams to play in Madison Square Garden (NY). Intersectional play was made possible through train travel from coast-to-coast. (Rosenthal 2003)

Hobson also changed the game by becoming one of the first coaches to analyze and evaluate the game of basketball statistically. It started in Oregon when he began a thirteen-year study of shooting percentages and the objective areas of basketball. He charted 460 games at all levels and styles of play to find that, on average, a shot was taken every 18.05 seconds; thus, he became the first advocate of the shot clock in basketball.

It was furthered when he took a leave of absence from the University of Oregon to complete his doctorate at Columbia University and write his dissertation on basketball statistics. In addition, he conducted 13 experimental games with the three-point field goal and the widened lane at 12 feet (at that time it was six feet and looked like a keyhole—later called the key or free-throw lane). He continued to push for a time limit/shot clock, doubling the 18 seconds to 36, and eventually recommending the shot clock at 40 seconds. As manager of the 1952 USA Olympic team, Hobby pushed for the 30-second shot clock for international basketball (FIBA), which was adopted soon after. About 1953, Hobson recommended the adoption of the NBA shot-clock at 24 seconds because of the higher skill levels in professional basketball. He derived this from his college research at 18 seconds and the international adoption at 30 seconds. Thus halfway between was 24 seconds, the shot-clock limit he recommended for the NBA. The NBA commissioner at the time, Maurice Podoloff, credits Hobby with "saving the NBA" by speeding up play when the shot-clock rule was adopted.

He continued to advocate for the wide lane and the three-point field goal. His reasons were to "curb violence." He said his three-point shot will "act like a good cough syrup and break up the congestion" around the basket because of the narrow key (Oregonian, June 17, 1974). His original recommendation was to have three scoring areas; award 1 point for close shots (0-12 ft), 2 points for mid-range shots (12-24 ft), and 3 points for long-range shots (over 24 feet). The NBA eventually adopted the three-point field goal in 1979; and the college game implemented the three-point shot in 1987. (Note: one of the co-authors, Krause, was chairman of the Basketball Rules Committee when the three-point field goal was adopted— ironically it was passed at the same distance Hobson used in his 1945 experimental games—21 feet from the center of the basket). The material he researched eventually became the source for his book, *Scientific Basketball*, published originally in 1945. Thus, it is seen that Coach

Hobson laid the groundwork for several rules milestones: the 12-foot widened lane, the shot clock, and the 3-point field goal.

Howard Hobson became president of the NABC and one of the game's most prominent scholar/authors. After retiring at Yale, Hobson returned to his native Northwest roots in Portland (OR), where he lived until his death until 1991. Hobby continued to lobby for his science-based rules changes, even in his last years. Howard "Hobby" Hobson will always be remembered as the scholarly coach who analyzed the game quantitatively.

SOURCE

Hobson, Howard. Vertical Files. Archives. Naismith Memorial Basketball Hall of Fame. Springfield, MA.

Hobson, Howard. (1948). *Basketball Illustrated*. New York: Barnes and Co.

Hobson, Howard.(1955). *Scientific Basketball*. Englewood Cliffs, NJ: Prentice-Hall.

Rosenthal, Rick. Interview with Jerry Krause, July 21, 2003.

THE SHOT CLOCK

By Howard Hobson

It was the season of 1935-36, my first year as coach of Oregon in the Pacific Coast Conference. Armory "Slats" Gill, a friend since high school days but now a worthy opponent, was the tutor at Oregon Agricultural College. "Slats" was an exponent of "percentage basketball" originated by Bob Hager, his coach when he played for the Aggies. The system was ball control all the way, with scores often in the twenties.

They beat our Oregon Webfoots this night 28-26 on our court, and the fans were up in arms due to the "stall" tactics. I went over to "Slats" and congratulated him on the win, but added, "some day I am going to propose a rule change that will demand that a team shoot within 15 seconds or give the ball to the opponents." The reply, in laughter, "you wouldn't dare." But I wasn't really joking. I had already been charting shots and keeping percentages, but not to any great extent.

That game really got me started in earnest, and in 1936-37, I started my 13-year research study of shooting percentages and all other objective phases of basketball. We covered 460 games, which showed a shot taken every 18.05 seconds on the average and by all kinds of teams—fast break, ball control, etc. We didn't just add shots taken, made, etc. but we used seconds—not minutes. The technical statistics 1,104,000 seconds divided by 61,167 attempts equals the 18.05 average. Further, in Madison Square Garden, all the games in 1944-45 were covered, involving all kinds of offensive styles from all over the country. That statistic for 52 games showed 124,800 seconds divided by 8,319 attempts or an average of almost exactly 15 seconds—just what I told Gill in 1936.

I immediately started to "sell" the time limit as soon as the study was completed which was in 1947-48.

When I moved to Yale in 1946, I tried to get the Ivy League to try the plan.

As manager of the Olympic team in 1952, I conducted a rules clinic for coaches of all countries. I persuaded Oswald Tower to go and interpret rules which he did, and he was favorable to the plan. Jim Coogan was also there and was also favorable.

The International rules went to the 30-second clock soon after, which was the time limit I had suggested.

John Bunn, then coach at Springfield College, and I played an exhibition game using the time limit, which I believe was in 1951 or 1952, but I do not have the records.

The NBA was having serious trouble in the early 1950s due to stalling, and low-scoring games that were keeping fans away. Commissioner Maurice Podoloff was really a hockey man and was not altogether familiar with basketball. He knew of my study, and we had numerous visits about the rules. I suggested the time limit to him years before it was adopted. Then, at Leones Restaurant at the Basketball Writers Luncheon, I made a plea to the coaches and the press for adoption.

I believe this was in 1953, soon after the Olympics. Maurice Podoloff sent me a letter which credits me with the plan prior to the NBA adoption, which occurred on April 22, 1954. However, he seems to have forgotten our visits and particularly how we

arrived at 24 seconds instead of 30 seconds. I told him of my statistics and explained while college teams perhaps needed 30 seconds to set up their plays, that the professionals who are more mature and playing a faster game could get along with a lower time limit which would speed up the game and be more attractive to the fans. So, we took the 30-second international rule and the 18-second statistic from my study and came up with 24 seconds. It has worked very well at the professional level.

Maurice Podoloff, at public gatherings in New Haven, twice gave me credit for the time clock and for "saving the NBA." The last time, I remember distinctly. It was at the Boys Club banquet in the spring of 1955. He introduced me as the speaker and the "Yale coach who first proposed the time clock and saved the NBA."

Regardless of where credit is given, I still believe the clock should be in the high school and college games for so many reasons I have explained over the years. It is now adopted for the Olympics; International play, the NIT, Women's NCAA, and why not by all?

I am extremely proud of my study which was my doctoral dissertation at Columbia and the basic material for my book, *Scientific Basketball*. It not only brought about the three-point goal, the widened lane, and the time limit, but numerous other proposals and rules changes as outlined in the book as well.

SOURCE

Hobson, Howard. (1981). The Time Limit. *NABC Bulletin*.

THE THREE-POINT SHOT

By Howard Hobson

Authors' Note: This article was written by Hobson in 1981 and provides rationale for the three-point field goal which was eventually adopted by colleges in 1987.

Violence in basketball? You mean it is NOT a no-contact game as intended by its inventor, Dr. James Naismith in 1891? Well, there has always been bodily contact, but it reached a peak in the National Basketball Association when Rudy Tomjanovich and Kareem Abdul-Jabbar were out for most of the season and other players were severely injured due to brutal violence. IT MUST BE STOPPED. Much of the problem lies in the fact that the game is played now almost entirely within a radius of about 23 feet from the basket, except for an occasional goal from a fast break or following an interception. Put ten big fellows in an area that small, and rough play is bound to occur. It's like putting two heavyweight boxers in a telephone booth and telling them not to clinch. Perhaps a review of an old plan, the 3-point play, may help solve this problem.

How did the game get the way it is today? It probably all started with the discovery and reporting of national shooting percentages. Struggling for a Doctorate at Columbia University in 1945, we decided to do a study of all objective factors of basketball but mainly on shooting percentages. We had statistics from college games all over the country, covering a 13-year period. There were isolated cases where coaches kept shooting records, but national records were unknown. Scoring and shot attempts had greatly increased since 1937—when a great idea by Sam Barry of University of Southern California was adopted (the elimination of the center jump after every basket). But

still, a player might score ten field goals in a game, but did he take ten shots or fifty-and what percentage should he be EXPECTED to make? A baseball background helped in doing our study. We knew that .300 was a good batting average and that a home run was more valuable than a single—and more spectacular. We knew, in basketball, that field goals scored near the basket would show a higher percentage than those from mid-court, but we never dreamed that the differences were so great. Shooting percentages and other findings indicated the need for a widened free throw lane, the shot clock, more severe penalties for the personal foul, and especially the need for an area method of scoring; hence the birth of the 3-point play.

The season of 1944-45 showed a shooting percentage of .339 in the area from the basket out to 12 feet, mostly dominated by the tall man; .206 from 12 feet to 24 feet; and .171 beyond 24 feet. The overall percentage was .259. Percentages are much higher today, of course, due mainly to publicizing of the percentages, greater specialization and better equipment, but the relative figures from various distances are quite similar. Actual statistics dictated that one point should be credited for a goal out to 12 feet; two points from 12 to 24 feet and three points beyond 24 feet. But we knew it would not be practical to divide the court into three areas, so we compromised by proposing two points out to 21 feet and three points beyond that distance. We claimed the following benefits from the plan:

1. It would relieve congestion under the basket and reduce bodily contact, as it would cause the defense to come out to cover the outer areas.

2. It would reduce the use of the zone defense and open up the court for drive-in plays.
3. It would decrease the value of the tall man and increase the value of the outside shooter—perhaps giving smaller players a better chance.
4. It would give the team that is behind a better chance to catch up.
5. It would keep the long 2-hand set shot in the game and would give us a HOME RUN OF BASKETBALL, which would have great appeal to both players and fans.
6. The plan would require no new equipment, merely an arc line on the court.

We presented the plan, along with our proposal to widen the free throw lane from 6 to 12 feet, to the New York Basketball Writers and Coaches at the weekly meeting on January 2, 1945. The *New York Times* and the *New York Herald Tribune* reported favorably on the plans and gave the reactions of several New York college coaches.

Nat Holman, City College of New York: "Liked both suggestions, but wanted them tested for a season first, just as the Pacific Coast Conference tried out the elimination of the center jump before it was incorporated into the rules."

Howard Cann, New York University: "Was more enthusiastic—there are two suggestions worth considering. I think the coaches association research committee ought to get to work on them right away."

The presentation resulted in an experimental game to try out the plans, which was played between Columbia and Fordham on February 7, 1945. Both plans were favored by sports writers fans, officials and coaches.

Wrote Hugh Fullerton, Jr., Associated Press, February 9, 1945: "There's a bigger kick in seeing a long shot swish through the basket—especially when so many big boys are trying to get under the basket that you can't tell who's who. And you should have heard the customers shouting 'THREE' when a kid was poised to shoot from just inside the 21-foot arc. As for the scoring, it's no more confusing than the difference between a base hit and a two-bagger, and we never heard a football coach, for instance, objecting to long passes or wide end runs because he preferred the more intricate teamwork of off-guard play.

Harry Grayson, NEA Sports Editor: "Howard Hobson's idea preserves the two-hand set shot. Eliminating it is tantamount to taking the home run out of baseball, although it is the most satisfying skill to the player and the most thrilling to the spectator."

Irving Marsh, *New York Herald Tribune*: "From the spectators' point of view, the new rules provided more wide-open basketball and a decided accent on set shooting. The crowd voted 60-50 in favor of the 3-point basket and 70-30 in favor of widening the free throw lane. The officials, Chuck Solodare and John Norton, liked the innovations, in spite of the added burden. To this observer, the new rules definitely provided a game with more action and more excitement."

Well, the widened lane got, in but we couldn't sell the rules makers on the 3-point play—although we served on the committee. Perhaps too many coaches liked the zone defense. It wasn't until 1962 that we persuaded Abe Saperstein, of Harlem Globetrotter fame and an old friend, to give the 3-point play a try when be became Commissioner of the newly formed American Basketball League. It met with instant success. An Associated Press story out of Chicago dated April 15, 1962 says: "The 3-point goal is here to stay and then

some. It could spread to the college ranks eventually. Chants of 'HIT A HOME RUN, HIT A HOME RUN' or "GO, GO, GO FOR THE LONG ONE' were common among fans at the ABL games. The 3-pointer has determined the outcome of many ABL games during the season. In a recent five-game championship playoff, the Cleveland Pipers made 22 and the Kansas City Steers 12. The Pipers won the crown."

The American Basketball Association succeeded the ABL and always used the 3-point play until its merger with the National Basketball Association. Faced with serious problems—not only of violence but also with the interpretation of the supposedly illegal use of the zone defense, the NBA has adopted the plan. It is difficult to legislate against the zone, but proper rules can make its use less advantageous.

But the NBA should give very careful consideration to the distance from the basket for which 3-point goals will be credited. If the distance is too far out, percentages will be low, and the defense will not come out to force play; the problems will remain. On the other hand, if the distance is too short, congestion under the basket will not be relieved. Abe Saperstein, in the old ABL, increased our 21-foot distance to 23 feet, 9 inches. The ABA used the same distance for many years, finally increasing it to 25 feet, which was too far out.

The current NBA distance is 23 ft., 9 inches, tapering down to 22 feet along the sidelines from the foul lines to the end lines. Our recommendation to them was no greater distance than 23 feet.

The exceptional shooter, of course, can hit from any distance. Did you know that Jerry Harkness, playing for the Indiana Pacers in the ABA, made a desperation 92-foot shot at the buzzer to defeat the Dallas Chaparrals 119-118; the three-point goal winning the game? That one, it seems, should have counted TEN.

It is obvious that the current problems mentioned in this story are similar to the ones we had 35 years ago—problems

caused because the percentage of the long shot was just not worth the risk and the shorter one-hand shot took over.

Wouldn't it be great to have that long shot back, giving us a HOME RUN OF BASKETBALL; a wide open game clear out to mid-court; and violence under control?

Professionals and amateur teams have similar rules problems, but the NBA again must be congratulated on stealing a march on the school and college game by adopting the 3-point plan. The pros must put on a show—they are dependent on the gate for survival and have led the way in important rules changes. The low scoring, stalling game led to their adoption of the clock-24 seconds to shoot, for example. Schools have refused to adopt the rule, electing to have the privilege of using slow-down, stalling tactics, regardless of spectator disapproval. But schools are becoming more aware of the importance of monetary return and spectator appeal so policies may change. A good start would be to adopt the 3-point plan.

SOUTHERN CONFERENCE LEADS THE WAY

Finally, one major nine-member conference, the Southern Conference, tried the 3-point play for the 1980-81 season. The distance was 22 feet-a good choice. It was a rousing success. Magazines, including *Sports Illustrated*, carried articles, and newspapers throughout the country wrote welcoming stories about the plan. We were in close touch with the conference during the season. J. Dallas Shirley, assistant to the Conference Commissioner, was deeply involved in the experiment and made a detailed report at the NABC in Philadelphia. It was a very favorable summary. Suffice to say here, the Southern Conference will use the plan again in 1981-82.

An important point should be made here. The pros have not used the plan to full advantage. It has been tried mainly as a catch-up weapon by the team behind in the last moments of the game. Most Southern Conference teams did the same but some of them did utilize other parts of the plan. The many other stated advantages will not be achieved until the three-point field goal is used throughout the entire game and becomes a major part of the team offense. This will come with experience and particularly when more outside shooters are developed.

The research experts and rules makers are still requesting more experimentation and favorable evidence before adopting the plan. Well, we had the Columbia-Fordham game in 1945, 20 years in three major professional leagues, and now a year in a major college conference—all favorable. What more is needed?

Perhaps the conservatist should take a look at basketball history. The major rule change since the very early years was the elimination of the center jump. We were coaching in the Pacific Coast Conference at the time. The plan was tried out by the Southern Division just ONE YEAR, in 1935-36. It was nationally adopted in 1936-37. No one has ever looked back. Nothing very exciting has happened to the rules of the game in the 44 years since.

Basketball is not the only sport with a Rip Van Winkle, doldrums philosophy and policy that may be some consolation. Football, for example, grants three points for a field goal, whether it is made from the one-yard line or from mid-field. They must keep per-

centages from various distances. Say the Cowboys are leading the Packers by four points late in the game. It takes a touchdown for the Packers to win so the fans are going for the exits. But suppose a field goal from say 30 yards or further counts four. As Mel Allen used to say, "HOW ABOUT THAT."

SOURCE

Hobson, Howard. (1981, Winter). The Three-Point Play-Answer to Violence. *NABC Bulletin*.

LEGACY OF
Nat Holman

- Only coach in basketball history to lead his team (CCNY) to both the NIT and NCAA championship in the same year (1950).

- Developed a street-smart style of play know as "The City Game."

- Led a double life of professional basketball player and college coach from 1919 through 1937.

- Played with the Original Celtics, the most celebrated barnstorming team of their day.

- Became the game's first superstar and was a national hero during the 1920s; nicknamed "Mr. Basketball."

- Recognized as the "Father of Israeli Basketball."

NAT HOLMAN

*"To be a coach is to be a teacher.
You have to teach people from different
backgrounds to work together
for the common good."*
— Nat Holman

BIOGRAPHY

Born: October 19, 1896 in New York, NY

Died: February 12, 1995

Inducted into the Naismith Basketball Hall of Fame in 1964

Nat Holman was a national hero during the 1920s and earned the title "Mr. Basketball" for his playing excellence. He was one of the game's most accurate shooters and dazzled fans with his wizardry ballhandling and passing. Holman played the majority of his career with the world famous Original Celtics, and made the team virtually unbeatable. He was one of the great pioneers of professional basketball, and his creativity on the court helped developed the pivot play in basketball. From 1919 to 1933, Homan lived the double life of professional basketball player and college coach. At the age of 32, Holman ended his professional playing career to concentrate on his coaching job at CCNY. During his 37-year coaching career at CCNY, Holman compiled a 423-190 record. In 1950, his CCNY team won, what has been called the "Grand Slam in College Basketball," the NIT and the NCAA tournaments. Holman is the only coach to ever win both titles in the same season. Holman was an international ambassador for basketball and held coaching clinics in Israel, Japan, Turkey, Korea, Taiwan, Mexico, and Canada. He wrote four basketball books, served as president of the NABC in 1941, and was presented with the Helms Foundation Award in recognition of his contributions to basketball. In 1951, Holman was selected National Coach of the Year.

Nat Holman...

Nat Holman grew up on New York's lower east side, with his parents, six brothers and three sisters. By the time Holman was twelve years old, he had earned the reputation as an excellent basketball player. He obtained that reputation the hard way—playing in the rough neighborhood games against men much older and bigger than him.

Even though the game of basketball was in its infancy, "It was not a new game on the lower east side," Holman said. "It was very popular. We played basketball all year, indoors, and outdoors. It was at the Settlement Houses that I really got my start. Saturday night was a big night out. We would schedule a game, and there would be a dance before the game, between halves, and after the game. Thanks to the Settlement Houses, we always had a place to play basketball." (Healy, 1988)

Holman recalled how difficult it was playing on a court with dance wax. "I cut two holes in the sole of each basketball shoe and filled them with petroleum jelly," Holman said. "This allowed me to have better traction."

A key person in Holman's life was his playground instructor, Jim Gennitty. "I really must tip my hat to him. I can honestly say he inspired me so much that I patterned my lifestyle after him," said Holman. (Healy, 1988)

While in the High School of Commerce, he earned the nickname "Kid" Holman for his athletic exploits. In football, he was the all-star halfback; in soccer he was the all-scholastic goalie; in baseball, he starred as a pitcher and his team came within one game of winning the city championship; and in basketball, he received his first taste of what might be considered professional basketball by playing on a touring team called the Busy Izzies that featured future Hall of Fame players Barney Sedran and Marty Friedman.

After Holman graduated from high school, the Cincinnati Reds offered him a baseball contract, but instead, he enrolled in the Savage School of Physical Education. While an undergraduate, Holman played basketball for Savage, and one of his teammates was future Hall of Fame referee, Dave Tobey. Holman financed his education by barnstorming with several professional basketball teams.

While in graduate school at New York University in 1919, Holman assumed the basketball coaching duties at the City College of New York (CCNY). From 1919 through 1933, Holman led a double life of professional basketball player and college coach. "Those were busy days," explained Holman. "There were times when I'd rush to

New Jersey after a game at the college and get into my pro basketball suit in an automobile while crossing the 125th Street Ferry." (Strauss, 1959)

Holman was one of basketball's most accurate shooters and the finest passer and playmaker of his era. Holman reached the top as a player with the Original Celtics, a team that won 720 games out of the 795 played between 1921 and 1928. The Original Celtics never lost a series and frequently played up to 150 games a year, averaging five or six games a week, including two on Sunday. "You had to be in good condition," Holman stated. "Your body would adjust. Saturday, we learned to hit the sack early to prepare for Sunday's two games. We'd play one at 2 p.m., and then rest before the next game at 8 p.m."

Holman was a national hero in the 1920s and was called "Mr. Basketball." Wherever the Original Celtics played, their clean-cut hero was the main drawing attraction.

The Original Celtics, as well as other teams in that era, wore heavy, woolen uniforms. They had padded pants and kneepads, and some players even wore elbow guards. "We had to wear heavy, woolen uniforms," Holman recalled. "We played in armories, dance halls, even on theater stages. The temperature would vary from one place to the next. In fact, in many of the armories, the fans would wear overcoats, and we'd be playing in shorts and a sleeveless top." (Healy, 1988)

The highlight in Holman's coaching career occurred in 1950 when his CCNY team won both the NIT and the NCAA championship for the first and only time in basketball history. "What a great thrill it was that night," remembered Holman. "When we left Madison Square Garden the students and fans were on Seventh Avenue waiting for us. Flags were being waved and the students were singing our Alma Mater. I will never forget it."

Holman was an outstanding teacher whose devotion to detail was overwhelming. CCNY was different from most schools. There was no tuition, so only the top academic students could gain admission. Holman did not have the best talent, but he masterfully developed his players into beautifully drilled teams that won far more games than they were entitled to win. His teams always portrayed his poise, confidence, and toughness. Even at the age of 60, Holman would often get on the floor during practice and show his players what he wanted and how to do it.

Early in his coaching career, Holman believed in the patient, deliberate Eastern style of play but later installed the Western style that featured the fast break and the one-hand shot. To Holman, the five most important ingredients in the game were ballhandling, shiftiness, endurance, shooting ability, and poise.

Holman's teams operated with very few set plays. "I want resourceful, flexible-thinking teams that are never stuck for an idea on what to do next." Said Holman. "I teach my players to recognize situations and know what will develop from a particular floor pattern. All basketball is a pattern. Get in that pattern and then you're going." (Padwe, 1970)

Holman retired from coaching in 1960, with an overall record of 421-190.

Holman believed there were many contributors to the game of basketball during his lifetime, but Hank Luissetti and Ned Irish were at the top of his list.

"Hank Luissetti of Stanford will be remembered for his famous one-hand shot," said Holman. "In my time, this was the first man who brought something new to the game. I tip my hat to him for all the thrills he gave me."

"Ned Irish made basketball a big-time sport," stated Holman. "He organized the first college doubleheader in Madison Square Garden in 1934, and in the 1940s, he introduced college basketball to television."

In 1949, one year after the birth of the State of Israel, Holman launched the nation's first basketball program. He has been recognized as the Father of Israeli Basketball. Holman served as president of the United States Committee Sports for Israel (USCSFI), an organization established to promote athletics and physical education both in the United States and Israel. In 1972, on only four hours notice, Holman flew to Israel to attend the memorial service for the Israel athletes slain during the Olympics in Munich. He was the only non-member of the Israel Olympic Committee who was invited to address the body during its days of grief.

Holman's contributions go far beyond his accomplishments on the basketball court. He worked more than half a century as director of Camp Scatico, a private summer children's camp in Elizaville, New York. His interaction with campers, counselors, and parents brought him great joy.

Holman said, "I loved every minute of it. You talk about recruiting basketball players. I recruited counselors! I spent a great deal of time looking for the right person to work with the campers. I wanted a person the campers could look up to and would be proud to introduce to their parents."

Nat Holman was a special human being. He was a gifted leader who touched every person he met. To each, he imparted that special "Holman magic," the power to believe, and the urge to excel and exceed self-imposed limits.

SOURCE

Healy, Jerry. (1988, September 12). *Nat Holman...Player and Coach*. Naismith Memorial Basketball Hall of Fame News Release.

Holman, Nat. Vertical Files, Archives. Naismith Memorial Basketball Hall of Fame. Springfield, MA.

Padwe, Sandy. (1970). *Basketball's Hall of Fame*. Englewood Cliffs, NJ: Prentice-Hall.

Strauss, Michael. (1959, February 8). Holman Figures His Age by Games. *New York Times*.

LESSONS FROM THIS LEGEND...

HOW WE CAN SAVE BASKETBALL

By Nat Holman

Authors' Note: A year after winning both the NIT and the NCAA championship in 1950, seven CCNY players were implicated in a point-shaving scandal.

Basketball is a great sport. It has come to serve youth throughout the world. City playgrounds are built around a basketball court. Bushel-barrel rims have become standard equipment on garage doors all along the American countryside. Today, more youngsters play basketball than any other sport.

It has developed a phenomenal following of millions of people. Giant arenas, on college campuses and in metropolitan main streets, have been built to house it. Schools have made money from it. Coaches have received better salaries because of it. Newspapers, radio, and television have recognized its growth into a major sport and have benefited from it.

Whether the present state of scandal exiles the sport to some professional limbo or not, basketball will always be "big time" to kids who love it as a clean, good game. Basketball will never die. Certainly this is a game worth saving.

But how? Here is a scandal, stunning in its bigness, horrendous in its implications. Boys have been fixed. Not just a few, but boys from CCNY, Bradley, LIU, Manhattan, and Toledo, boys from many sections of the land. And we all ask: will this kill basketball?

I don't know. It may, if we do nothing but sit back in righteous indignation and take pot shots at the currently popular social pariahs. Like it or not, we have a fight on

our hands, all of us; a fight that must be fought today. Next year will be too late.

But again, how? There are so many facets to this terrible problem. Now evils shoot out with almost every newspaper headline. There is the gambler, an outside evil that must be eradicated. There are the inside evils, the recruiting system, the concentration on gate receipts. There are the coaches, the officials, the public, the press, the boys themselves, the very temper of our times—all must be subjected to examination. As basketball stands at its particular crossroad, we're on the spot. Let's do something about it now, not later.

Let's understand, first off, what's been happening. I do not like platitudes, but I think it is obvious that there is a general relaxation of morals in the country. The war hysteria, impending inductions, boys at loose ends have brought this on. In such a state, there are boys ready to take risks regardless of consequences, despite repeated warnings by coaches and parents, and in this climate, the responsible authorities of big-time basketball have failed in their duty. They have allowed the game to fall into the hands of the boys.

There has been recruiting without conscience. Boys have been bought, subsidized, catered to, pampered. They have been invited to tap the till. If a boy wants more meal money, he gets it, because the school is afraid that otherwise he might leave. The boys know their demands will be met. A coach tries to train them, motivate them, seeks to inspire them to play the game for the joy of honest competition, for the camaraderie it develops, for the thrill of winning, for the greater thrill of playing the

game; then they turn around and sell out. If you have been educated to have a price, there is no need for a teacher.

The thinking of the boys must be reshaped. We must condition them to know the right and wrong of behavior patterns, to be able to stand up in the strong winds of temptation, before they arrive on the college scene, instead of pointing the way to the gate receipts. We must eliminate the original bribe, which is unrestrained recruiting. If we fail in this, we must be prepared for them to continue to sell out by making deals with gamblers.

I have been so close to the scandal that it has been like a death in the family. After all the NYCC boys did for the school, for the alumni, and for themselves with their twin tournament championships, this explosion was a bitter experience to all of us. They are basically good boys. Unfortunately, when they were asked the big question, they weren't quite strong enough. They needed toughness!

I felt that I had control of my boys. I spoke often to them of the shady deals that would be thrust at them. I warned them to be careful. But the easy money was a great temptation. The rumors about dumps had been prevalent for some time, but I swore my boys wouldn't dump. They were good boys, and they had been warned.

Oh, I was slightly suspicious of some players on other teams, who would make glaring mistakes out on the court. But I couldn't be suspicious of my boys. No coach could and still do his job. Before many a game, I would warn my players, even citing these blatant errors by other players. But when my players were making similar bad moves, I saw them as technical errors, basketball mistakes. When I chastised them for their mistakes, to them it must have sounded like an expression of suspicion on my part. But it wasn't. I was seeing basketball mistakes.

I would keep moving the boys in and out. I've always done this. I'm known as a disciplinarian, and when a player goofs off on the court, out he comes. It would seem that such practice would kill any attempts to dump a game, but I had seven of them against me. My first seven men were all in on the fix. I was strapped.

Even on the train coming home from Philadelphia on the night the first three boys were picked up, I cautioned them, not only for their occasional lapses on the court but about the need to keep up their class work, too. That evening, in the game, a couple of them had made awful plays, and I bawled them out. An hour later, they were picked up for shading the points.

Knowing these boys as I did, having a truly fatherly pride in them, and sincerely believing that they are good boys, I still say there must be a penalty. This is part of the toughness that must come into the game. The boys knew they were doing wrong. Some of them even tried to stop. But they went back to it, after accepting the argument that "you're in it already. Why pass up the easy dough?"

What the punishment should be is a question that a higher authority than I am must answer. It may be that the suffering they've gone through already is sufficient. The degree of guilt must also be established, for they are not all equally guilty. Many of them were just stupid wrongdoers, while other went on to become fixers themselves. It is the responsibility of the proper dispensers of justice to determine the penalties that fit the crimes.

Of course, I realize that in many quarters it is argued that the boys are being made to

burden more than their share of the blame. This is true but it is also inevitable, for they have committed a crime for which the law has prescribed penalties. Basically, the colleges for their policies and practices governing moneymaking basketball must carry the greater burden of blame. Now, this is not a cry against big-time basketball. There is nothing inherently wrong in collegiate basketball being a major sport. The trouble has been that college administrations, with a long view to the counting of gate receipts, have totally neglected to scrub the evils out of the game as they went along. After such laxity in leadership, the job of cleaning up basketball is monumental, but it must be done.

The college administrations have to get into the act. It is time for college presidents, trustees, and administrative officers to accept the responsibility for the athletic programs they have molded and that have given such great financial service to their schools. I urge the colleges to waste no time doing this.

I also submit the following changes in the collegiate athletic picture:

1. Formation of a national ruling body to set standards of procedure and govern any irregularities or breaches of prescribed practice. A national clearinghouse, so empowered, could, in making a ruling in one region, establish the precedent for the entire collegiate family. The same standardization should be applied to the playing rules themselves.

2. Formation of conferences for all schools playing basketball. Each conference would be a member of the national agency and be committed to its rules of procedure.

3. Uniform treatment of athletes. The schools that persist in recruiting must be ready for the evils that will follow.

4. College qualification for admission should be re-examined and re-evaluated, with a design for

uniformity. The tendency has been to cater to the athlete who is not a bona fide student.

5. College cooperation on athletes dismissed from school for breaches of conduct, so that schools cannot bid for the services of an athlete who has been dropped from another college for a serious offense.

6. The formation of a permanent college commission to supervise and guide the athletic policies of all colleges.

7. Probably as a first move, it will be necessary to form a series of national seminars—including coaches, college officials, the press, radio, television, referees, the national and regional athletic bureaus, and the proper federal agencies—to examine all the problems now bedeviling basketball and athletics generally.

Naturally, any success in saving basketball requires the cooperation of all our colleges. Again, I call for the schools to meet this responsibility. No school that fails to observe the agreed formula should be allowed intercollegiate athletic competition by the national agency. I repeat, let's get tough!

The press must accept its share of responsibility in this tragic situation. On many occasions, newspapermen have been asked to refrain from publishing betting odds on games. But, for the most part, the press has failed to listen. We must look to the basic evil of gambling. Here is the root of the tragedy. All else may be in vain if this cannot be stamped out. I am not suggesting that all gambling can be erased, but surely we can block off the evil influence of the professional gambler, the fixer, by:

1. Limiting the circulation of wire and phone information.

2. Withholding names of referees until game time, as done in boxing.

3. Halting the publication of national tip sheets forecasting

regularly scheduled games with odds, betting information, and probable winners.

4. Eliminating the point spread. There is a unique betting situation in basketball where a team can lose but its backer can win. The testimony of the boys involved in the scandal reveals that most of them were not willing to fix a game if it meant actually losing, but would go along with "shading points," that meant winning under the point spread, but still winning.

5. Eliminating summer competition. It is a choice area for gamblers to establish their contacts with basketball players and impress them with flashy clothes and large rolls of money.

Let the cockeyed, pretentious critics be damned. Play the game and fight to play it always in accordance with our highest ideals; that's how we will save basketball.

SOURCE

Holman, Nat. (November 1951). How We Can Save Basketball. *Sport*.

LEGACY OF
Alvin F. "Doggy" Julian

- Led Holy Cross to the 1947 NCAA National Championship without having a home gymnasium.

- Brought about a renaissance of basketball in New England during the 1940s and 1950s.

- Coached in five NCAA and two NIT tournaments.

- Known as a "builder" of basketball programs.

- Wrote the popular textbook *Bread and Butter Basketball.*

- Admired and respected by his peers for his cooperative, appreciative, and modest nature.

ALVIN F. "DOGGY" JULIAN

"If you can't rebound, you can't win."
—Doggy Julian

BIOGRAPHY

Born: April 5, 1901 in Reading, PA

Died: July 28, 1967

Inducted into the Naismith Basketball Hall of Fame in 1968

Alvin "Doggy" Julian coached at Albright, Muhlenberg, Holy Cross, and Dartmouth, and the NBA's Boston Celtics during his 41-year coaching career. His basketball teams at Muhlenberg compiled a 129-71 record and won one Middle Atlantic Conference title and tied for three others. Julian spent three seasons at Holy Cross, where he led the Crusaders to 65 wins in 75 games. Under his direction in 1947, Holy Cross became the first New England school to win the NCAA championship. The Crusaders returned to the Final Four in 1948 but were defeated in the semi-finals. Julian then coached the Boston Celtics for two years, before returning to the college ranks at Dartmouth. His Dartmouth teams won three Ivy League championships and appeared in three NCAA tournaments. Overall, Julian's basketball teams won 435 games and competed in two NIT and five NCAA tournaments. Julian was president of the NABC and wrote a popular basketball textbook, *Bread and Butter Basketball*.

Alvin F. "Doggy" Julian...

Alvin "Doggy" Julian was an outstanding athlete at Reading H.S. (PA), where he won twelve letters. He was known for his intensity and competitiveness. Julian attended Bucknell University and excelled in football, basketball, and baseball. He received notoriety as a baseball catcher and signed a professional contract after graduating from Bucknell in 1923. He was playing in the International League, advancing towards the Major Leagues, when a foul tip shattered a finger on his throwing hand and abruptly ended his diamond career. Julian also played professional football for the Pottsville (PA) Maroons.

During part of Julian's 41-year coaching career, he simultaneously coached football, basketball, and baseball. His path to success in basketball wasn't easy, according to his wife, Lena. "He had come up a very hard way. From Albright College to high school football coaching in Ashland, Pennsylvania to Muhlenberg College to Holy Cross, which had no athletic facilities. He went on to win the NCAAs with a bunch of boys who had given everything by going off to war, and, then came back and worked so hard to become such a great team, for nothing but the joy of doing it. He was a builder. That's why I think he went to Holy Cross, for the challenge. I also think that's why he went to the Celtics." (Fink, 1997)

Alvin "Doggy" Julian was regarded as the coach whose genius, creativity, and genial personality brought about a renaissance of basketball in New England. Even though Holy Cross had no real basketball facilities, and his teams were forced to practice in a made-over barn on a long narrow court with walls as out-of-bounds barriers, he led the Crusaders to the NCAA championship in 1947. It was the first-ever NCAA title for a school from New England.

The saga of the 1947 Holy Cross basketball team was one of the greatest sports Cinderella stories of all time. To begin with, Julian was hired from Muhlenberg College as an assistant football coach and told that an additional responsibility was to coach the school's basketball team. There was no gym on campus, only an old barn that had been converted for practice use. Nor was there any money in the budget for extensive recruiting.

The first class that reported to Julian in 1945 included George Kaftan, a 6-3 center with extraordinary jumping ability. "It never dawned on me that Holy Cross didn't have a gymnasium," Kaftan said. "I just liked the school." (Gergen, 1987)

The Crusaders won twelve of fifteen games during Julian's first season, including a victory over national power City College of New York (CCNY) at Madison Square Garden. The following year, Julian added service veterans Joe Mullaney, Frank Oftring and high-school sensation Bob Cousy to his roster. This team, even though uncommonly short in stature, could run the court and handle the ball. The media called them the "Fancy Pants A.C." for their slick style of give-and-go basketball.

Authors' Note: The letters A.C. stood for "Athletic Club" and was a playful reference to the athletic-club teams of that era.

Without its own gym, Holy Cross scheduled games at the Boston Garden, where the Crusaders soon outdrew the professional Celtics. A caravan of cars followed the Crusaders all over New England. In only its second-year of major-level competition, Holy Cross was selected to play in the Eastern playoffs in New York City. They met CCNY in the finals played before 18,000 fans. It was nearly eight minutes into the game before Holy Cross made their first field goal, but they steadily came back to take a slight lead at halftime. The second half belonged to Holy Cross, as George Kaftan dominated the backboards and scored 30 points in the Crusader's 60-45 triumph.

Holy Cross faced Oklahoma in the NCAA championship game. The outstanding player in the West was Oklahoma's service veteran, 25-year old Gerry Tucker. The match-up between Tucker and Kaftan was predicted to be the key to the game.

Before the opening tip, Tucker said to the 19-year old Kaftan, "So you're the young hotshot I've heard so much about. Kaftan quickly replied with a smile, "Hang it up, Gerry. It's a young man's game. The two proceeded to stage a sensational battle in the first half, and Oklahoma held a slight three-point lead at intermission.

Julian made a strategic change in the second half. He assigned reserve Bob Curran to guard Tucker, and the Crusaders began to step up the pace of the game. With an edge in speed and depth, Holy Cross took the lead. Holy Cross scored ten of the last twelve points in the game and prevailed 58-47. The team without a gymnasium was the champion in college basketball.

The excitable Julian always rubbed the heads of his players just before they stepped onto the court. He admitted "I did it once about ten years ago, and we won. Since I am superstitious, I've been doing it ever since." (Sampson, 1947)

Julian won the admiration and respect of all those around him. The news media called Julian "cooperative, appreciative, and modest." He patiently answered all their questions with a smile, even the most difficult ones. Sportswriter Arthur Sampson said, "We've never heard a coach give credit to so many persons and accept so little

himself. "Doggy" sees something good in every basketball coach's style of play. He thinks officials do a remarkable job considering the conditions, and he's thankful that the authorities at the Boston Garden have seen fit to allow Holy Cross to use the facilities there. It's all so simple the way "Doggy" wins friends that it is as refreshing as ice cream on a hot day." (Sampson, 1947)

SOURCE

Fink, Craig. (1997). Four Building Blocks. *1997 Enshrinement Program*. Naismith Memorial Basketball Hall of Fame. Springfield, MA.

Gergen, Joe. (1987). *The Final Four*. St. Louis: The Sporting News Publishing Co.

Julian, Alvin. Vertical Files, Archives. Naismith Memorial Basketball Hall of Fame. Springfield, MA.

Sampson, Arthur. (1947, March 4). Secret of Success Simple to Julian: Respected by All. *The Boston Herald*.

26 WINNING BASKETBALL PRINCIPLES

By Alvin "Doggy" Julian

Success in basketball is dependent upon 26 principles. These winning principles are fundamentally sound, simple to teach, easy to remember, and apply to any style of play or age group.

1. PROTECT THE BALL—IT'S 20-KARAT GOLD!

- Too many players and teams are careless with the ball.
- Protect the ball and make good passes.
- Be determined to hold onto the ball until you or one of your teammates gets a good shot.
- Bad passes and low-percentage shots are the trademarks of a poor team.

2. BE CAREFUL ON A LAY-UP—IT'S MONEY IN THE BANK!

- More games are won on lay-up shots than on any other, and more games are lost because of poor lay-up shots than by any other shot.
- The lay-up is often missed because shooters want to be fancy, or they don't slow down before releasing
- When shooting lay-ups, players should learn to shoot with the left hand on the left side of the basket and with the right hand on the right side of the basket.

3. BASKETBALL IS A GAME OF MOTION—IT'S YOUR MOVE!

- Motion on the court is vital. Too many players stand still and beg for the ball.
- Players should always pass and move. This action will take their

defenders away from the ball and open up the court for a teammate.

4. ALWAYS FAKE DIRECTION—REMEMBER "WRONG WAY" CORRIGAN!

- Faking is important because it tricks opponents into making mistakes.
- Learn to watch the defender and react accordingly.

5. MOVE TO MEET THE PASS—BE WHERE YOU AIN'T!

- Moving and meeting the pass is the stamp of a good ballplayer.
- Players who move and meet passes make it easy for teammates to get them the ball.
- Another option is to fake receiving the pass and execute a reverse cut. This is especially effective when the defensive player is overshifting.
- After receiving the pass, a player should be in position to do one of the following: pass and cut; feed the pivot player; or shoot the basketball.

Authors' Note: A reverse cut in this article is commonly called a backdoor cut in today's game. Coach Julian's phrase "when the defensive player is overshifting" refers to a defender denying the lead pass.

6. WHEN IN TROUBLE, MAKE A V-CUT FOR VICTORY.

- A player in the wrong position on the floor should make a V-cut. This will open the floor and take the defensive player away from the ball.

- This is an important fundamental and is particularly good when more than one player cuts at the same time.

Authors' Note: A V-cut in this article refers to a clear out. Today coaches refer to a V-cut as a fake in one direction and movement in the opposite direction in order to receive a pass or get open.

7. DON'T THINK FOR THE OPPONENTS—BE YOURSELF!

- Some players are more concerned with what they think the opponents are thinking. This will only help the opponents play their defense better.
- Play our game and do not spend time trying to figure out what our opponents are thinking.

8. ONE PLAYER CUTS AT A TIME—STAY OUT OF THE ACT!

- Always remember—only one cutter at a time.
- If a teammate is cutting and you are in the way, V-cut out of the play.
- When a player starts a cut and sees that a teammate is also cutting, a V-cut should be made.
- Two players cutting at the same time will allow the defense to be in a position to either double-team the ball or stop the play.

9. GRAB IT—DON'T TAP IT!

- Effective rebounders grab and secure the ball rather than tapping it.
- Many times players make the

mistake of tapping the ball under the defensive basket. This is bad because the ball often goes out of bounds or is tapped into the hands of the opponent.

- Under the offensive basket, it is all right to tap the ball back up, but it is generally better to grab the rebound and then go back up for a shot.

10. NEVER FORCE A SHOT—LOOK BEFORE YOU LEAP!

- Never shoot a shot if closely defended. Look for open teammates when guarded closely.
- Before attempting a shot, make sure that you have teammates in rebounding positions.
- Good balance is essential for effective shooting. All offensive players should be sure their opponents are not forcing them to shoot unnaturally (bad arch on the ball, shooting from a spot too far, attempting shots they seldom practice).
- The opponents will never block a good shot. A shot should never be blocked if it is attempted at the right time.

11. DRIBBLING IS AN EMERGENCY MEASURE—BRING YOUR OWN BALL!

- Nine out of ten players dribble or bounce the ball before they do anything else. This is a bad habit and bad basketball because it limits a player's opportunities.

12. TALK TO YOUR TEAMMATES— I'VE GOT A SECRET!

- Talking on offense and defense builds team play.
- Talking encourages teammates. Talking on defense is vital when picking up loose opponents and calling "stay" or "switch."
- A word of praise for a good play or effective offensive or defensive

rebounding makes for a close-knit team.

- However, players should not be traffic cops—they should not stand in the backcourt and tell teammates what to do.

13. NEVER TURN YOUR HEAD ON DEFENSE!

- Players should never turn their heads to watch the ball when playing man-to-man defense. Naturally, there are times when screens and picks force defensive players into situations in which this rule must be violated. In these situations, teammates must communicate and help out.
- When players change from offense to defense, they should backpedal so that they can locate their personal opponent, or help in case of a fast break.
- When players change from defense to offense, they should keep their eyes on the ball.

14. DON'T CROSS YOUR FEET ON DEFENSE!

- Defensive players should not cross their feet on defense, especially on the first step.
- Players should move only one foot at a time in defensive play. Successful defensive players move their feet in short steps when playing defense. This type of defensive shuffling allows defenders to go just as fast as running sideways and crossing their feet.

15. HANDS UP ON THE DEFENSE!

- Keeping the hands up is important to body balance and good defense. Tight-rope walkers use their hands for balance, and the good defensive player does likewise.
- Movement of the hands and feet discourages passing and shooting

and shows that the defensive player is on the ball. All offensive players dislike being harassed.

16. WATCH YOUR OPPONENT'S BELLY BUTTON—THE HANDLE OF THE BREADBASKET!

- We like our defensive players to keep their eyes glued to a part of the offensive ball player that can't fool them—the belly button.
- Wherever the belly button goes, the opponent must go.

17. PICK UP THE FIRST MAN - FIRST COME, FIRST SERVED.

- When you are back or coming down the floor ahead of the rest of your teammates, pick up the first offensive player down the court, whether it is your assigned player or not.
- Call out to the teammate who is closest to your assigned player and ask for that player's assistance.

18. DON'T LEAVE YOUR FEET ON DEFENSE!

- Good defensive players keep their head up and their feet on the ground.
- Don't be a jumping jack just because your opponent makes a ball fake.
- Defensive players should keep their feet on the floor unless they are rebounding, jump shooting, jumping for a held ball, or trying to block a shot.

19. GET POSITION FOR REBOUNDS —POSITION IS EVERYTHING IN LIFE!

- Instinct and sensing the direction of the shot and the angle of the rebound enables players to move into the correct rebounding position.

- Too many players stand still and watch the flight of the ball instead of securing the best rebounding position.

20. IF YOU CAN'T REBOUND, YOU CAN'T WIN—JOIN THE UNION!

- Good rebounding limits the opponents' shots and this is key to winning basketball games.
- Players do not have to be tall, but it is vital that they block out and want to rebound.
- You could almost, though not quite, say that basketball today is: rebound and shoot.
- We have a mythical organization on our team. We call it the Union. The big players must make double figures (number of rebounds) to warrant membership. The smaller players must average six rebounds per game to qualify.

21. THE FIRST FAST-BREAK PASS MUST BE PERFECT—A GOOD BEGINNING, A PERFECT ENDING!

- The fast break must get started with a quick outlet pass.
- If the first pass is a good one, the fast break is underway. After the fast break is started, it is hard to stop.

22. YOU MUST MAKE 70 PERCENT OF YOUR FREE THROWS—LOOK A GIFT HORSE IN THE MOUTH!

- Free throws are more important today than at any other time in the history of basketball. The value of free throws has been increased chiefly because of the bonus free throw.
- Practice, confidence, and the proper technique are the keys.
- There is no excuse for being a poor free-throw shooter.

23. KEEP THE DEFENSE BUSY!

- If all five offensive players keep moving, their opponents cannot afford to sag or float.
- Moving with or without the ball forces the defense into making mistakes because the offensive players know what they are trying to do and the defensive players do not know what to expect.
- The offensive team that moves keeps the opponents worried about their defense, and this stress upon their defense affects their offense.

24. DON'T CROSS THE BACKBOARD TO SHOOT—YOU TAKE THE HIGH ROAD!

- Many players cross the backboard to take a shot with their favorite hand. This is a definite weakness, because the big objective is to get to the basket quickly and to get the shot away.
- A defensive player can catch up with the cross-over shooter because of the extra distance and the time required to cross-over.
- A player should learn to shoot from both sides of the basket and with both hands.

25. NEVER UNDERRATE AN OPPONENT—TALL TREES FALL HARD!

- Be ready to play every game. Never underestimate an opponent.
- Overconfidence can affect a team's play, and it is wise to remember that it is only the underdog who can do the upsetting.
- Years ago a five-point lead, with ten minutes to go, was big. Today, a twenty-point lead with ten minutes to go does not mean the game is over.

26. PRACTICE DOES NOT ALWAYS MAKE PERFECT—DO IT RIGHT!

- Practice does not make perfect—if you practice the wrong techniques.
- Players often work long and hard and make little progress because they are practicing incorrectly. Stop them! Start all over! They will make better progress.
- Supervise all practices. In shooting, start all practices with lay-ups. Too many players start with long shots that they will never use in a game.

SOURCE

Julian, Alvin F. "Doggy". (1960). *Bread and Butter Basketball*. Englewood Cliffs, NJ: Prentice-Hall.

LEGACY OF
George Keogan

- Led Notre Dame to the Helms Foundation national championship in 1927 and 1936.

- Popularized the defensive switch, which he called the "shifting man-for-man defense" to combat the popular offense of that time, the "Figure 8."

- Directed Notre Dame to 20 consecutive winning seasons, his whole tenure at Notre Dame.

- Won 77 percent of his games during his coaching career.

- Hired at Notre Dame in 1923 by football legend Knute Rockne as an assistant football coach.

- Built his teams on speed, aggressiveness, and strong pivot play.

GEORGE KEOGAN

"Players should respect their opponent but always consider themselves equal or superior."
—George Keogan

BIOGRAPHY

Born: March 8, 1890

Died: February 17, 1943

Inducted into the Naismith Basketball Hall of Fame 1961

George Keogan directed Notre Dame to 20 consecutive winning seasons from 1923 to 1943. At the time of his arrival in 1923, basketball was not highly regarded at Notre Dame. Keogan quickly changed that way of thinking and led the Fighting Irish to the Helms Foundation national championship in 1927 and 1936. His coaching record at Notre Dame was 327-96-1 for a .771 winning percentage. Prior to Notre Dame, Keogan coached on the college level at Charles City (IA), Superior State (WI), St. Thomas (MN), Allegheny (PA),and Valparaiso (IN). His overall collegiate record was 412-124-1. Keogan's innovative and visionary style of play featured the defensive switch and strong pivot play. He was a student of the professional game and built his coaching strategies from the Original Celtics and the Buffalo Germans. Keogan coached future Hall of Famers Edward "Moose" Krause and Ray Meyer. Keogan died of a heart attack during the middle of his 20th season as head coach of the Fighting Irish.

George Keogan...

George Keogan was born and raised in Minnesota Lake, Minnesota. He graduated from Detroit Lakes (MN) High School and began his coaching career at Charles City (IA) College. He had coaching stints at Lockport (IL) H.S. and Riverside (IL) H.S. before leading Superior (WI) State Teachers College to a 17-5 record.

Keogan attended the University of Minnesota and St. Louis University. While attending St. Louis, Keogan took several dentistry courses and was referred to as "Doc." He also coached the basketball team to a 13-5 record.

After serving as an instructor in World War I, Keogan coached at St. Thomas (MN); Allegheny (PA); and Valpariaso (IN). While at Valpariaso, Keogan's football team battled heavily favored Notre Dame to a relatively close game. Legendary football coach Knute Rockne was so impressed with Keogan's coaching effectiveness that he offered him a position on Notre Dame's football

staff. Keogan's responsibilities at Notre Dame also included being the head basketball and baseball coach.

When Keogan took over at Notre Dame in 1923, the team's record the preceding six years was a dismal 35-64. The program was not highly regarded, and the facilities and equipment left much to be desired. Instead of a sharply lined hardwood court, Keogan had nothing but a dirt base with dry lime markers to form the outline of the court. The uniforms were of various colors.

Keogan quickly turned things around and built a nationally acclaimed program. He led the Irish to back-to-back 19-1 seasons in only his third and fourth seasons as coach. In twenty seasons at Notre Dame, Keogan won 327 games, second in Irish history, while losing just 97 for a .771 winning percentage. The Helms Foundation named Notre Dame national champions in 1927 and 1936.

Keogan was one of the game's more notable innovators. To defend against the Figure 8 offense, which used screening and blocking tactics, Keogan popularized the screen-switch defense. He called it the "shifting man-to-man" defense. Keogan instructed his defenders to switch opponents whenever a block or screen was encountered. This enabled the defenders to be in a better position to stop an uncontested shot.

The three characteristics that Keogan insisted upon were speed, aggressiveness, and alertness. He wanted his players to "love basketball, live clean, work hard, and play with all that they had."

He constantly studied the game of basketball and always looked for new ideas. When future Hall of Fame player Ed "Moose" Krause enrolled at Notre Dame, Keogan combined ideas from the Original Celtics and the Buffalo Germans in order to better use the talents of

Krause. The Original Celtics utilized a play where their star pivot man Dutch Dehnert stationed himself on the foul line with his back to the basket. His teammates would pass to him and then cut off of him, trying to run their defenders into a screen. Keogan designed an offense, combining the Original Celtic's pivot man with the cross-court offense, that he had developed from the Buffalo Germans.

Describing his offense, Keogan said: "Picture, if you can, a basketball court hung on the wall like a clock. The pivot man under the basket is the top of the pendulum. The rest of the team is the weight on the pendulum. They swing back and forth across the court, passing the ball to one another until they see an opening. Then, they pass the ball into the center man who either shoots, passes, or fakes a pass to one or more men breaking for the basket." (Petritz, 1932)

Adolph Rupp, whose Kentucky teams were defeated the first six times they met Notre Dame, said, "He (Keogan) taught me a rugged kind of basketball. I'm sure our teams are much better because of the whippings we took from Notre Dame."

Hall of Fame coach Tony Hinkle from Butler stated, "Notre Dame is the most powerful, under-the-basket team I have ever seen anywhere." (Petritz, 1932)

In 1936, the Helms Foundation named Notre Dame national champions with a record of 22-2-1. The tie occurred on December 31, 1935 in a game played at Northwestern's Patten Gym. Late in the game, future Hall of Famer and Irish star Ray Meyer went to the free-throw line and made two free throws. The scoreboard at one end of the gym read 20-19 in favor of Notre Dame. At the other end of the gym, the scoreboard read 20-19 in favor of Northwestern. As time expired, both teams left the floor celebrating and thinking they had won the game. There was much confusion. After newspapermen rechecked their books, it was discovered the score was 20-20. But by this time, the players had showered and were dressed in street clothes. It was then decided to leave the game tied at 20-20.

"There are two ways of coaching," stated Keogan. "They'll play for you because they hate you or because they love you." (Meyer, 1987)

Ray Meyer (2003) said, "Coach Keogan was the best at preparing a team for a game. If I could select only one coach to get a team ready for a game, I would definitely select George Keogan. He was an outstanding coach. He was also very demanding and particular. He expected his players to have their hair cut, dress accordingly, and represent Notre Dame in the proper way. It was very simple. You did what he said, or you didn't play. Period."

Keogan and "Doc" Carlson from Pittsburgh were archrivals and had many fiercely contested games. Meyer remembered the game that occurred during his freshmen year in these words. "Notre Dame was leading by eight or ten at halftime. The second half started, and we had played around ten minutes when it was discovered that the clock had not started. Keogan went up to the officials and said that we had played about ten minutes and the clock should be adjusted accordingly. Carlson disagreed and said that the clock indicated that we had not played at all so they should start the half from the beginning. We ended up playing the whole half over again, and Pittsburgh won the game. Keogan was so mad that he took the clock and threw it against the wall, and it broke into a thousand pieces. There were many other times that "Doc" Carlson drove Keogan crazy. Notre Dame would have a great team, and before the game, Carlson would announce that he didn't think the Irish were that good and that he was going to start his second team. Keogan would come into the locker room and he would be raving mad. Carlson did it just to torment him."

Basketball lost a great coach and leader when George Keogan died of a heart attack at the age of 53 during the 1943 season.

SOURCE

Keogan, George. Vertical Files, Archives. Naismith Memorial Basketball Hall of Fame. Springfield, MA.

Meyer, Ray. Interview with Ralph Pim. September 5, 2003.

Meyer, Ray. (1987). *Coach*. Chicago: Contemporary Books.

Petritz, Joseph. (1932, March). Release from Department of Sports Publicity, University of Notre Dame.

THE REQUISITES OF A GOOD BASKETBALL PLAYER

By George E. Keogan

Any basketball coach who has enjoyed a certain degree of success will be called upon to answer many queries as to how this has been accomplished. I will try to cover carefully a few important factors in the development of a team.

OBSERVATION

Observation is a very important factor in developing and improving a young player. Anyone who is a good player is always looking for pointers that might be used for personal improvement. No player should ever be satisfied. There are in basketball, as well as in other sports, people who play for years and never seem to improve their game.

There are players who have been stars during their high school days but who never make their varsity college teams. Possibly, they lack experience; they may not have the mentality to improve; or they may be physically unable to do better. Then again their failure may be attributed to self-satisfaction and to the fact that they never try to learn new things. They are satisfied with themselves as they are. High school players will never improve unless they have the will to do so.

A very excellent way to improve a team by observation is through a round-table discussion after each game. Here should be discussed honestly, the faults the players displayed during the contest, and the ways to correct them. Also, the good moves and plays the players made during the game should be talked over. The fine points of the opponent's game should also be considered.

Whenever someone has the opportunity to see good players in action, they should by all means do so. This also applies to the coach. Coaches can learn from watching good players in action, and by studying the game tactics of other successful coaches.

BRAIN POWER IN BASKETBALL

I do not know of a more convenient way to classify basketball players than to place them into two groups: those who use their "gray matter" and those who do not. Possibly the most striking feature I find in reviewing the many players I have coached or observed in action is the ease with which they fall into one or the other of the above classes. To my way of thinking, it is one of the distinct compliments in the game of basketball and separates the good players from the great ones.

I admire the thinking, planning, clever-type of player who carefully thinks out each move. Such a player gives form and structure to the game and makes basketball enjoyable to the spectator.

As players and as a team, basketball should be played with a purpose. There must be a purpose to every pass and cut for the basket, just as there should be a purpose to every move on defense. In the case of the individual, especially when two players of equal ability meet, it becomes a matter of brain against brain, with the quick, alert, thinking player holding the edge.

CONCENTRATION

There are players who have wonderful physical selves and are very skillful from years of experience and competition but who never become top-notchers because they cannot concentrate during the entire game. Players who cannot concentrate thoroughly will be found to be the mechanical or impulsive sort of players whose execution never varies much, but is always the same. Such players may have some success due to their great physical prowess, but basketball as a team game is not benefited much by their presence.

Players who have the ability to concentrate on their game, both in practice and in actual competition, will greatly improve their playing skills. They must learn to disregard remarks made from the sidelines and those coming from the opponents.

Concentration requires self-control, and this is absolutely necessary to a great basketball player. Players must remain calm and never worry when things go badly in a game. It is skill, stamina, determination, plus concentration that bring success. At no time is concentration so necessary as when a player is shooting a basket. Sometimes an opponent raises a hand in an attempt to distract the shooter. The eyes of the shooter must stay focused on the target.

While working on offense, players must always concentrate and study the manner and style of their opponents. They should plan their moves and remain undisturbed by any annoying occurrences.

CONFIDENCE

Players who have confidence in their abilities are usually dependable and courageous, and never get panicky. They are not conceited but rather self-reliant, and when put to the real test, they produce.

Great shooters have confidence in their shooting. Some players go into a shooting slump when someone tells them they are off form. When the shots are not going in, a shooter should ask the following questions:

- Am I shooting high enough?
- Do I hurry my shots?
- Am I gauging the distance properly?
- Am I holding the ball too tightly?
- Am I off balance?

Players will come out of their slump quicker if they discover there is not much fundamentally wrong with their shot. A coach should never tell players that they are shooting poorly. Correct the fundamental that needs to be corrected and always attempt to build the confidence of your players.

Players should never regard themselves inferior to any other player. If this ever happens, a player's game is bound to suffer.

Players must overcome this fear. Players should respect their opponent but always consider themselves equal or superior. A player's confidence will bolster individual and team play and is a key ingredient for success.

SOURCE

Keogan, George E. (1928, December). The Requisites of a Good Basketball Player. *The Athletic Journal.*

LEGACY OF
Bob Knight

- Highly principled coach who believes his primary role is to prepare his players for success in life.

- Led Indiana to three national championships (1976, 1981, 1987).

- One of only three coaches to win the "Triple Crown" of coaching.

- Regarded as one of the all-time best teachers.

- One of the top five winningest coaches in the history of basketball with more than 800 wins.

- Demands the absolutely best effort possible from his players.

- Played on the 1960 national championship team at Ohio State.

BOB KNIGHT

*"The will to win is not as important as
the will to prepare to win."*
—Bob Knight

BIOGRAPHY

Born: October 25, 1940 in Massillon, OH

Inducted into the Naismith Basketball Hall of Fame in 1991

Bob Knight has earned the reputation as one of the top coaches of all-time and has won three NCAA championships (1976, 1981, 1987). He won 763 games at Indiana University and the United States Military Academy. Currently he is the head coach at Texas Tech. In 2005, Knight earned his 850th college victory and recorded his 27th NCAA Tournament appearance, which equals the top mark held by Dean Smith. His Indiana teams won eleven Big Ten Conference titles and made five Final Four appearances. His Army teams led the nation in team defense for three consecutive years. Knight is one of only two coaches to both play on and coach national championship teams. As a player, he played at Ohio State for Hall of Fame coach Fred Taylor. Knight was selected National Coach of the Year in 1975, 1976, 1987, and 1989. He coached the U.S. Olympic team to a gold medal in 1984.

Bob Knight...

Bob Knight learned the game of basketball while playing at Ohio State University for Hall of Fame coach Fred Taylor. A native of Orville, Ohio, Knight was a member of Buckeye teams that won Big Ten titles in 1960, 1961, and 1962. Ohio State posted an overall record of 78-6 during those three years and won the 1960 national championship. In 1961 and 1962 the Buckeyes finished second in the NCAA tournament.

After graduating with a degree in history and government, Knight was an assistant coach at Cuyahoga Falls, (OH) H.S. one year, before entering the U.S. Army, where he was assigned to assist Coach Tates Locke at West Point. When Locke became head coach at Miami University (OH), Knight became the head coach at West Point in 1966, earning the distinction of becoming the youngest head coach in major college history at the age of 26. Knight's Army teams finished 102-50, led the nation in team defense three consecutive years, and participated in four NIT tournaments in five seasons. Among his players at West Point was future Hall of Fame coach Mike Krzyzewski.

When Knight left West Point in 1971 to accept the position at Indiana University, he called the decision "the toughest in his life." During his first decade in the Big Ten, Knight's coaching strategies changed the style of play from run-and-gun to ball control. His hard-nosed approach reaped large benefits. During his 29-year stint at Indiana, the Hoosiers won 662 games, including 22 seasons of 20 or more wins. Under Knight, Indiana won 11 Big Ten Conference titles, three national championships, and one NIT championship.

Knight became the head coach at Texas Tech in 2000 and immediately turned the program around during his inaugural season. The Red Raiders compiled a 23-9 record and earned an NCAA berth during Knight's first season. The year before Knight's arrival, Texas Tech won only nine games.

On February 5, 2003 Knight earned his 800th victory. Only Dean Smith of North Carolina (879), Adolph Rupp of Kentucky (876), and Jim Phelan (Mount St. Mary's (827) have won more than 800 men's games in Division I.

Coach Knight stands for high principles. He demands excellence and possesses the uncanny ability to extract the full potential from his teams. He is demanding of himself, his players, and the officials. Knight does not demand victory; he demands the absolutely best effort possible. He has said that you aren't just playing against opponents, but the higher calling is to play against the game.

Knight believes that the majority of players never understand how to win. "When players understand what has to be done to win, then you've got a chance to be pretty good. And the very first thing that has to be done to win, in any team sport, is playing well defensively. I mean, there's never been a team that has won championships, in whatever the sport, that has not been very good defensively." (Packer, 1999, p. 102)

"From a coaching standpoint, the greatest fear I've ever had is that in some way I might not have prepared my team as well as I could have," said Knight (2002). "I'm always afraid I've left something out, or overlooked something. If you've done that, you've shortchanged your players. They're not as well prepared as they should be."

Discipline is an important component to Knight's success. "To a lot of people, discipline is a very negative word," said Knight. "I've always felt it was a positive word, and I defined it in that vein a long time ago. I said discipline is doing what has to be done when it has to be done. You do it as well as you can do it, and you do it that way all the time. That's what a disciplined person does, and that's how a disciplined person plays." (Packer, 1999, p. 114)

three-point shot has taken a lot of the science of coaching from the game."

Coach Bob Knight is truly a legend. He is a four-time national Coach of the Year and he is one of only three coaches to win the "Triple Crown" of coaching, winning NCAA and NIT titles and an Olympic gold medal. He has been an outspoken critic of illegal recruiting practices and prides himself on his violation-free programs at Indiana and Texas Tech. Knight takes immense pride in the graduation rate of his players. All but two of his four-year players completed degrees, a ratio of nearly 98 percent. Equally impressive is the fact that 27 former players and assistants have gone on to become successful head coaches.

When asked about the changes in college basketball during his career, Knight (2002) responded in these words. "Certainly the pay is enormously better. But that's about the only change I'd consider positive. I hate the elements that recruiting has brought into college basketball — the know-it-alls, but know-nothings, who have made fortunes by feeding the national recruiting frenzy with gossip and guessing that is passed off as inside information; way out-of-control AAU summer programs; shoe-company financial involvement that attracts unqualified and sometimes undesirables into basketball. The worst effect of all this may be the damage done to the egos of sixteen and seventeen-year-old kids, in way too many cases convincing them they're far better than they are."

Regarding rule changes, Knight (2002) said, "I don't like the three-point shot and the shot clock. Those two changes take away some of the control I felt I had on the outcome of the game. The three-point shot exclusively favors raw talent — the ability to shoot the basketball, period. I think the intent of the rule was to take the zone defense out of college basketball by awarding three points for an outside shot over the zone. I don't think rules should ever be made to favor the team with the most talent. And in my opinion, both the shot-clock and the three-point shot are talent-oriented rules. I think the

SOURCE

Knight, Bob. Vertical Files, Archives. Naismith Memorial Basketball Hall of Fame. Springfield, MA.

Knight, Bob and Bob Hammel. (2002). *Knight: My Story*. New York: Thomas Dunne Books.

Packer, Billy and Roland Lazenby. (1999). *Why We Win*. Chicago: Masters Press.

LESSONS FROM THIS LEGEND...

BASKETBALL CORNERSTONES AND CREDOS

By Bob Knight

CORNERSTONES

I coached for eight seasons at West Point. In those years, I developed an interesting relationship with probably the three most prominent people in New York City basketball history—Clair Bee, Joe Lapchick, and Nat Holman.

Joe Lapchick had played on one of the first great professional basketball teams. There were two in New York in the 1920's—an all-black team called the Rens, or the Renaissance, and the other, an all-white team called the Original Celtics. Lapchick was the Celtics' center, and he later became a great coach at St. John's, then with the Knicks, then back at St. John's. Every time one of my Army teams played in Madison Square Garden, when I would walk out on the floor, I would look over to where he always sat. He'd put his thumb under his chin, which was telling me: "Lift your head up." He had a phrase: "Walk with the kings." And he lived it. This was a man whose schooling had stopped in the sixth grade, and he had the intellect, the great vocabulary, of a doctor of philosophy.

The first time I really got to know Coach Lapchick was a significant moment in my coaching career. At one of the Metropolitan Coaches Association luncheons, as I was getting ready for my first season as a head coach, I asked him if I could sit down and talk with him sometime. I was twenty-four, and I was looking for some guidance. I went to Yonkers just as soon as we could work it out.

We hadn't talked very long before he said: "What kind of training rules are you going to have?"

"That's one thing I wanted to talk to you about," I said.

What his recommendation amounted to was no training rules at all. I'm sure people would think I'd have a rigid set of rules players would have to live by—be in by this time or that time, don't do this, don't do that.

All those years as a coach, because of that evening I spent talking with Coach Lapchick, I had one training rule: If you do anything in any way, whenever or wherever, that I think is detrimental to the good of this basketball team, to the school, or to you yourself, I'll handle it as I see fit.

I think that was absolutely the best plan, and certainly he did. He told me why: "You're going to have a player who is a real problem, and you're going to be happy to get rid of him. And you're going to have a player who is a good person who makes a mistake. You can't set down rules and then treat players differently. You decide, based on your knowledge of the situation, what you're trying to do with it, what's best for the player, and go from there.

His second question that night was: "How important is it to you that people like you?"

I hadn't thought about that. I did for just a minute or so and said, "I'd like to be respected as a coach, but I'm not concerned about being liked."

He said, "Good. If you worry about whether people like you or not, you can never made tough decisions correctly."

Of the four cornerstones I have about coaching basketball, that was one of them:

the whole idea of running a basketball team—team rules, my approach to training, and clearing away inconsequential matters to allow good decision-making, all of those things were influenced by me talking with and observing a master of the game: Joe Lapchick.

The second cornerstone came from one of the game's first truly great coaches, Clair Bee. It was the critically important role of teaching in basketball—teaching the game's fundamentals and philosophies, including all things involved in a team approach and a determination throughout that coaching the team not just to play well, but to win.

Clair Bee dominated basketball during the 1930's as the coach at Long Island University, where he also coached football and baseball. His career as the basketball coach there carried into the early 1950's, and he has the best won-lost percentage of any coach in major-college history.

I was fortunate enough to meet him in my very early coaching years, and he willingly became a mentor to me.

His .826 winning percentage did not just happen. The sustaining, significant thing with him was his determination to win. One summer he and I were relaxing at a camp he ran at Kutscher's up in the Catskills Mountains. Without having any point to make, but just musing out loud, he said, "You know, there was a nine-year period when my teams lost twenty games."

I could tell how proud he was of that. Winning was a very important thing to him—not winning by breaking the rules in any way, shape or form, but winning by working harder, being better prepared, and teaching better than the other coaches.

He pounded into me that the very first thing you had to be was a teacher, and you had to teach players how to play basketball. You had to teach them the game. You couldn't ever assume that they knew what they needed to know, or that they were going to do the right thing, unless you had taught them the right thing. This was a man who early in his coaching career developed a way to teach the two-handed set shot, which up until World War II, was the basic method of outside shooting in basketball. People familiar with the history of basketball know a landmark game was December 30, 1936, when a player named Hank Luisetti introduced the one-handed shot when Stanford came out East to play. Stanford ended a forty-three game winning streak for Clair Bee's Long Island University team before 17,623 people at Madison Square Garden, 45-31.

Almost immediately, the loser in that game became one of the best teachers of the one-handed shot. His explanation of the mechanics and his phraseology of those mechanics were exceptional. He had a great phrase, the "elbow squeeze": catch the ball, and when you're getting ready to shoot, squeeze your elbows in. It puts your shooting elbow right under the ball. Coach Bee's ability to go from being victimized by the one-hand shot to being a master teacher of it and its successor, the jump shot, was just one more illustration of his ability to observe details and break down a facet of the game to its essential steps and parts—its "fundamentals."

He watched a game on television once, and a team working against a press had its best player take the ball out-of-bounds. "No," he almost shouted, "get him in the middle of the press where he can make all the decisions and handle the ball." It was one illustration of his advice that I heard more than once and can still hear today: make sure your best players are in their absolute best roles. Then use your supplementary players in just that, supplementary roles—against a press, they make the in-bounds pass, or they catch the in-bounds pass, then they get it to the player who can do the most with it.

Coach Bee qualified as a lifelong inspiration for me in other significant ways, including the most significant of all—human relations. On Thanksgiving Day in 1939, his LIU football team played Catholic University at Ebbetts Field and lost 35-14. LIU's end, Dolly King, caught a touchdown pass. That night, at Madison Square Garden, King played in LIU's season basketball opener. Coach Bee coached both games and was honored at an alumni reception in between.

Dolly was black. LIU played Marshall in basketball at Huntington, West Virginia. At the hotel where the LIU team stayed, Dolly was told he couldn't eat with the team in the hotel's dining room. Coach Bee marched his entire team into the kitchen, sat everybody down, and said, "Serve us."

There never was a thought in Clair Bee's mind about color or religion or anything like that. I've tried to follow him in that way, too.

My third coaching cornerstone was an appreciation of basketball as something never to be mastered but always, every day of every year, to be studied with an unflagging zeal for answers—and a duty to pass them on. That was brought into focus for me by playing at Ohio State for another Hall of Fame coach, Fred Taylor, and it also gave me a better understanding of some things I learned from a couple of other coaches as I was growing up.

As a basketball coach, Fred Taylor was very well organized, and he was articulate in his explanation of how to play and what he wanted done. Somebody told me once:

All my life, I've had six honest serving men. They taught me all I knew. Their names were What, Where, and When; How, Why, and Who.

As a college basketball coach, Fred Taylor put everyone of those "serving men" to work for him. The how and the why are so important in basketball. When I was a freshman at Ohio State, we practiced against the varsity almost every night, so I saw him work daily. That was his first year as a head coach, and obviously—having played the game himself and having coached the Ohio State freshman team under Floyd Stahl before succeeding him—he went into it with some ideas and thoughts on how to play. But after that first year, he knew that he had to make his teams better on defense to have the kind of success he wanted to have. Maybe as important as anything I ever learned from him was that a coach should never be afraid to ask questions of anyone he could learn from. That's what he did to improve his defense (he went to the defensive genius of the day, Pete Newell) to the point where he raised the level of the whole Big Ten through his teams' consistent success. Other teams had to try to match him if they ever hoped to beat him or compete with him for championships.

Pete Newell was the fourth cornerstone in the construction of my philosophy of coaching. He was a good friend of Coach Taylor's, and he helped me and befriended me in many ways. I got him to come to West Point a couple of times and to Indiana almost every year. He was articulate, and he always had a basketball message for our players. He'd talk with each player—about what the player could and should do, and what he had to work on.

CREDOS

Among all the things that I've gathered from the people who have influenced me, I think one tops the list: the importance of preparation.

We talk in coaching about "winners," and I've had a lot of them, players who just will not allow themselves or their team to lose.

Most coaches call that a will to win. I don't, because it puts the emphasis in the wrong place. Everybody has a will to win. What's far more important is having the will to prepare to win.

Playing smart, in discussing how to play basketball, is a function of percentages. Playing smart is a function of positioning, or placement, or recognition. Playing smart is a major key to winning in all sports.

We try to teach our players to play intelligently. A key to that is getting them to understand not just that something works but why.

Identifying what each player can do and can't do is important. I can't expect any player to do everything well. Part of my teaching process is to tell our players: "Learn what you do well. Learn your strengths and weaknesses. You can, on occasion, improve your weaknesses. You can work to steadily improve your strengths, but there will be some inherent weaknesses that you have as a player—or as a team— that you just can't improve greatly. In your play, stay away from weaknesses like those."

Great players maximize their talent and make everybody around them better. It's not an accident that they do this. They understand the game, and they understand the strengths and weaknesses of their teammates and their opponent. That comes from thinking. There's nothing more important that a basketball player can do. Above all else, think!

The worst phrase ever used in teaching players how to play a sport is, "Don't think, just do it."

If you can't think, you can't play.

I use the word "understand" often. I want my players to understand why teams lose: poor shot selection, bad passing, failure to block out defensively, lack of pressure on the ball. Often, the reason players and coaches give for losing a game is how well the other team shot, when the actual reason is how poorly their own team played defensively in giving up so many good shots.

To me, concentration is basketball in a nutshell. Concentration leads to anticipation, which leads to recognition, which leads to reaction, which leads to execution.

The concentration I'm talking about involves four key words. The first two are "look" and "see." Very few players train themselves to use their eyes. Not everybody has the same shooting ability as everybody else, or the same size, or the same quickness. But each person who's playing this game can develop the ability to see what's happening on the court— see the open man, see where to take the ball, see the player who's being defended, see who's open on the break.

"Hear" and "listen" are the next two words. Most people only hear. The key is listening to what you're being told, what's being said, what is expected of you in your role as part of any team.

A basketball player who learns to see and to listen has improved tremendously without doing a single thing involving physical skills. Once learned, "seeing" and "listening" are valuable traits for anyone doing anything.

We all want to win. We all talk about winning. But I'm a great believer in understanding what goes into losing, because if we know how we can lose, if we know those factors or reasons that cause us to lose, and we eliminate those things, we stand a much better chance of winning.

I don't apologize to anybody for really wanting to win or for hating to lose. Win at any cost? No, absolutely not. I've never understood how anybody who cheated to get a player, or players, could take any satisfaction whatsoever out of whatever winning came afterward.

There are fundamentals that have to be adhered to and mastered in any business. Some people grasp those fundamentals, and teach them or learn them, and others don't. And those who don't are never as successful as those who do. That's what coaching is all about.

In basketball, it's a matter of having a sound fundamental base, both offensively and defensively.

On offense, your players don't take bad shots. They don't throw the ball away. They move without the ball. They help each other get open.

On defense, your teams don't give up easy points on conversion, on fast breaks. They don't commit bad fouls—unnecessary or dumb fouls that keep the other team on the free-throw line. Your players never foul a player who is in the act of taking a bad shot or a three-point shot. And they have to control the lane, and know where the ball is at all times. A good defensive player can never lose sight of the ball, because it is the ball that has to be stopped, not a particular player.

When a shot goes up, they have to be consistently good at blocking out, because that one thing eliminates a lot of problems. There's nothing more demoralizing to a defense than playing well and forcing the opponent to take a shot that he misses, and then giving up a point-blank basket because a player who wasn't blocked out sneaked in and got the rebound. The first thing you have to do defensively as a coach is to eliminate cheap points, and nothing is cheaper than that.

I spend hours looking at tapes as preparation for a game. I've always felt that preparation is much more important than anything else you do. If you have prepared correctly, your team plays well, but you can't make adjustments once the game is played that cover up lack of preparation. That's a point I've tried to make in almost every clinic I give. In any walk of life, the best-prepared person creates advantages that help him or her be the most successful.

In all of sports and pretty much in all of life, the mental is to physical as four is to one. And one thing more almost supersedes everything else. Enthusiasm.

Emerson said, "Nothing great is ever accomplished without enthusiasm."

LESSONS FROM THIS LEGEND...

Norman Vincent Peale said, "Enthusiasm makes the difference."

Players have to understand that you, as the coach, aren't going to be satisfied with just winning. Play can be sloppy, things can be poorly executed in games you win, but before you can be good and beat better teams, that kind of play has to be straightened out and eliminated. Players will be satisfied with what you tolerate. If a coach tolerates mistakes, players will be satisfied with mistakes.

The most essential thing in a team being ready for a game is that the coach is ready —that the coach understands the importance of keeping everything on an even keel.

Winning is the last of all criteria that I think you should use to determine how well you're playing. When the way you've won a game just isn't good enough, you show your players why: you talk about turnovers, missed block-outs, fast-break points allowed, fouls committed—to show your team, "We just didn't play well."

I do that, and then I point out some games that we still have left to play where we can't play poorly and win. You're trying to get players to understand that how they play is a lot more important than whether or not they win.

When I was a youngster, Ash Hall, an outstanding Ohio high school coach at

Rittman told me, "Basketball is not a game of great plays and great shooting, it's a game of mistakes and errors. If you ever see a state championship game, you'll see errors and mistakes made, and the team that makes the most of them will be the team that gets beat, almost without exception."

Basketball is a game of not making mistakes. The more you cut down on mistakes, the better your chance of winning.

SOURCE

Knight, Bob and Bob Hammel. (2002). *Knight: My Story*. New York: Thomas Dunne Books.

LEGACY OF
Mike "Coach K" Krzyzewski

- Passed Dean Smith in 2005 for the most wins in NCAA tournament history.

- Led Duke to three NCAA national championships (1991, 1992, 2001) and ten Final Four appearances.

- Graduated from West Point and played for future Hall of Fame coach Bob Knight.

- Established programs built on hard work, commitment to excellence, teamwork, and attention to detail.

- Regarded as an excellent teacher and a person of the highest character.

- Believed the primary responsibility of a leader is to inspire.

- Selected NABC Coach of the Decade for the 1990s.

MIKE "COACH K" KRZYZEWSKI

"When our goal is to try to do our best, when our focus is on preparation and sacrifice and effort—instead of numbers on the scoreboard—we will never lose."
—Mike Krzyzewski

BIOGRAPHY

Born: February 13, 1947 in Chicago, IL

Inducted into the Naismith Basketball Hall of Fame in 2001

Mike Krzyzewski has been one of the most dominant college coaches during the past two decades and was selected the NABC Coach of the Decade for the 1990s. Krzyzewski led Duke to three NCAA national championships (1991, 1992, 2001) and ten Final Four appearances. His three national championships place him third on the all-time list, tied with mentor Bob Knight and trailing Adolph Rupp (4) and John Wooden (10). "Coach K" passed Dean Smith in 2005 for the most wins in NCAA Tournament history. His ten Final Four appearances place him second on the all-time list behind John Wooden (21). Krzyzewski won a Gold Medal in the 1992 Olympics, serving as an assistant coach. He is a graduate of the United States Military Academy, where he played for future Hall of Fame coach Bob Knight. Krzyzewski returned to West Point and began his head coaching career in 1976. He led Army to an NIT appearance, before accepting the position at Duke in 1980. He has been named national Coach of the Year 11 times.

Mike "Coach K" Krzyzewski...

They still can't spell or pronounce his name (Krzyzewski which sounds like Sha-shef-ski), but they know that "Coach K" is associated with the highest level of success in the college basketball world. But what sets him apart from thousands of coaches striving for success in the basketball coaching fraternity? It is one word—"leadership." He believes that the main job of a coach is to motivate, and the primary job of a leader is to inspire, and how well he does that. Grant Hill, former Duke All-American player, said it best. "My first team meeting in 1990 was an awesome day. I remember being excited, anxious, and nervous when Coach K. walked in; the first thing he said was that we're going to win the national championship. That's one of his most valuable qualities. He's inspiring. He makes you a believer." (Krzyzewski, 2000). An even more important question is how he became such an exceptional leader?

Mike Krzyzewski had humble beginnings filled with early involvement in sport and a strong support system; father William (an elevator operator at Willoughby Tower in downtown Chicago), mother Emily (a homemaker and cleaning woman at the Chicago Athletic Club), brother Bill, and best friend, Moe Mlynski. There were few material things but lots of love and pride in the family. The family sacrificed so Mike could attend a private all-boys Catholic high school in Chicago, Weber. This may be why he has developed such a strong sense of confidence in what his family/his teams can accomplish together. His strong sense of unconditional support and commitment to success he attributed to his mother; he stated that her happiness, commitment to family, and not being afraid to fail came directly from her. In fact, before each game, he puts his hand over the pocket where he carries his mother's rosary and says this prayer, "Please God, help me to do my best, help me be myself, and help me lead from my heart."

When Mike decided to attend the United States Military Academy at West Point, a difficult decision, it was again because of his parents. Even though he didn't want to go, he had the discipline to believe and trust in his parents at a moment's notice. This is another coaching trait he felt was important for success. During his four years at Army,

he was exposed to the teachings of future Hall of Fame coach Bob Knight, as well as being absorbed in the Academy, and it's claim as one of the best leadership development programs in the world. Not only did he assimilate the West Point honor code: "I will not lie, cheat, or steal—nor tolerate those who do" but he took to heart the academy purpose "to develop leaders of character for service to the nation." His coaching videos stress absolute honesty (instant belief in each other), complete responsibility for your own actions (no excuses), and shared experiences (the Army code of soldiers depending on each other). When Mike left West Point as an officer/leader, he went on to another military service leadership development experience that led to his eventual promotion to Captain. He still attributes his formative years at the USMA as a strong factor forming his character in the West Point crucible of leadership.

Coach K views coaching as being focused on two essentials:

- **TEACHING**—he states that "I am a teacher and a coach". Our whole approach to coaching revolves around teaching. "We need to always find better ways to become better teachers. Teaching is what I love most." (Krzyzewski, 2000). He also believes in exposing his players to teaching; to force them to learn themselves and serve others, and to teach is to learn twice. Coach K has said that teaching is the heart of his coaching style.

- **LEADERSHIP**—like most coaches, he believes strongly that the coach is a leader, but his background and development have forged a new definition of leadership in the coaching world. The lessons learned from his family, the Academy experience at West Point, the leadership laboratory in the Army, plus his varied coaching experiences have produced a new leadership model. This is reflected in his belief that leaders need to do their best, learn their limits, and try to extend them as a proper leader perspective. He believes that the main job of a coach is to motivate and the main job of a leader is to inspire. (Krzyzewski, 2000). These are sound principles for all to follow.

.....SCOUTING REPORT.....SCOUTING REPORT...

Coach K's emphasis on leadership and teaching has produced the following milestones at Duke:

- **Three national championships (1991, 1992, 2001)**

- **12 National Coach of the Year honors in eight different seasons**

- **21 NCAA Tournament bids**

- **Ten Final Four appearances (third all-time)**

- **Seven ACC tourney championships (first to win four straight in 2002)**

- **Nine ACC season championships**

- **Passed Dean Smith in 2005 for the most wins in NCAA tournament history.**

- **NABC Coach of the Decade (1980s)**

- **Coach K Court naming honor at Cameron Indoor Stadium in 2001**

- **Duke's all-time winningest coach**

- **Naismith Basketball Hall of Fame in 2001**

- **John Wooden Legends of Coaching award in 2000**

- **NABC President in 1998-1999**

- **Named "America's Best Coach" by Time/CNN in 2001**

- **Coached players selected as National Defensive Player of the Year seven times**

- **Named Sportsman of the Year in 1992 by *The Sporting News*.**

SOURCE

Krzyzewski, Mike. Vertical Files, Archives, Naismith Memorial Basketball Hall of Fame. Springfield, MA.

Krzyzewski, Mike. Interview with Jerry Krause. 2001.

Krzyzewski, Mike. (2000). *Leading with the Heart: Coach K's Successful Strategies for Basketball, Business, and Life*. New York: Warner Books.

THE CORE OF CHARACTER

By Mike Krzyzewski

COURAGE

Courage is a word that comes up a lot in leadership. And it does take courage to walk down that dark alley where others don't want to go. But true bravery in leadership really revolves around the degree to which a person maintains the courage of his convictions.

That kind of courage takes persistence to believe in yourself – and resilience to keep picking yourself up after every loss, every stumble, and every fall. Following through with your plans, your commitments, and your dreams – even when everyone else is saying you can't do it – that's courage.

And why does a leader need courage?

Because someone is always trying to pull you down when you're a leader. And you cannot be vacillating back and forth with the wind. There can be a wind where you're successful and everyone agrees with you. Or there can be a wind where you're not successful, and everybody disagrees with you. Courage gives a leader the ability to stand straight and not sway, no matter which way the wind blows.

A strong gale might change a leader's strategy, but it should never change his core beliefs. If you believe in your system, in the people around you, and in your own abilities, then going 11-17 will not change what you do. But if you don't believe in those things, if you don't have the courage of your convictions, then going 11-17 might change everything that you do.

A leader has to know who he is and what he stands for. And he also has to say it, demonstrate it, and mean it if he ever hopes for people to follow him. And, believe me, when you stand strong in those vacillating winds for the first time, it's easier to have courage again and again.

CONFIDENCE

In 1988, when Elton Brand completed his freshman year, the press, the sports analysts, everybody said that he was a great, great basketball player. I knew he was going to be a great player. But, Elton himself did not yet know it.

Because he was out with an injury for seven weeks of the season, when he finally did come back, he wasn't the dominant player that he could have been. He simply wasn't up to par physically. So he just naturally figured that he wasn't as good as everybody was saying he was.

That summer, Elton had a mental obstacle to overcome. He had to overcome the thought that his reputation was better than he really was. So Elton and I sat down in my office one day and talked about it. He told me that his dream was to play in the NBA, but he didn't know if he'd ever be good enough. I told him that he would definitely be good enough to make it to the NBA and that everything the media was saying about him was true. He just had not come all the way back from his injury. So I advised him to play some off-season basketball and tryout for the Goodwill Games.

Several weeks later, when he made the team, I flew up to New York to watch some of his practices and take in a few of his games. The main reason I did that was so I could reinforce to him that he was good – really good at playing basketball.

You can talk about a pitcher throwing shutouts or striking out twelve batters in a game. But until that pitcher does it, he never really knows he's that good. Elton Brand did not know he was that good. We utilized the summer, then, for him to get to know that he was an outstanding player. He had to have the confidence in himself in order to realize his own full potential – in order to achieve his true greatness.

As a leader, I have to have confidence in myself. That goes without saying. But I also want my players to have confidence in themselves. If I'm a manager of a company and I have a terrific director of personnel, I want him to think he's great, too. I want him to think he's so great that he'll set the world on fire.

So how do I make sure he knows it? Well, it's important for me to tell him what I think. But simply telling him that he's terrific won't really accomplish all that much, except that he knows how I feel. In order for him to know deep within himself that he's really good, he has to prove it to himself. So my job as a leader is to put him in the position where he can do so.

That's what I did for Elton Brand. I advised him to participate in the Goodwill Games, because I was certain he would shine in that venue. And he did shine. In fact, he was a star. So when he came back to Duke for his sophomore year, he was armed with the confidence that comes from experience and knowing.

With accomplishment comes confidence, and with confidence comes belief. It has to be in that order.

LESSONS FROM THIS LEGEND...

CONTINUAL LEARNING

When we're born, are we given three baskets of potential? Do we stay with three baskets our entire lives? Or when we fill up two of those baskets, have we developed even more possibilities so that now we have eight baskets of potential? Maybe one of the potentials in the third basket is to learn how to make more baskets.

I feel like I have a lot more potential at this stage of my life. Of course, I may be less likely to set the world record in a 100-meter dash. Some of the baskets that contained physical potential are full. But scientists say that we use only 10 percent of our brain, so there have to be other things that can be focused on and then achieved.

The beauty of leadership is that there are no complete or perfect recipes. You cannot say: "Do these ten things, and you will be a leader." Those ten things might help you become a leader, but doing them alone won't make you one.

Any blueprint to leadership has to be used as a guide. It can only be structured so much. There has to be room for personal creativity. And every leader has to put his signature on his leadership style.

Continual leadership is a key to effective leadership, because no one can know everything there is to know. In leadership, things change. Events change, circumstances change, people change. As a matter of fact, leadership is all about change. Leaders take people to places that they have never been before.

Because leaders are always encountering new situations, they have to learn how to meet new challenges, to adapt, to confront, to master, to win. A leader's job is ongoing. It's like a ring. There is no end. Leadership never stops.

We have to think of different ways to learn and grow every day. Because when you stop growing, you start to decay. And life goes on, win or lose. Either way, you just have to try to figure out what you can do better the next time.

I believe that every person has to learn from success and failure. We should never forget a defeat. Defeat can be the key to future victory.

HARD WORK

My mom and dad never missed a day of work cleaning floors and operating the elevator. If they were coughing or sniffling in the morning, it was: "I gotta go to work." If one of them had a fever, it was: "I gotta go to work." They never missed work – I mean, never.

That's what I learned growing up. Show up every day, even if you have to sweat it out. And you know what? I became amazingly dependable – just like my parents.

For some reason, "hard" and "work" have been associated with other four-letter words that have negative connotations. But I believe work is good. There is dignity in work. I also believe that a hard-work ethic forges strong leaders.

I have found that when people achieve something that they've really worked hard for, it makes them feel great, superb, and wonderful. In that context, rather than causing pain, work brings people joy, fulfillment, and self-esteem.

In order to be a winner, you have to look for ways of getting things done and not for reasons why things can't be done. People who live with excuses have things that can't be done hovering around them all the time.

The only way we lose is if we don't try our best. There is always a way to win. Never say you cannot do it. Find the way to win.

HONESTY AND INTEGRITY

A lot of our success in Duke basketball has to do with character. And at the heart of character are honesty and integrity.

We all know what honesty means. And integrity is nothing more than doing the right thing no matter who's watching you. Are you going to show integrity only when someone is watching you – or are you going to show it all the time?

In our program, the truth is the basis of all that we do. There is nothing more important than the truth, because there's nothing more powerful than the truth. Consequently, on our team, we always tell one another the truth. We must be honest with one another. There is no other way.

In addition, as a leader, I believe I must be honest with myself. If a leader is honest with himself, it'll be a lot easier to be honest with everybody else. I consider my biggest achievement to be anytime a kid knows I've been honest with him.

Whenever I go back to Chicago, I find myself thinking, "Gee, I'm so lucky, it's amazing."

Not because my family was poor or that I had humble beginnings – but, rather, that I had it so good. And also because of all those values my folks taught me. They were great values – and they proved to be the basis for how I would conduct myself for the rest of my life.

Back then, you grew up believing in God, you told the truth – and you loved your country and playground basketball.

It was really very simple.

Source

Krzyzewski, Mike. (2000). *Leading With The Heart*. New York: Warner Books.

LESSONS FROM THIS LEGEND...

RANDOM THOUGHTS

By Mike Krzyzewski

"I don't look at myself as a basketball coach. I look at myself as a leader who happens to coach basketball."

"Your heart has to be in whatever you lead."

"Confrontation simply means meeting the truth head-on."

"Believe that the loose ball that you are chasing has your name on it."

"During critical periods, a leader is not allowed to feel sorry for himself, to be down, to be angry, or to be weak. Leaders must beat back these emotions."

"It takes courage not only to make decisions, but to live with those decisions afterward."

"You have to work hard at staying in contact with your friends so that the relationships will continue and live on… Friendships, along with love, make life worth living."

"During the season, your team should be led with exuberance and excitement. You should live the journey. You should live it right. You should live it together. You should live it shared. You should try to make one another better. You should get on one another if somebody's not doing their part. You should hug one another when they are. You should be disappointed in a loss and exhilarated in a win. It's all about the journey."

"In our program, the truth is the basis of all that we do. There is nothing more important that the truth, because there's nothing more powerful than the truth.

Consequently, on our team, we always tell one another the truth. We must be honest with one another. There is no other way."

"Throughout the season, I look into my players' eyes to gauge feelings, and confidence levels, and to establish instant trust."

"Every leader needs to remember that a healthy respect for authority takes time to develop. It's like building trust. You don't instantly have trust, it has to be earned."

"Too many rules get in the way of leadership. They just put you in a box…People set rules to keep from making decisions."

"Leadership is ongoing, adjustable, flexible, and dynamic."

"Mutual commitment helps overcome the fear of failure—especially when people are part of a team sharing and achieving goals. It also sets the stage for open dialogue and honest conversation."

"When you first assemble a group, it's not a team right off the bat. It's only a collection of individuals."

"When a leader takes responsibility for his own actions and mistakes, he not only sets a good example, he shows a healthy respect for people on his team."

"Discipline is doing what you are supposed to do, in the best possible manner, at the time you are supposed to do it."

"Goals should be realistic, attainable, and shared among all members of the team."

"There are five fundamental qualities that make every team great: communication, trust, collective responsibility, caring and pride. I like to think of each as a separate finger on the fist. Any one individually is important, but all of them together are unbeatable."

"You develop a team to achieve what one person cannot accomplish alone. All of us alone are weaker, by far, than if all of us are together."

"Confidence shared is better than confidence only in yourself."

"In leadership, there are no words more important than trust. In any organization, trust must be developed among every member of the team if success is going to be achieved."

"Two are better than one if two act as one."

"A leader may be the most knowledgeable person in the world, but if the players on his team cannot translate that knowledge into action, it means nothing."

"Erect no artificial walls that might limit potential, stifle creativity, or shackle innovation."

"Leaders should be reliable without being predictable. They should be consistent without being anticipated."

"A leader has to be positive about all things that happen to his team. Look at nothing in the past as failure."

"Courage and confidence are what decision-making is all about."

"Leaders show respect for people by giving them time."

LESSONS FROM THIS LEGEND...

"I believe God gave us crises for some reason—and it certainly wasn't for us to say that everything about them is bad. A crisis can be a momentous time for a team to grow—if a leader handles it properly."

"Encourage members of your team to take the initiative and act on their own."

"People want to be on a team. They want to be part of something bigger than themselves. They want to be in a situation where they feel that they are doing something for the greater good."

"Never set a goal that involves number of wins – never. Set goals that revolves around playing together as a team. Doing so will put you in a position to win every game."

"When teaching, always remember this simple phrase: "You hear, you forget. You see, you remember. You do, you understand.""

"Members of your team need to see themselves through your eyes – so that they may see how they *really* are, not how they *think* they are."

"Don't let a single game break your heart."

"People talk to you in different ways – through facial expressions, moods, mannerisms, body language, the tone in their voice, the look in their eyes."

"Sometimes a leader has to draw a line in the sand."

"The people on your team expect you to be upbeat, positive, confident, and certain they can win."

"Take time to get refreshed. Clear you head, rest and recharge your batteries, and then get after it."

"The worse the crisis, the more people will tend to think as individuals rather than as members of a team."

"Before you ever utter a word, the team sees your face, the look in your eyes, even your walk. Show the face your team needs to see."

"A leader's job is to remove any obstacle that can negatively impact his team's performance."

"Sometimes, all the good things you try to provide for your team members do not make a difference. Sometimes, people have to move on."

"Hunger not for success, but for excellence. And don't let anyone else define excellence for you."

"Enjoy the journey."

SOURCE

Coach K – The official website for Coach Mike Krzyzewski. Website: http://www.coachk.com

Krzyzewski, Mike. (2000). *Leading With The Heart*. New York: Warner Books.

LEGACY OF
Branch McCracken

- Coached Indiana to NCAA national championships in 1940 and 1953.

- Emphasized an aggressive, fast-breaking style of play and his Indiana teams were known as the "Hurrying Hoosiers."

- Detested dribbling and wanted his players to handle the ball like it was a "hot potato."

- Authored the popular book, entitled *Indiana Basketball*.

- Received the NAACP Award for his role in breaking the color barrier in the Big 10.

- Played for Everett Dean at Indiana and was a consensus first team All-American.

BRANCH McCRACKEN

*"Our style of play is very aggressive,
both offensively and defensively.
We have a reputation of being a running ball club.
There is no substitute for speed in our game."*
—Branch McCracken

BIOGRAPHY

Born: June 9, 1908 in Monrovia, IN

Died: June 4, 1970

Inducted into the Naismith Memorial Basketball Hall of Fame in 1960

As a player, Branch McCracken played for Hall of Fame coach Everett Dean and led Indiana in scoring three straight years. His versatility allowed McCracken to play the center, forward, and guard positions during his career at Indiana. He was a ferocious competitor and earned the nickname "Big Bear" because of his size and tendency to scowl. McCracken won 457 games while coaching at Indiana and Ball State and was selected National Coach of the Year at Indiana on two occasions. He led his Indiana teams, known as the "Hurrying Hoosiers," to the NCAA championship in 1940 and 1953. At the age of 31, McCracken was the youngest coach to win the NCAA Division I national championship. He directed Indiana to Big 10 championships in 1953, 1954, 1957, and 1958. McCracken authored *Indiana Basketball*, a very popular book for coaches. McCracken coached at Indiana from 1938 until his retirement in 1958.

Branch McCracken...

Branch McCracken was a native Hoosier and played his high school basketball at Monrovia (IN) High School He led his team to the championship at the Tri-State Tournament in 1925 and 1926 and was selected the most valuable player of the tournament both years.

McCracken attended Indiana University and was a three-year letter winner for Hall of Fame coach Everett Dean. McCracken was selected All-Big 10 Conference first team in both 1929 and 1930. He led Indiana in scoring three straight years, and as a senior, set the Big 10 record for points scored in one season. McCracken was named first team All-American by the Helms Foundation, Grantland Rice, Press Foundation, and the Coaches Poll. McCracken stood 6-foot 4-inches and weighed 215 pounds during his playing career. He also played football at Indiana University and was selected All-Big 10 in that sport.

Besides his athletic prowess, McCracken took a stand against the ritual of freshman-sophomore hazing on college campuses. Until the late 1920's, at least 14 students in this country died in collegiate freshman-sophomore hazing. Administrators railed against the practice to little avail. McCracken, who was highly respected by his peers, spoke out against hazing and the Indiana University student newspaper published his remarks. McCracken's stand, as a student, helped reduce hazing not only on the campus of Indiana University, but also nationwide. Only one death related to freshman-sophomore hazing rituals has been reported since 1930. Hank Nuwer has written three books on hazing behaviors and recognized the importance of the stand made by McCracken. "It took a united front of administrators and concerned students to end this scourge," said Nuwer (1999).

After graduation from Indiana, McCracken played professional basketball with the Fort Wayne Hoosiers, Oshkosh All-Stars, and the Dayton Metropolitans. McCracken teamed up with Hall of Fame player Bud Foster to lead the Oshkosh All-Stars to the Midwest championship.

McCracken coached at Ball State University from 1931 to 1938 and compiled a 93-41 record. In 1938, McCracken replaced Everett Dean as coach at Indiana University and introduced a different style of play. Dean coached what many people called the "scientific game," stressing precision passes and a slow-down type offense that methodically created good shots from relatively close range. McCracken emphasized an aggressive, fast-breaking style of play.

"Our style of ball is very aggressive," said McCracken (1955). "We have the reputation of being a running ball club. We are always trying to get into offensive territory before the defense has time to get organized and set up. The opponent doesn't have time to wait for us to play ball. There is no substitute for speed in our game. We all realize the importance of height. But for height to be effective, we must have speed to go with it. Naturally, we are going to make more mistakes playing this style of ball than we would playing a slow deliberate game. However, we feel that we more than compensate for the mistakes by getting many more good scoring opportunities."

McCracken detested dribbling and wanted his players to handle the ball like it was a hot potato. He taught his players the importance of getting the ball down the floor quickly by passing, rather than dribbling. Marv Huffman, Indiana's standout guard, said, "I remember at one of our first practices, I got a rebound and dribbled the ball a couple of times. Branch blew his whistle and threw two balls up on the backboard. I got one and dribbled before I passed. He took the other ball and just threw it downcourt. Then he looked at me and said, 'OK, now which one got there faster?' That was the last time I ever dribbled the ball like that." (Gergen, 1987)

In 1940, McCracken's second season, the Hoosiers were 17-3 in regular-season play and finished second to Purdue in the Big 10. Purdue's legendary coach, "Piggy" Lambert was not a proponent of post-season play and since Indiana had defeated Purdue twice during the season, the selection committee picked Indiana to represent the Upper Midwest in the second NCAA national tournament.

Indiana, known as the "Hurrying Hoosiers" for their run-and-gun style, ran past Kansas to win the NCAA national championship. The final score was 60-42, and it would be 10 years before another team scored as many points in an NCAA championship game. Kansas newspapers called the blitzing Indiana team a "tornado" in the wake of the one-sided final.

McCracken was a Navy Lieutenant, Senior Grade, and commanded in the Pacific Theatre during World War II. He returned to Indiana for the 1946-47 season after a three-year leave of absence.

In 1948, McCracken was instrumental in breaking the color barrier in the Big 10 Conference when Bill Garrett became the first black full-scholarship basketball player to play in the conference. Garrett was a natural fit with McCracken's brand of fast-breaking, up-tempo basketball. "Bill must have been closer to 6-foot 1-inch than 6-foot 3-inches," said teammate Phil Buck. But he was agile; he had finesse. He played smarter basketball than most guys." (Newlin, 1998)

The news that Garrett would attend IU raised eyebrows around the Big 10. Although black students played other sports, basketball coaches had maintained an unwritten agreement against integrating the indoor game. Teammate Bill Tosheff said there were only a couple of instances where the racial thing came up. "In St. Louis, they made special arrangements to let him stay in our hotel, but they wanted him to eat in a private dining room. So we went out as a team and walked until we found a place that would serve all of us. We protected him, without making a big deal out of it. But we never heard any racial slurs or had any problems at games." (Newlon, 1998)

Garrett, through his career as a coach and educator, until his untimely death at age 45, was as admired for his personality and character as for his athletic achievements. Garrett knew that he always had the unqualified backing of his college coach. "Branch was very loyal to Bill for the rest of their lives," recalled Garrett's widow, the former Betty Guess.

Entering the 1952-53 season, McCracken had won nearly 75 percent of his games at Indiana, struggled through only one losing season (in the aftermath of World War II), and directed the Hoosiers to the championship of the second NCAA tournament. The only thing missing from McCracken's portfolio was a Big 10 Conference championship, as Indiana had finished second on seven occasions in his 11 years. His teams executed the fast break as well as any team in the nation, but Indiana had been ham-

pered by a lack of size. Don Schlundt solved that problem. He was a skinny 6-foot 6-inch center when McCracken recruited him out of South Bend (IN). By the time Schlundt was a sophomore at IU, he had grown to 6-foot 9-inches. He led the Hoosiers to a Big 10 record of 17-1 and their first undisputed conference championship.

In the 1953 NCAA Tournament, Indiana slipped past DePaul and soundly defeated Notre Dame to advance to the Final Four. In the semifinals, the Hoosiers defeated LSU, led by future Hall of Fame player Bob Pettit.

In the title game Indiana faced the defending champions, the Kansas Jayhawks. In a classic match-up, Indiana's Bob Leonard supplied the decisive point by hitting one of two free throws with 27 seconds left to give the Hoosiers a 69-68 victory. In the locker room, a beaming McCracken told reporters that Leonard "had ice water in his veins."

The fiery McCracken had a habit of drinking more than 30 cups of coffee a day. The legendary coach who dressed in a blue suit and red tie was a bona fide workaholic, and his teams always reflected his character with aggressive and spirited play.

Besides his coaching honors, McCracken received the Leather Medal for the outstanding faculty leader, the Brown Derby Award for the most popular professor, and the NAACP Award for breaking the color barrier in the Big 10.

SOURCE

McCracken, Branch. Vertical Files, Archives. Naismith Memorial Basketball Hall of Fame: Springfield, MA.

Nuwer, Hank. (1990). *Broken Pledges: The Deadly Rite of Hazing*. Atlanta: Longstreet Press.

Gergen, Joe. (1987). *The Final Four*. St. Louis: The Sporting News Publishing Co.

Newlin, Ron. (March/April 1998). "Shooting down the Color Barrier," *IU Alumni Magazine*.

THE COACH AND HIS PLAYERS

By Branch McCracken

In a basketball game, the spectators are able to see many things—team play, excellent ball handling, a variety of shots, clever footwork, good defense, and field goal-shooting accuracy. The important factors that mean the difference between a great ball club and an average one, even though the players are of equal ability, are the unseen assets that must be developed by the coach and his players during the years they are together. An outstanding team isn't built up merely during the basketball season. The spirit, understanding, and desire must be developed from the time a coach and his players first meet until the boys' playing days are over. What are these unseen assets?

1. Team spirit: moral and cooperation
2. Driving desire: to learn, to improve, to excel, to win
3. Self-discipline: mental, emotional, physical
4. Pride: in himself, his teammates, his chool, his coach, and the community
5. Confidence: in himself, in his own and his teammates' ability, in his coach, in the system of play
6. Leadership: to direct, to encourage, to take responsibility

If every member of every squad acquires these assets, a coach, given players of average ability and coordination, can develop outstanding teams. A coach, then, must be a man of many professions: a teacher, a salesman, and a psychologist. Yet, he must practice all three simultaneously.

THE COACH AS A TEACHER

Thorough knowledge of basketball fundamentals, drills, team offense, and team defense does not mean necessarily that a coach will be successful. In spite of having players were press clippings declaring that they were a great basketball player and knew how to execute all fundamentals and systems, a coach may still fail. Neither knowledge nor press clippings will develop a good team unless the coach is able to teach. He must be able to present the material so that every player clearly understands and learns quickly. The coach uses the same methods of teaching that are used in every field. Fortunately, he is able to concentrate on individual instruction when necessary.

KEY POINTS WHEN TEACHING

1. Clear, simple, precise presentation
2. Progression: correlation of new with previous knowledge
3. Whole and part presentation: present over-all subject, and then teach step-by-step
4. Demonstration: coach shows how
5. Participation: players learn by doing
6. Repetition: doing until the action is automatic
7. Criticism and correction
8. Use of various teaching media: movies, pictures, diagrams, and chalk talks

ADVICE FOR TEACHING

1. Keep your teaching simple and easily understood.
2. Be sure the players thoroughly understand and learn each step as it is presented.
3. Have each boy do well in everything he learns.
4. Always remember that demonstration is one of the best teaching methods. Seeing is believing. If players see how a play is run and that it will work, they learn and perfect it quickly.
5. Teach individually for correct and thorough learning.
   - Take the player off by himself.
   - Work patiently.
   - Demonstrate and correct until the work is mastered.
6. Don't over-coach. It is better to do a few things well than many things poorly.
7. Simplify your system and do it well, rather than use a complicated system, doing everything haphazardly.

Almost no other field of our school curriculum demonstrates good or poor teaching better than does athletics. It would be very interesting if other instructors had to demonstrate the results of their teaching before fifteen or twenty thousand critics each week for three months each year, especially if each critic considered himself an authority on the subject demonstrated. I imagine several professors would turn gray in a hurry and develop ulcers, too.

THE COACH AS A SALESMAN

The coach must be a salesman. He must sell himself to the players, to the faculty, and to the public. He must be sincere and honest in his salesmanship.

The players must have confidence in the coach as a person. They must believe in him, his experience, and what he is teaching. Every player must be sold on what he is taught, how to do it, and be convinced that by doing properly what he learns, he and the team have a good chance of being successful. The coach must sell the players to each other, and teach the players how to sell themselves to one another.

The coach must have the faculty be for him. He must enter into faculty functions and be willing to cooperate in every way possible. It is easy for all of us to get so wrapped up in our own field that we can't sympathize with another person, see his problems, or understand his point-of-view. The other person's field is just as important to him as your field is to you. Also, his field may be as important to your player as basketball is. I honestly believe that because a coach must work with so many people whose interests and problems are widely varied, he is less apt to get into a rut and be intolerant. But it is wise to keep reminding ourselves that public interest in our field does not make us all-important. Conceit makes a poor salesman.

The coach must sell himself and his players to the public. Since nearly everyone in the state of Indiana has played basketball of some kind—from the barnyard to the well-coached, competitive type—or is a basketball spectator, most people have an idea of how the game should be played. There are the "they don't teach reading like they did in my day" fans who can't understand what ever happened to the stationary back guard. They think that nowadays a coach just throws the ball out, and the boys run up and down the floor with no set plays. Nobody knows anything but run and shoot. Then there are the "as I see it, you started holding the ball too soon" second-guesser fans. They may be right. As soon as the game is over, win or lose, most coaches are as rabid second-guessers as any fans. Then there are the "spectator sport" fans. They go to the game to enjoy themselves. Besides eating hot dogs and popcorn, for them enjoying the game may include berating the official, the coach, and the players, booing and cheering all in the same breath. But almost all fans are sincerely loyal followers, interested in the boys as a team and in their coach. Everyone is entitled to his opinion about how to do everything—remember that. You, as a coach, just hear more of these opinions about your business than other people hear about theirs.

1. Sell the public on what you are trying to do in basketball and with the boys.
2. Sell the boys as players and individuals to the public.
3. Take as much interest in community affairs as the fans take in your basketball.
4. Listen to criticism without losing your temper. Everyone has a right to his opinion. Don't antagonize the fans.

In a short time, a coach will find the community taking pride in the team, and the team working harder to deserve the respect of the public.

THE COACH AS A PSYCHOLOGIST

A coach is a practical psychologist. His is the applied psychology of common sense and understanding. His greatest asset is his ability to remember his own problems when he was young and see the boys' point-of-view. He works not only with the squad as a unit, but also with each individual player. The coach can develop those assets that make for a great team only if he has a thorough understanding of and sympathy for each boy who plays for him. A coach's job would be comparatively easy if all he had to do were to teach fundamentals and systems, make schedules, and coach during ball games. A ball player is a temperamental individualist influenced by home and school environment, emotional tensions, friends, and responsibilities. A coach must learn what makes the boy tick—why he does what he does, what his attitudes are, and how best to approach the boy to help him.

A coach must be sincere in his interest in the boy, not just as a ball player but also as a man. A boy isn't easily fooled and can spot a fraud quickly. The coach who can establish an easy, confidential, friendly relationship with each boy can do his job much more effectively. Get to know the boy's parents and home conditions. When a player needs help, coach and parent cooperation can solve many problems. But a coach must know whether or not the boy will resent involving his parents. If he does, the parents can be of little help. Usually the coach and parents working together can handle most situations.

Friends and school environment influence a ball player greatly. Sometimes a ball player's close friends are not desirable. They are insubordinate, have bad habits, and are troublemakers. A man is known by the company he keeps. The player must be influenced against the bad habits, attitudes, and conduct of those friends—not against the friends personally. All boys have an intense loyalty. A coach defeats his purpose when he tries to turn a player against his friends. Concentrate on teaching the player appreciation and desire for virtues, not vices. Help him develop his good points and become self-confident. Remember too, that youth is the age of daring, recklessness, and bravado. We all went through that stage. Even the best boys make serious mistakes because they are young, easily influenced, and want to be accepted by a group. Help them improve their sense of values, judgment, and confidence.

As a psychologist, a coach must help every player realize that he is a good player because his teammates make him one. The boy who rebounds well, passes accurately, sets up a scoring opportunity, or plays a great defensive game is just as important and just as valuable as the boy who does the most scoring. There can be no jealousy or envy in a successful team. It's the coach's job to spot signs of these feelings and iron out personal antagonisms before they develop fully. Players soon learn that it is the coach's job to criticize, not theirs. Razzing, griping, and criticizing only antagonize a teammate. The sooner a player learns this, the better off he is.

In every player's make-up there is a valuable asset. It is the will or desire to learn, to improve, to excel, and to win. In some boys this is strong, in others latent. It is the coach's job to develop this asset into a driving force. He can do this in many ways. He can appeal to the player's pride in his own ability and that of his teammates. The coach can arouse interest in learning by talking over new material and respecting the boy's judgment of it. The coach must always work to make the learning process interesting. Competition with teammates is invaluable to develop in a boy the driving desire to improve and excel. Just criticism and deserved praise of both the boy and his teammates are the coach's two most valuable methods. The desire to win must be developed through pride, a feeling of responsibility to his coach, his teammates, the school, and the fans.

A coach must develop personal pride and confidence. Confidence and pride are not to be confused with cockiness and over-confidence. Confidence is a secure inner belief in one's self. Cockiness is shouting that belief to the world. One thing a player learns early at Indiana: "Respect all —fear none."

A coach must develop leadership. Some boys are natural leaders—with that intangible something that makes other boys follow them. With these boys, a coach's only responsibility is to see that the boy leads in the right direction. Other boys may be great game generals, respected for their knowledge and ability. They assume leadership on the floor unconsciously. Help them carry over this ability to lead in basketball to other activities. If they fail, help them find out why. Don't be content to let a boy be a good leader for you, and a poor one elsewhere. Every boy should be given responsibility, authority, and praise for a job well done. Help him to learn to make keen decisions quickly.

It's quite a job, this coaching: full of headaches, criticisms, disappointments, success, and some glory. But a coach is paid not in money or winning teams, but in the men his players become.

SOURCE

McCracken, Branch. (1955). *Indiana Basketball*. Englewood Cliffs, NJ: Prentice-Hall.

LEGACY OF
Arad "Mac" McCutchan

- Led Evansville to the College Division NCAA national championship in 1959, 1960, 1964, 1965, and 1971.

- Was the first Division II coach elected to the Basketball Hall of Fame.

- Designed a points-per-possession chart and analyzed each possession to determine its point value.

- Used the t-shirt style of uniform and it became the trademark of Evansville basketball.

- Believed basketball was an integral part of education, and he never cut a player for lack of ability.

- Switched his team's jersey color from purple to orange because he believed it improved his players' ability to see one another.

ARAD "MAC" McCUTCHAN

*"What your players do after they graduate,
their successes in life, means far more
than the score of a basketball game."*
—Arad "Mac" McCutchan

BIOGRAPHY

Born: July 4, 1912 in Evansville, IN

Died: June 16, 1993

Inducted into the Naismith Basketball Hall of Fame in 1981

McCutchan excelled in basketball and football at Bosse, (IN) High School (1926-30) and went on to dupli-cate that achievement at Evansville College (1930-34). He coached nine years in high school before a three year service stint in U.S. Navy (1943-45). McCutchan coached at high school alma mater (Bosse, IN) and then returned to Evansville to compile a magnificent 515-313 record in 31 years. He won 14 Indiana Conference titles and five NCAA College Division Championships in 1959, 60, 64, 65 and 71. His 1965 team went 29-0, earning him his second straight NCAA College Division Coach of the Year award. McCutchan coached the Olympic Trials teams in 1960 and served as an assistant coach for the Gold Medal Pan American Team in 1971. He was the Indiana Hall of Fame Silver Anniversary Coach award winner in 1973. Along with Coach John Wooden, McCutchan is one of only two coaches in collegiate basketball history to win at least five NCAA championships.

Arad "Mac" McCutchan...

Arad Allen McCutchan was born and raised in the hotbed of basketball – Evansville, Indiana. Arad grew up on the family farm north of Daylight, Indiana, where his older brothers put up one basket on their barn and another at their one-room schoolhouse. Mac, as he was affectionately called, attended Bosse High School and excelled in basketball and football. He was the leading scorer on the basketball team for four years and earned All-State honors for two years. Arad reportedly became one of the first players in the area to employ a one-hand jump shot.

McCutchan then attended Evansville College, and he led the basketball team in scoring for three years. After graduating from Evansville in 1934, Mac accepted his first position at Sulligent, Alabama, where he taught mathematics and coached the high school basketball team. The school had no gymnasium of its own, so all games were played on the road. McCutchan also played amateur basketball with the Golden Tornadoes, and taught and coached one year at Guin (AL) High School before heading back to Indiana.

In 1935, McCutchan became an assistant to Harry King at his alma mater, Bosse High School. King was a renowned player on the 1921, 1922, and 1923 Indiana High School Champions dubbed the "Franklin, Indiana, Wonder-Five." When King was called to active duty with the National Guard in 1941, McCutchan became head basketball coach.

In 1943, Arad joined the U.S. Navy. After World War II, McCutchan was stationed at the Pensacola Naval Base in Florida when he received a letter from Evansville College President Lincoln Hale offering him a position as head basketball coach and assistant football coach. McCutchan, with a wife and two children to support, decided to decline the offer because of monetary reasons. A few hours after sending the letter of refusal, he began to have second thoughts. "Down deep, I knew coaching was what I wanted to do," McCutchan said, "so I phoned Hale and said I'd take the job."

Thus began a career spanning 31 years of basketball which included: five NCAA College Division championships; 15 Indiana Collegiate Conference (ICC) titles; 12 ICC Coach of the Year awards; induction into the Indiana Basketball Hall of Fame; and induction into the Naismith Memorial Basketball Hall of Fame.

Even though McCutchan retired from basketball coaching in 1977 with a record of 514 victories and 314 losses, he continued to teach mathematics at Evansville. He always believed that basketball was never an end in itself and insisted that the scoreboard victories don't mean as much as the way a coach molds a young man's life. "What's most gratifying," said McCutchan, "is the number of former Aces who now hold a doctor's degree. That's the kind of record I'm most proud of."

McCutchan was proud of the fact that he never cut a player, walk-on or otherwise, who showed up daily for practices. Mac said, "I never cut a player for lack of ability. Of course, I had to dismiss players who did not comply to training rules or who missed practice, but I would never cut a player for lack of ability. After all, if we as educators claim that athletics is an integral part of schooling, then we'd be two-faced if we denied participation to some players. To make my team, a player simply had to meet eligibility requirements, demonstrate a desire to play ball, and abide by the rules."

Mac was an advocate of a high-scoring, fast break style of basketball. Utah Jazz head coach Jerry Sloan was an All-American player under McCutchan and said, "Mac wanted us to get up and down the floor and push the ball as much as we could. If the final score was 103-102, it was OK with him – as long as we had the 103." (Johnson, 2005)

Evansville won the 1964 NCAA College Division Championship with a 26-3 record. After the 1964 season, Jerry Sloan had an opportunity to play for Baltimore in the NBA but turned it down so he could receive his degree in education. With that decision, Sloan not only received his degree but also led the Purple Aces to an undefeated season and a second consecutive national championship. "From the start of fall practice, we were committed to being as good as we could be," said Sloan. "We had tremendous confidence. We felt like if we came out and played hard, we could win every game."

The Aces went on to average a school-record 95 points per game that season. They scored more than 100 points nine times and were in the 90s on nine other occasions. McCutchan usually used just a couple of substitutes, and the starters normally played all but a minute or two.

Herb Williams, a sophomore starter on the 1965 team, remembered the starting five received most the headlines and accolades, but everybody on the squad played a part in the unbeaten season. "Coach McCutchan did a masterful job of building cohesion – from the freshmen all the way up to the seniors," said Williams. "He made everybody feel like part of the family."

Teammate Sam Watkins agreed and said, "Everybody had his role, and they were well laid out by Coach McCutchan and assistant coach Tom O'Brien. Only five guys can start, and even though we were only seven or eight deep, there was no tension, no bickering. All I can say is thank God for all those guys who challenged us in practice and helped us get better."

Jerry Sloan earned back-to-back All-American honors at Evansville and then spent 11 seasons as a player in the NBA. Sloan became head coach of the Utah Jazz in 1988 and is the winningest coach in Jazz history. "I learned so much from Coach McCutchan," said Sloan. He taught me how important it is for a team to be committed, to stay together, and to do what the coach tells you."

Sloan remembered a regional tournament game against Bellarmine when one of his teammates questioned McCutchan. "Before the game, Mac told us he wanted us to press. We got down by 10 points in the first half, and during a timeout one of the guys said to him, 'Coach, what are you doing? We're getting killed out there.' Mac said, 'I don't care what you guys think. We're going to run the press. But I need five guys to do it; we can't do it with four.'

"We were up 10 points at halftime," Sloan said, "and wound up winning by seven."

McCutchan was the mastermind and architect of Evansville's basketball success. He was an innovator and switched the team's jersey color from purple to orange for road games. "I've taken some kidding about putting my Purple Aces in orange uniforms," McCutchan said, "but I took a course that rated the various colors on ease of visibility. Orange was rated the best. You see, the average crowd at a winter game is dressed in dark and when we used purple uniforms, the players seemed hidden in the crowd. There's no surer way to ruin a fast break than to lose sight of your teammate."

McCutchan dressed his early Evansville teams in robes. When the players made their initial appearance, the pep band struck up "When the Saints Go Marching In," providing a lively atmosphere. "On the road, we play in places that are small and cold," explained McCutchan. "The robes kept my player's legs warm." Mac also believed warm-ups with long pants hindered quick substitutions. "It takes too long for a substitute entering the game to get out of those long pants some teams wear," McCutchan said.

In 1947, McCutchan introduced jerseys with sleeves and it became the trademark of his Purple Aces. In a 1964 interview McCutchan said, "I use the T-shirt style of uniform because I feel that is what most players wear in practice, and therefore, what they are most comfortable in. It's also more flattering to the thin ballplayer." Evansville, a school rich in basketball history, maintained the "jerseys with sleeves" tradition until the 2002-03 season.

Using his mathematical expertise, Arad calculated the importance of each possession. He called this points per possession (PPP) and charted each possession during the course of a game. McCutchan said, "How much is a basketball possession worth? I figure it's worth about one point to the team in possession. We keep points per possession charts that tell exactly how much a ball is worth for any given game or any given season. We use the PPP charts to help us make judgments on whether to keep possession or to shoot in certain situations. When we use our delay game we know, that if we handle the ball perfectly, we will eventually end up at the free-throw line. We know that the free throw with the bonus is worth 1.2 points. Of course, a 70% sure shot is worth 1.4 points. Obviously, we should shoot the 70% sure shot."

On December 13, 1977, during the first season after McCutchan's retirement, the entire Evansville basketball team was killed in a crash shortly after takeoff from the Evansville airport. This tragedy haunted McCutchan the rest of his life. Arad and Evansville athletic director, Jim Byers, attempted to identify the bodies. McCutchan said, "I've never had to face anything like this." It was the hardest task of his life. (Wiesjahn, 1995)

After McCutchan's death in 1993, an anonymous friend donated $300,000 to the University for a football stadium, with the stipulation it be named Arad McCutchan Stadium.

SOURCE

Johnson, Dave. (2005, March 15). The Perfect Season. *The Evansville Courier Press.*

McCutchan, Arad. Vertical Files. Archives. Naismith Memorial Basketball Hall of Fame. Springfield, MA.

Wiesjahn, Lisa (1995, January 8). Robes, Orange Uniforms Part of McCutchan Legacy. *The Evansville Courier.*

Wiesjahn, Lisa (1995, January 8). Identifying Bodies was 'Hardest Task of Life' for McCutchan. *The Evansville Courier.*

LESSONS FROM THIS LEGEND...

JUMP BALLS

By Arad McCutchan

Authors' Note: This article, taken from the Winter, 1974 NABC Basketball Bulletin is a reflection of Coach McCutchan's attention to detail and emphasis on fundamentals. At the time, more held balls occurred but they are still important, though fewer, in number, today.

From records kept at Evansville, we have six to seven "jump balls" per game. As the quality of officiating decreases, the number increases to as high as 15-20 per game.

Since scoring averages about one point per possession (more on offense, less on defense), the value of the jump ball is two points. Therefore, any jump where possession is gained is an advantage of two points for Evansville.

RULE #1

Tap the bottom of the ball with your fingertips. Most jumpers in a held-ball situation tap the side of the ball. We ask our players to tap near the bottom of the ball, thus gaining 3-6 inches of effective tapping of the ball. Players will feel they can't tap it far enough, but we feel it can be done easily and effectively near the bottom of the ball.

RULE #2

Place your biggest non-jumper on the circle towards your basket directly in front of the jumper. This allows your best jumper/rebounder to move toward the tapped ball, angle jump to it with two hands, and gain possession. In addition, a scoring play can be designed with right and left lanes being filled upon the tap to this person who can turn and pass to the cutters filling the lanes.

RULES #3

Tap with the arm that is further away from the opponent's jumper. The jumper's body should face the sideline, and he attempts to get his head under the ball, bringing the near hand down, and tapping with the far hand. This also increases the jumper's effective jumping height and prevents the opponent jumper from getting to the ball. This is a difficult, unnatural skill that must be taught and practiced.

RULE #4

Use the momentum of the far leg (swing and stamp the leg before the jump) and the swing upward of both arms. Effective jumping height also depends upon changing forward momentum of legs and arms into the upward momentum of the whole body.

RULE #5

Tap over the referee's head or to an open spot where you have two player's with no opponent between. This is another option if you choose not to tap to your next best jumper/rebounder.

The jump ball is a small part of the game, but practice and perfection of these skills can make a difference—maybe a few points per game.

SOURCE

McCutchan, Arad. (1974, Winter). Jump Balls. *NABC Basketball Bulletin.*

COACHING THOUGHTS

By Arad McCutchan

Authors' Note: Arad McCutchan presented the following address at the National Association of Basketball Coaches Convention at the Shoreham Hotel in Washington D.C. on March 18, 1966.

Gentlemen, I am not at all sure you will remember anything I say here this afternoon, but I hope you will allow me just a moment to tell you one thing that I hope will help you remember me a little better.

When I grew up in the country, my name was A-rad, not Arid, as I have been introduced, and you might wonder why I want to make a point out of this. In the past few years, we have been what we think is successful in basketball, and I want to be identified with something successful. If you have watched television as I have in the past several years, you realize that we have a lot of problems we can't solve, including that of underarm perspiration. With that in mind, how would you like to be introduced as ARID?

At clinics, I have heard one speaker get up and say, "A good defense is the finest offense you can have;" and the next speaker gets up and states, "A good offense is the best defense you can have." We keep records on this. Through the years we have statistics, based on Keller out of Ohio, that tells us how many times the ball changes hands. You do realize that you are going to have the ball about every other time. It seems to me, then, that we need to spend half of our time on offense and half on defense, and the idea that one overshadows the other is not true.

STATIONS

I would like to start by talking about "stations" as a way of working with your team in the fall. It is our way of practicing the important skills, and we have approximately 22 stations. I assign two players to each station. At these various stations, we have such things as isometrics, leg lifts, free-throw shooting, and field goal shooting using the golf idea where there are marked spots and we record them each time. We have a McCall's Rebounder where we do four or five things on that. We have a Tip-omatic.

We also have a "defensive rack" that helps keep your players in the defensive stance. I got a local builder to construct mine. It has a roof on four legs so the roof will be over the player's head while he plays defense. It is my theory that the head must move on a straight level and the knees must remain bent. I arrange my players by height and make the roof approximately two inches higher than the tallest player. This forces players to stay low in the defensive stance. We do this approximately two to three minutes a day.

We use rope jumping to improve our foot quickness. Additionally, I want players to work on hand position and hand quickness. Arms and hands must be active and held upward.

In a two-minute time period at each station and 22 stations, I can give my players a 44-minute workout. Then if you use another 40 minutes or so, you've got practice lasting one hour and half. I think it is our responsibility with college boys that we do not keep them away from their studies three hours a day. So our practices, except when we have scrimmages, generally last within this time frame.

MAN-TO-MAN DEFENSE

Now I want to move over to defense and talk about what we try to teach. I have been kidded a good deal about the fact that I think the word "zone" is profane, and I have not in my 20 years of college coaching to this point used a zone defense except to press with occasionally. I have never used a zone that would fall back under the basket. It is not any real feeling against it other than I don't know how to get the job done with it. So we work real hard on the man-to-man and use zone concepts within that framework.

FLAILING YOUR ARMS ON DEFENSE

Probably 25 to 30 years ago, I saw Chuck Taylor demonstrate the importance of faking prior to passing. He would first bring someone up from the audience and have that person attempt to keep their hand with his. It was impossible. Taylor's hand was always quicker.

It is an important concept that is often overlooked. He explained that a passer, by using a fake, could get the defender's hand out of the passing lane. A fake down results in the defender's hand being lowered, and then the passer can throw over. It can be done the opposite way; fake up and throw under.

LESSONS FROM THIS LEGEND...

This, coupled with the advice of Hank Iba, is crucial to all coaches. I heard Coach Iba at the first clinic I attended after becoming head coach at Evansville, and I have never forgotten his words. He said that coaches should look for a style of play that will enable them to beat all the teams they are supposed to and a few they are not supposed to.

Then what I am saying is, if the player out here in front of me is equal to me and I am playing defense, he is going to be able to fake me and get that ball past me. So what we want our men doing is flailing their arms wildly, and moving in as close to the ballhandler as we think we dare. We use this concept in all of our defenses. When our opponent takes the ball out after a made basket, we want to be right up there close to the out-of-bounds line, flailing our arms. There are pretty good odds that the ball might hit the defender's hands. We also pressure all shots. I want my defensive players to attempt to block every shot. I always tell my players to block the shot so that it hits the nose of the shooter. If each of my players block one shot in a game, I know that we will win.

In order to practice this, we spend 20 minutes every day doing a drill we call three-on-three. It is a defensive drill, and I do not pay much attention to what the three offensive players are doing. I want the defenders to get through screens and flail their arms and try to block every shot. We generally work 10 minutes, with the idea of staying with your man, don't switch, and don't help anybody else. The basic principle is stopping your man and getting through.

During the next 10 minutes is when we practice a switch every time two men cross. Our emphasis is to jump up and make him go back the other way on the switch. We have learned not to be too upset about the fact that the screener may roll. If you go up there and flail those arms, the possibility of passing to the player rolling is not nearly as good as it is if you just switch and follow along.

MAINTAIN DEFENSIVE PRESSURE

After every free throw, we will cover you tight man-to-man defense all over the floor. We want to fight you and make it difficult to get the ball across the time line. I have seen quite a few teams that seem happy once they have gotten over the centerline, and I think this may be the best time to try and steal the ball.

ALWAYS SEE THE BALL

We find a lot of players, after they make a basket, will turn and run down the court with their eyes on the floor. I call them "hard-board examiners." We do a lot of preaching to our players that they must see the ball one hundred per cent of the time. This means both on offense and defense.

BENCH ROBES

One of the things that we have been doing for 10 years, and we haven't been copied on, is our bench robe. It is a complete robe that is ankle length. Last week in our tournament, I saw a coach call for a substitute, and it was two minutes before the player could get out of his sweat pants and report to the scorer's table. In this time, several baskets may be scored. Most of us, at some time or another, sit on metal chairs, and if you come out of a game hot and sit down on a metal chair, you know the shock. We think robes are a real good idea.

HAIR CUTS

One of the other little ideas that I think helps is this: I have a barber friend who will come to my house every two weeks and cut the boys' hair. It saves a little money, and the boys look a lot better on the floor.

CLOSING

Several years ago I heard another coach say this, and I would like to close with this remark. Have you ever finished your practice and said, 'We had a bad practice today?' Probably all of us are guilty of it, but we need to examine somebody at this point. There are 10 or 15 players out there on the floor, and you come away saying, 'We had a bad practice.' One, two, three, or four of those kids may have had a bad practice, but if everybody had a bad practice, *who* had the bad practice? The answer of course is you, and you had better examine yourself.

SOURCE

McCutchan, Arad. (1966, March 18). National Association of Basketball Coaches Convention, Washington D.C.

LEGACY OF
Al McGuire

- Led Marquette to the 1977 NCAA National Championship in the final game of his coaching career.

- Regarded as one of the great "bench coaches" of all time.

- Designed the triangle-and-two defense while an assistant coach at Dartmouth.

- Possessed a charismatic and engaging personality and had multiple interests outside of basketball.

- Described by his peers as eccentric, controversial, philosophical, street smart, and candid.

- Spoke in his own language, called "McGuireisms," using quick quips and New York street wisdom.

AL McGUIRE

"I've never blown a whistle, looked at a film, worked at a blackboard or organized a practice in my life."
—Al McGuire

BIOGRAPHY

Born: September 7, 1928 in New York, NY

Died: January 26, 2001

Inducted into the Naismith Memorial Basketball Hall of Fame in 1992

Al McGuire coached at Marquette University and Belmont Abbey and had a career record of 404-144. The charismatic McGuire led Marquette to eleven post-season appearances including the 1977 NCAA championship and the 1970 NIT title. The AP, UPI, and USBWA named McGuire National Coach of the Year in 1971 following Marquette's 28-1 season. In 1974, he was named the NABC Coach of the Year. At Belmont Abbey, McGuire led his teams to five postseason tournament appearances. McGuire began his coaching career as an assistant to Hall of Fame coach "Doggy" Julian at Dartmouth. As a player, McGuire led St. John's to a 65-19 record, including three NIT appearances and one NCAA appearance. He captained the 1951 team that finished third in the NIT. He also played professionally with the New York Knicks and Baltimore Bullets. McGuire was enshrined in the Naismith Memorial Basketball Hall of Fame in 1992. His brother Dick, a star player in the NBA, was inducted into the Hall of Fame as a player a year later. They are the only brother duo residing in the Naismith Basketball Hall of Fame.

Al McGuire...

Al McGuire grew up in Queens and often teamed up with his brothers, John and Dick, on the basketball court near his family's tavern in Rockaway. It became known as "McGuire's court." Dick was the more gifted basketball player and later became one of the flashiest playmakers of his era during an eleven-year NBA career with the New York Knicks and the Detroit Pistons. Al attended St. John's Prep and was all-city in football and basketball.

Al followed his brother Dick to St. John's University and appeared in three NIT tournaments and one NCAA tournament. After his senior year, Al was not selected in the NBA draft but talked New York Knicks coach Joe Lapchick into a tryout. He made the team and played for the Knicks for three years. Al's brother Dick was a star player for New York during that time. Before the 1954-55 season, Al was traded to the Baltimore Bullets, but the team folded 14 games into the season and McGuire's professional career was over.

Hall of Fame coach "Doggy" Julian hired McGuire in 1954 at Dartmouth, where he coached the freshman team for two seasons. McGuire's first head-coaching job was at Belmont Abbey in North Carolina. After leading his team to five postseason tournaments, McGuire accepted the head basketball coaching position at Marquette University.

Al asked Marquette's assistant coach Hank Raymonds to stay on the staff. Before McGuire returned to North Carolina to gather his possessions for the move, he surprised his new assistant by giving him a blank check and telling him, "Go buy my house for me." (Raymonds, 2003). Raymonds bought a house that McGuire lived in until his death in 2001.

There were many words to describe Al McGuire. Eccentric. Controversial. Philosophical. Street fighter. Candid. Witty. But most notably, McGuire won basketball games doing things his way.

McGuire's teams won 79 percent of their games in his 13 years at Marquette. He led Marquette to 11 consecutive post-season tournaments, including a runner-up finish in the 1974 NCAA tournament and a national championship in 1977.

McGuire's basketball roots were firmly planted in the concrete courts of the New York City playgrounds. He would venture into the worst neighborhoods of the inner cities to find his players. McGuire said, "My rule was I wouldn't recruit a kid if he had grass in front of his house. That's not my world. My world was a cracked sidewalk."

McGuire called himself the "greatest kitchen recruiter in the world." McGuire said, "I grew up in the kitchen. I never got into the living room until somebody died. The drapes were always drawn, because the sun faded the furniture." (Castellano, 1980)

McGuire's teams exhibited his brashness and cockiness, which sometimes did not sit well with some of Marquette's rivals. Notre Dame's coach Johnny Dee once had his team hand Marquette starters mustard packs during the pre-game introduction and handshake.

Dean Smith, Hall of Fame coach from North Carolina, stated "Al never got enough credit for being a truly great coach, because he didn't use the same X's and O's as many other coaches did. Al was a maverick. He did it his way."

Hall of Fame coach Ray Meyer called McGuire "the best bench coach I ever coached against—the best I ever saw. Al was unorthodox, but he was usually right."

As a coach, McGuire developed teams that played tough defense and disciplined half-court offense. Marquette was annually one of the nation's top defensive teams in fewest points allowed per game. McGuire insisted that his team's defense was their offense. Marquette's defense forced opponents into turnovers and created scoring opportunities.

.....SCOUTING REPORT.....SCOUTING REPORT...

"I conceived the triangle-and-two defense on a train ride," said McGuire, "when I was the freshman coach at Dartmouth under "Doggy" Julian. We were going to play Holy Cross, who had Tom Heinsohn and a good back-court man. I told "Doggy" that they're 20 points better than we are. We started to work on the triangle-and-two, and then in the end, we didn't use it. I finally got to try it at Belmont Abbey, and it's been a part of our defensive system ever since."

McGuire's message to all his players never changed: You must use the game of basketball to better yourself. Don't let basketball use you. He stressed the importance of making the most of opportunities.

Bo Ellis who led Marquette to the 1977 NCAA championship called McGuire "a caring man, a giving man, and a major influence in my life. He was a disciplinarian, a motivator, a father figure, a teacher, and a fighter."

Tom Crean, the current coach at Marquette, said that McGuire was a unique individual who taught many life lessons to those who came in contact with him. "The impact he had on people will go on forever," stated Crean. "Al had a unique way of making you feel better about yourself. The highlight of my coaching career is the year-and-a-half friendship that I had with him."

McGuire retired from coaching at the age of 48 and became one of the country's most colorful sports commentators. He often seemed to be speaking in his own language with his quick quips and New York street wisdom. The following are examples of "McGuireisms" that became part of the sport's vocabulary:

1. Aircraft carrier—a dominant big man
2. Seashells and balloons—those times in life when everything is joyful and beautiful
3. Thoroughbred—a gifted athlete
4. Dance-hall player—one short on talent, but big on effort
5. Checkerboard—black-white relationships
6. Dunkirk—a disaster or extremely poor team performance
7. Uptown—post-season tournament invitation
8. Zebras—referees
9. White-knuckler—a close game
10. French pastry—a player or game with style
11. Back-room lawyers—professional agents
12. Curtain time—game time
13. Cupcake—an easy opponent
14. Memos and pipes—college administrators
15. Whistle-blower—a coach who uses a lot of drills and likes his team to wear look-alike sport coats.

But as much as McGuire was known because of basketball, he had a wide variety of interests outside the game. "Al almost didn't want to be labeled as a coach," said Rick Majerus, McGuire's former assistant. "He wanted his life to be more expansive, rather than the one-dimensional box that most coaches have a tendency to put themselves into. He would go off into these tangents. He went the photography tangent. He went the travel tangent. He took me to my first play. He had a great intellectual curiosity." (Wolfley, 2001)

McGuire was committed to helping charitable projects. He started "Al's Run," a five-mile run in Milwaukee with proceeds benefiting Children's Hospital of Wisconsin. In the 15 years that the run carried his name, the event raised a total of 2.9 million dollars. McGuire also served on the President's Council on Physical Fitness and Sports.

Longtime assistant Hank Raymonds (2003) said, "Al loved the limelight, but by nature, he was a loner. He liked to go on his motorcycle. In fact on the afternoon of the 1977 NCAA championship game, Al was off riding a motorcycle. He didn't get back until close to game time. He liked to take walks. He liked to think. There was a big contrast on the court and off the court. And what people saw was not the real Al McGuire. The real Al McGuire was a compassionate man. He always kept his word. He liked to do little things for people, whether it be a janitor or an executive."

SOURCE

Castellano, Joe. (1980, April 12). McGuire really a bananas man. *St. Louis Globe-Democrat*.

Crean, Tom. Interview with Ralph Pim, November 13, 2003.

McGuire, Al. Vertical Files, Archives. Naismith Memorial Basketball Hall of Fame. Springfield, MA

Raymonds, Hank. Interview with Ralph Pim, July 17, 2003.

Wolfley, Bob. (2001, January 26). Al McGuire, Marquette coach, dies at 72. *Milwaukee Journal Sentinel*.

BASKETBALL AND LIFE

By Al McGuire

Every coach must be himself. Here are some of the things that I feel are important in life as well as in the game of basketball. Only take what fits your personality and your style of coaching.

LIVE IN THE MOMENT

When I was 12 or 13 year old, I was down at the beach, body-riding the waves. I came home for lunch, and my grandmother fixed me a triple sandwich on fried bread with catsup. I loved them, and I used to eat them all the time. When I finished, there was this big beautiful yellow banana. She said, "Alfie, take the banana." And I said, "No Granny, I want it, but I'll take a pass." She said, "Why?" And I said, "I want it, but if I eat the banana, I'll have to stay out of the water for an hour because of cramps." I rushed back to the beach. The wind kicked up, and it got too cold to swim. I sat on the boardwalk stairs looking out at the ocean, too young to understand what I was thinking. But I thought, it's too cold to go swimming; I wish I had eaten the banana. When I was 21, I thought about life and finally said to myself, "I will eat the banana." Live in the moment that you are in. Make your life exciting. Do what you have to do, as long as you don't hurt people.

DREAM BIG

Everyone must dream. I don't care what your dreams are, but dream big. Want something. Don't let things pass you by. Don't get caught in the corner. Don't be another guy going down the street and going nowhere. Get on the top shelf. Touch the Camelot, the Shangri-La, and that type of stuff. Live for the moment.

There are two ways to travel in life. One is with the eagles in the mountains. The other is at the nauseous level of your feet; you can play handball against the curb, you're so small.

FEAR OF FAILURE

Most people in our profession are afraid they might be wrong. I can understand this. I'm wrong too, almost all the time. But I can't wait until the fifth time-out to make a correction. I can't wait until they chart it or take a picture of it. When a coach sees something, he can't hold anything back. Don't be embarrassed. Don't be afraid to be wrong. You're not an executive who can postdate a memo. What you do as a coach is out there in the open. There is no equity in your profession. You have to accept that. It's a very, very manly type of pressure. When you win a national championship or a state championship in high school, you have got one-year equity. You have one year of grace; you can't let it pass by.

Don't fear failure. Get out of the shallow water. Take the tide out. There is no problem if you go out and come back without a fish. The only disgrace in life is not going after it. If you go out and don't catch the fish, what's the difference? But you must go out. It's a beautiful, beautiful life.

BE YOURSELF

Be yourself. All the X's and O's are not worth it. You've got to like the person who you are. I always liked being Al McGuire. I didn't want to be a Bart Starr, a Mickey Mantle, or a Joe Louis. I just always liked my way of living. There are a lot of people who didn't like it, but I always enjoyed it.

DO WHAT YOU THINK IS RIGHT

You're all going to leave your profession. The moment will come when you have to gently pack coaching away—everyone else had to do it so why not you? No one can keep it up. Enjoy it while you're at it. Do what you think is right. Don't try to please the administration. They will jump ship on you if they need to. Your loyalty should be to your family first, your players second, and your school third.

STAY TOGETHER IN THE COACHING PROFESSION

One of the things I am most proud of in my coaching career is that I think I started a little more love between the coaches. I remember going to a major conference tournament, and all the big-time coaches refused to associate with each other. This has been changing, and in the past seven or eight years, we've seen coaches showing much more consideration for each other. So stay together in your profession, because it's certain that none of your superiors will help you. No one can help you but yourself. You are born alone, and you die alone. Don't try to climb over anybody in your attempt to get a better position. Do the best you possibly can with the material you have and without fear.

GIVE NO EXCUSE - ACCEPT NO EXCUSE

All you have to do in life is to give no excuse and accept no excuse. I don't care about the 106-degree temperature. I don't care about a sprained ankle. You either win or lose the game. And you cannot have indecision in your program.

LESSONS FROM THIS LEGEND...

I didn't allow any fooling around on the court. You talk about disciplined teams. The most disciplined team ever on the court was Marquette University. We didn't have a fast break all the years I was there. You want to thrill me, do it out-of-bounds. No bad shots. No surprises. You've got to be dictatorial but always pick them up before the end of practice.

ELIMINATE THE FIFTH COLUMN

The fifth column is the column from within. The fifth column is internal jealousy and selfishness. This must be eliminated. It is the cancer that destroys teams. Get that cancer out before it grows. The competition is not the problem. The problem is from within.

I try to teach players in a rough way to avoid jealousy. You have to make them work together and the only way to have teamwork is to eliminate jealousy. Eliminating jealousy is the answer; it's the key to the game, so you've got to work on it. All I really did was work on the minds of the players and hope that we succeeded together. If we all went uptown together, it was all worthwhile.

MAKE FIVE PEOPLE ONE

All I ever did at Marquette University was to make five people one. Sometimes you have a situation on your team in which one guy constantly throws the ball to a buddy. They come to practice together and leave together like a husband and wife. You must break up the husband and wife act on your team. All teams have this husband and wife act, and you must watch them closely. A lot of times this happens subconsciously. I

don't care. They have to knock it off. If they don't break up this act, I let one go early or rearrange the locker room. Don't allow your lockers to sit there for the school year with the same guy going to the same spot. This is how cliques form. It's up to you to watch these things and to take care of them.

KEEP COACHING SIMPLE

Keep things simple. We try to get too complicated much of the time. When the national anthem was played, I'd say to myself "Keep it simple, stupid." Don't get complicated. You forget the obvious when you try to force knowledge into young people who can't absorb our knowledge. Give them only what they can absorb.

ARE YOU AN OFFENSIVE OR DEFENSIVE COACH?

You must know whether you are an offensive or a defensive coach. You can't be both, and you can't please everybody. I was a defensive coach. My reasons were: (1) if you practice defense, you know what you are doing; and (2) defense is like water. It finds it level. It is there day-in and day-out. Plus, when I played, I couldn't shoot, so I taught defense.

YOU MUST ACT THE PART OF A LEADER

You are the leader and must set the example. Don't let your players see you tight. They pick up on it, and then they get tight. It's like free throws. One player misses, and they all start to miss. The rain barrel becomes a teacup.

You must set the example for your people. As a coach, you must have no indecision—none! That's why at the end of the game, when it's prime time, you must have automatic moves. For 23 years, if the opposing coach called a timeout with 10 or 15 seconds left in the game, I'd automatically go to a combination defense, such as a box-and-one or a triangle-and-two. If the score was tied, and we were at home, we drove to the basket for the shot. If the score was tied, and we had the ball on the road, we went for the fifteen-foot jump shot. I did that because of the subconscious of the official. At home, he's not going to call me for charging, on the road he is.

I have no problem knowing who the boss is. I know I am the boss. I know when the score is 62-62, everybody will be quiet, and I will make the decision on what to do. I am not trying to prove to anyone that I am running the show. If you've got to prove you're the boss, you're not the boss.

KNOW YOUR PLAYERS

The only reason I yell at a player is because he has talent. If I didn't think he had talent, I would not yell at him. It would be a mortal sin if I didn't get the talent out of a person. I had a player who was the nicest young man that I had ever met in my life. I had to hurt him. I had to hurt him because the guy played without knowing the score. To him everything was beautiful. He was so nice that all he wanted to do was play. That's all right if a player doesn't have talent, but when a player has talent, it was my obligation to get him to produce. Just because you have ability doesn't mean that you are going to produce or reach a certain level. You must study your players to know

LESSONS FROM THIS LEGEND...

what is the best for each particular person so that you can get the most out of his talent.

ALWAYS LEAVE THE DOOR OPEN WITH YOUR PLAYERS.

Never give them an either-or. That's the first step of insanity. It's like ice fishing. Always try to leave a crack so both of you can get out of a situation with dignity. Remember, cracks get bigger. Don't accept them. Only accept what you want.

ELIMINATE SURPRISES

You want no surprises in a game. You tell the players, "You can do what you want off the floor, but on it, I am the discipline." That's why I could let a player yell at me on the sideline. When he stepped back onto the playing court, he did what he was supposed to do.

PLAY THE GAME TO WIN

If you don't see a fish in a poker game, get up and leave because you're the fish. Know yourself. Remember, you drive at home, pull up on the road. The first thing you decide in a game is whether the official has a quick or slow whistle.

They are three crucial times in a game: 1) the first three minutes; 2) the last three minutes; and 3) the first three minutes of the second half. Always make sure your team is warmed up properly before the game and at half.

NEVER TALK TO A PARENT

Never talk to a parent, because it only leads to trouble. When I signed a player I'd say to the parents, "The next time that you will see me smile is when your son graduates." And that's the way it was. A parent can only think of their son or daughter. I had a player whose father was a cookie salesman. After one game, he came up to me complaining about his son's lack of playing time. I told him, "I don't sell cookies, and I don't know anything about cookies. You don't coach basketball, and you don't know anything about basketball. Leave me alone."

COACHES ARE THE LAST OF THE COWBOYS

A lot of us go into coaching because we don't grow up. Coaches are the last of the cowboys. I got out of coaching because now to be a cowboy, you have to work at it.

DON'T MAKE THE GAME OF BASKETBALL YOUR MISTRESS

We treat coaching as a mistress. We neglect our families. We all want to improve our station in life. We keep trying to advance, and sometimes find ourselves running toward an impossible goal. I did it myself. I'm not saying everyone else is wrong. I was wrong. Moving my family down to North Carolina—why? I was running toward my mistress. Basketball was my mistress. Basketball was my world. Be careful. It is a beautiful thing you are building as a coach, but don't get it all mixed up. You have to take care of your home first.

SOURCE

McGuire, Al. (1982). Basketball Reflections. *Medalist Flashback Notebook.*

McGuire, Al. (1981). Basketball and Life. *Medalist Flashback Notebook.*

McGuire, Al. (1976, Fall). Thoughts on Coaching. *The Basketball Bulletin.*

LEGACY OF
Dr. James Naismith

- Invented the game of basketball and its 13 original rules in 1891 at Springfield College.

- Preached the doctrine known as "Muscular Christianity," a belief that physical activity enhances the mind, body, and spirit.

- Strongly opposed the suggestion of getting a patent on the game and did not profit financially from his invention.

- Regarded his invention as a mere step in a career devoted to helping mankind enjoy leisure time.

- Remembered as a kind, softhearted, intelligent professor who truly cared about the welfare of his students.

DR. JAMES NAISMITH

"In basketball there is no place for the egotist."
—Dr. James Naismith

BIOGRAPHY

Born: November 6, 1891 in Almonte, Ontario, Canada

Died: November 28, 1939

Inducted into the Naismith Basketball Hall of Fame in 1959

James Naismith received his B.A. degree in 1887 from McGill University and was named the Best All-Around

Athlete at the school. He participated in soccer, rugby, track, lacrosse, and tumbling. Naismith eventually

earned four degrees in the diverse fields of philosophy, religion, physical education, and medicine. He was

first and foremost a physical educator and taught at McGill University, Springfield College, the YMCA of

Denver, and the University of Kansas. His career goal was to leave the world a little better than what he found

it. Naismith invented the game of basketball in 1891 at the International YMCA Training School, which is

now called Springfield College. He was given the task of creating an indoor game in order to provide college

students an athletic alternative during the winter months. As the game's popularity grew, Naismith did not

seek publicity or attention. He attended basketball's debut as an Olympic sport at the 1936 Berlin Games.

To honor his historic invention, Naismith's name adorns the Basketball Hall of Fame.

James Naismith...

James Naismith was born in 1861 and his parents died when he was eight years old. He was raised by his bachelor uncle and older sister in the farming country of Almonte, Ontario, Canada. Naismith worked the farm with his uncle but also proved to be quite an athlete in the different games played by his peers.

In 1883, Naismith left Almonte to study for the ministry at McGill College, Montreal. One evening, while watching the football (rugby) team practice, Naismith was recruited to join the team. His decision to join the team led to a career choice that eventually changed the course of sport history. The turning point occurred when one of his teammates who used profanity during a football game later apologized to him for the indiscretion. Naismith concluded from the experience that there might be another way other than preaching to combine his passion for helping mankind and his love for athletics.

Naismith made the decision not to enter the ministry after talking to the director of the YMCA in Montreal. "In our conversation," Naismith said, "I brought up the point that I thought that there might be other effective ways of doing good besides preaching." (Padwe, 1970). The director told Naismith about the International YMCA Training School, which is now Springfield College. After graduation from McGill, Naismith enrolled at Springfield.

At Springfield, Naismith had the opportunity to meet Dr. Luther Gulick, the dean of the physical education department. Dr. Gulick was a dynamic young man who shared with Naismith the doctrine known as Muscular Christianity, a belief that "proper cultivation of the body could further, rather than hinder, proper mental, and spiritual growth." (Young, 1996)

Naismith was an athletic and robust man who took great pride in presenting a picture of health and vitality. As a student at McGill, Naismith was named the school's best all-around athlete. He was very outspoken against things that he felt detrimental to a person's health and enjoyed participating in sports and recreational activities that aided the overall well-being of the body.

Naismith became a professor at Springfield College, and one of his colleagues was Amos Alonzo Stagg, the legendary football coach. The two of them created the first football helmet. It resembled a cotton stocking cap with a strap under the chin. Years later, Stagg credited basketball with the development of the forward pass in football.

In 1891, Naismith was a graduate at Springfield. He was given an assignment from Dr. Gulick to create an indoor game that provided physical exercise during the brutal New England winters and keep the male students out of trouble. After unsuccessful attempts of bringing outdoor games such as soccer and lacrosse inside, Naismith borrowed from various sports to develop the original 13 rules of basketball. Based on a childhood game called "Duck on a Rock," Naismith decided to have the ball tossed at a goal. A goal on the floor would be too easy to guard, so he planned to put boxes on the balcony railings. When the janitor couldn't find any boxes, peach baskets were used. The game proved to be an instant success with the class. The students wanted to call the new game "Naismith Ball" but the inventor wanted nothing to do with that name. It was finally decided to call it basketball.

News spread quickly of Naismith's invention. The game became popular both domestically and internationally because of its association with the YMCA Training School. The school's newspaper, which was the primary publication of the YMCA, printed a description of the game and the rules in January 1892. Graduates of the school introduced the game in YMCAs all over the world. Colleges and universities were slower to adopt the game, because many college coaches and physical educators were not familiar with the new sport. The game became more widely accepted once boys who learned the game at YMCAs started to enter college. Naismith was especially pleased that many theological schools took up the game because promoting Christian values was always the underlying vision for the new game.

In 1895, Naismith left Springfield to become the director of the YMCA in Denver. He also attended medical school and received his degree in 1898. Instead of practicing medicine, Naismith became the director of chapel and professor of physical education at the University of Kansas. He directed the physical education department until 1925 and continued to teach physical education classes until his retirement in 1937.

Naismith coached the Kansas basketball team from 1898 to 1907. One of his pupils, "Phog" Allen succeeded him as coach. Naismith attended nearly every Kansas home game but always remained an inconspicuous spectator. It was his belief that basketball did not need a coach because it was just a recreational game for the participants.

Naismith's life was dedicated to helping mankind. The fact that he invented a game that captured the fancy of both competitors and fans gave him less satisfaction than his 39 years of teaching at the University of Kansas. He regarded the game of basketball as a mere step in helping the physical condition of succeeding generations. Even though lawyers encouraged him to seek a patent on the game, he strongly opposed the suggestion and profited little from his invention.

Naismith was sponsored by the National Association of Basketball Coaches to witness basketball become an Olympic Sport at the 1936 Games held in Berlin. The fundraising effort to send him to the Olympics also included finances to buy the Naismith's a home in Lawrence, a testimony to the few materialistic things possessed by the family.

The kind, softhearted, and considerate professor was stricken by a cerebral hemorrhage and died in 1939.

SOURCE

Naismith, James. Vertical Files, Archives. Naismith Memorial Basketball Hall of Fame. Springfield, MA.

Padwe, Sandy. (1970). *Basketball's Hall of Fame*. Englewood Cliffs, NJ: Prentice-Hall.

Swalgin, Kenneth. (2001, Fall). "Duck on the Rock" - The Origins and Mysteries of Basketball." *Journal of Kinesiology*.

Young, D.C. (1996). *The Modern Olympics: A Struggle for Revival*. Baltimore: John Hopkins University Press.

THE ORIGIN OF BASKET BALL

By James Naismith

Authors' Note: Dr. James Naismith presented the following address at Springfield College on January 5, 1932.

I have been asked to speak on the origin of basketball and I feel a little embarrassed about this because it is more or less personal, but wherever I go, no matter how fine a talk or lecture I may give, always two questions are asked of me.

1. How did you come to think of it?
2. Has it changed much since that time?

In order to get an idea of the origin of the game, it is necessary for us to know something of the situations in which we were at that time. I look at the young people coming into physical education today with all the facilities for work and with all the different sports; in fact, we have come to the point where a great deal of physical education is games and the policy of many institutions is games.

In 1890, when I first entered this institution *(Authors' Note: Naismith is referring to what is now called Springfield College)* there were practically no games with the exception of football, baseball, and track; football in the fall, baseball and track in the spring. Soccer was played very little. From the time that we stopped playing football in the fall until baseball began in the spring, we had nothing but work on the horse, buck, and different pieces of apparatus, along with calisthenics. I wonder what men in physical education today would do with that limited sphere to work in; how would we get along? That was the condition that we had, and we all felt, Drs. Seerley, Clark, Gulick, and Stagg, that we should get together and talk it over. We needed some sort of game that

would be interesting and could be played indoors. We had three games: three-deep, line ball, and Dr. Gulick's game called cricket.

We had a seminar in which we discussed these things quite frequently. It was a seminar in psychology, and one day we discussed inventions, and Dr. Gulick made this statement, "There is nothing new under the sun, but all new things are simply a recombination of the factors of existing things." We simply recombined the factors of the old and made the new.

After thinking it over, I said to Dr. Gulick, "If that is true, we can go to work to invent a new game." Nothing much more was said about it, but Dr. Stagg said he assigned that as our home work for the next meeting, but no one brought in any record at all.

There was a class of secretarial men, twenty to twenty-five years of age. Most of them played on the football team, and when the winter season came and they were put on the parallel bars, etc. they had no interest in learning it, and there was no fun in it. Dr. Clark, who is present today, one of the finest athletes and gymnasts we had in the institution, a graduate of Williams, a medical man, everything in the world that could make a man efficient in work of this kind, found the same condition. It was not individuals at all, but existing conditions.

At a faculty meeting Dr. Gulick spoke and told how different it was to handle these men. He made another statement saying, "The difficulty is with that particular group of men what we want is recreative work; something that will please them and something they will want to do."

I told Dr. Clark that if he would play games, he would get the attention of these fellows. After a little while, Dr. Gulick said, "Naismith, I wish you would take charge of that class." If I ever tried to back out of anything, I did then. I did not want to do it. I had charge of a group interested in boxing, wrestling, fencing, and swimming, and I was perfectly satisfied with my work. Dr. Gulick said he wanted me to do it. I thought Dr. Gulick had imposed on me by giving me something I did not want to do and compelling me to do it. As we walked along the hall, talking about it, he said, "Naismith, this would be a good time for you to invent that new game you said you could." I closed my fist, but I saw a peculiar twinkle in his eye, which seemed to say "put up or shut up."

He said I could do two things: 1) I could invent a game; and 2) the game had to be fun. Whether or not he realized the importance of what he did at the time, I don't know, but it turned out to be the best thing that could have been done.

I took that class—neither in very good humor, nor grace. We tried to play football indoors, but broke the arms and legs of the players. It proved to be too rough. And it was not long before the boys rebelled against it. We then tried soccer, but broke all the windows. Then we tried lacrosse and broke up the apparatus. We found that this did not work.

I sat at my desk one day, scratching my head, trying to work something out. This thought came to me: They all like to play football. Why can't we play it indoors? — Because it is too rough. Why is it rough? — Because we tackle. Why do we tackle? — Because we run the ball. If we did not run

LESSONS FROM THIS LEGEND...

with the ball, there would be no need for tackling. We need a game to play indoors ——— I had it!! Just by asking myself those few questions, I think that it is one of the biggest things in the world today.

If we don't let them run with the ball, what are we going to do? Think of a goal of some kind. In soccer and lacrosse, we had a perpendicular goal and a goal keeper, but the difficulty with that was in order to make a goal you had to throw the ball with as much speed as possible. The harder you threw, the more chance there was for you to make a goal. That again made for roughness. I thought of the underhand swing. That is a negative rule, and negative rules do not work efficiently.

I was stumped for a while. By and by, I began to think of a little game I had played near Affleck's home—Duck on the Rock. We found a rock two feet high and two feet across. Each one took a stone about the size of his fist. One put his stone on the rock, and the rest of us got behind a line and tried to knock it off. We would throw our stones as hard as we could, and if we happened to hit it, it was all right, but if we missed it, we went way down. Once in a while, we threw the ball in such a way that it would knock his off and come back again, and we would walk up and get it.

I think I have it! Instead of throwing the ball straight for the goal, let us throw it in a curve, and we cannot throw it hard. You must take your time and use skill instead of power and speed. I first thought of putting a mark on the floor; just a circle, and use that for the goal. But then, I thought if the goal was put above his head and no one can stand in it, you would have a chance of making a goal once in a while. I decided that the goal would be horizontal and high in the air.

My next thought was how was I going to put the ball in play? I used Gulick's idea of taking parts of other games. In polo, the ball is in the center and the teams line up at both ends and rush for the ball. There

would be a mix-up in the center of the floor when that happened so that idea was thrown out. I recalled in playing English rugby that when the ball goes out-of-bounds, two forward lines line up at right angles to the side line where the ball goes out; the umpire stands outside, back of the line, and throws the ball in between the two lines. But I remembered that when we jumped for the ball, the elbows interfered and there was much roughness. If we took two men out of that group and put them in the center, there would be no roughness. I did not appreciate the ingenuity of American boys, for I have seen some pretty rough things done. We threw it from the outside in on the floor. Then I thought that the ball must be thrown in such a way as to fall between two center players.

We went to work and jotted down some of these thoughts. There was 13 of them—until that time thirteen was an unlucky number for me, but since then it has changed. I had these typed and carried down and pinned them up on the bulletin board. As I was going down with a soccer ball in my hand, as I had concluded we would want a round light ball, I met Pop Stebbins. I said, "Have you got a couple of boxes eighteen inches square?" He said, "No, but I have a couple of old peach baskets." He brought them up, and I nailed one at each end of the gallery—ten feet from the floor. If the gallery had been eleven feet high, the goals probably would have been at that height today.

I got things ready, and the class came down. Frank Mahan, a big burly Irishman who played tackle on the football team, came down among the first, and my mind was pretty well disturbed. I had a soccer ball in my hand, two peach baskets on the wall, and an idea in my head. I did not know how to go about it. My future, as I looked at it then, depended on the throw of the ball. When Mahan came down and looked up and saw one basket, then he looked around and saw another one. "Humph," he said, "another new game." That was the attitude they all had, and they

were ready to scrap anything brought before them. They did not want to give in to me, but I called them up. There were eighteen men in the class. I was center on one side, Patton on the other. I tossed the ball between them, and I never had any more trouble with the class or the game. The class took to it, and the only difficulty I had was to drive them out when the hour closed.

There was a school not very far away. Our gymnasium was down in the basement, and the door opened onto the street. A number of schoolteachers used to come in and watch the boys play games and added incentive to playing. The regular hour was between 11 and 12. At the close of that hour every day, the girls would come in, and the boys would play for them. Soon there were as many as 100 people watching the game from the gallery. It was not long until some of the teachers came to me and asked why they could not play the game. I did not see any reason why they could not. I thought it was a good game and would be all right for them.

After consultation, they were given a certain hour to practice. You boys don't know what clothes the girls wore then—bustles, hoops, and high heels—and they played in them. It was not long until the stenographers of the school got up another team. Some of us young unmarried men got our sweethearts interested in it, and we got a ladies' faculty team. The girls asked me to umpire. I agreed to, but I didn't know as much about ladies as I do now. We got along nicely until I called a foul on one of the girls. She asked, "Did you call a foul on me?" She then told me where I came from, where I was going to, and what my character was! I tried to pacify her but couldn't do it. The only way was to toss up the ball, and then she had to fall into her place.

That girl was not different from other girls. They never had a chance to take part in any game where sportsmanship was required. It was something new for them. She had played some shuttlecock and a few other games similar to that. They had not even

LESSONS FROM THIS LEGEND...

played tennis. For a number of years the rules were adopted as unsportsmanlike conduct among women. This is not true today. Some of the finest sportsmanship has been exhibited in women's basketball games.

Going into physical education in 1890 was a very different proposition than it is now. When I decided to enter physical work and spoke to a young man whom I expected to be my brother-in-law, he asked, "What are you going to do now?" I replied, "I am going to Springfield and take up athletics." Then he said, "Athletics to the devil." When I first played football on the McGill team in 1883, a group of my chums got together and had a prayer meeting over me because I was playing on the varsity team. You would not realize that now, but it is a fact. The change of attitude is illustrated in a letter, which I received from the man who started that prayer meeting. He wrote, "In thinking over our old class I don't think any one has made a bigger contribution to the building of character than the one who invented basketball." People have a different outlook today regarding physical education than what it once was. Men had to enter that work against general opinion, and they had to have more or less of a missionary spirit in working out their ideas of what good could be done.

I hope you will pardon a personal experience, but it may help you. Way back in my college days, I was lying on the bed on Sunday and thought: What is this all about? What is life about? What are you going to do? What are you going to be? What motto will you hold up before you? I put up on the wall, not in writing, but in my mind this thought: "I want to leave the world a little bit better than I found it." This is the motto I had then, and it is the motto I have today.

The best definition of character I know is: It is that combination of reflexes within me, which determine how I shall act under unforeseen circumstances. The reflexes you build on the floor are going to be part of your character. The best illustration of this is: An old watchman was riding a horse through the main street close to the university, just as the students were going out. His hat blew off, and he couldn't very well get off the horse. I wondered what the students would do to this old man. How would they react to the situation? Two boys ran out from opposite sides of the street, and one of them got the hat and returned it to the owner. Those two boys were brothers, brought up in the same home, athletes of the finest type, track and football men. I thought what an opportunity there is for

men in physical education to develop those characters that will live with them through life.

That is what we are after. It is not the money we are going to get out of it. I had a man write me thirty years after saying, "I have just been thinking over things, and I am mighty glad I knew you."

I did not know I had any influence on him. It is your inner life, the things you do and say that will influence those fellows and make them men. I wish every one of you boys the pleasure not only of having a successful football team, but also of having a bunch of fellows come up and say, "I am glad I knew you. You have been a help in my life."

SOURCE

Naismith, James. (1932, January 5). The Origin of Basket Ball. Speech given Springfield College.

Naismith, James. Vertical Files, Archives. Naismith Memorial Basketball Hall of Fame. Springfield, MA.

LEGACY OF
Charles Martin "C.M." Newton

- Renowned as a builder of programs, both as a coach and as an administrator.

- Promoted integration and removed racial barriers at every school that he worked.

- During his reign as Chair of the Rules Committee, the 45-second shot clock, three-point shot, and coaches' box were implemented.

- Served as President of USA Basketball from 1992 to 1996 and was instrumental in the selection of the Original Dream Team in 1992.

- Compiled a 509-375 record during his 32-year coaching career.

- Played for Adolph Rupp at the University of Kentucky and was a member of the 1951 NCAA National Championship team.

CHARLES MARTIN "C.M." NEWTON

"The culture of sports teaches athletes and coaches to be takers. I've always tried to give back to the game that has been so good to me".
—Charles "C.M." Newton

BIOGRAPHY

Born: February 2, 1930 in Rockwood, TN

Inducted into the Naismith Basketball Hall of Fame in 2000

Charles Martin Newton, better known as C.M. Newton, attended the University of Kentucky and was a letterman on the Wildcat's 1951 National Championship basketball team. C.M. was also a star pitcher on Kentucky's baseball team and pitched five years in the New York Yankees' minor league system. From 1956 to 1989, Newton coached at Transylvania College, the University of Alabama, and Vanderbilt University and compiled 509-375 record. He led Alabama to SEC championships in 1974, 1975 and 1976 and appearances in four NIT and two NCAA Tournaments. He led Vanderbilt into the 1988 and 1989 NCAA Tournament. Newton became athletic director at the University of Kentucky in 1989 and is credited with hiring Bernadette Mattox, the school's first African-American women's basketball coach (1985) and Orlando "Tubby" Smith, the school's first African-American men's basketball coach (1997). Newton was President of USA Basketball from 1992 to 1996, when the U.S. Olympic Team went from college to professional players, and was instrumental in the selection of the original Dream Team in 1992.

Charles Martin "C.M." Newton...

C.M. Newton was an all-state performer in football, basketball, and baseball and won eleven letters while participating in sports at Fort Lauderdale High School in Florida. An important mentor in Newton's life was his high school basketball coach, Clois Caldwell. Newton was only ten years old when Caldwell took him under his wing. Caldwell encouraged C.M. to attend practice and go on road trips. They had a very special relationship during a period of time when Newton's father was struggling with his sobriety. Caldwell was an outstanding teacher/coach who commanded respect without raising his voice or swearing.

Newton wanted someday to play professional baseball, but there weren't too many schools that offered baseball scholarships at that time. Coach Caldwell wanted C.M. to look at Oklahoma A&M, Duke, Illinois, Kentucky, and Tennessee. Newton wanted to go to Tennessee because of his family's roots, but the Vols wouldn't recruit him as anything other than a football player. When C.M. visited Kentucky in June 1948, Kentucky was playing host to the Olympic Trials. "I couldn't have been in Lexington at a more exciting time, and I wanted to come to Kentucky and play in Coach Rupp's program after that experience," stated Newton. Another key factor was that the Wildcats were also going to let C.M. play baseball.

Under Coach Rupp in basketball and Paul "Bear" Bryant in football, Kentucky was in the midst of a golden era of athletics. "Coach Rupp and Coach Bryant were more alike than they were different," said Newton (2000). "They both motivated with fear. Heck, I stayed scared of Coach Rupp the whole time I was in school. Both were also sticklers for detail. I used to watch the football practices, and I probably learned as much about coaching basketball from Coach Bryant as I did from anybody. He emphasized situation practices, saving timeouts until the end of games, things like that. Coach Rupp emphasized fundamentals, pressure

defense, game preparation, and paying attention to little things. His practices were timed to the second and they were all business. He had a saying. 'Don't speak unless you can improve the silence,' and that's the way he ran our practices."

For a player to be successful under Rupp's reign, he had to be able to take Rupp's sarcasm and profanity. In one scrimmage, Newton was attempting to guard Kenny Rollins, who had been the captain of the "Fabulous Five" in 1948, and Rollins was just too quick for him. Finally Rupp had seen enough and took C.M. out and said in his sarcastic way, "Go sit down, Newton. You know what you remind me of? A Shetland pony in a stud-horse parade." (Newton, 2000).

"Playing for Coach Rupp was very, very difficult," stated Newton (2004), because he was a dictator, and he motivated by fear. Some players were able to overcome it, and some weren't," said Newton. "I wanted to please him so badly that it *did* bother me. But it taught me something that was useful to me later: You can't treat everybody the same way. Some players need to be patted on the back, and some need to be disciplined. Later, I saw a lot of guys who went into coaching who tried to be like Coach Bryant and Coach Rupp, but they failed. You've got to be yourself. And motivation by fear is not always the best way."

C.M. was a letterman on the 1951 Kentucky team that compiled a 32-2 record and won the NCAA championship. Newton roomed with Kentucky's center Bill Spivey, a 7-footer from Georgia who quickly developed into the nation's best big man. The basketball world was hit by a point-shaving scandal in 1951 that involved members of the Kentucky basketball team, including Spivey. What unfolded in the wake of the scandal drastically changed the life of C.M. Newton. C.M. received a phone call from Coach Rupp, telling him to call the athletic director at Transylvania College. It seems that officials from Transylvania were talking with former Kentucky player Walt Hirsch about their head-coaching

.....SCOUTING REPORT.....SCOUTING REPORT...

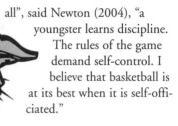

job until Hirsch was implicated in the scandal. This opened the door in the world of coaching for Newton. Even though C.M. had not graduated yet, his coaching career began as the head coach at Transylvania.

During Newton's 32 years in coaching, he guided Transylvania, Alabama, and Vanderbilt to 509 wins. He led Alabama to three SEC Championships (1974, 1975, 1976), two NCAA Tournaments and four National Invitation Tournaments. He directed Vanderbilt to the NCAA Tournament in 1988 and 1989. Newton became known as a builder of programs.

Newton became athletic director at Kentucky in 1989 and re-established integrity, honor, and class to a University that had been swimming in a pool of rules violations. He earned the reputation for doing the right thing.

C.M. promoted equality in college athletics and shattered racial barriers. He integrated his teams at Transylvania, recruited the first black player at Alabama, hired the first black coach at Kentucky, and hired Orlando "Tubby" Smith as the first black head men's basketball coach at Kentucky.

Newton served basketball in nearly every capacity imaginable – NABC Board of Directors, NCAA Basketball Rules Committee Chair, Officiating Committee, Tournament Committee Chair, USA Basketball President, and FIBA Central Board. A clear pattern of service and leadership emerged – not only did he serve basketball, but he rose to the top of the ladder and strongly influenced the game both as a coach and as an administrator.

Hall of Fame coach Bob Knight said, "There's nobody I've met in all of athletics whom I respect more or like more than C.M. He was one of the very best coaches of any era. He has gone on to be the very best administrator in all of college athletics, although there aren't that many great ones."

Newton believed that through the game of basketball, young people could learn valuable life lessons. "First of all", said Newton (2004), "a youngster learns discipline. The rules of the game demand self-control. I believe that basketball is at its best when it is self-officiated."

"Another important lesson is being able to handle winning," Newton said. "I think learning how to win is a more difficult lesson to learn than the losing. Being able to win graciously is an essential part of the game."

Newton believed the key person in promoting life lessons through basketball is the coach. The ability of a coach to lead and inspire is crucial. His expectations, demands, and coaching style set the tone for the entire program.

"Whenever I'm asked about my legacy, I don't know what to say," said Newton (2000). "If there is such a thing, it's up to others to decide, not me. I just hope that if and when I'm remembered, it will be as somebody who tried to make a difference as both a coach and an administrator. By that, I mean trying to be a mentor, as well as a coach. Caring about student-athletes as human beings, instead of just looking at them as a labor force whose main task is to win games and make money. Pushing them to get an education and teaching them how to live and be productive citizens, no matter whether they're going to be NBA players or insurance agents or farmers. If we are to maintain our integrity as educators, that always must be at the core of our philosophy."

C.M. Newton has been a winner his entire life and has won while playing by all the rules. Coach "Bear" Bryant described Newton perfectly when he said, "C.M. Newton is a winner, and that's important, but more than anything else, he wins or loses with class, and that's more important." (Newton, 2002)

SOURCE

Newton, C.M. Vertical Files, Archives. Naismith Memorial Basketball Hall of Fame. Springfield, MA.

Newton, C.M. (2000). *Newton's Laws*. Lexington: Host Communications.

Newton, C.M. Interview with Ralph Pim. September 10, 2004.

LESSONS FROM THIS LEGEND...

BUILDING A
BASKETBALL PROGRAM

By C.M. Newton

Authors' Note: As a coach, C.M. Newton loved to take a program, build it to the championship level, and move on to other challenges. This article gives great insight as to how he accomplished this daunting task.

This whole business of building a basketball program is, at once, the most exciting and interesting aspect of our profession, yet also the most frustrating. I think if most of us are really honest about it; the biggest obstacle we face is being itchy or anxious about our jobs, and we should be. In our business, 75 to 80 percent of us will either be fired or forced to quit eventually. The days of a coach like Adolph Rupp, with all those years at Kentucky, are gone at just about every level of basketball.

So, the truth is, we'd all like to have a job with an established program. I'm talking about the quality of the facilities, the available monies and the tradition. These are the most desirable items no matter what level of coaching we are talking about. If you go into a situation with all of these things, obviously your job should be a little easier, but what I'd like you to think about is taking a program that is down, a situation in which you can build, not just sustain. To me, that's the really fun part of coaching, and in my career, I'm now involved with the third opportunity I've had to build a program.

I recall the first year I was at Transylvania. I came there fresh out of Kentucky with a lot of ideas, figuring we'd win all of our games and not being even slightly concerned about the fact that the team had not won a game the year before. The only reason I got the job was because no one else wanted the position. Well, my first year we won just one game. But I was able to stay with it; we began to give scholarships on a limited basis and eventually built a very fine program which remains intact today.

One afternoon I was sitting in my office when my secretary came in and said Coach Bryant from Alabama was on the phone. He asked me if I was interested in the Alabama basketball job, and we talked a bit about it. I asked him when he would like me to come down for an interview because I was definitely interested. He said "I don't want you to come for an interview, I want to know if you want the job!" I asked how soon he needed a decision, and he said he would call back that evening. He did, and I accepted, but there were three questions I asked of him and I think they are very important ones for any coach to ask before looking at any program.

First, is there a real commitment to wanting a quality program by those who count? The second thing, are they realistic in what they want? If Coach Bryant would have told me they wanted me to win a national championship within three years, I'd still be at Transylvania today. Third, what kind of tools are they going to make available to you?

I don't think you should be concerned about the so-called incompatibility of other sports. I think you should want your football team to be a winner, because success breeds success. The same with the women's program. You want them to be successful for the same reasons.

No, it's very important before taking any job to ascertain who it was that hired you because that's who will fire you. Was it the superintendent? Was it the school board? Was it an athletic committee? It's very important to know who you are working for because the degree of the essentials (commitment, finances, and expectations) will come from that source.

I recall as a young coach sitting with Adolph Rupp and asking for some of his thinking about going into coaching as a profession, as opposed to some other kind of work. He allowed that it was a tough business, but he said the one great thing about it was the security. This was in the 1950s and obviously is far from being true today. In fact, it's about 180 degrees the other way. Today, any coach in any situation needs a contract, and I would advise you to have a contract that is a legal document. You see that the superintendent or school board may lose some of its courage when times get a little tough, and the media starts jumping on you because there aren't enough wins being produced.

A contract protects both the institution and the coach involved. The key to it is not the salary or the fringe benefits but the length of time when we are talking about building a program. When you are talking about the college level, there's no way anyone is going to come in and quickly turn everything around. To illustrate how important I think the length of a contract is, I recall the most

LESSONS FROM THIS LEGEND...

difficult aspect of leaving Transylvania for Alabama was explaining to my wife why I would leave the relative security of Transylvania to take a job which everyone said was a bad one at $2,500 less per year. When Coach Bryant said four years, I jumped because I felt that was adequate time, and there was a commitment on his part so a basketball program could be built or at least vastly upgraded in that period of time.

Once you've accepted the job, there are a number of things to consider. The first consideration is the people who are already at your institution. You need to find out as quickly as possible about the players you have, who you can count on and who you can't count one. When I went to Vanderbilt; there were a couple of players who talked about transferring. The only thing I said was, "please do it now." I had to get those who were staying and working toward achieving their potential and understanding what I am trying to do as soon as possible.

The next thing you need to consider is your staff. I want, first and most important, people who are going to be loyal to me. That's so much more important than ability because during that time when you're gonna get your fanny beat, and when you're trying to get your own people in there, loyalty and support from the assistant coaches are absolutely essential.

The second thing in looking for a staff member is compatibility. Can you work with these guys? I'll tell you, your nerve endings get raw, and having a good group

of assistants can really help. I think every coach ought to have one of those 4-20 seasons. My first year at Alabama, I was hired to turn the program around, and we sure did a job. We went from seven wins the previous year to four in my first year. I will assure you, though, you learn more about the guy who hired you, about the people around you, and about yourself in one of those years than in any season you'll ever have.

The third thing you need is a willingness to work. There's no easy way to sustain a program and certainly no easy way to build one. Those are some very key elements in setting up a program and getting ready to start. It's like a foundation under your house; it must be sturdy because there's a lot of weight going to be sitting on top of it.

Turning to the program itself, you must begin by establishing good work habits and improving attitudes. You must understand that these will be two major problems that you'll see in any losing situations. If they had good working habits and winning attitudes, you wouldn't be there.

It's important not to try and change any attitudes with gimmickry, but rather with a subtle approach. Maybe a newly decorated weight room or a remodeled dressing room, something to start building some honest pride. It's a message to them which says, we care about you and want you to succeed.

I believe in goal setting. We ask our youngsters to try very hard to determine what

things they want to achieve in their college careers. I think you need to be realistic, but I think, if you are ever going to achieve anything, you must first understand what it is you are trying to achieve. When I went to Alabama, our staff looked at our basketball schedule and our players and determined that if we won nine games, we would have had a winning season. Nine games. You may say that's ridiculous, that your goals should have been to win all of the 24 games. Well, I believe you have to be realistic, and we felt if we could get to that level, we were on the right path. Ultimately, of course, our goal became to win the conference championship, but in the beginning, we tried to be very realistic.

SOURCE

Lazenby, Roland, David Meador and Ed Green. (1987). *Championship Basketball*. Chicago: Contemporary Books.

MOTIVATING YOUNGER PLAYERS

By C.M. Newton

Authors' Note: As a way to sell the game to parents and younger players, Coach Newton developed a program that emphasized ballhandling. His well-known program called "Lil Dribblers" was featured at halftime performances of colleges where he coached. It was a strong motivator for many beginning players.

BENEFITS THAT CAN BE DERIVED FROM A COACHING CLINIC

1. Reinforcement in something you already believe
2. New ideas
3. Personal relationships

MY BASIC BELIEFS ARE:

1. Basketball is the most difficult game to learn to play well.
2. I believe the sport you learn early is the one you tend to be proficient in as an adult.
3. Basketball coaches at all levels have an obligation and responsibility to promote basketball.
4. The most important function of basketball coaches is public relations—sell your program.

AREAS OF FUNDAMENTALS THAT HAVE TO BE TAUGHT ARE:

1. Ballhandling
   a. dribbling
   b. passing
   c. catching
   d. related footwork

Catching comes in two ways—catch by feel and look the ball into the hands

2. Shooting
   a. layups
   b. jump shots
   c. power shots
3. Defense
4. Rebounding

You can't dictate the tempo without ballhandling. Every shot is preceded by some form of ballhandling.

In relation to young players, motivation is the key to learning. You can teach, but the players must learn.

FACTORS NECESSARY TO BECOME A SUCCESSFUL PLAYER

1. Size
2. Quickness
3. Footwork
4. Speed
5. Strength

When working with young players, you minimize the above factors and stress by:

1. Putting the young player and keeping him in a situation where he can be successful.
2. Making the goal of good ballhandling a homework situation for the young player. Competition is within himself.
3. Having suitable equipment

QUALITIES OF A GOOD BALL-HANDLER

1. Finger tip control
2. Confidence—You can make the ball do what you want it to do—use both hands equally well
3. Quickness of hands

SUGGESTIONS FOR DRILLS

1. Name them
2. Categorize them
3. Arrange in order of difficulty

OFFENSIVE DRILLS

DRIBBLING DRILLS

1. Basketball position (ball in front)
2. Dribble right
3. Dribble left
4. Dribble—alternate hands
5. Punching bag
6. Knee dribble
7. T.V. dribble
8. Laying down dribble
9. Standing figure 8
10. Standing behind the back
11. Feet fast—ball slow
12. Feet slow—ball fast
13. Speed dribble (left, right, alternate)
14. Stop-start dribble (left, right, alternate)
15. Dribble at angles (change hands, then behind back)
16. Dribble in circle (left and right)
17. Dribble pretzel
18. Dribble—"do your thing"—(one minute)

BALLHANDLING DRILLS

1. Banana drill
2. Pendulum
3. Pretzel
4. See saw
5. Rhythm drill
6. Ricochet
7. Bullet ricochet
8. Body drill

9. Pass in air, catch behind back
10. Bounce in air, catch behind back
11. Behind the back, over the shoulder (right and left)
12. Running Pretzel
13. Ballhandling—"do your thing"— (one minute)

SPINNING DRILLS

1. Proper spin
2. Spin and pat
3. Change fingers
4. Knuckles
5. Bounce off fist, arm, head, knee, and shoulder
6. Spin, lay down and get back up

7. Between the legs
8. Spin inside out
9. Spin outside in
10. Spin off head—layup

PASSES

1. Chest pass
2. Bounce pass
3. Overhead pass
4. Baseball pass
5. Right and left hand pass (air and bounce)
6. Behind the back (right and left)
7. Behind the back bounce (right and left)

SHOOTING

1. Layup (right and left)
2. One-hand push shot
3. Free throw
4. Jump shot
5. Hook shot (right and left)
6. Power move

SOURCE

Newton, C.M. (1976). Motivating Young Players. *Medalist Flashback Notebook*

LEGACY OF
Aleksandar "Aza" Nikolic

- Produced a legion of Nikolic basketball disciples that shaped European basketball, both as players and coaches.

- Recognized as the best basketball coach in European history.

- Called the "Father of Yugoslavian Basketball."

- Developed a system of play known as the "Nikolic Method" built on the components of supreme physical conditioning, repetition, intense focus on execution, and physical play.

- Demanded perfection and pushed players to their maximum.

- Known as "The Professor."

ALEKSANDAR "AZA" NIKOLIC

*"In the United States you have the legends
of Allen, Iba, Rupp and Wooden;
In Europe we have Rubini, Ferrandiz, Gomelsky and
Nikolic, with Nikolic voted as the best ever"*
—Dan Peterson,1997 • Editor, Giganti del Basket

BIOGRAPHY

Born: October 28, 1924 in Sarajevo, Bosnia and Herzegovina

Died: March 12, 2000

Inducted into the Naismith Basketball Hall of Fame in 1998

Known as the "Father of Yugoslavian Basketball," Aleksandar Nikolic led the Yugoslavian National Team to its first-ever international medal (silver) in the 1961 European Championships. He attended King Alexander H.S. in Belgrade where he graduated in 1943. Nikolic played basketball and soccer in club and professional system in Belgrade. He attended the University of Belgrade, studying medicine and law, graduating in 1946. He was an integral part of Red Star club team of Belgrade in 1947-49, when they won three consecutive national championships. He won gold medals in the 1977 European Championships and the 1978 World Cup as national coach. He excelled at both the club and national team levels. A two-time European Coach of the Year (1966, 1976), Nikolic won three national titles, three European titles, three Italy Cups, and two Intercontinental cups as coach of the Italian club team Ignis Varese. His Ignis team has been called the best club team in European history. He was the recipient of the Yugoslavian Order of Merit, and also founded the Yugoslavian Institute of Physical Education.

Aleksandar "Aza" Nikolic...

"Aza" Nikolic had a rather nondescript upbringing in Belgrade, Yugoslavia that somehow lit the fire to produce the "Giant of Giants," the European coach that would dominate basketball on the continent for over 40 years. European writers came to call Nikolic the "Bosnian Devil," executives labeled him the "Father of Yugoslavian Basketball," and coaches, in reverence, called him "The Professor."

His real story began when the Yugoslavian Federation asked Nikolic to leave his hometown of Sarajevo, in the Southern Republic of Bosnia-Herzegovina, to re-assemble the leftovers from the national team after the disaster of their only attempt in international play: 13th place in the 1947 Europeans (next to last). They were ready to drop the sport completely.

He had a plan, eventually called the "Nikolic Method or System," that would revolutionize Yugoslavian and European basketball. He knew he would be working with one of the tallest races of people on Earth, that it would take time to teach them how to play his system, that the country needed to absorb his method, and that he was going to develop the "Yugoslavian School of Basketball," a large task indeed.

He struggled early on in European competition (1953-59), as he was laying the foundation. Coaches sensed the revolution; they flocked to his practices, his assistants became head coaches, and the players he cut stayed around the master to become assistants. "The Professor" had the attention of the nation, and basketball class was in session.

The competition breakthrough occurred in 1961, when the host Yugoslavian team won the Silver Medal (USSR was champion), their first in any international competition. It was the first of many to follow, as Aza became a coaching legend. His national team coaching successes produced offers from club teams all over Europe.

The club system involves coaching at a much different level and situations than that of coaching a national team. Competition for club teams is organized as "CUP" play:
- Cup of Champions—the highest level of competition, for national champions only
- Cup of Cups—for league runner-ups or winners of a nation's cup, a slightly lower level of competition
- Korac Cup—for teams who finish 3-6 in league play

As Aleksandar Nikolic swept into Cup play, his teams again dominated. The peak was reached from 1969-73, when his Ignis Varese team swept Cup play twice, becoming National Champions, European Champions, and World Club Champions. Experts called the 1973 Ignis team the best team in European basketball history.

In 1970 and 1973, Ignis swept all four competitions— league, national, European and World Cup—for club teams. This "Grand Slam" is the rarest of records: It can be equaled but never broken. In fact, no other coach or other team has ever done it before or since.

Now Nikolic had achieved the rare distinction of dominating competition as a national team coach and as a club team coach, an unheard of feat. And the beat went on— Nikolic was repeatedly called back to the national team and continued his success at both levels. His team's amazing records at both levels followed. Aza, during his club coaching era, also stunned the European Basketball World in 1973 by resigning from Ignis to return to his adopted home town of Belgrade to spend more time with his family. He took over the local club team, cellar dweller Red Star, and everyone predicted failure. Red Star took 2nd in Yugoslavia, won the European cup of Cups, and his "bad apple" star player had his greatest year, so the legend continued until his "official" retirement from coaching in 1985.

YUGOSLAVIA

HE'S BACK!

This was the worst possible news for his European coaching colleagues who hoped that Nikolic had gone the way of the Tyrannosaurus Rex into retirement. In 1990, the John Wooden of Europe would return in the shadows, heeding the many SOS calls from his coaching brethren. The coaching juggernaut continued on its own with frequent calls to "The Professor" for a refresher course and a team makeover. He sorted out the many calls, answering only those who had worked under him and, of course, for his country. He was asked were to put things in order and help organize things. His response was generally to:

- run every practice
- put in offense and defense
- plan every strategy
- program conditioning and training
- set up lineups and substitution plans
- develop mental preparation

Amazingly, his reverent disciples allowed him full control and access. Champion coaches stepped aside for the coaching giant. This continued until his death in 2000.

Thus, many teams developed the Nikolic signature. Former assistant Mauro Di Vicenzo said, "Nikolic basketball is as recognizable as a still life by Morandi". A Nikolic-coached team had "that look," they are as identifiable as the Eiffel Tower, the London Bridge, Adolph Rupp's "guard around", Bruce Drake's "shuffle," or John Wooden's "high post." His influence has spread all over Europe—former players, former assistants and a legion of Nikolic Method disciples. In addition, a host of European players developed with his method have reached the highest professional levels of basketball—Kresimer Cosic, Toni Kukoc, Dino Radjo, Vlade Divac, Stojan Vrankovic, Sasho Danilovic, and Drazan Petrovic, to name a few. What a living testament to the father of Yugoslavia basketball, the revered "Professor" of European basketball.

SOURCE

Nikolic, Aleksandar. Vertical Files, Archives. Naismith Memorial Basketball Hall of Fame. Springfield, MA.

LESSONS FROM THIS LEGEND...

THE NIKOLIC METHOD OF COACHING

By Aleksandar Nikolic

Authors' Note: So what is the "Nikolic Method" that became his basketball signature? It consisted of a number of key components:

1. PHYSICAL CONDITIONING AT THE HIGHEST LEVEL.

The workload, in time and intensity, that he imposed on players was the "stuff of legend" that they passed on in the lore of their generation. To survive was to tell the story. He brought out more than the best of players physically.

2. REPETITION

He ran the same five set plays, but there was intense focus on execution. Every practice, there was extended work against live defense on a half-court basis, then on the full-court (two and one-half hours a day, 15 minutes/play). His players could execute in the dark and make automatic responses to defenders.

3. CLARITY

Aza was very clear about demanding perfection and having high expectations. He would return to the gym after poor performances for lengthy practices with his teams.

4. DEFENSE

In 1969, Nikolic brought the "body check" and more physical play to European basketball. His straight-up, "eye-hand-chest," man-to-man defense, developed with his famous Ignis team, stopped other teams and players. His teams played tough, but clean basketball.

5. COURAGE

Nikolic, though a bundle of nerves and a chain smoker, was a gutsy strategist. He introduced the use of the "6th man" to change the game, as well as such things as starting a little used substitute to wear down and "dog" the opposition's star player.

6. SPORTSMANSHIP

He taught players to compete, but as sportsmen. He never had a technical foul, an expulsion, or a disqualification. He expected the same of his players, and they conformed to his demands.

7. HARD WORK

He transformed coaching from amateur to professional. He regularly outworked the opposition.

8. PLANNING

He often took undesirable, later practice times so he could have unlimited time to practice at night. Aza was also very organized and paid strict attention to detail.

9. PERSONALITY

He was a "Doomsday" pessimist who kept a low profile but he was always a favorite with the press. Nikolic had a "human touch" that turned out champions and developed players and coaches who led their teams and loved the game. No other European coach has approached this unparalleled influence on the game.

SOURCE

Nikolic, Aleksandar. Vertical Files, Archives. Naismith Basketball Hall of Fame. Springfield, MA.

LEGACY OF
Jack Ramsay

- Recognized for his extraordinary attention to detail and knowledge of the game.

- Viewed the game of basketball as an art form and compared the movements in basketball to those in ballet.

- Designed conditioning regimes that produced teams that were in superior physical condition.

- Regarded as a master motivator and was known as "Dr. Jack."

- Led Portland to the NBA championship in 1977.

- Led St. Joseph's (PA) to 10 postseason appearances and a third-place finish in the NCAA tournament in 1961.

JACK RAMSAY

*"Well-coached teams are never surprised;
they can adapt to anything they see."*
—Jack Ramsay

BIOGRAPHY

Born: February 21, 1925 in Philadelphia, PA

Inducted into the Naismith Basketball Hall of Fame in 1992

Jack Ramsay was a head coach at the professional, college, and high school levels for almost fifty years, and his overall coaching record includes 1,164 wins. He coached Philadelphia, Buffalo, Portland, and Indiana in the NBA and guided the Trailblazers to the 1977 NBA championship. Ramsay was general manager of the Philadelphia 76ers in 1976, when the 76ers won the NBA championship and set a league record for most victories in one season. He coached at St. Joseph's (PA) from 1955 to 1966 and compiled a 234-72 record, including ten post-season tournament appearances. Ramsay led St. Joseph's to the Final Four in 1961. The Hawks were defeated by eventual champion Ohio State in the semi-finals but came back to win the third-place trophy by beating Utah 127-120 in four overtimes. He played basketball and baseball at St. Joseph's and captained the Hawks basketball team his senior year. He also played professional basketball for six seasons in the Eastern Basketball League. Ramsay received a Ph.D. in education in 1963 from the University of Pennsylvania.

Jack Ramsay...

Jack Ramsay was born in Philadelphia but soon moved to Milford, Connecticut, where he grew up shooting baskets at a goal nailed to the side of a barn. His family moved to Upper Darby, Pennsylvania, a suburb of Philadelphia, when Jack was in high school, and he starred in basketball, baseball, and soccer. He then entered St. Joseph's University and earned a starting position on the basketball team. Ramsay left school after his first year and joined the Navy. He was commissioned an ensign in 1944 and served with underwater demolition teams in the Pacific. After his discharge, Ramsay returned to St. Joseph's and made the All-Philadelphia team during his junior and senior years.

When he became head coach of the Portland Trail Blazers in 1976-77, Ramsay inherited a team that in it's six years of existence had never had a winning record or made the NBA playoffs. In Ramsay's first year, the Trail Blazers shocked the basketball world by winning the NBA championship. Ramsay transformed his players into a smooth functioning, confident team. His positive approach made all the difference in the world. Ramsay (2003) recalled stopping a training camp scrimmage following a brilliant segment of play to tell his players, "We can win if we play like that! I mean the whole thing ...the NBA championship." Ramsay believed that in coaching, a positive approach makes all the difference.

In the championship series, Portland lost the first two games to the Julius Erving-led Philadelphia 76ers. The Trail Blazers had not played well, and Ramsay detected a bit of nervousness among his players. He knew that it was

After graduation from St. Joseph's, Ramsay coached six years on the high-school level and played in the Eastern Basketball League. In 1955, he was named head coach at his alma mater, St. Josephs. In his first year, Ramsay led the Hawks to a 23-6 record, the school's first Big Five championship and a trip to the NIT tournament. During his eleven years at St. Joseph's, his teams compiled a record of 234-72, with ten postseason appearances.

In 1966, Ramsay accepted the position of general manager of the Philadelphia 76ers. In his initial campaign, the 76ers set an NBA record for victories and won the world championship. He stayed in the front office one more year before returning to the sidelines. During his NBA career, Ramsay coached in Philadelphia, Buffalo, Portland, and Indiana.

crucial that he portray confidence in his players. Instead of changing his line-up or altering his offense and defense, Ramsay reminded his team about how they had blown out the 76ers in a regular season game. He told them that he was confident that they could duplicate that kind of performance if they played their game. The players responded to his message, and Portland stormed back to win four straight games.

Ramsay's coaching genius was instrumental in creating the phenomenon, Blazermania. In 1993, Portland retired jersey number 77 in Ramsay's honor, symbolically recognizing the 1977 NBA Championship.

Ramsay continually talked to his players about the will to win. He believed that everyone has the will to win, but that some individuals have a greater desire than others. Ramsay (2003) listed the following players as the most determined that he had seen throughout his years in the NBA—in chronological order—George Mikan, Bill Russell, Jerry West, Dave Cowans, Larry Bird, Magic Johnson, Michael Jordan, Hakeem Olajuwon, Shaquille O'Neal, and Kobe Bryant.

When asked to describe the game of basketball, Ramsay (1978) stated, "The game is unified action up and down the floor. It is quickness, it is strength; it is skill, it is stamina; it is five men playing as one. It is tenacity on defense; it is quick penetration on offense. It is taking advantage of every offensive opportunity. It is stifling the opponent; it is jamming up the one-on-one player. But most of all, it is the spirit of winning as a team. It is the solidarity of a single unifying purpose, the will to overcome adversity, the determination never to give in."

Ramsay often compared the movements in basketball to those in ballet. "Basketball is a graceful sweep and flow of patterned movement, counter pointed by daring and imaginative flights of solitary brilliance," said Ramsay (1978).

Ramsay believed coaching was a means of self-expression. Ramsay (2003) said, "A foundational principle of success —in any endeavor—is to be yourself. Trying to be someone else, no matter how admirable we may think that person is, just doesn't work."

To become a successful coach, Ramsay (2002) believed there were five key factors:

1. Know the game and have your team play their best within the rules of the game.
2. Develop an effective game plan that gives your team its best chance to win.
3. Teach the game to your staff and players. Use the whole-part-whole method. Give the players an overall view of what the end product looks like, break it down into its essential parts, and then put all the parts together.
4. Coach the game. Go over the game plan with your players and simulate at practice the game that you expect them to play. At the same time, you must prepare them to meet the unexpected.
5. Obtain quality personnel. A good coach makes maximum use of the talent that he has, but if he has less than standard quality players, he can't win. Talent is the coach's lifeblood, and good talent has to be well-coached.

Ramsay has always been highly respected by his peers. Jim Calhoun, head coach at Connecticut, said, "There are only a few 'teachers' we all learn from, and Dr. Jack is one of them."

Hall of Fame coach Harry Litwack (1992) described Ramsay in these words, "Jack is an outstanding competitor and motivator, and his knowledge of the game is incredible. He's an outstanding individual, a wonderful family man, and regarded by everyone as a genuine human being."

SOURCE

Ramsay, Jack. Vertical Files, Archives. Naismith Memorial Basketball Hall of Fame. Springfield, MA.

Ramsay, Jack. (2003). *Dr. Jack's Leadership Lessons Learned From a Lifetime in Basketball*. Hoboken, NJ: John Wiley & Sons.

Ramsay, Jack. (2002, September 19). My secrets to NBA head coaching success. ESPN.com.

Ramsay, Jack. (1978). *The Coach's Art*. Forest Grove, OR: Timber Press.

LESSONS FROM THIS LEGEND...

"ABSOLUTES" IN BASKETBALL COACHING

By Jack Ramsay

I always had a great fascination for the game of basketball. As a player, I was schooled in crisp passes, quick give-and-go cuts, flash post-ups, and tough man-to-man defense. No frills, or gimmicks. It was just good, solid, fundamental basketball. Years later, I heard that style referred to as "Eastern" basketball.

CONTRASTING STYLES

During my four years at St. Joseph's, I played against some of the best teams, players, and coaches of that time. It was fascinating to see the different styles that some of the giants of the coaching profession brought to Philadelphia. Coach Frank Keaney's Rhode Islanders were the first to race up and down the floor with what he called "fire-horse" Basketball. In contrast, Coach Hank Iba's Oklahoma A&M teams played a physical, bruising defensive game; then stressed a ball-control offense. Eddie Diddle combined the two styles at Western Kentucky, with an array of tall, talented, agile players; and CCNY's Nat Holman had a slick, quick game that won both the NIT and NCAA championships in the same year (1950)—the only grand slam in history.

My Navy duty game me the chance to play briefly with the San Diego Dons while awaiting re-assignment. The Dons employed a "western"-style offense, using weakside screens and ball reversals, rather than the give-and-go "Eastern" style I had grown up with. I was lost in the system, and was transferred before I had time to really adjust to it. But I learned again, this time from a first-hand experience, that there were other ways to play the game effectively.

THE CHALLENGE OF COACHING

I came out of my playing years with a strong desire to coach. There was something intriguing about taking a group of players, teaching them to play your game, and finding a way to win with it. I wanted the opportunity to help increase the players' skills; to get them to play selflessly as a unit; to demand that they go at it with intensity and poise; and to play only to win in the same way those great coaches appeared to have done.

My adjustment to coaching was more difficult than I had expected. I had thought because I played against great teams, players, and coaches, I could easily transfer those experiences to my players. It wasn't quite that simple.

COACHING IS TEACHING

I learned that a major part of coaching was teaching, not just showing and telling. I found that, although all coaches had a system of play, the good ones often adapted it to fit the special skills of their players. Well-coached teams were never surprised. They seemed prepared for anything that happened in a game. They could make an effective adjustment for any quickly changing situation.

I watched opposing coaches do a better job of motivating their players and teams. I wanted my players to exhibit more poise under pressure, but understood that I could not expect it from them until I could demonstrate it myself. I needed to become a better coach.

STUDY THE GAME

To improve my coaching ability, I carefully observed coaches and noted their attention to detail and their inner-team relationships. I sent to the NCAA office for game films of the tournament finalists. I attended coaching clinics to hear the great coaches speak about their techniques. Defense, these coaches said, was the key to winning. And it didn't have to be the conventional man-to-man. At that time, teams were having success with various zone defenses—match-ups, traps, and combinations, like the box-and-one. These were different tactics from those I had experienced as a player, and I gave them full attention—ultimately incorporating some of them into my system.

EXECUTION DETERMINES SUCCESS

Through the years, championship coaches have used varying styles of offense and defense. It proves that theory, however sound, is less important than execution in determining success. Legendary coach John Wooden achieved enormous success with zone trapping during his incredible run at UCLA.

The match-up zone defense reached its peak of effectiveness with Harry Litwak's great Temple teams of the late '50s. Then Frank McGuire won an NCAA title with North Carolina in 1957 with a standard 2-1-2 zone defense.

I first saw aggressive, jump-switching, man-to-man defense used successfully at the college level by Pete Newell at California (1959 NCAA champions) and by Eddie Donovan at St. Bonaventure. Their defenses wrought

LESSONS FROM THIS LEGEND...

havoc with the opponents' carefully executed plays. Dean Smith did the same thing at North Carolina, and added an in-and-out, shuttling system of substitutions.

Red Auerbach's Boston Celtics brought pressure defense into the NBA, and combined it with the shot-blocking and intimidation threat of Bill Russell to win eight consecutive titles (1959-1966). Russell was the first player to make the blocked shot an offensive as well as defensive weapon. He blocked the shots, and his teammates ran for fast breaks with the possessions. I believe that Bill Russell had a greater impact on the game than any other player in history.

Offensive styles also changed during my period of observation. In the late 1940s and early 1950s, the half-court series run by Adolph Rupp at Kentucky was totally different from the five-man weave of Ken Loeffler at La Salle—but they both won NCAA championships. Ed Jucker showed it wasn't necessary to fast break to win, when he took his Cincinnati team to consecutive NCAA championships in 1961 and 1962 with a ball-control game similar to that of Newell's at California.

Bob Knight used a passing, screening game —somewhat related to the old, "Eastern" style to win three NCAA titles for Indiana; while Mike Krzyzewski's Duke teams won back-to-back with a combination passing game and pro-type screening offense. Both schools played rock-ribbed, man-to-man defense.

In the NBA, the Celtics used the same six half-court plays during their reign of terror, on those occasions when they weren't fast-breaking. The plays were fundamentally sound, yielding shots well-suited to the abilities of their players.

My championship Portland team (1977) used the consummate passing skills of Bill Walton to feed cutters at the basket. Magic Johnson was the master floor general of Pat Riley's fast-breaking Lakers that dominated the 1980s, although Boston bounced back to win two championships sparked by the all-around wizardry of Larry Bird.

Then Detroit won back-to-back titles with a three-guard attack orchestrated by Chuck Daly; and later Chicago won its celebrated "Three-peat" with Michael Jordan, the game's greatest player, at center stage. Bulls coach Phil Jackson didn't just give Michael the ball and clear the floor. Chicago used an offense that assistant Tex Winter developed in college. It designated spot positions on the floor and required specific screen, pass and cut continuities. The positions were interchangeable to accommodate Jordan's considerable skills, and the offense was flexible enough to afford M.J. some one-on-one bursts to the hoop.

"ABSOLUTES" IN BASKETBALL COACHING

Since ending an active coaching career, I have stayed close to the game, mostly as a television analyst, but also giving coaching clinics around the world for the NBA. But no matter where or when I have seen the game played, it has always had constants— indigenous, never-changing concepts. Here are my dozen "absolutes" in basketball coaching:

1. Basketball, like every other sport, is predicated on the execution of fundamentals.
2. The coach is a teacher; his subject is the fundamentals.
3. Teams attain the highest level of achievement with the best-conditioned players.
4. Even the greatest players have a level of improvement to achieve.
5. Even the greatest players accept coaching and value the need for discipline and the order that it brings to the team.
6. Winning is more related to good defense than good offense.
7. Breakdown drills, under simulated game conditions, are essential to team success.
8. Teams that play together beat those with superior players who play more as individuals.
9. There are no physical limits to individual achievement.
10. Although the game has become more sophisticated, simpler is better in developing and teaching a system of play.
11. Players draw confidence from a poised, alert coach who anticipates changing game conditions.
12. Teams that never concede defeat can accomplish incredible victories.

SOURCE

Ramsay, Jack. (1994, October). My 60 Years in Basketball. *Scholastic Coach*.

LESSONS FROM THIS LEGEND...

COMMUNICATE, COMMUNICATE, COMMUNICATE

By Jack Ramsay

Most people want to know where they stand. They want to do their job well, want recognition for their work, want to learn how to do the job better, and want to receive the appropriate compensation for what they do. They also want the same ground rules to apply to everyone – from the most capable to the least. Telling people where they stand – on a team, in a relationship, in a family, at work – requires the ability to communicate effectively. Without it, success in any endeavor is hard to come by, and success in a leadership position becomes virtually impossible.

Yet for all its importance, communication appears to be one of humankind's most serious shortcomings. How does positive communication begin? Simply enough: eye contact, a smile, a handshake, a pleasant nod of the head, a simple "hello" or "how ya doin" may be the start of something positive and enduring. Conversely, the lack of the same may forestall any communication at all.

MAKE EYE CONTACT

Eye-to-eye contact is the first and strongest bond that establishes good communication between two people. If the eyes are "the windows of the soul," as someone once wrote, then eye contact enables two people to look into the very depths of each other's being.

To that end, I made it a practice to speak to every player on my team each day that we met, which was almost every day during the season. I tried to make eye contact with them as well, and if that proved impossible, it was a clear sign that I had to try harder to communicate.

READ BODY LANGUAGE

Like making eye contact, the ability to read body language is imperative for effective communication. The posture of a person speaks volume. Those who stand or sit in a slouched position, facing away from the speaker, are saying that they're neither happy nor comfortable being there. Arms crossed across the chest, feet set apart, and eyes narrowed impart a defiant attitude. Clenched fists signal anger or extreme nervousness or anxiety. Knowing how to read those unspoken signals and, then how to put such people at ease can help defuse a potentially damaging situation.

GET PERSONAL

The door to effective communication opens wider when you get to know the people you work with – whether staff or players – on a personal basis. As a coach, in addition to talking directly with each player on my team every day, I took an interest in their families, as well as their general well-being. And I gave players who weren't getting any playing time extra, personalized practice from me. I kept them longer to work on their game skills, so that they'd be ready to contribute if called on. I found that if players sensed they were benefiting from the work, they'd do whatever I asked of them, volunteer for more, and show appreciation for my interest.

SAY IT STRAIGHT

Alex Hannum, my predecessor at Philadelphia, had great rapport with his players, and was a stand-up guy. Though he'd had only modest success as an NBA player (averaging six points per game over nine seasons), he had a great sense of the game as a coach. Known as "Sarge" for his no-nonsense approach with players, he was widely admired by players throughout the league. As general manager of the Sixers for the two years Alex coached them, I was able to listen in at team meetings. When he spoke of strengths and weaknesses of his team, he indicated which players were doing enough and which needed to contribute more. He was direct; he told it like it was. He also invited comments from the players, which they often accepted. Everything was out in the open.

MAKE YOUR POINT

My first team meeting as coach of the Portland Trail Blazers was set for 7:00pm before the opening day of training camp. Everyone was there at the designated time – except three key players: Bill Walton, Maurice Lucas, and Herm Gilliam. They strolled in together at 7:05. I knew my authority was being challenged. I pointedly checked my watch, then announced that the three players – and I named them – who were five minutes late would be fined $5 a minute, an accepted rate for tardiness in those days. I added that, henceforth, starting times for all team events would be observed to the second and that any stragglers would be penalized.

Years later, Larry Steele, a reserve swingman on that team, observed that fining those three players was my most significant act in getting the team off to a good start. He said that it established team unity and made it clear that everyone would be treated the same.

LESSONS FROM THIS LEGEND...

HEAR YOURSELF SPEAK

Adjustments are almost always necessary in any leader's communication, to account for changes, especially in personnel. One episode from my coaching career stands out in my mind.

In my third season at Portland, after many personnel changes, we were no longer a championship team. I was exasperated with the way we were playing and communicated that emotion to anyone within hearing distance. I often became angry on the sidelines and, at times, chewed out players for their mistakes. Soon, team morale was sagging, and I tried to turn things around by calling a team meeting before the next practice. At the meeting, I went over the areas where we needed to improve, told each player where and how I thought he could upgrade his performance, and then asked what I could do to help him achieve a new level of play.

Maurice Lucas was the last to respond. He said that I should calm down, that the players were getting negative vibes from my conduct on the sidelines, and it was hurting their confidence. Instead of jumping all over players at timeouts, Lucas suggested that I just tell them they "messed up" and let it go at that. With that, everyone in the room, including me, broke up laughing. I agreed to be more patient, but said that I still wanted each player to lift his game. There was a united nodding of heads, the meeting ended on an upbeat note, and our play picked up after that.

HAVE THE LAST WORD: RESPECT

One of the best at successfully communicating with his players – with the championship rings to prove it – was legendary Celtics coach Red Auerbach. When the old Boston Garden was being razed in 1995 to make way for the upscale Fleet Center, *Courtside Magazine* asked me to write a piece on Red, who was 78 years old at the time, but whose recollections were amazingly clear.

During our conversation, I complimented him on the marvelous rapport he had had with his players, evidenced by the way they all talked about him. Whenever any of those players spoke of their unique reign of championships – 8 in a row, and 9 in 10 years with Red as coach – they always mentioned Auerbach prominently – most often prefacing some story about their involvement with the Celtics with "Red said this" or "Red did that." Many of them played their entire career with Boston: Bill Russell, Bob Cousy, Tom Heinsohn, John Havlicek, Sam and K.C. Jones, Satch Sanders, Frank Ramsey, and Bill Sharman were among those who wore only Celtic green during their pro basketball lives.

I asked Red how he had handled so many star players so well. "First of all," he said, "you don't *handle* people. You handle animals; you treat people like human beings. That was always the most important thing with me." And that's what Red did. He treated each player with respect and got the same in return.

SOURCE

Ramsay, Jack. (2004). *Dr. Jack's Leadership Lessons Learned from a Lifetime in Basketball.* Hoboken, NJ: John Wiley and Sons.

LEGACY OF
Cesare Rubini

- Called the "Father of Italian Basketball."

- Elected first president of World Association of Basketball Coaches and served in that capacity for over 20 years.

- Coached the Simmenthal Club of Milan for 31 years and compiled a 322-28 record.

- Won 15 Italian Basketball Championships, five as a player (1950-55) and 10 as a coach.

- Pioneered the globalization of the game by recruiting American players, such as Bill Bradley, to play for European club teams.

- Was the first foreign coach inducted into the Naismith Memorial Basketball Hall of Fame.

CESARE RUBINI

"The team in basketball reacts according to general plans prepared ahead of time, in which the individuals are constructive elements of a complex whole."
—Cesare Rubini

BIOGRAPHY

Born: November 2, 1923 in Trieste, Italy

Inducted into the Naismith Basketball Hall of Fame in 1994

In 1994, Cesare Rubini became the first foreign coach to be inducted into the Naismith Memorial Basketball Hall of Fame. Rubini single handedly built the Simenthal Club Team of Milan into a major European basketball force. His teams won 15 Italian basketball championships, five as a player (1950-1955) and ten as a coach. Rubini spent 31 years as coach of the Simenthal Club and compiled a 322-28 record. He coached the Italian National Team to a silver medal at the 1980 Olympics. Rubini led the Italy to the European Championship in 1983 and a third-place finish in 1985. He was very active in international basketball and was the founder of the World Association of Basketball Coaches (WABC). Rubini served as president of the WABC from 1979 to 2002 and was named Honorary President of the WABC at the time of his retirement. Rubini was also a member of the Italian Olympic Water Polo team and led Italy to a gold medal in 1948 and a bronze medal in 1952. Rubini was inducted into both the Water Polo Hall of Fame and the Naismith Memorial Basketball Hall of Fame.

Cesare Rubini...

Cesare Rubini holds the distinct honor of being inducted into two international Halls of Fame for his athletic accomplishments in basketball and water polo. Whether Rubini was on the basketball court or in the water, he was a winner of games and hearts. His involvement and influence went far beyond the depth of the water or the length of the court.

Rubini was born in Trieste, Italy and graduated from G. Oberdan High School in 1941. During Rubini's youth, water polo was his first love. As a youngster, he aspired to emulate fellow countryman Mario Majoni as one of the leading water polo players in Europe. At the age of 24, Rubini teamed up with Majoni and led Italy to the 1947 European Championships. The following year, the dynamic duo captured the gold medal at the London Olympic Games. The gold medal was Italy's first championship in Olympic water polo history and was the beginning of his country's superiority in international water polo. Majoni graduated to National Team Coach and Rubini to National Team Captain. As captain, Rubini's team won the bronze medal in the 1952 Olympic Games, behind the great Hungarian and Yugoslavian teams. Italy finished third behind the same two countries at the 1954 European Championships.

During Rubini's water polo career, he won six Italian National Championships as a player and coach for Olona of Milan, Rari Nantes of Naples, and Camogli of Genoa. He played 84 matches with the National Team, 42 of them as captain.

Cesare Rubini methodically built Italian basketball from scratch. Through his hard work and perseverance, Italy became an international contender in the game of basketball. During his career, Rubini won 15 Italian basketball championships, five as a player and five as a coach. He was the head coach of the Simmenthal Club of Milan for 31 years and compiled an outstanding record of 322-28. The Simmenthal Club was often referred to as "the team with red shoes" because of the color of their shoes.

When Rubini was elected into the Naismith Memorial Basketball Hall of Fame in 1994, headlines of his achievement blazed across newspapers in his native country. It was a joyous day for the native son who had given five decades of his life to the establishment, structure, refinement, and advancement of Italian basketball. The name Cesare Rubini and Italian basketball are inseparable.

Dan Peterson, longtime observer and expert of world basketball, called Rubini a "true giant among coaches and among men." As the "Father of Basketball" in Italy, Rubini is considered the architect who built the cathedral for basketball in Europe. He is as revered in Italy for basketball the same way that James Naismith is respected in the United States.

Rubini, as a basketball coach, was a strict fundamentalist. He taught thousands of Italian players the correct fundamentals and a sound approach to the game. Rubini was a quiet disciplinarian and was highly respected by his players. He stressed sportsmanship and fair play. Rubini's teams always exhibited great chemistry and team play. He masterfully designed solid game plans that were followed by his teams. Rubini's players maintained their poise even under the most adverse circumstances.

Rubini was the founder of the World Association of Basketball Coaches (WABC) and served as president from 1979 until his retirement in 2002. He was named honorary president of the WABC in 2002.

SOURCE

Rubini, Cesare. Vertical Files, Archives. Naismith Memorial Basketball Hall of Fame. Springfield, MA.

ITALY

LESSONS FROM THIS LEGEND...

TEAM FUNDAMENTALS

By Cesare Rubini

What is the definition of team sport? Certainly, it does not propose to achieve determined goals by bringing together individual or coordinated acts; this is the case of a track and field meet, doubles in tennis, or the "eight" of crew. The cooperation of individuals in a team sport, however, must be of a different nature, not simply the addition of multiple individuals' efforts or the division of labor.

The "team" is a complex unit, inspired by tactical principles, not to be confused with management, which is but a contingent code of conduct, guided by particular demands of the competitive moment. Nor does it refer to the banal "one for all, all for one," which implies a plurality that is not necessarily operative. The pieces in a game of chess may be considered a "team," not because the operational objective of "check-mating" the opposing king brings them together, but rather because they all obey the tactical plan devised by the chess player himself. Every individual piece assumes a value often higher than its own intrinsic value; the humble pawn can, in fact, become the "check-mater."

So the team in basketball reacts according to general plans prepared ahead of time, in which the individuals are constructive elements of a complex whole. Very simply, there are two objectives—shoot the ball into your goal and prevent your opponent from scoring. For the purpose of custom and convenience, these two aspects are called offense and defense. Some American college teams still practice zone-pressing for long stretches of a game, if not for the entire game. Even on our courts, where the importance of defense has long and mistakenly been passed, it is not rare to participate

in bouts of pressing, not only in the ideal moments of play (when one is behind late in the game), but also after a basket's been made, with the scope of surprising or somehow disconcerting the opponent

Obviously a more aggressive defense carries with it risks; the danger of committing fouls increases, and the expenditure of psychophysical energy can bring many players to the extreme before the game ends. The relative lack of reserves, generally endemic in our sport, not only in just basketball, the poverty of adequate substitutes for the ideal quintet, all this induces the coach to renounce the paroxysm defense. But in overtime, as the breeding ground continues to bleed the already poor ranks, there can be no doubt that defensive planning will undergo radical revisions.

We know the behaviors and the weapons that are at the disposition of the basketball player in both the phase of attack and that of defense. Now let us see how the individuals establish themselves in the complex unit known as a team. Between two teams of equal strength, that which imposes its own defense to impose play will be better. It will always be the attacker who must adapt his game plan if the opponent has guessed the appropriate defense, never the contrary. This conclusion leads to another consideration. Every team must possess sufficient defensive eclecticism to adapt to any condition.

It is all good and well to specify that any type of defense, if applied with rigorous observance of its fundamental principles, is good against almost any type of offense. The opposite is not the case. It seems logical, therefore, to begin the exposition of

team play with the defense, or rather with the collected means studied to consent one unit to prevent its adversary from reaching its goal.

There are two collective means of defense— by man or by zone. Within the two types, there are unlimited nuances, each just as valid as it is contaminated. The polemics between the supporters of one versus another type are destined to last probably so long as basketball exists.

Zone defense is accused of preventing the attackers from playing a spectacular game, in other words, of preventing high scores. The accusation is recognition of the zone defense's validity; like every other scheme, it has its defects, but not for this should it be insulted or banned. There was a revival of zone defense in many American universities following the anathema group of Adolph Rupp, one of the patriarchs of basketball in the United States. From it was born zone pressing, the latest fashion in defense. Obviously, one would not chose zone defense as a team's primary defense, if it will not result congenial to the mental state of its components. We are not talking about an inability to apply it; rather every self-respecting basketball player must be able to do everything. The ABCs of defense are obtained, anyway, marking by the man, the boy at the beginning, the youth of great hopes must always be brought up in this way. In addition to perfecting and completing their technical skills, from them will spring a personality, individual pride, and the spirit of initiative.

Man-to-man defense aspires to an elementary and instinctive principle; for every defender, there is an adversary to mark, an expression of varied significance, which range from being a generic obstacle to aggressive anticipation. Zone defense, at least in its most pure form, is the defense of a territory precisely that presided over by the quintet that rolls ahead of the ball, orienting themselves both along with its displacements like the needle of a compass attracted to a magnet that moves before it. The goal of a zone defense is the marking of the ball, prohibiting its entrance into to defensive territory.

Now let us see the ways of carrying out man-to-man defense, its derivations, its plusses, and its minuses. Every defender has a man to mark. One will not allow a center to guard a player of too small stature. It will be either the tallest player of the team or the person who can jump the highest.

Knowledge of the opponent will inspire the defensive positioning. The most agile adversary will be entrusted to the fastest defender, as will the one with the best ball control to the defender most gifted with marking skills. The good rebounder should defend someone who is good at clearing the ball. Regarding the playmaker, it is worth mentioning in the most advanced line of defense, a very fast player will react quickly and is capable of intercepting a pass and escaping in a counterattack.

But one cannot discuss man-to-man defense as a collective scheme, returning to that is to the team sport, ignoring particular devices; otherwise, it would resolve itself in a series or sum of individual acts. The base procedures, which we can more aptly name helpful norms, have the purpose of creating, in the favor of the defense, a situation of numerical superiority with respect to a single attacker, that is double coverage, the additional man. The floater of these helpful devices is the active one and eliminates the passive one. The first consents to two defenders—to attack an attacker simultaneously, or at least to put one of the two in an advantageous position. The second ensures that another defender, while prepared to recover the ball, from being overcome by an adversary.

Other procedures are carried out in order to ensure that the man-to-man defense maintains its integrity, to prevent an attacker from remaining, not even for a moment, free from his direct adversary. There are three of these: the scissor, the change-over (defensive), and the slide. The scissors are a movement carried out by the defender in which he distances himself from his respective opponent just enough to enable a defender-attacker to pass through the space created. The danger of the allowed passage, for example, discourages doing a scissor in the vicinity of the basket. The adversary of the defender who carried out the scissor move would then have the possibility of an easy shot.

The change of coverage is an exchange carried out when an attacker escapes from one's teammate's coverage. The beaten man will move to cover the man left open, after his teammate has moved to cover the man with ball and called out the switch.

The slide (forwards and backwards) is a movement carried out by the defender in order to not lose contact with his direct adversary, preventing a pick-off, between oneself and that other, of a teammate or opponent. The switch has the grave defect of bringing, sometimes, even if for just a moment, a defender of small stature against a much taller adversary, or a very tall and immobile defender against a quick and agile attacker. But there are situations, the defense against a counterattack for example, which do not permit any alternate solutions. Obviously, the switch-over must be organized. All the players must have trained themselves and be able to both call it and obey.

Scissors, the switchover, and the slide are the elementary procedures that an individual defense must know how to carry out in order to avoid the danger of blocks and screens, the principle weapons the attacker uses against that type of attack. Training oneself is of determinant importance. A humorous sport columnist once wrote that the frantic management of defenders and attackers in a relatively constrictive space is reminiscent of the image of roosters who fling themselves against a handful of bird-

seed. In reality, the disorder is only apparent. Moves and countermoves take place in the space of moments, all guided by a logical design, never without sense.

Man-to-man defense has obviously evolved in its methods of application. The "normal" type by now serves merely an educational function, it is the "school of defense" for excellence and has the overall scope of developing the players by refining their set of techniques, instilling within them individual pride, the spirit of the initiative, and a sense of responsibility and combativeness. The base rule is to always keep oneself on the line between the adversary and the basket. The distance of coverage is a function of the length of the adversary's stride and the distance to the basket. The man with the ball will always be covered closer. Limiting the attackers' zone of action, in the phase under the basket, the adversary can be anticipated: the defender will take care to situate himself between the attacker and the man with the ball, discouraging a pass, which could put the entire defense in a very critical situation.

The first evolutionary step is an aggressive man-on-man defense. It dictates much more severe ways of marking, with the intent of inducing the adversary to check himself before taking the initiative. The most severe pressure on the man with the ball is already a notable obstacle to the successful execution of predetermined offense schemes: the possibility of slowing the marking of the men without the ball and of carrying out defensive changes becomes a great instrument against teams with poor ball control or that are afflicted with technically weak players. That distancing from the direct adversary and from the attacker to basket guiding principle introduces to the further perfecting of the man-to-man defense. It is, in other words, the principle of floating. The player who floats abandons the direct adversary (considered relatively dangerous for his distance from the basket or for the scarce shooting ability) to help teammates in difficulty. That is, he will bring himself into an intermediate position that is the vertex, towards the basket to be defended, an isosceles triangle that has at the other two vertexes—the man with the ball (and the relative direct adversary) and the abandoned attacker. The floating defender can decide to bring himself decisively against the man with the ball, coming to the side of his teammate, when he believes there is the concrete possibility of stealing the ball, or when he is constrained to knocking the ball free towards the lateral line, or anyway in a position at which he makes it very difficult to make a good pass. Otherwise, the floating player can move to cover another attacker at the defender's back. In either case, he realizes a double-coverage, the extra man.

Obviously, one who is not agile enough to readily return to closely cover the original adversary is not able to float. Floating will also not permit itself use in the moment in which the man with the ball is not marked closely enough to prevent a pass to the abandoned man.

Floating and double-coverage indicate extreme teamwork, collaborative spirit, and sense of sacrifice, but they are also weapons, which can resolve a game. A double-coverage of a center can prevent that he receive passes or makes it extremely difficult for him to attempt a lay-up, which is the key shot of the well covered center.

The individual procedures, in the three types of man-to-man defense, it is said, are those consecrated in the individual's fundamentals. Particulars which are apparently insignificant, but which are in reality essentials in the set of a first class defender, must not go completely ignored. For example, the player who floats will always keep in front the foot on the side of his man, who can suddenly become important if the ball is passed to him: and that is the position that allows him to most rapidly return to covering his original man. The good defender, again will always search to set himself up with his weakside (correspon-

ding to that foot advanced) towards the part of the court where he knows he can find help: for a change-over, for example, in the event that his adversary beats him with ballhandling. In every case, the defender will try to direct his adversary towards the least favorable side of the court; or towards a lateral line in order to limit the attacker's range of action, or to gain time permitting his teammates to reconstitute the defensive setup, or towards the center where the defense is most fit.

SOURCE

Rubini, Cesare. Archives, Pedro Ferrandiz Foundation. Samaranch Library. Madrid, Spain.

LEGACY OF
Leonard "Lenny" Sachs

- Adapted the professional game to college basketball by using the post player as a goaltender, screener, and passer.

- Laid the groundwork for Loyola's pioneering endeavors in desegregating sports.

- Designed a 2-2-1 zone defense, prior to the goaltending rule, that enabled taller players to stand under the basket and swat away shots.

- Respected for taking players of average ability and developing them into cohesive, overachieving teams.

- Led Loyola to a 31-game winning streak from 1928 to 1930.

- Directed Loyola to a second-place finish in the 1939 NIT.

LEONARD "LENNY" SACHS

"Len knew his basketball, and he knew how to teach it—his ideas were his own. He played the game clean. He won and lost like a man."
—Jimmy Corcoran
Chicago Herald - American • October 28, 1942

BIOGRAPHY

Born: August 7, 1897 in Chicago, Ill

Died: October 27, 1942

Inducted into the Naismith Basketball Hall of Fame in 1961

A native of Chicago, Leonard "Lenny" Sachs graduated from Carl Schurz High School in 1914, where he was president of the senior class and earned eleven letters as an all-around athlete. Sachs was in the U.S. Navy during World War I and played on the Cleveland Naval Reserves football team. In 1918, he received honorable mention status on the Walter Camp All-Service football team. Sachs was also a standout basketball player and led the Illinois Athletic Club to the AAU national championship in 1917. Lenny played professional football for the Chicago Cardinals, Milwaukee Badgers, and the Hammond Pros. He joined the Chicago Public School coaching ranks in 1919, first at Phillips High School and then at Marshall. Sachs was the basketball coach at Loyola University from 1923 to 1942. He coached the Ramblers to a record of 224-129, including an undefeated season in 1928-29. Loyola won 31 consecutive games from 1928 to 1930 and finished second in the NIT in 1939. Sachs developed a 2-2-1 zone defense that enabled his tallest player to swat away shots prior to the goaltending rule. Sachs served as chairman of the NABC Research Committee in 1937. Loyola annually names the Lenny Sachs Male and Female Student-Athlete of the Year.

Leonard "Lenny" Sachs...

Lenny Sachs was a prolific athlete at Chicago's Schurz High School, and earned 11 varsity letters before he graduated in 1914. He joined the U.S. Navy during World War I, and was named honorable mention on the all-service football team in 1918.

Sachs returned to Chicago in 1919 and attended the American College of Physical Education. To work his way through college, he coached basketball at Wendell Phillips High School from 1919 to 1921, and at Marshall High School from 1921 to 1923. Lenny led Marshall to the city's basketball title in 1922.

But that wasn't all. While attending college and coaching high school basketball, the 5'8", 176 pound Sachs played offensive end for the fledging Chicago Cardinals of the NFL from 1920 to 1922, and scored the first points in franchise history. In one game in 1920, Sachs blocked three punts in the same quarter, and ran the first one back for a touchdown,

Upon graduating from the American College of Physical Education in 1923, Sachs signed on as the basketball coach at Loyola. His Loyola teams went 8-11 in 1923-24, and 4-11 in 1924-25. It was not an impressive start for Sachs, but he might have been a little distracted. At the same time that he was coaching at Loyola, Lenny played for the NFL's Milwaukee Badgers during his first year, and

the Hammond Pros in his second season. After a brief NFL coaching stint with the Louisville Colonels in 1926 (they were 0-4 before disbanding), Sachs focused his full attention on Loyola basketball.

That's when the winning really began. Over the next 17 seasons, Sachs' Loyola teams went 212-107. Using a 2-2-1 zone defense that focused on the play of big men, the Ramblers won 31 consecutive games from 1928-1930, and finished a perfect 16-0 in 1928-29. Sachs designed the defense so that his tall players could stand under the basket and swat away shots. The strategy was so effective that it eventually forced the adoption of the goaltending rule.

In 1938-39, the Ramblers were a perfect 21-0 going into the NIT Championship game at Madison Square Garden. They had won their games by an average margin of 14.5 points per game during an era when dominant teams typically scored in the 40s. But Long Island University, coached by Clair Bee and encouraged by the home crowd, manhandled Loyola 44-32 in the championship. It was the lowest point total of the year for the Ramblers.

While at Loyola, Sachs earned a graduate degree, and was hired as athletic director upon graduation in 1935. He is often credited with being one of the greatest Jewish athletes of all time, and recognized for taking players with mediocre talent and turning them into winners through infusing determination and strategy. His philosophy took a struggling basketball program at a Midwestern Jesuit Catholic school and turned it into a national powerhouse.

After the disappointing loss in the NIT Finals, Sachs began to rebuild the Loyola squad that was depleted by graduation. His team won only five games in 1939-40, but improved to 13-8 and 17-6, respectively, the next two seasons.

In addition to his role as Loyola basketball coach and athletic director, Sachs coached the all-black Wendell Phillips High School football team. While preparing for a dramatic match up at Soldier Field with cross-town rival DuSable, Sachs had a massive heart attack just outside the physical education building at Phillips High School.

Leonard David Sachs passed away on October 27, 1942 at the age of 45. Loyola's Dean of the College of Arts and Sciences, Rev. William A. Finnegan, issued the following statement on behalf of the University:

.....SCOUTING REPORT.....SCOUTING REPORT...

"The sad news of the sudden death of Mr. Sachs was a terrible shock to the faculty and students of Loyola University. It will be extremely difficult to find another coach of basketball who combines in himself all the qualities we observed in him during the long years of loyal service to the University. We regarded him as the finest basketball coach in the country, one who not only taught basketball to his students and produced many basketball stars, but a coach who exercised a profound influence on the young men who came under his direction. His memory will endure at Loyola as a molder of men, an excellent Catholic gentleman and a Loyola friend."

The night after Sach's death, one of his great basketball stars, Charley "Feed" Murphy appeared on WGN radio to highlight his former coach's career. Members of the 1939 and 1942 Loyola basketball team served as pallbearers at his funeral.

The death of Lenny Sachs during the midst of World War II was a major factor in the suspension of the Loyola basketball program from 1943 to 1945. After the war, Loyola resurrected its basketball program under Thomas Haggerty. And thanks in part to the strong foundation built by Sachs, the Ramblers were back in the 1949 NIT Finals, this time losing by only one point to San Francisco.

Before and throughout his tenure at Loyola, Lenny Sachs coached African-American athletes in the high school ranks. As a coach of a Division I college program that played teams from large and small communities all over the country in the 1920s and 1930s, he may not have had the ability to bring African-Americans onto his teams at the college level, but the commitment was certainly there. His legacy was to lay the groundwork for Loyola's pioneering endeavors in desegregating sports.

In 1961, nineteen years after his death, Lenny Sachs was inducted into the Naismith Memorial Basketball Hall of Fame. In 1963, Loyola finished what Sachs had begun forty years earlier by winning the NCAA national championship with four African-American starters.

SOURCE

Sachs, Leonard. Vertical Files, Archives. Naismith Memorial Basketball Hall of Fame. Springfield, MA.

Thomas, John C. (2002). *Lenny Sachs: A Loyola Legend.* http://www.ramblermania.com/sachs.htm

THE MODERN ADAPTATION OF THE PRO GAME

By Len Sachs

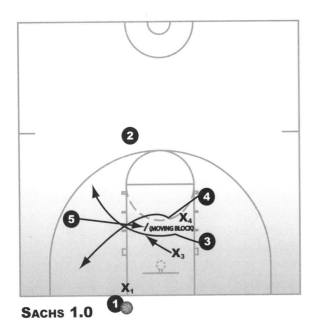

SACHS 1.0

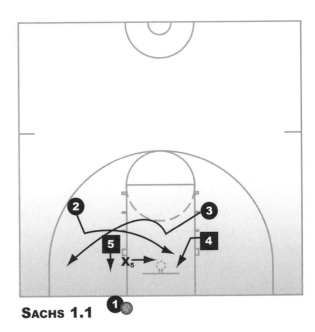

SACHS 1.1

Authors' Note: This article by Lennie Sachs first appeared in the December 1937 Athletic Journal, one of the first athletic publications for coaches. It centers on the lessons to be learned from the demise of the early versions of professional basketball. It reveals how he incorporated the more free-lance movements of the pros with his knowledge of basketball rules to produce his Loyola basketball system, with the post player as a screener (blocker) and passer.

With the passing of the professional cage league, basketball lost its greatest supporter of the ready-made pickoff offense, yet many schools find that it provides them with a first-class power attack, one that requires the greatest of basketball skill, with perfect ballhandling a necessity. This style of play, used by Loyola University of Chicago, does away with the mechanical style. It means that the players must be wide-awake at all times.

The diagrams depict some of the differences between the "new" and "old" types of basketball.

In **Diagram 1.0,** an out-of-bounds play under the offensive basket is pictured in "old style." Player 05 has deliberately blocked out X4, who is guarding 04 in order that 04 may cut for the basket. This is an obvious block and is illegal.

Diagram 1.1 shows a typical modern block play which is entirely within the rules. Instead of going out of his way to block a defensive man, the pivot man has taken his position on the free-throw line, facing his teammate who has the ball out of bounds under his own basket. Guards 02 and 03 have run their men into the pivot man and are cutting around him to receive the pass from out-of-bounds. They have used him, the pivot man, as a blocking post, and there has been no deliberate illegal block on his part.

In case 01's man drops back to switch, as in **Diagram 1.1,** he is free to receive the pass from out-of-bounds.

Diagrams 1.2 and 1.3 show the type of play used by professional and other teams which have fine ballhandling clubs. Practically every play involves a so-called block. However, the play is legal, for when contact takes place, it is because a smart offensive player has maneuvered his opponent into such a position that it is impossible for the defensive man to cover his man.

In **Diagram 1.2,** player 01 has been dribbling towards his basket; while doing so, his teammate, 02, has cut around him from the side, and 01 has bounced the ball to him without slowing down; as a result, X2 has run into 01, and unless the man X1 who is guarding the offensive player 01 switches, 02 will dribble into the basket.

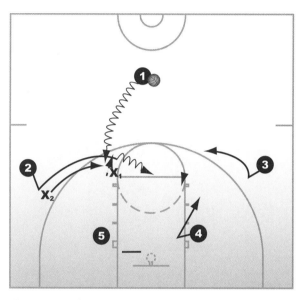

SACHS 1.2

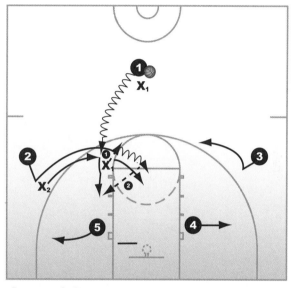

SACHS 1.3

In **Diagram 1.4** we have the typical "old" pickoff or block play, much on the order of the old out-of-bounds play. Player 5 is picking off the defensive man in order that his man may cut through, free, towards the basket. This and similar plays are closely allied to blocks used in football games, the amount of contact and blocking depending upon time, place, etc.

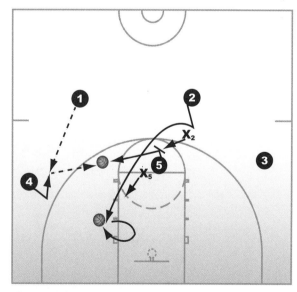

SACHS 1.4

SOURCE

Sachs, Len. (1937, December). The Modern Adaptation of the Pro Game. *Athletic Journal*.

LEGACY OF
Dean Smith

- Recorded 879 wins during his 36-year coaching career and is the all-time winningest Division I men's coach in the history of the game.

- One of only three coaches to win the "Triple Crown" of coaching.

- Held the NCAA Tournament record for most appearances, most consecutive appearances, and most tournament victories at the time of his retirement.

- Had teams that were known for their unselfish play, outstanding teamwork, and a tenacious man-to-man defense.

- Popularized the four-corner offense and the run-and-jump defense.

- Created a basketball program based on integrity, honor, and respect.

DEAN SMITH

"What to do with a mistake—recognize it, admit it, learn from it, and forget it."
—Dean Smith

BIOGRAPHY

Born: February 28, 1931 in Emporia, KS

Inducted into the Naismith Basketball Hall of Fame in 1983

In thirty-six years at the University of North Carolina, Dean Smith compiled a record of 879-254, a winning percentage of .776. The 879 victories are the most by any men's coach in Division I college basketball history. He led North Carolina to the NCAA championship in 1982 and 1993. Under Smith, the Tar Heels made twenty-three consecutive NCAA appearances. His Carolina teams also won or shared a record seventeen ACC regular-season titles and won a record thirteen ACC tournament championships. Smith was head coach of the 1976 U.S. Olympic basketball team, which won the gold medal. He was highly regarded as an innovator and developed the four-corner offense and run-and-jump defense. Smith played for Hall of Fame coach "Phog" Allen and was a member of the 1952 University of Kansas NCAA championship team. ABC and ESPN named him one of the seven greatest coaches of the twentieth century in any sport.

Dean Smith...

"We Are Family," the 1978 hit by Sister Sledge, aptly describes Dean Smith's North Carolina teams during his illustrious 36-year coaching career. The lyrics depict the togetherness and camaraderie of the North Carolina basketball family. If you were tuned into the radio during that era, the words will come back with comfortable familiarity:

"Everyone can see we're together
As we walk on by
(Fly!) and we fly just like birds of a feather
I won't tell no lie
(All!) all of the people around us they say
Can they be that close
Just let me state for the record
We're giving love in a family dose
We are family!"

Smith's Tar Heels flew "like birds of a feather" past their opponents with amazing consistency. Under Smith, North Carolina had an all-time record of 879-254 and his teams won more games than those of any other college coach in history. The Tar Heels won at least 20 games for 27 straight years. North Carolina was the dominant force in the Atlantic Coast Conference and finished in the top three for 33 successive seasons. In that span, the Tar Heels won the ACC 17 times and finished second 11 times.

Despite such success, victories were secondary in the North Carolina's "We Are Family" environment. Smith's number one priority was developing people of high character. He placed this above everything else, including winning. "Coach Smith was concerned about preparing players for life after college and the game of basketball was a platform for him to do that," said James Worthy, a member of the 2003 Basketball Hall of Fame enshrinement class.

Smith structured the North Carolina basketball program on the tenets of respect and loyalty and created a fraternity like no other in the basketball world. "His program was very much a different style than most college basketball programs," stated former Tar Heel and NBA coach George Karl. "He built his program around team and family and togetherness and camaraderie and helping each other. There was always a family kind of unity that I don't think existed anywhere else."

Smith's emphasis on family values developed during his childhood in Emporia, Kansas. His parents, both public school teachers, reinforced the important life lessons of integrity, compassion, industriousness, humility, and love. "I was raised in a relatively strict home, and I learned most of my values from a very loving mother and father," said Smith.

"Value each human being" was a central theme in Smith's household, and he was taught to treat every person with respect and dignity. Smith had been in Chapel Hill just one year when he and his pastor escorted a black student into a restaurant where blacks were not served. It was not a popular move in the segregation-inflicted South of the 1960s, but that did not concern Smith because he would not tolerate racial injustice.

Smith transferred the lessons he learned as a young man into his basketball philosophy. He created a basketball program based on integrity, honor, and respect. Players learned how to live with people from different backgrounds and different cultures. They gained an appreciation for working hard and playing according to the rules. They learned the importance of teamwork and unselfishness. They were provided daily opportunities to experience success in an arena much larger than basketball.

Smith's players received a daily practice plan with a "Thought for the Day" at the top of the page, and they were expected to memorize it. It usually had nothing to do with basketball, but rather was a philosophical statement that put basketball into a larger context. Smith used the Serenity Prayer on occasion or a statement, such as "Don't let one day pass without doing something for a person who cannot repay you." Smith started each practice with a few comments and then asked a player to recite the "Thought for the Day." If for any reason a player failed to give the correct response, the entire team had to run. Players made sure they learned the "Thought for the Day," because they didn't want their teammates to run for their mistake.

The basketball program at North Carolina was built on three goals: 1) play together, 2) play hard, and 3) play smart. The goals were clear and concise, and Smith seldom discussed winning with his players. He believed that winning was merely a by-product of players demonstrating unselfishness, hard work, and proper execution.

Smith promoted rituals that encouraged togetherness and teamwork. One ritual was pointing to the passer to acknowledge the unselfish act of passing the ball to an open teammate. Coach John Wooden told Smith that he always wanted the receiver of a pass to say a quick thank-you to the passer or wink at him. Smith decided that he wanted a more obvious gesture and asked his players to point to the passer. He hoped this gesture would alert fans and members of the media to the importance of passing. It became a ritual not only with the players on the floor but also with the coaches and players on the bench. It wasn't long until Tar Heel fans adopted the ritual and were showing their appreciation for unselfish play.

Another North Carolina ritual was to have everyone on the bench stand and applaud when a player was taken out of the game. "We told our players that if the president of the United States entered the room, we'd stand out of respect," said Smith. "To our way of thinking, a teammate was more important than anybody. So when a player came out of the game, his teammates showed their appreciation by standing and applauding. The coaches also stand to applaud, even if the player hasn't played well. That did wonders to promote unselfishness."

Smith treated every player as an important member of the team. He did not differentiate between the lesser-skilled and higher-skilled athletes. "Whether you were a starter or a twelfth man, he made us all feel like we were the most important player who ever played for him," remembered former player and future Hall of Fame coach Larry Brown.

Smith created a practice environment that was conducive to learning and was recognized by his coaching peers as a master teacher. "Dean Smith is a better teacher of basketball than anyone else," said legendary UCLA coach John Wooden.

Each session was carefully planned and meticulously organized. Players sprinted from one drill to the next. As they moved, they were reminded of the specifics of the North Carolina philosophy. Virtually everything during practice was graded based on execution.

"Practice was the foundation of everything that we did," explained Smith. "We used practice and repetition to teach our players what we wanted. Our players always felt that our practices were harder than games, and that's the way it should have been. The teaching I did in our practices was what I really missed the most when I retired."

Smith's goal in coaching was not to become the all-time winningest coach. He does not talk about the 879 wins. He talks about the people behind the victories...their successes and their accomplishments. Like a proud father, he smiles when reflecting on the fact that 97 percent of his players graduated, and almost forty percent later attained post-graduate degrees. His greatest desire is that his players succeed as people and find happiness in life.

Smith has always been there for his players. When Michael Jordan's father was murdered in the summer of 1993, it was Smith who met Jordan at the Wilmington, North Carolina Airport. "The two most important men in my life have been my father and Dean Smith," said Jordan.

David Chadwick, a forward on the great North Carolina teams in the late 1960s and early '70s, wrote a book entitled, *The 12 Leadership Principles of Dean Smith,* based on what he considered were Smith's guiding principles. During one of his conversations with Coach Smith, the phone rang in Smith's office, and Smith looked puzzled. "I don't understand," said Smith. "I gave explicit instructions not to be interrupted." The phone stopped ringing and Chadwick continued his conversation with his mentor. The phone started ringing again, but this time, Smith wasn't puzzled.

"Excuse me for a moment," said Smith. "That must be my private line. It's either one of my children or another former player. They're the only ones who have my private number. They are the only ones who can get to me any time they want."

All-American Phil Ford may have described it best when he said, "I always tell Coach that he's the only father in the world with three hundred children, and only five of them are his own."

Bill Bradley said, "Dean Smith epitomizes what a coach can be — teacher, counselor, mentor, example, friend." During his stellar career, Smith has received numerous awards, including *Sports Illustrated's* 1997 Sportsman of the Year and the 1998 University Award, the highest honor given by the Board of Governors of the 16-campus University of North Carolina.

Smith is more than the all-time winningest coach in the history of college basketball. He is a man of unyielding integrity whose "North Carolina basketball family" is an internationally recognized symbol of what intercollegiate sports should represent.

SOURCE

Chadwick, David. (1999). *The 12 Leadership Principles of Dean Smith*. Total/Sports Illustrated. New York.

Pim, Ralph. (2003). Family Style. *Naismith Memorial Basketball Hall of Fame Enshrinement Program.*

Smith, Dean. Interview with Ralph Pim. June 18, 2003.

Smith, Dean. Vertical Files, Archives. Naismith Memorial Basketball Hall of Fame. Springfield, MA.

Smith. Dean. (2002). *A Coach's Life*. New York: Random House.

PLAY HARD; PLAY TOGETHER; PLAY SMART

By Dean Smith

I never went into a season as North Carolina's head coach thinking we'd just plug things into the previous year's plan and duplicate ourselves. We never had the same team return, and there were any number of variables from one year to the next. We couldn't have had the long run of success that we enjoyed if we'd been too stubborn to change and come up with new ideas and different ways to play the game.

Don't fear change. Sometimes change can refresh a stale team; sometimes changing personnel mandates it; sometimes the rules of the game change. We adapted each year to hide our weaknesses and accentuate our strengths.

Although we didn't have a system at North Carolina, we certainly had a philosophy. We believed in it strongly and didn't stray very far from it. It pretty much stayed the same from my first year as head coach. It was our mission statement, our strategic plan, and our entire approach in a nutshell: Play hard; play smart; play together.

Hard meant with effort, determination, and courage; *together* meant unselfishly, trusting your teammates, and doing everything possible not to let them down; *smart* meant with good execution and poise, treating each possession as if it were the only one in the game.

This was our philosophy; we believed that if we kept our focus on those tenets, success would follow. Our North Carolina players seldom heard me talk about winning. Winning would be the byproduct of the process. There could be no shortcuts.

Making winning the ultimate goal usually isn't good teaching. Tom Osborne, the great former football coach of the University of Nebraska, said that making winning the goal could actually get in the way of winning. I agree. So many things happened in games that were beyond our control: the talent and experience of the teams, bad calls by officials, injuries, bad luck.

In teaching our players, I tried to concentrate on the process, rather than the results. I think it is the best way to teach. If a coach starts out on the first day of practice talking about winning, that approach can actually get in the way of winning.

Building a team takes patience and planning. We went through the process step by step, no shortcuts. We repeated drills until good habits were established. We stressed sound fundamentals. We drove home the point that basketball is a team game, and the team members need to depend on one another. We talked about the soundness of putting the team first. We taught players not to dwell on the consequences of failure. We valued each possession, and I encouraged the players not to look at the scoreboard until it became smart to do so with a few minutes left, although that was difficult for them to do. We went to great lengths to reward unselfish behavior, and we profusely praised those acts we wanted to see repeated.

By sticking to our philosophy, we asked realistic things from our players. A player could play hard. He could play unselfishly and do things to help his teammates succeed. He could play intelligently, if we did the job in practice as coaches. We measured our success by how we did in those areas.

When we put these elements together, the players had fun, one of my goals as their coach. I wanted our players to enjoy the experience of playing basketball for North Carolina. Each player on our team knew he was important. Each did a terrific job of sharing the ball, which also made the game enjoyable for more players. All won and lost as a team.

Of course, it is easier to talk about playing hard, playing smart, and playing together than it is to do all three. It begins by the recruiting of unselfish players, who subscribe to the philosophy of team over individual.

PLAYING HARD

Maybe a player wasn't the fastest, the tallest, or the most athletic person on the court. In the course of any given game, that was out of his control. But each of them could control the effort with which he played. "Never let anyone play harder than you," I told them. "This is part of the game you can control." If another team played harder than we did, we had no excuse for it. None. We worked on it in every practice. If a player didn't give maximum effort, we dealt with it right then. We stopped practice and had the entire team run sprints for the offending player. We played a style of basketball that was physically exhausting and made it impossible for a player to go full throttle for forty minutes. When he got tired, he flashed the tired signal, a raised fist, and we substituted for him. He could put himself back in the game once he had rested. We didn't want tired players on the court, because they usually tried to rest on defense. That wouldn't work in our plan. Therefore, we watched closely in practice and in games to make sure players played hard. If they slacked off, it was important to catch them and get them out of the game, or if it occurred in practice, to have the entire team run.

PLAYING TOGETHER

One of the first things I did at the beginning of preseason practice was to spell out for our players the importance of team play. Basketball is a game that counts on togetherness. I pointed out that seldom, if ever, did the nation's leading scorer play on a ranked team. He certainly didn't play on a championship team. I made them understand that our plan would fall apart if they didn't take care of another: set screens; play team defense; box out; pass to the open man. One man who failed to do his job unselfishly could undermine the efforts of the four other players on the court.

PLAYING SMART

We taught and drilled until we made the things we wanted to see become habits. The only way to have a smart team is to have one that is fundamentally sound. We didn't skimp on fundamentals. We worked on them hard in practice and repeated them until they were down cold. We didn't introduce something and then move away from it before we had nailed it. Our entire program was built around practice. Practice, competitive games, late-game situations, and my relationship with our players are what I've missed most since I retired from coaching. If we practiced well and learned, we could play smart. It was another thing that we could control.

If you asked me to define my coaching and leadership style, I'd describe myself as an open-minded dictator. My basketball philosophy boils down to six words: play hard; play together; play smart.

SOURCE

Smith, Dean. (2004). *The Carolina Way*. New York: The Penguin Press.

BUILDING CONFIDENCE

By Dean Smith

I've never believed that there was a magic formula for building confidence. I think it comes out of the process. The working equation is: hard work equals success, which equals confidence.

Confidence can be as fragile as an eggshell. Coaches can't talk players into being confident, although praising players when praise is deserved can help them become more confident.

There are some who believe a leader can trick subordinates into being confident. I know of a Columbia University experiment many years ago involving twenty young people who flunked a math quiz. Ten of them were told they had flunked, while the others were told they had made Cs. When they all took the exam again, the ten who had been told they'd made Cs improved more than the others. Ten of them had been conned and improved, but I think that type of confidence is short-term. The truth will be revealed at some point, and those who were conned into believing they were improving will suffer a significant setback. They could lose trust in themselves and their coach or teacher.

I believe strongly in positive reinforcement. I looked carefully to determine that we praised behavior that we wanted to see repeated. In the case of at least one player, I even made a note on the top of my practice plan to try to find some reason to praise him. He did not have much self-confidence and needed a boost. His play reflected it. However, I waited for it to happen before I praised, and then I made a big show of it to make sure every player on the team heard it. I wasn't going to offer false praise, because I believe it is counterproductive.

Maybe something good would come of it in the short term, but not for the long haul. Years later the player might look back on the incident and realize his coach had conned him or lied to him. The truth will prevail.

Every coach wants a confident team. Players who enter games intimidated or doubting themselves don't have much chance to succeed. There's a fine line in athletics between confidence and complacency. I wanted our players quietly confident but not overconfident, because overconfidence leads to complacency. Overconfident people think they're better than they really are, and they're ripe for a reality jolt. Sometimes players act cocky to hide being scared.

While most of our teams were confident, I also like the players to feel a little nervous before they played. Senior leadership also was crucial in having a confident team. Those players had been in our program for four years and knew what we wanted and what it took to get it. They were able to mentor the youngest players and give them a heads-up on what to expect in different situations, especially on the road, where we faced hostile crowds. They told them that is was okay to be nervous and to expect some adversity in the game.

I was not a locker-room orator along the lines of Knute Rockne. The players would have been shocked to hear me stand before them and give a "Let's win one for the Gipper" speech. However, I did challenge them. For example, if an opponent had played harder than we had in the first half, I challenged them during our halftime talk to reverse that in the second half. On most occasions, though, I would just go over our

strategy at halftime, review the first half, and talk about what we needed to do in the second half. On road games, I would say, "Remember, after we win the game, no celebrating on their court. Let's come back down here and celebrate the victory in our locker room as a team."

One of the best ways to instill confidence is through good preparation. We tried to put our players through every situation in practice that they might experience in a game. For instance, we would give our second team a fifteen-point lead with five minutes on the clock to see if our starters could go to their "hurry-up" offense and overcome it. The first team pressed and gambled on defense, shot three-pointers on offense, and if it missed, fouled the defensive rebounder.

When a situation came up like this in a game, I could say to them, "We've done this before in practice. Let's go out and repeat it now." In such a situation, players can gain confidence from their coach, because they have been prepared to face it. It is also important for players to see their coach poised and prepared to face any situation.

We wanted every player on our team to feel confident and needed. It's one reason, among several others, that I never wanted a so-called go-to-guy on our team. A team is more dangerous when each man on the court can score or make a play in a crucial game-deciding situation. If you have one player designated to take most of the crucial shots, the opponent knows it and could take steps to defend it. I preferred having five go-to guys on the court. Every one of our players could make the shot if left open; otherwise he shouldn't have been on

LESSONS FROM THIS LEGEND...

the team. I didn't want our team to think it had a go-to-guy. My goal was for all of them to feel they had an important role, which they did.

Practice is where we built our foundations, and that included building confidence. For example, I didn't use a player's name when practicing a play. Instead of calling the name of the starting point guard, I would say, "This is what our number one man needs to do in this situation." That way the reserve point guards also felt more a part of the team and gained confidence from it. After all, they were very much part of the plan.

Confidence is elusive but a great thing for anyone, not just college basketball players, to have. I see no shortcuts to get it. Hard work plus success equals confidence. Remember, if you think you can't, you're correct; if you think you can, you're halfway there.

SOURCE

Smith, Dean. (2004). *The Carolina Way*. New York: The Penguin Press.

LEGACY OF
Pat Head Summitt

- Became the all-time winningest Division I basketball coach on March 22, 2005.

- Selected the Naismith Coach of the Century.

- Became the first woman to reach the 800-win plateau.

- Has led the University of Tennessee to six national championships.

- Coached the 1984 U.S. Women's team to their first gold medal in Olympic competition.

- Builds her teams on the premise that defense wins games, and rebounds win championships.

- Teaches life skills through the game of basketball.

PAT HEAD SUMMITT

*"Sometimes, basketball is the
least of what I teach."*
—Pat Head Summitt

BIOGRAPHY

Born: June 14, 1952 in Henrietta, TN

Inducted into the Naismith Basketball Hall of Fame in 2000

Pat Head Summitt became the all-time winningest Division I basketball coach on March 22, 2005, breaking the record held by legendary Dean Smith. To commemorate her incredible achievement, the University of Tennessee named its basketball court at the Thompson-Boling Arena, "The Summitt." Pat, who took over the reins of the University of Tennessee program at the age of 22, has led the Lady Vols to six national championships and 16 Final Four appearances. During her 31-year tenure, Summitt's teams have an incredible 15 seasons of 30-plus wins. She has been named the NCAA Coach of the Year on seven occasions. In 2000, she was named the Naismith Coach of the Century. In 1999, Summitt was the first woman to receive the Naismith Basketball Hall of Fame's John Bunn Award. In 1984, Summitt coached the U.S. Women's team to their first gold medal in Olympic competition. As a player, Summitt was co-captain of the 1976 U.S. Olympic Team that won a silver medal. She was enshrined in the Women's Basketball Hall of Fame in 1999 and the Naismith Memorial Basketball Hall of Fame in 2000.

Pat Head Summitt...

No coach in women's college basketball history has been to more NCAA tournaments, coached in more Final Fours, or won more national championships than Pat Summitt.

Pat Head Summitt was the fourth of five children of Richard and Hazel Head and the first girl. Her father was a strong disciplinarian, and "Tricia," as she was known as a youth, grew up competing with three older brothers and working hard on the family farm. She learned that laziness was not tolerated, and that excuses weren't accepted. When she wasn't working in the fields or attending school, Summitt was playing basketball in the hayloft with her brothers. She was a four-year starter at Cheatham County (Ashland, TN) High School and was an All-District 20 Tournament selection in 1970.

Summitt attended the University of Tennessee at Martin and received her degree in physical education. She led the Lady Pacers to a 64-29 record and two appearances in the national championship tournament. Summitt scored 1,045 points during her career and graduated as UT-Martin's all-time leading scorer.

Summitt was a member of the 1973 U.S. World Games team and co-captain of the 1976 U.S. Olympic team. She earned two silver medals and had the opportunity to play for coaches such as Cathy Rush, Billie Moore, Sue Gunter, and Alberta Cox, some of the greatest coaching minds in women's basketball.

Summitt was only 22 years old when she took over the program at the University of Tennessee. In her first year, she led the team to a 16-8 record, attended graduate school, taught physical education classes, and earned a playing spot on the U.S. Women's World Championship team.

To win championships, it takes talented players. Summit believes two key ingredients of a championship team are a go-to player in the paint and a point guard who is the quarterback of the team. Her system is built on great defense and rebounding. Summitt said, "Offense sells tickets, defense wins games, and rebounds wins championships."

Summitt preaches the team concept, and every player is expected to understand and play her role. "I've always felt that you had to go out and play great defense every night and board with people," said Summitt.

Summitt is an intense, demanding, and focused competitor. She instills a pattern of success in her players and constantly challenges them to reach their maximum potential. "I'm someone who will push you beyond all reasonable limits," said Summitt (1998). "Someone who will ask you not to just fulfill your potential but to exceed it. Someone who will expect more from you than you may believe you are capable of."

Player Semeka Randall said, "Having Pat is like having a second mom—tough love." Teammate Kristen Clement added, "Yeah, Coach will get on you and she'll make you feel really bad at times, but I think she brings out the best in you, and you really grow to love her."

To her athletes, she is "Pat" from the minute she meets them on a recruiting trip to the day they receive their diploma.

Summitt believes her primary mission is to prepare players to win at the most important game of all—life. "We're teaching life skills," said Summitt. "I don't want average people. Average people cut corners. Winners know there are no shortcuts."

If a player does not go to class, she cannot play. Players are expected to sit in the first three rows in class and pay attention. They are to complete all assignments on time and treat everyone with respect. Every Lady Vol who has completed her eligibility at Tennessee has received her degree or is in the process of completing her degree requirements.

To Summitt, a coach assumes many different roles such as a teacher, a parent-figure, a friend, a counselor, or a psychologist. Her program is concerned with three dimensions: the person, the player, and the student. "It's more than X's and O's," said Summit. "It's about caring about individuals. Basketball is a way in which we teach life skills." (Packer, 1999)

Summitt said that some of the best advice on how to develop championship teams came from Hall of Fame coach Billie Moore. "She's the most professional person I've ever known. Her advice to me was to always do things the right way and be a professional. There's a right way and a wrong way to do things. Things are black and white. Do not live in the gray. Do not move into the gray for any decision. Keep things as they should be, and do them the right way." (Packer, 1999)

On March 22, 2005, Summitt led her Lady Vols past Purdue, 75-54, in the second round of the NCAA Tournament. The victory was the 880th of her coaching career, which moved her past the legendary Dean Smith of North Carolina (879) as the all-time winningest coach in NCAA basketball history, men or women.

Assistant coach Dean Lockwood (2005) said, "If you had been in our staff meetings on a daily basis, you would not have known that record was imminent or on the horizon. It was not brought up or discussed by Pat. Her only focus was that of our basketball team. All the other things were peripheral to Pat. I think that speaks so much to Pat's genuine and true humility. She is so unconcerned about personal glory and personal recognition. Pat is probably the most humble person I have ever been around."

"Even as great a coach as Pat is," continued Lockwood, "she is even a better human being in terms of how she cares about our players and how seriously she takes her responsibility as a leader and a role model. It is sacred to her. She is totally committed to preparing young people for success in life. As much as she has accomplished as a coach, and as many Hall of Fames as she is in, there is nothing that means more to Pat than acting with character and integrity."

SOURCE

Lockwood, Dean. Interview with Ralph Pim. March 26, 2005.

Packer, Billy and Roland Lazenby. (1999). *Why We Win.* Chicago: Masters Press.

Summitt, Pat. Vertical Files, Archives. Naismith Memorial Basketball Hall of Fame. Springfield, MA.

Summitt, Pat and Sally Jenkins. (1998). *Reach for the Summit.* New York: Broadway Books.

THE DEFINITE DOZEN SYSTEM FOR SUCCESS

By Pat Summitt

The Definite Dozen System is more than just a formula for success. It is a set of principles that has evolved over my coaching career and is my blueprint for winning. You don't often hear ethics discussed in the same breath as success. But to me they are inseparable. Long-term, repetitive success is a matter of building a principled system and sticking to it. Principles are anchors; without them, you will drift.

1. RESPECT YOURSELF AND OTHERS

- Respect is the first step toward team building.
- Treat people the way you'd like to be treated.
- There is no such thing as self-respect without respect for others.
- Hard work breeds self-respect.
- When you ask yourself, "Do I deserve to succeed?" make sure the answer is yes.

2. TAKE FULL RESPONSIBILITY

- To be successful, you must accept full responsibility.
- Responsibility never ends. It's not a step or just a chapter. Responsibility is a constant state of being.
- The only effective way to teach responsibility to younger people is by making them accountable for the small things day in and day out.
- Being responsible sometimes means making tough, unpopular decisions.
- Admit to and make yourself accountable for mistakes. How can you improve if you're never wrong?

3. DEVELOP AND DEMONSTRATE LOYALTY

- Loyalty is not unilateral. You have to give it, to receive it.
- The single most common reason organizations self-destruct is disloyalty, especially when they are made up of young people who have a tendency to talk behind each other's backs.
- You win with people. I don't care how good you are. If you don't have a good, loyal staff, you will not succeed.
- The absolute heart of loyalty is to value those people who tell you the truth, not just those people who tell you what you want to hear.
- Loyalty must be tended to on a daily basis.

4. LEARN TO BE A GREAT COMMUNICATOR

- A clear understanding of what's expected of each person is crucial.
- Listening is crucial to good communication.
- Make good eye contact.
- We communicate all the time, even when we don't realize it. Be aware of body language.
- Silence is a form of communication, too. Sometimes less is more.

5. DISCIPLINE YOURSELF SO NO ONE ELSE HAS TO

- Discipline is the internal structure that supports your organization.
- Discipline fosters achievement and self-confidence.
- The ultimate goal of discipline is to teach self-discipline.
- When disciplining others, be fair, be firm, and be consistent.
- Discipline helps you finish a job, and finishing is what separates excellent work from average work.

6. MAKE HARD WORK YOUR PASSION

- There is a direct correlation between our record and our work ethic, and if there is one thing I cannot abide, it's a lack of effort.
- The harder you work, the harder it is to surrender.
- It is important to surround yourself with people who have the same work ethic that you have.
- Plan your work, work your plan.
- Think big, focus small. You have to focus small, because attention to everyday, ordinary detail is what will separate you from everyone else.

7. DON'T JUST WORK HARD, WORK SMART

- Smart work is a combination of efficiency and effectiveness that helps you succeed without wasted motion, and with perspective.
- Peaking is a matter of timely work. It's a matter of knowing when to sweat and when to rest.
- Success is about having the right person, in the right place, at the right time.
- Know your strengths, weaknesses, and needs.
- When you understand yourself and those around you, you are

better able to minimize weaknesses and maximize strengths.

8. PUT THE TEAM BEFORE YOURSELF

- Teamwork does not come naturally. It must be taught.
- Teamwork is really a form of trust.
- Teamwork allows common people to obtain uncommon results
- Teamwork is an emotional cohesion that develops from mutual respect and reciprocity and from coping with good times and adversity
- Not everyone is born to lead. Role players are critical to group success.

9. MAKE WINNING AN ATTITUDE

- Belief is at the core of everything I teach our players. I ask them to believe in each other and to believe in our principles.
- Attitude is a choice. Maintain a positive outlook.
- No one ever got anywhere by being negative.
- Confidence is what happens when you've done the hard work that entitles you to succeed.

10. BE A COMPETITOR

- Competition is one of the great tools for exploring yourself, and surprising yourself.
- People rise to the level of their own expectations and of the competition they seek out.
- Each time you go beyond your perceived limit, you become mentally stronger.
- Your competitors make you better. Having worthy adversaries stimulates your work ethic, and brings out qualities you may not have known that you had. So don't resent them.

11. CHANGE IS A MUST

- Change is good. How can you grow if you never change? Change forces you out of your comfort zone and pushes you to places you haven't been before.
- Overcoming fear is the most broadening thing in the world.
- The most successful organizations are those that are always looking for the new idea, the new way of doing things—or at least improving upon what they know.
- Take risks. You can't steal second base with your foot on first.

12. HANDLE SUCCESS LIKE YOU HANDLE FAILURE

- You can't always control what happens, but you can control how you handle it.
- You can't have continued success without experiencing failure.
- Most of us overreact when we lose, and overcelebrate when we win. We established a rule to make us move on. We have twenty-four hours to enjoy the win or recover from a loss.
- Sometimes you learn more from losing than winning. Losing forces you to reexamine.
- It's harder to stay on top than it is to make the climb. Continue to seek new goals.

SUCCESS IS A JOURNEY

Success is a lifelong endeavor. You can't solve every problem in your life, and you can't make yourself perfect. Somehow, you have to make a commitment to get better every day. At Tennessee, we make our practices harder than games. And we play a schedule that forces our team to cope with both success and failure, and get over it. To me, success is not overcomplicated. The truth is, it's a simple matter of focus. The most successful organizations tend to have a signature. They do two or three things extremely well.

FIVE CRITICAL AREAS IN BASKETBALL:

We emphasize five critical things every year, no matter whether we have won or lost. We teach them meticulously. The five things we emphasize are:

1. Pressure defense
2. Dominating the boards
3. Taking care of the basketball
4. Taking good shots
5. Making lay-ups and free throws.

"REAL" SUCCESS

I only promise what I can deliver. I don't guarantee success. I tell our players, "If you work with me, I'll help you be the player you should be." I give our players structure and discipline. I give them the tools and the opportunity to be successful. But at the end of their four years, they have to walk through that door to continued success by themselves. I'll get them to that point—but they have to take those final steps. Real success is when they don't need me anymore.

SOURCE

Summitt, Pat and Sally Jenkins. (1998). *Reach for the Summit.* New York: Broadway Books.

LEGACY OF
Bertha Frank Teague

- Coached 42 years at Byng (OK) High School and compiled an amazing 1,152-115 record.

- Known as "Mrs. Basketball of Oklahoma."

- Was a dignified coach, who stressed individual confidence and team conditioning.

- Won 98 consecutive games from 1936 to 1939.

- Led Byng High School to eight Oklahoma state titles.

- Founded the first girl's basketball clinic and first summer camp for women in the Southwest.

- Authored landmark girl's basketball coaching book in 1962.

BERTHA FRANK TEAGUE

"Good basketball players don't just happen. It takes time and plain hard work to develop unskilled material into game-winning players. There is no magic formula."
—Bertha Frank Teague

BIOGRAPHY

Born: September 17, 1906 in Carthage, MO

Died: June 13, 1991

Inducted into the Naismith Basketball Hall of Fame in 1985

Few coaches in any sport can match Bertha Teague's coaching success or her dedication to the game. Although she never played the game she so successfully mastered, Teague compiled an astonishing 1,152-115 record for a winning percentage of .910. Bertha held the record for most wins at the girl's high-school level until 1991. Teague coached 42 years (1927-1969) at tiny Byng High School in Ada, Oklahoma and guided her teams to eight Oklahoma state championships and finished as runner-up seven times. From 1936 to 1939, the Lady Pirates won 98 straight games and three state titles. The Jim Thorpe Athletic Awards Committee named Teague the Coach of the Decade for the 1930s, 1940s, and 1960s. In Teague's last game as coach in 1969, Byng won the state championship by one point. She founded the first girl's basketball clinic and camp in the Southwest. She also helped organize the Oklahoma High School Girls Basketball Coaches Association in 1962 and served as president for eight years. Teague served on the National Rules Committee of the Division of Girls and Women's Sport from 1949 to 1960. She was enshrined in the Women's Basketball Hall of Fame in 1999 and the Naismith Memorial Basketball Hall of Fame in 1985.

Bertha Teague...

In 1969, Judy Corvin of the Byng (OK) Lady Pirates hit a short jump shot at the buzzer in a 46-45 victory over Elk City in the Class 2A state championship girls basketball game. The shot (and the win) provided a storybook ending to what may stand forever as Oklahoma's most brilliant high-school coaching career.

The win was the final game for Mrs. Bertha Frank Teague, the only girls basketball coach that Byng had known in its almost half century of existence and served as an appropriate finish to her improbable and almost incomprehensible coaching career, by any standard in any sport.

The 1969 title was the eighth state championship for a Coach Teague team. Seven other times they reached the finals in Oklahoma's arduous single-elimination playoff process, in what was at that time, the state's largest school bracket. During her remarkable 42-year career, the Lady Pirates won 40 district championships, 22 regional titles and 38 conference crowns. All, of course, stand as state prep records. But the unsurpassed and unbelievable record of the Teague teams is best viewed by a review from 1927-69, a span which saw her construct not only the most well-known girls basketball program in the nation, but also witnessed her significant impact on the growth of women's sports in Oklahoma and across the nation.

THE BEGINNING

The Bertha Frank career began in 1927 at the small, rural school located six miles north of Ada, in south-central Oklahoma. She had no playing experience in basketball and certainly never coached at the competitive level. But her husband, Jess Teague, had been hired to teach at Byng (he later became the school's first superintendent; a tenure that lasted 40 years), and so Bertha not only became a first-grade teacher (a position she held for 39 years) but also became—by default—the high school girl's basketball coach.

Early on, the competition was not as stiff as it became in the latter years of her reign, but even in the beginning, she distinguished herself as an extraordinary mentor, as she developed the young country girls into stellar athletes —long before the breakthrough days of Title IX for women's sports.

Mrs. Teagues' first five teams compiled records of 16-2, 15-3, 18-2, 20-1, and 31-2, before a playoff system was developed, a total record of 100-10. And this was only the beginning, a scenario that took place without an indoor court.

THE DECADE OF THE 1930'S

This was clearly the record highlight of her career. Between the Great Depression and World War II, her team's accomplishments were truly legendary:

- Overall record of 289-8 (wining percentage of .973)
- Eight district, six regional, and four state titles
- 98 wins in a row from 1936-39, with three straight state championships

THE DECADE OF THE 1940'S

After winning the state title in 1940, Byng went for 10 years without another state championship. They were hardly unsuccessful, with an overall record of 310-17 (a winning percentage of .948). The Lady Pirates gathered in seven district crowns, and five regional titles during this "down period."

THE 1950'S DECADE

The early 50's were a time of huge growth in other Oklahoma girls basketball programs, as well as the zenith of Teague's storied career. From 1950-52, Byng won three district and regional crowns and two state titles with an incredible record of 97-8 against stiff competition. Her clubs put together a similar remarkable streak from 1955-57, winning 97 and losing 8 again. The Pirates lost in the state finals all three years. This decade's totals were 288-38, an unbelievable winning percentage of .883.

THE 1960'S FINALE

Coach Teague described the first three years of her final decade at the Byng helm thusly, "We had a slump." This meant records of 15-10, 13-7, and 13-8, the closest to losing seasons her teams would ever garner.

But the final seven years wiped out any thoughts of a lowering of the Teague standards of excellence. Her teams won six district and regional crowns and two state championships. The 1965 team went undefeated at 27-0—one of five Teague-coached teams to accomplish this extremely rare feat in basketball (men's or women's). Two other clubs lost only once, and her final 1969 team, with three underclass players out of the six starters, lost only twice. The 60's record was 222-44 (.835) with the final seven years a glittering 181-17 (.914).

THE FINAL LEDGER

A summary of the accomplishments of this coaching icon pinpoints a career that is almost impossibile to fathom:

- 1,152 wins and 115 losses (a .910 winning percentage)
- Average record over 43 years, 27-3
- Eight state titles
- Seven state runner-ups
- 22 state tourney appearances
- 40 district titles
- 38 conference crowns
- 22 regional titles
- Won 98 consecutive games and 3 state championships from 1936 to 1939
- Five undefeated seasons
- Eighteen-30 plus win seasons
- Thirty-six-20 plus win seasons
- Undefeated in conference play for 27 straight years

Coach Teague is the most celebrated female sports figure in Oklahoma sports history and, along with Hall of Fame coach Henry Iba and legendary Jim Thorpe, the most decorated sports figure in the state's history.

In addition, Bertha Frank Teague positively impacted basketball and the women's sports world in the following ways:

- Organized the Mid-America Girl's Basketball Tournament in 1973, which became the elite prep girls basketball tourney and always attracted the best teams from surrounding states.
- Organized an accompanying clinic for basketball coaches, the first of its kind in the nation.

- Founded the first summer camp for women in the Southwest.
- Launched the Oklahoma Girls High School Basketball Coaches Association.
- Influenced girl's basketball rules/ formation and changes (e.g. change from three-division court to two-division court).
- Won a national AAU Championship.
- Authored what is believed to be the first book devoted entirely to girls basketball (*Basketball for Girls*, Ronald Press, 1962).

And what of Bertha as a coach. She once stated "I wouldn't play a girl if she was not a top girl in school. It is what I demanded." And those demands were:

- No horsing around—her players worked hard at basketball.
- Do your best at all times—train and stay in top shape at all times.
- No crying after games, until you got behind closed doors in the locker room. Keep emotions level.

Teague believed girls basketball was special and preached to never give up or quit. She wanted to her players to develop the will to win.

Bertha Teague taught basketball, grace and poise, and the goodness and beauty of life.

SOURCE

Teague, Bertha. Vertical Files, Archives. Naismith Memorial Basketball Hall of Fame: Springfield, MA.

BASKETBALL SUCCESS

By Bertha Frank Teague

NO MAGIC FORMULA

Good basketball players don't "just happen." It takes time and plain hard work to develop unskilled material into game-winning players. There is no magic formula.

Since neither science nor alchemy has produced anything resembling that formula, coaches still must take the untrained, often awkward, adolescent girl and work toward developing her into a part of a smooth, closely knit unit—the team.

Before any player enters into the special training required to become a basketball player, she should consider two aspects not involved in her technical training for the game, but which are equally essential if she wishes to become an outstanding athlete. These two essentials are (1) the desire to win, or the "will to win," and (2) physical condition.

The desire to win is the most important factor in becoming a basketball player. Without it, players seldom pay the price to get in top physical condition. During my experience as a coach, I have been fortunate to have had the opportunity to coach many players who have had a burning desire to play the game and give it everything they possessed. It is almost impossible for a team to win, although it may display superior technical skill, if players do not possess more of this "will-to-win" quality than their opponents.

Superior physical condition is the other quality a team must possess in order to win. Basketball is a game of constant maneuvering. It is a strenuous game that requires near perfect physical condition of its players. No game is important enough to risk impairing the health of a player. You, as a player, should have an annual physical examination and, if necessary, additional checkups during the season. This is necessary for the team's protection, as well as for your own. A healthy player is less likely to get an injury. A player who is continually out of action because of ill health or lack of conditioning is worth very little to the team.

Often basketball is a battle of superior thinking. Mind and body are close associates in the fast-moving game of modern basketball.

Basketball rules and techniques of the game have changed so much in recent years that the day is past when a player can become a "star" by developing one certain skill or specialty.

The game has become so highly skilled that major emphasis is on all-round performance. Basketball is a game for the competitor who has gained self-confidence and poise through training and practice to meet varied and difficult situations which arise in a fast-moving game—one who thinks it's fun to "out-compete" a rival who is equally good.

The player must be able, of course, to think on the playing court. For some, this is easy. In general, however, this is the hardest quality to develop in the team as an over-all unit. Six individuals are on the court; and if just one is not thinking in terms of basketball skills, the whose team is affected. (*Authors' Note: At the time Oklahoma girl's basketball was a 3 offense, 3 defense, 6-on-6 player game*).

As a prospective player, you may improve your basketball "thinkability" on the court by the work you do in practice sessions. Then you must study the game. Read all you can about it. Watch outstanding players and well-organized games. Think basketball as much as you possibly can.

Certainly, brainpower is the "open-sesame" to a lot of doorways; and probably, if you're a smart girl, you'll be a better athlete. You'll find, however, that basketball sense is a bit different from academic aptitude, and you'll discover you need many rehearsals to think clearly as a part of a team during a tight game.

Athletic competition presents many situations that test a player's self-control. Often, you may feel irritation or anger at a rival. Remember, it's never permissible to use unethical playing tactics. Play hard, be aggressive, but adhere to the spirit of the game. Remember, you are the representative of your family and your school. You owe it to them, to your coach, and to yourself to have poise enough never to become rebellious or upset to the point that you lose your self-control. Win honestly and modestly. Lose courageously.

If you are playing under the directions of a coach, she has probably spent many hours working out what she thinks is best for you and your teammates. You should accept her decisions. The manner in which you accept the coach's authority determines whether you are an asset or a detriment to the team.

The player who scores most is not always the best player on the team. Remember, scores result from combined team effort. Someone has to be high-point girl in every

LESSONS FROM THIS LEGEND...

game. (It makes more colorful copy for the sports writer if each contest has its heroine.) Don't permit a jealous attitude toward a teammate to creep in and cause you not to support her and your team. Remember, basketball victories are never one-player triumphs. The team is always more valuable than the "star." You may never make headlines; but when you have done your assigned job, you have the satisfaction of knowing you have played an important part in your team's success. The more you progress as a player, the more you will realize how important your individual contribution is to the team's success, and the more you'll realize jealousy and envy have no place in your life on or off the basketball court.

If you expect to become an outstanding player, you should start in junior high school. Your general development is important during those years. It will have a bearing on your later performances.

The following is a general summary of hints to help you become a better player:

1. Keep hustling. A winner never quits, and a quitter never wins.
2. Learn the rules of the game.
3. Learn the fundamentals—and the essential elements of a winning team.
4. Be on time for every practice session.
5. Put a supreme effort into the game.
6. Be alert. Listen to your coach. Be responsive.
7. Remember, the only personal glory you may derive must be a result of teamwork.
8. Get in the best possible condition.
9. Practice "getting along" with team members.
10. Do that something extra. If you do, your membership on the team will make the difference.
11. Never get so "good" you think the team cannot do without you.
12. You are in school to get an education. You must make passing grades.
13. After you have made the first team, concentrate upon your special weaknesses and strive to improve by putting in extra time to correct those weaknesses.
14. A good basketball team is built on the work it does in practice.
15. You must want to win. That is what the game is all about. Those who do not mind losing will seldom win.

The opportunity to match your skill and ability against that of another individual is one of the prime goals of basketball. Accept defeat courageously, but do not reach the point where it makes no difference whether you lose or win.

SOURCE

Teague, Bertha. (1962). *Basketball for Girls*. New York: The Ronald Press.

LEGACY OF
John Robert Thompson

- Compiled a 596-239 record during his 27 years at Georgetown.

- Was the first African-American coach to win the NCAA Division I national championship.

- Respected as a coach-educator, motivator, and leader whose teams were known for discipline, mental toughness, and hard play.

- Compiled a 97 percent graduation rate for his four-year players.

- Kept a deflated basketball near his office to remind players that life goes on when the ball quits bouncing.

- Known as a man, who knew himself, set high goals and stood up for what he believed was right.

JOHN ROBERT THOMPSON

"The biggest con in education is kids saying they were exploited. If the kid doesn't get an education, it's his fault.
—John Thompson

BIOGRAPHY

Born: September 2, 1941 in Washington D.C.

Inducted into the Naismith Basketball Hall of Fame in 1999

John Thompson coached 27 years at Georgetown University and compiled a record of 596-239. His teams were physical, disciplined, and built around defense and a strong inside game. Georgetown appeared in three NCAA Final Fours (1982, 1984, 1985) and won the national championship in 1984. The Hoyas made 24 consecutive postseason tournament appearances (20 NCAA, 4 NIT) and won seven Big East championships. Thompson had a 97 percent graduation rate amongst his four-year players. Prior to his arrival at Georgetown, Thompson coached at St. Anthony High School in Washington D.C. and had a five-year coaching record of 122-28. He served as an assistant coach for the 1976 gold medal Olympic Team. In 1988, Thompson was the head Olympic coach and led the United States to the bronze medal. As a player, Thompson led John Carroll High School to 55 consecutive victories and two city championships. At Providence, he led the Friars to the 1963 NIT Championship. Thompson played for the Boston Celtics on two NBA championship teams and was the back-up center to Bill Russell. Thompson served as president of the NABC and was on the Board of Directors for the Black Coaches Association.

John Robert Thompson...

Many things can be said about John Thompson: Stubborn, confrontational, self-serving, bombastic, bullying, and paranoid. He is clutch-fisted, iron-willed, and very persuasive. The secret of his success is that John Thompson knows himself. Even when surrounded by the hurry and shouting of a tense Georgetown game, he moved at his own pace, paused like a bemused professor to weigh, consider, and ponder. Even as he walked along the sidelines with his trademark white towel thrown over his right shoulder, his 6 foot 10 inch frame dwarfing players, fans, and writers, Thompson seemed lost in thought. But he was not removed from the game. Suddenly, he was in action, challenging an official, benching a player, or hugging another. His focus and control are what made Thompson a great coach and a powerful man.

But because Thompson is black, outspoken, and accomplished and his teams were predominantly black at a predominantly white school, his motives were sometimes seen as racist. Because his Georgetown teams played an in-your-face defense and a physical, intimidating style, many called the Hoyas "thugs." But in truth, Thompson cannot be defined in black and white. "He's not a racist; he's a realist," said Patrick Ewing in a soft, reflective tone. "He prepared you for what life will be like in a predominantly white world."

Thompson knew what he wanted and had the confidence to define his world, his goals, and his achievements on his own terms. Thompson's power to shape his own life and lives of others came from his balance: competitive fury restrained by conscience; a hunger to win matched by a refusal to let heated emotion take over; a seething perfectionism tempered by sharp intuition and a deep understanding of human frailty. "I'm not perfect," Thompson told author John Edger Wideman, shortly after his Georgetown Hoyas won the 1984 NCAA men's basketball championship, "and I resent every minute of not being perfect. I work hard to get better." (Aronson, 1993)

More than just shaping winning teams, Thompson guided individuals toward winning lives. He always had a deflat-

ed basketball near his Georgetown office as a reminder that life goes on when the ball stops bouncing. Over 97 per cent of his players, who stayed four years, graduated. He taught players to know their limits and find the inner strength to rise above those barriers.

A black man from a poor neighborhood in segregated Washington D.C., Thompson had one huge asset – his family. Though illiterate, his hardworking father woke up each morning at 5:00 to earn what he could. The only work his mother could find was housekeeping. Determined to give their son a better start in life, John's parents sent him to Catholic school. But, hampered by a vision problem that made it hard for him to read, Thompson fell behind. By the fifth grade, the frustrated nuns had decided that Thompson was a slow learner and asked that he not come back.

Thompson's parents were not about to let someone else write off their son. A determined public school teacher got him glasses and made sure John caught up. His mother inspired him to meet any challenge and to find the way to win. Thompson's mother taught him, "You can do anything you think you can. It's all in the way you view it. It's all in the start you make. You must feel that you're going to do it." (Shapiro, 1991)

Thompson's challenges as a youth stirred his desire to help others. "I want my players to graduate," stated Thompson, "but I'm not responsible for them getting an education. If they understand that they are responsible, they'll get it. The product we are trying to produce is not necessarily love and affection. It's education."

John demonstrated and modeled the importance of education by graduating from John Carroll High School, Providence College (major in economics), and the University of the District of Columbia (degree in guidance and counseling). He also enjoyed great success on the basketball court: at John Carroll, he led his teams to 55 consecutive victories and two city titles; at Providence, he led the Friars to the NIT championship in 1963; and with the Boston Celtics, he won two NBA championships in 1965 and 1966.

When Thompson began his coaching career, it was at the high school level in Washington D.C., where his teams

.....SCOUTING REPORT.....SCOUTING REPORT...

were 122-28 from 1966-1971. This was enough to launch his Hall of Fame coaching career and land him the head coaching job at downtrodden Georgetown University in 1972. The school had never won a national championship and had a dismal 3-23 record and the low spirits to match.

The day Thompson took over, he gathered the ragtag Georgetown team, pointed to the wall in the gym, and predicted, "Someday, a national championship flag is going to hang there." Then he took his team into the gym and told them to start running.

According to Felix Yeoman, who was on that team, "Our practices were brutal. If you were fooling around, he'd put you on the line for what he called hamburger drills, a hundred of them. You run from the baseline to the foul line and back. That was one hamburger. A killer drill."

Mike McDermott, a specialist for the FDIC, learned all about success and failure from Coach Thompson. "He told us that we were always measuring and being measured. You can't fool yourself or anybody else when it's all out there on the court for everybody to see."

These are lessons for life, not just game time. One of Thompson's first appointments at Georgetown was Mary Fenlon, an ex-nun who had taught Latin and English in high school. Thompson referred to the determined, fiercely loyal, and bulldog-tough Fenlon as his "academic conscience."

"I'm a basketball coach," he said, "and if it were up to me, I'd spend all our time on basketball. Mary won't allow me to do that. She'll shoo the players out of the gym if she has to." Thompson knows one of the great secrets of being a great leader: "Your team will always go the extra mile if they believe you want them to succeed at everything they do. Your dedication inspires theirs."

Thompson was at his best coping with defeat. Anyone can rack up a win or two. Only the greatest coaches can turn devastating losses into even greater victories.

In 1982, Georgetown cruised through the early rounds of the NCAA Tournament playing outstanding basketball. The championship game pitted Thompson against Dean Smith's Tar Heels. North Carolina also had an outstanding team led by Michael Jordan, James Worthy, and Sam Perkins. The teams exchanged leads until, with just 17 seconds in the game, Jordan hit a shot and gave the Tar Heels a 63-62 lead. Now, the game, the season, and the championship were in the hands of Fred Brown, the point guard for Georgetown.

In the heat of the moment, Brown made a terrible mistake. He threw the ball straight to North Carolina's James Worthy, giving North Carolina the title. All eyes turned to the terrifying presence of Thompson, whose coaching style the media was calling "Hoya Paranoia." Instead of throwing a tantrum, Thompson walked over to the crestfallen player, as millions watched on television, and hugged him. The gesture changed Brown's life.

"I was really down on myself," Brown admits. "Coach Thompson's action made me realize that it wasn't the end of the world, and I think it affected me in other ways. I've learned not to view a goal as the end of the action, and it means I'm never really done."

In 1984, for the third time in four years, Georgetown made it to the NCAA Finals. This time they won easily, beating Houston 84 to 75. As the final seconds ticked off, Thompson walked over to Brown and hugged him again. The national championship Thompson had predicted in 1972 was coming to Georgetown.

On Jan. 8, 1999, Thompson stunned the basketball world when he resigned at Georgetown, but his legacy had been firmly built. In 27 years, Thompson compiled a 596-239 (.714) record. His teams appeared in three NCAA Final Fours (1982, 1984, 1985), played in 14 consecutive NCAA tournaments (1979-92), made 24 consecutive post-season appearances (20 NCAA, 4 NIT) and won seven Big East Tournament championships.

SOURCE

Aronson, Marc. (1993, June). He Creates Winners. *Success Magazine.*

Shapiro, Leonard. (1991). *Big Man on Campus.* New York: Henry Holt.

Thompson, John. Vertical Files, Archives. Naismith Memorial Basketball Hall of Fame. Springfield, MA.

Tuttle, Dennis. (1999, January 18). Practicing What He Preaches. *The Sporting News.*

LESSONS FROM THIS LEGEND...

MOTIVATION AND COMMUNICATION

By John Thompson

SELECTION OF PLAYERS

We have all discriminated against players based on our own little idiosyncrasies, and that is what I call selection of players. I have never taken the best 12 or 15 guys on my teams since I have been coaching. I think the input the player gives, the psychological welfare that is involved in the composition of the team—his attitude, how he deals with things, are just as important to me as his physical attributes and being able to play the game.

Show me coaches who just take players based on the fact that they have the ability to play and play alone, and I will show you guys that are going to lose. Physical ability is definitely necessary. However, you can't coach character, but you will have a lot of problems if you don't have it.

When we go into a player's home, he is making an assessment of us. If a player disrespects his parents, his coach, teachers, counselors and other adults, then I am not interested. If a player respects his parents, I feel that he will respect me. In most cases our players respect their parents and high school coach.

It is very important to you when you're dealing with a kid because of the nature of athletics. Athletics is something that everybody is interested in; it's a form of entertainment for people, a way of life for some people, it's a way out for other people. It has various aspects for everyone. People often speak to me concerning the relationship that players have with the principal, teachers, and the administration. Sure, the

principal is going to try and coach. Sure, the teacher is going to coach, because he thinks he knows more about the game than you ever knew. You try to coach too, on Monday night football. It is very important, when you get a young player, to sit down with him and explain some of the pressures and things he is going to have to deal with. When he walks through the halls, the principal is going to ask him why he didn't win. When he goes to the math class, the teacher is going to say he is stupid. We try to do this with our players. We try to sit down and let them know that these are some of the things that are going to occur to him, before they happen. We try to explain why they happen. It is extremely important when he gets on the court, that he does not listen to professor X in the stands. Who is going to cut you. If you tell him first that it's going to happen, and tell him that it's a part of sports, and how to deal with it, he will better be able to deal with it.

Now we're talking about motivation-communication. You can motivate people all you want to, coaches. I don't know in the beginning who's been motivated; who you can't communicate with. You can communicate with a lot of people who aren't motivated. You have to explain things logically and intelligently. Basketball is no longer a game where a group of kids go out to the park and play for exercise, period. I enjoy the girls, Title IX, and women's athletics. They say that they will not be like the men. Do you want to make a bet? Your competitive instincts and the time aren't always the controlling factors around us. They want recognition, to excel, they want to keep

their jobs. I see it happening now. Some of my best friends are women involved in athletics.

The first person I hired was a woman. I hired a woman assistant coach. Things are going to happen to players and it is of extreme importance that you deal with them in an intelligent manner. When you are in a dormitory, it is different than high school. In high school, you could go home and get away from me. While you're studying in the dorm, someone will knock on your door, and ask you why you threw a pass away. It will have an effect on you, because it means something to you. That same idiot, who asked you why you lost a game in Indiana, is going to ask you why you flunked out of school, if you give up.

I think you have got to deal with these things before kids overreact to them in a hostile way. Yes, it is important for you to build discipline in matters that pertains to off the court. When I asked my players to leave, they understand that about me; they get up and leave. It is extremely important to show your players order in the total perspective of what you are doing. Gentlemen, that's programming. Coaches tell me "our program" is this. What does "our program" mean? To me it means from day one, the introduction, you have to know what you're trying to achieve when you go in the house. It's going into the classroom and talking to them about how we do things at Georgetown. It's expecting them to attend classes, that is some of the things we say. Too often, we try to be like the kids we coach. I have never played for a coach who wanted to be like me. I didn't want my junior high school coach to come on the court and give me five. I wanted a symbol of respect. Too very often, we are afraid to impose discipline and order in the everyday lives of our players and then wonder why we don't have it on the court.

I came here in 1972. You all know what happened in the late 60's to our society. That was when the youth took over. Anything that an adult said was challenged. Whether you were selecting the president of the college or a basketball coach. All committees had to have student representation. Students were paying to go to school, so they could teach teachers. Someone said to me, you can't do this or that with players of today. I just came out of St. Anthony High School. I have never been an assistant coach and realistically I didn't know that much about coaching. Luckiest man in the world to get the job. The timing was right. There were a lot of people with more qualifications.

My father could not read or write. But I loved him. He had a lot of common sense. They split up the family; half had to work, half went to school. It wasn't his choice. One of the things that he told me was, there is one thing in this world that you want to remember son, you've got to do it your way, don't you ever forget that. You fail or you succeed your way. I was not Aristotle, Socrates, or Plato. I didn't know how the kids were going to react. I want you to go to school, and you to be in class, and this is how we do this. Gentleman, do not be afraid to do things the way you think they should be done.

It is extremely important when it comes to motivation-communication that you do it your way. If you make a mistake, what do you do? I see coaches grabbing people's thumbs when they shake hands, making all kinds of signs, wearing clothes that are out of context with their cultural habits, trying to relate to someone.

When the level of my intelligence is geared to a handshake, then I'm in a sorry situation. If you make a mistake or offend someone, the thing to say is I'm sorry. I'm sorry is in order. My junior high school coach made many mistakes, but he didn't say anything. My God, he knew how to motivate.

He carried a little pool stick. When he said jump, you jumped. I never saw him hit anyone with that stick. I never saw anyone challenge him either. We won the junior high school championship. Getting back to an early thought, I have never played for a coach who wanted to be like me. Don't ever forget that.

When you try to be like the kids you're coaching, you're making a tremendous mistake. Most kids, regardless of how they respond to it or how they rebel, have a tendency to want leadership and guidance. It is a fact. What happened in the late 60s and early 70s is gone. Forget that democracy experiment.

Most kids are very well committed. Adults have a little more sanity in their lives with age and experience in their thoughts. It is extremely important for you to understand one thing, that if you are giving kids discipline and order, you better expect it on and off the court.

We talk to our players about the dormitories and the cafeteria. I don't want one of my players going into the cafeteria, and because he is an athlete and has received a lot of attention, telling the cook in an ungentlemanly manner, gimme this, gimme that. No son, I don't allow that. He is representing me, his parents, and himself.

Bobby Knight had nothing but praise for John Duren, when he was with the Pan-American Team. Bob Weinhauer, head coach at Penn, spoke very well of Ed Spriggs, when he was with the ECAC All-Stars in Yugoslavia this summer. Talk to Steve Martin or Craig Shelton or any of my

players. We didn't make them that way, they came here that way. We looked at them very carefully. Those kids don't want me to be like them.

You've got to make them understand, that when they go through the line and the cook gives them something, they must tell him "thank you". When a manager brings me a towel, I say thank you. Whenever our players go to the cage for equipment, they must thank the equipment manager. That's very important. All the kids are not going to say thanks, but you got to keep saying it. That's where conduct and respect from the program initiates. That's where the informal education comes from in relation to you teaching them good habits off the court.

LOCKER ROOM

We try to let our players know the locker room is their private domain. I don't let anybody in my locker room without permission, and that includes the players' family. If someone is in there who does not belong, our players will politely ask them to leave. I am very conscious of player locations in the locker room. I spend at least 30 minutes making locker assignments, based on their personalities. It is the responsibility of the players to keep the locker room clean and neat.

MANAGERS

Our managers are treated with respect. Managers set the tone at practice, they sprint to all assignments during practice. Managers must keep the coaches informed; like who is missing class, or who is having some kind of academic problem, etc.

TRAVELING

I ride in the back of the bus so I can feel the mood of the players better. I can also observe everything from that location. Freshman carry all extra luggage.

LESSONS FROM THIS LEGEND...

RESTAURANTS

Players must be polite and courteous. Order what you want, but eat what you order.

ASSISTANT COACHES

I am the "WE" person. They are the "JOHN" person.

BENCH

I went to Europe with John McClendon, and one game he sat in the middle of the bench. I wasn't playing much, but I felt very comfortable, I could hear the things he was saying. I have never sat on the end of the bench since I've been coaching. It's very convenient for me to sit in the middle of the bench. I can communicate better with my players. All players are near a coach. When a player comes out of the game, our bench stands and cheers for him. The player sits next to a coach when coming out of the game. Players are never given a towel or warm-up when coming out of the game. We do this because the player could be upset with himself, and throw them down in disgust. Most people would interpret that as a player with a bad attitude. I want the player to sit down and be relaxed before the manager brings him a towel. Players are instructed to run in and out of the game.

WARM-UP LINES

Players must be neat. Managers count missed lay-ups; for each missed lay-up, players run in practice the next day.

GAME

Captains are polite when meeting officials and opposing players-players or managers always wipe-up the floor. We never let an official wipe the floor. Our players never criticize an official. After the game, shake hands, sprint to the locker room.

SOURCE

Thompson, John. (1979, Winter) Motivation and Communication. *Basketball Bulletin*.

LEGACY OF
Lily Margaret Wade

- Known as the "Mother of Modern Women's Basketball."

- Pioneered an unprecedented dynasty in women's basketball, which led to the growth and popularity of the sport during the 1970s.

- Directed Delta State to three AIAW national championships from 1975 to 1977 and a 51-game winning streak.

- Believed the difference between a good team and a great team was the heart, drive, and desire to push past fatigue and overwhelming obstacles.

- Namesake of the Wade Trophy, which is presented annually to the top women's collegiate basketball player.

LILY MARGARET WADE

"The X factor is the difference between a good team and a great one—the heart, drive, and the desire to push past fatigue and overwhelming obstacles to play better than one ever thought possible."
—Coach Margaret Wade

BIOGRAPHY

Born: December 30, 1912 in McCool, MS

Died: February 16, 1995

Inducted into the Naismith Basketball Hall of Fame in 1985

Lily Margaret Wade pioneered a dynasty at Delta State, which led to the growth and popularity of women's basketball in the 1970s. At the age of 60, Wade resurrected a 41-year dormant women's basketball program and won a national championship within two years. From 1975 to 1977, Delta State won three AIAW national championships, compiled a 93-4 record, and had a 51-game winning streak. She retired from Delta State in 1979 with a collegiate coaching record of 157-23. Wade coached in the high-school ranks between 1933 and 1954 and compiled a record of 453-89. Her Cleveland (MS) High School teams won 14 county titles, 11 regional crowns, and lost three consecutive state championships by a total of four points. Wade's overall coaching record was 610-112, for a winning percentage of .845. She is the namesake of the Wade Trophy, which is presented annually to the top women's collegiate basketball player. She was the first woman enshrined in the Mississippi Sport Hall of Fame and the Delta State University Hall of Fame. Wade was enshrined in the Naismith Memorial Basketball Hall of Fame in 1985 and the Women's Basketball Hall of Fame in 1999.

Lily Margaret Wade...

Lily Margaret Wade proved to be a legend in her own time. She was born in McCool, Mississippi and never left her roots in an amazing career spanning over 60 years. Margaret earned all-conference honors in 1928 and 1929 at Cleveland High School. She enrolled at hometown Delta State College and was team captain of the school's first women's basketball team. Unfortunately, Wade's playing career came to a screeching halt in 1932 when college administrators deemed the game too strenuous for girls. Protests that involved the burning of uniforms went unnoticed.

Wade did not let this setback deter her from her love of the game. She continued her career by playing semi-pro basketball with the Tupelo Red Wings. She served as team captain and ultimately led the team to the Southern Championship. While playing with the Red Wings in 1933, Wade began her coaching career at Marietta High School. She then coached at Belden High School for one year. A knee injury ended Wade's playing career after only two seasons, but her coaching career was just beginning. Wade returned to her high school alma mater, Cleveland High School, and coached

women's basketball from 1935 to 1954. During her high school coaching career, Wade compiled a record of 453-89. Her teams won 14 county titles, 11 regional crowns, and lost three consecutive state championships by a total of four points. Margaret retired from high school coaching following the 1953-54 season.

In 1959, Wade returned to Delta State as the school's director of women's physical education. She was an exemplary teacher and administrator, and at the same time, courageously won battles with cancer, survived a near fatal car accident, and overcame severe bouts of arthritis.

In 1973, the women's basketball program was reinstated at Delta Sate after a 41-year hibernation. President Aubrey Lucas appointed 60-year-old Margaret Wade head coach. Her first team produced a record of 16-2. The following three campaigns brought three AIAW national championships, an overall record of 93-4, and a 51-game winning streak.

Dr. Kent Wyatt served as president of Delta State from 1975 to 1999 and remembered the hiring of Margaret Wade. He said, "My father, as head of the health, physical education, and recreation department in 1959, hired Margaret Wade to come and teach at Delta State. And then, when women's basketball started back up in 1973, Margaret was already working for us at Delta State and had a tremendous high school coaching record. My father, Dr. Lucas, and I talked with her whether she would want to continue coaching in college. Thank goodness that she wanted to. What a phenomenal success she was. The first two years of my presidency, she won the national championship. That made three years in a row, that we were the dominant power in women's basketball in this country. And Margaret was a wonderful lady. We used to call her "Queen," because the city of Cleveland recognized her many years ago at the Charity Ball, as the queen of the Charity Ball. So we called her, not just coach, but Queen Margaret. She was a very, very good friend and a wonderful individual. She was a tough disciplinarian with her basketball team. She expected them to perform the way she had asked them to, and they did. She knew basketball inside and out, and was a wonderful coach."

The formula for success for the Lady Statesmen under Coach Wade, or "Aunt Maggie" as she is often referred to, was fundamentals, teamwork, and offensive execution. Wade attributed her great teams to the "X factor," which represented the heart, drive, and desire to push past fatigue and overwhelming obstacles to play better than one ever thought possible.

.....SCOUTING REPORT.....SCOUTING REPORT...

Margaret Wade had a John Wooden-like demeanor and was a "sly ol' fox." Wade treated her players with a blend of mothering, discipline, and humor. Lusia Harris Stewart, three-time All-American and Naismith Basketball Hall of Fame inductee, said, "Coach Wade was the type of person who always encouraged you to do your best. She demanded that we played as a team, and she wanted us to be young ladies both on and off the court. She truly cared about us as individuals. On the light side, I always remember her having a pin that she wore like a button on the inside of her coat. And whenever we played, she would open up her coat and the pin said, 'Give 'em hell, girls.' I will always remember that!"

Wade pioneered an unprecedented dynasty in women's basketball, which led to the growth and popularity of the sport during the 1970s. Her legacy is remembered and symbolized through the oldest and most prestigious award presented in Division I women's basketball, "The State Farm Wade Trophy." Before she passed away in 1995, Margaret Wade said, "My last will and testament to the "Margaret Wade Trophy" will be the satisfaction that prospects of the award will create and stimulate desires in young women athletes throughout the country, which will propel them to their greatest achievements in athletics; if their athletic accomplishments can be recognized by the award, then my life has been worthwhile."

SOURCE

Wade, Margaret. Vertical Files, Archives. Naismith Memorial Basketball Hall of Fame. Springfield, MA.

The Margaret Wade Collection. Delta State University, Library Archives. Cleveland, MS.

A FORMULA FOR SUCCESS

By Margaret Wade with Mel Hankinson

Authors' Note: This Margaret Wade philosophy contribution was taken from a 1980 coaching class booklet developed and used when she was teaching Delta State coaching classes.

FOREWORD

The original press announcement told of an expansion in Delta State University's physical education program to include women's participation in basketball, tennis and badminton. It was a very inauspicious beginning for what was to become one of collegiate athletics most miraculous and exciting dynasties.

It all began in the spring of 1973, when the Delta State President Aubrey K. Lucas called in Margaret Wade to inform her that the school was reinstating its women's basketball program after a 40-year layoff. Upon the recommendation of Forest Wyatt, chairman of the department of physical education, as well as athletic director Horace McCool, President Lucas was seeking to bring Margaret Wade out of a 14-year coaching retirement.

"As I recall, she had mixed feelings and didn't know if she wanted to get back into coaching," Dr. Lucas, now president of the University of Southern Mississippi, said. "Her main concern was that I would expect too much, and she offered that, it's going to take some time."

Later that summer, President Lucas asked Coach McCool to take on the responsibility of women's basketball as a part of the athletic department. Little did we know that two years later on a cold March night in Harrisonburg, Va., Delta State would be thrown into the national spotlight, a

national champion, setting in motion three of the greatest years far too few communities ever experience. For the true basketball fan, they would soon learn Cleveland, home of Delta State University, was located in Mississippi, not Ohio.

Margaret Wade's appointment as head coach of the Lady Statesmen basketball team was met with rapid fire approval since Clevelanders knew she would once again have the opportunity to reach a goal she had missed while coaching at Cleveland High School—a state championship.

She had spent 17 years coaching the women's basketball team at the local high school before taking a position in the physical education department at Delta State in 1959. Three straight years, her Wildkittens had advanced to the Mississippi state finals, only to lose those three championship games by a total of four points.

It would have been easy for Margaret to have turned aside President Lucas' coaching request, but the challenge before her wasn't nearly as great as she had faced in the past. After all, she had won a bout with cancer and survived a near fatal auto accident during the years away from the court. Coaching styles and player attitudes may have changed, but no one doubted her ability to run the club, no matter the changes.

The results of her comeback are a matter of record—four Mississippi AIAW championships, three AIAW Region III crowns, and a national record, three straight AIAW National titles (shared with Immaculata). When her retirement finally came after the 1978-79 campaign, Margaret Wade had guided the Lady Statesmen to an almost

unbelievable 157 victories and only 23 defeats, including a national record 51 straight wins. Added to her high school coaching record of 453-89-6, Margaret Wade ended her coaching career at 610-112-6. As the saying goes: "That's incredible!"

While the success at Delta State brought much joy, it was accompanied by pain for the lady we have all come to love and respect. The cancer and automobile accident had taken its toll. Severe attacks of arthritis, especially to her knees, made us wonder how she kept going. At the time, the travel was murder, especially one night in the Louisiana Superdome next to Madison Square Garden. Having lived across Dean street from "Coach" for seven years, I had often watched from my window the many times when it would take almost five minutes for her to get out of her car and into her home. The urge was always there to scurry over and help, but it didn't seem appropriate, because deep down, I knew this giant of a woman the Rogers children, Laura and Bill, grew up calling "Aunt Margaret" would find the strength to carry on. For the most of us, the return to coaching wouldn't have been worth it, but for Margaret Wade, it was just another chapter in her successful life.

Success is measured in so many ways. Behind the X's and O's is a composite of intangible ingredients of a successful coach. Such ingredients are found in and demonstrated by Margaret Wade, who has been called the mother of bigtime women's basketball and lends her name to the trophy which recognizes the nation's outstanding female player each year. Of Margaret, current Delta State President Kent Wyatt says:

LESSONS FROM THIS LEGEND...

"Having the most prestigious award in women's basketball (the Wade Trophy) named in her honor further recognizes her as the most respected coach in America. Throughout her career as a head coach, she touched many lives and earned a great love and respect from the people associated with women's basketball."

She's the first to admit much of her success at Delta State came about due to a strong list of graduate assistant coaches and the recruiting of Melvin Hemphill. But on the court, coaching was just part of the total Lady Statesmen success story, which has been called some of the most amazing accomplishments in sports history, from no team at all to national champion in just two years.

While attempting to teach her players the value of winning, she also emphasized the art of maintaining their image of being ladies. "The best way to describe Margaret Wade," says former Lady Statesmen captain Wanda Harriston, "is that she is a real Southern lady. And while she never preached it to us per se, because of her style, we tried to go out and prove you can be an athlete and a lady at the same time. She was much more than just a coach. She was a mother away from home."

Even though she needed no new fields to conquer, the most impelling factor in her return to coaching was a great love for Delta State, working with young people, and basketball. For this expression of love, we will be forever grateful.

Langston Rogers
November 18, 1980

PHILOSOPHY - A FORMULA FOR SUCCESS

The question that I am asked most often is "How have you been so successful on the high school and collegiate level," and "What is your formula for success?" Without being over simplistic, it would read:

SELECTION OF PLAYERS + EFFECTIVE COMMUNICATION = SUCCESS

X FACTOR

Selection of players: these are the key qualities that I have looked for when selecting my teams.

1. CHARACTER

— References from the girl's past coaches, counselors and teachers give us a track record to examine her behavioral pattern. I'd look for players who have developed stability in their lives. Were they good students and in regular attendance at school and practice; even tempered and dependable in all facets of their lives; and respectful to authority figures and their peers? Then in the personal interview with the prospective athlete, I would make a subjective judgement on their character and coachability.

2. ATTITUDE

— After evaluating her overall character, I would look more specifically into her attitude toward the game of basketball.

Factors which need to be considered are as follows: Is the person goal oriented? Is her desire to excel in the game? (Many times I may ask if she is desirous of winning a national title.) Is she willing to work toward maximizing her talents? Is she competitive during the game? (I've found the more success experiences a young girl has had, the harder she'll fight not to lose.) These are just some of the ingredients that are characteristic of an individual who has a winning attitude. These are qualities difficult to describe but readily observed.

3. ABILITY

— Certainly her over-all ability to play the game is important. My staff would weigh such physical characteristics as her size, quickness, and shooting skills. Also, her court sense and over all "feel" for the game would be taken into consideration during this evaluation.

4. TEAM INGREDIENTS

— After evaluating the skills of the prospective athlete, we would next ask if her abilities fit into what we needed. In our system, I was looking to be two-players deep at each position. To recruit any more players than this at any one position may lend itself to the unhappy circumstance of having too many talented players "riding" the bench.

5. LASTLY AND MOST IMPORTANTLY, DID THE PROSPECTIVE STUDENT-ATHLETE WANT TO COME TO OUR UNIVERSITY AND PLAY FOR ME?

— This is very important, because there is less anxiety from a student adjusting from high school to college environment if she has made up her mind that she is at the school of her choice. If the athlete recognizes that it is a privilege to be coached by you, immediate loyalty is gained, and this player-coach relationship enhances learning.

EFFECTIVE COMMUNICATION

If there is one strength that I have as a coach, it is to know what I want to have my team do, effectively communicate that knowledge to them, then convince them to do it! Several important facets of communication are:

1. KNOWING THE GIRLS

— Consideration must be given to their age, maturity, plus sensitivity for the coach to "stay in time" with the times:

- High school
  On the high school level, I was much more of a disciplinarian than on the college level. The girls were younger, needed more guidance, and during those teen-age years, when many young people rebel against the authority of their parents, many fathers and mothers would call asking for my support, simply because "coach, you are the only one she'll listen to." Because of this close interpersonal contact that the coach will have with her players, it is imperative that the high school coach assume the responsibility of guiding the girls through this sometimes troublesome adolescent maturing period.

- College
  A new type of communication must be established by the athlete once she arrives on a college campus. She no longer has lifetime friends, or mom and dad to talk with concerning her immediate problems, so she reaches out first to the coach, then her teammates and other people at the university.

2. KNOWING THE COACH

— It is not only important that the coach learns as much as possible about her players, but she must also open herself to the players so they may get to know her. This type of vulnerability requires self-discipline, emotional control, and continual self-evaluation in order to make judgements on those rules in the program which we need to change or not to change. Therefore it is imperative to:

- Drop the mask that is hiding your personality and let the girls know you.

- Care—There are many ways that a coach can show that she personally cares for her players including:
  ✓ Learn the names and something about everyone in her family; occasionally ask how they're doing and call them by name or mention their activity.
  ✓ Stop by the dorm and chat with them concerning their room, roommates, cafeteria food, etc.
  ✓ Know the students academic schedule. Be able to recall at least two of her teachers' names. Ask how she's doing in her various classes and if she needs any tutoring assistance.
  ✓ Encourage the parents to contact you in case of any emergency at home. This will make the parents and players feel that you are more interested in their well being than simply how well they dribble or shoot a basketball.

- Be accessible—The coach's schedule is a hectic one; teaching responsibilities; in-season scheduling; speaking at various functions; contacting prospective athletes; maintaining a relationship with friends, family, faculty, and community sometimes leaves little time to those who are most important to your program—the players.

  In the first team meeting, tell them that your office is always open to them; then go one step further and tell the players that you have several time blocks during the day which is "their" time. If they want to see you about a problem or just wish to come by and chit-chat, encourage them to come by at those times. Set specific "contact times, which will "insure" one-on-one conversation at least once a week.

  We all must remind ourselves that many young women come to the coach's university primarily to be tutored by her; it is then the coach's responsibility to make sure that she is available to meet personally with those students.

- Instill confidence—Even the most outstanding players and teams that I have had experience periods of self doubt. All have needed encouragement and assurance of self and team worth in order for them to continue being positive contributors to the team. Some significant factors when building confidence in a player/team are:

✓ Look for reasons to give honest praise—The coach needs to recognize when a player or team is "down" and be willing to give encouragement. Everyone likes to be complimented on a job well done, and our players are no exception. As coaches, we often "expect" players to do everything correctly and spend much of our time criticizing those few areas that are not up to the coaches' level of performance. This type of "negative" atmosphere may inhibit the learning process and therefore must be guarded against by the coach.

Caution must also be given to false praise. The coach should never attempt to simply "pacify" her players by a few insincere compliments. Although this is sometimes difficult, remarks need to be genuine evaluations of performances well done.

✓ Self pity—Self pity is a nemesis to everyone in our society, and not an ingredient in the formula for success. Our game is structured such that the greatest coach or the most outstanding player will always fail if she chooses to do so. A coach may win every game, but stay frustrated, because she dwells on errors that were committed which prevented perfect play, or the player may stay unfulfilled if she does not play the perfect game. The coach must continually remind the player that the primary measurement of success comes from knowing that you have given

your very best at practice and in the games. This is a carry-over quality of life. It is our responsibility in any task that we undertake to approach the job with this "giving-your-all" type of attitude. And if a player fails, or a team loses, emphasize that many times "our greatest glory is in rising every time we fail." We are God's greatest creation on this earth and do not need to live in our past failures. We are to learn the lessons from losing, gain strength from the setback, then bounce back from the defeat with all the spiritual and human fibre in us.

✓ The challenge must always be there.—No matter what the circumstances, the coach must always give her team a feeling of hope. If we've just experienced a loss, the challenge is to come back the next game for a victory. If we are winning, then we attempt to see how many games we can win in row. They must believe that there is always success tomorrow if they are willing to accept the challenge of today.

And there is a fine line between being "ready to play" and "overconfidence." If the coach senses that her team feels that the next opponent is a "push-over," then it would be wise for her to have a tough mental practice the night before the game, emphasizing some of the strengths of the team which must be neutralized, or challenge the team to beat their opponent in the first few minutes of the game. Share with your team that if

we let the opposition stay close in the first half, that may give them the confidence to make a game of it.

Other effective techniques that I've used to motivate our players when playing a weak opponent is to set individual challenges, such as—how many rebounds can you get in the first half? Or how many points can you hold the opponent to? These types of challenges keep your team focused on maximal performance rather than the weak team they're playing.

However, if it appears that your team is a hopeless underdog, share with the players your expectation of the coming upset. Give concrete examples of teams who have overcome great odds and won victory when everyone thought them doomed to defeat. If they can visualize themselves playing a great game before the event, this will increase their opportunity for a maximal performance. This mental process is called "memory vision."

Although trick defenses and offensive plays will never replace a team that is well schooled fundamentally, your players may gain added confidence before the game if they know that they are going to use something against the opposition that they have never shown before. If you normally play a zone and rarely press, you may shake your opponents up by starting in a full-court press, or if you often play person to person, you might want to start in a zone. If the opposing team has an outstanding offensive player, you may construct a "Chinese-checker" defense and begin the game in a box-and-one. These tactics will give your team confidence entering the game and may throw your opponents off balance enough for you to upset them.

Lastly, never forget that the players need the coach the most in tight situations. They must share an innermost belief in the coach's aptitude to solve the problems brought on by a formidable opponent. True leadership springs forth in this time of crisis.

LESSONS FROM THIS LEGEND...

THE "X" FACTOR—ON HEART ALONE

Although the areas we discussed concerning the selection of players and effective communication contain constants which I believe are sound based on my experiences, success is not guaranteed simply because we follow these tenants. There seems to be another dimension of competition difficult to describe, but responsible for success. At Indiana University, Dr. Counsilman, their great swimming coach, calls it the "X factor."

I do not pretend to have "the" answer when explaining why some people seem to "get the breaks in life" and are "at the right place at the right time;" but I have observed these types of experiences occurring consistently in successful peoples lives—our society calls them "winners"—individuals who believe in their own abilities, then are able to see and develop the best qualities in those that are around them.

In order to develop this quality in your players, the coach must first believe in her own abilities. Believing in yourself requires great preparation. Ask your players to memorize this quote; "I will be ready, for my opportunity will come."

This type of expectation develops a pattern of thinking among your players which makes them hungry for a great challenge. You are teaching them to believe in themselves. And in a tight situation, they are confident that they can be victorious. This was never more apparent than in our drive to our first AIAW National Title.

We were 25-0 and going against a very good team from the Washington D.C. area. With 9:50 left in the game, we were behind 53-43, and our great Olympic center, Lucy Harris, fouled out of the contest. One could approach this crisis situation as "hopeless" or as an "opportunity." "We have said throughout the year that we were not a one-woman team, and here's a great chance to prove it." I knew we could still win, and so did the players.

We forced the game into overtime as Wanda Hairston, Ramona Von Boeckman, Mary Logue, Debbie Brock and Cornelia Ward rallied around one another and patiently worked the ball for the open shot. This team effort gave us our first championship.

The second title was not any easier. In our semi-final game, we were behind a team from Texas by seven points at the half-time. And I'll never forget Debbie Brock coming up to me and saying "Coach, don't worry I'll handle this one for us." With five seconds left in the game, Debbie sank two free throws giving us a 61-60 victory and placing us in a position to win our second consecutive National Championship.

Our third championship brought still another challenge. The University of Tennessee constructed a defense that completely shut down our inside game; this placed the game pressure on the outside shooting of our guards, and Cornelia Ward came through. She consistently scored on long-range shots that gave her 19 points and us the win. Without her performance, another "heroine' would have been called on to meet the opportunity of this great challenge.

This is a big part of my success story. Calling on players to reach back and give more than they ever dreamed they had, and to look at a crisis as an opportunity to overcome a great challenge.

The "X factor" is a dimension that affects all levels of competition. It includes an innate quality that some coaches seem to have that enables them to: call the right play in a critical situation; to motivate that girl to push on when she is tired and she appears to play on heart alone; or it manifests itself in the players we have described, who put forth super human effort permitting us to achieve three national titles in a row. It is that quality of life where preparation meets opportunity, and I am thankful that success has continually fallen my way.

SOURCE

Wade, Margaret and Mel Hankinson. (1980). *Basketball*. Cleveland, MS: Delta State Office of Public Information.

LEGACY OF
Leonard "Lenny" Wilkens

- Became the all-time winningest coach in NBA history on January 6, 1995.

- Earned a pair of Olympic gold medals as an assistant coach in 1992 and as a head coach in 1996.

- Selected as one of the 10 greatest coaches in NBA History and one of the 50 greatest players during the NBA's Golden Anniversary celebration.

- One of only three people to be elected to the Naismith Hall of Fame as both a player and a coach.

- Participated in more games as a player or coach than anyone else in NBA history.

- Quiet, fierce competitor who is recognized for his integrity and perseverance.

LEONARD "LENNY" WILKENS

"You can either allow your circumstances to be a trap and ensnare you for the rest of your life, or you can use them to learn what it takes to succeed in a world where things won't always go your way."
— *Lenny Wilkens*

BIOGRAPHY

Born: October 28, 1937 in Brooklyn, N.Y.

Inducted into the Naismith Basketball Hall of Fame as a player in 1989 and as a coach in 1998.

Leonard "Lenny" Wilkens played 15 seasons in the NBA with St. Louis, Seattle, Cleveland, and Portland and is considered one of the top point guards to ever play the game. He was a nine-time NBA all-star and was voted the Most Valuable Player in the 1971 All-Star Game. At the time of his retirement, as a player, Wilkens ranked second on the all-time assist list. He served as a player/coach for three seasons with Seattle and one with Portland. Wilkens has also coached Cleveland, Atlanta, Toronto, and New York. In 2004, he completed his 31st year as an NBA head coach. Wilkens surpassed the legendary "Red" Auerbach as the all-time winningest coach in the NBA on January 6, 1995. He has led his teams to nine 50+ win seasons, two divisional championships, and two appearances in the NBA Finals. In 1979, Wilkens directed Seattle to the NBA title. During the NBA's Golden Anniversary celebration in 1996, Lenny was selected as one of the 50 greatest players and one of the 10 greatest coaches. Wilkens has earned two Olympic gold medals—one as an assistant coach with the original 1992 Dream Team, and the other as head coach at the 1996 Olympic Games in Atlanta. He played college basketball at Providence College from 1956-1960 and was selected as the MVP in the NIT and the East-West All-Star Game in 1960. Wilkens is one of only three people to be elected to the Naismith Basketball Hall of Fame as both a player and a coach.

Leonard "Lenny" Wilkens...

Leonard "Lenny" Wilkens fought his way up from the Bedford-Stuyvesant area of New York City to the top of the NBA. He epitomized the potential of the human spirit, as he successfully met the challenges of a difficult life.

Born in Brooklyn, Wilkens, was the son of Leonard and Henrietta Wilkens. At the age of five, Wilkens' father died, making Lenny Jr. the man of the household. Wilkens (Chappell, 1999) stated, "A lot of times, people didn't think I was going to make it, but I was determined to prove them wrong. When you grow up without a dad in a tough neighborhood, you have to prove yourself all the time. I didn't mind doing that, because it was a way of life. I was going to prove to you that I was as good as you."

Responsibility at such an early age made Lenny grow up fast. "I'm not a very emotional person," Wilkens said. "I don't know if that came from having to have a lot of responsibility at a young age. I was told 'You're the man of the family now' when my father died. So, I've always been fairly serious about what I do."

The Wilkens' family was forced to go on public assistance to make ends meet. "We didn't have anything," remembered Wilkens. "It was a struggle. We didn't have new clothes like everyone else, but what we had was respect and love. My mother often told us, 'God doesn't look at your clothes. He looks at the person inside the clothes.' She said that with such conviction that, after a while, I believed it. It amazes me today at what my mother was able to go through. I never saw anyone pray as much as she did. I'm a testament that prayer works."

Henrietta became the first beacon in Lenny's life. The persever-ing, loving mother supported her four children on her part-time job in a candy factory and welfare. She provided direction and a strong sense of values. Henrietta believed that happiness was the result of strong faith and hard work.

Wilkens remembered his mother's dislike of laziness. "My mother didn't like anyone who was lazy," stated Wilkens (Chappell, 1999). "She wouldn't tolerate laziness among her children. I have always had a job since I was seven years old. I delivered groceries. I was a stock clerk in a store. I washed floors in this lady's house. I've tarred roofs, painted houses. I've loaded sugar trucks."

"Working at a young age gave me confidence," Wilkens (2000) said. "I knew that if I had to take care of myself, I could. I learned that the only way most people got anywhere in the world is by making their own way. You had to work. You had to understand there were going to be roadblocks, setbacks, and even heartbreaks. I'm not saying I ever liked any of those things, but I understood that they didn't have to defeat me. Some people act as if responsibility is a dirty word. But it was a big part of my life, and I grew to like it."

Another important figure in Wilkens' life was Father Thomas Mannion at Holy Rosary Church. Father Mannion became a father figure and mentor for Lenny. He got him focused on education, staying out of trouble, and developing his basketball skills at Holy Rosary gym.

"Father Mannion kept encouraging me," said Wilkens. "He was always telling me that 'the only thing that holds you back is you. You can accomplish anything you want.'

Another of Lenny's role models during his youth was baseball legend, Jackie Robinson. Robinson played for the Brooklyn Dodgers and was the first African-American to play Major League Baseball. "I

.....SCOUTING REPORT.....SCOUTING REPORT...

remember sitting in the bleachers as a kid and watching him play," Wilkens said. "The thing about Jackie Robinson was that he never complained about his situation. He went out there to show you he was as good as you. He was my role model. He never made excuses for himself. So, I wasn't going to."

Wilkens played only one year of basketball at Boys High School in Brooklyn, but he had acquired excellent skills on the playgrounds of New York City. "Back then, especially in the areas that I played," stated Wilkens, "if you couldn't play, they wouldn't let you on the court. When I say, couldn't play, I'm talking about making a good pass, setting a good screen, defending, and rebounding. That's the way the guys played there. It wasn't just slam-dunking and three-point shooting. We played, and we wanted to stay on the court."

Father Mannion wrote Providence College, encouraging the school's athletic director to consider Lenny for a scholarship. Providence hesitated at first, but after watching him score 36 points in a summer-league tournament game, coach Joe Mullaney offered him a scholarship.

Wilkens said, "In fairness, no one from Providence had seen me play until that summer-league game. That one game drastically changed my life."

At Providence, Wilkens led the Friars to the NIT Finals in 1960 and was named Second Team All-American by *The Sporting News*. He was also selected the Outstanding Player in New England in 1960.

During his 15-year professional career, Wilkens was a nine-time NBA All-Star and averaged 16.5 points per game, 6.7 assists, and 4.7 rebounds per game. He is considered one of the greatest point guards in NBA history.

In 2004, Wilkens finished his 31st year as an NBA coach. During his coaching career, he has become the all-time winningest coach in NBA history. Wilkens also led the Seattle Supersonics to the NBA title in 1979. "People want to know how I've survived this long in the NBA, and I point to my faith and my family," said Wilkens (2000). "I love basketball, and there is nothing I'd rather do than coach, but basketball or beating Red Auerbach's record isn't everything to me—and I think that is healthy."

"When I was younger," Wilken's said, "I'd worry that I wouldn't live very long. Because my father died young, and I was never sure exactly why he died, in the back of my mind, it made me wonder if that would happen to me. But later, when I had a better idea of the circumstances of his death, I realized I could have a long life, and I've had an amazing life. But, I sometimes wish my father could've seen it. I stare at that picture of my father, and I see a man who wanted to raise his children the right way, a man who set out to support his family. He's a man whom I barely remember, a man who died when I was five years old, but a man who still means a lot to me today. I'd like to think I learned all the things he'd have wanted me to know. When I stare hard at his picture, I see myself."

SOURCE

Chappell, Kevin. (1999, April). Lenny Wilkens: The Winningest Basketball Coach of All Times. *Ebony*.

Wilkens, Lenny. (2000). *Unguarded*. New York: Simon & Schuster.

Wilkens, Lenny. Vertical Files, Archives. Naismith Memorial Basketball Hall of Fame. Springfield, MA.

LESSONS FROM THIS LEGEND...

LIFE LESSONS

Authors' Note: This article was written by the authors.

RACE AND PREJUDICE

One drop of blood is all it takes to define you as black. Wilkens, of African-American and Irish-American ancestry, was never listed or recognized as African-Irish-American, but only as black. In the land where all are created equal, what is the purpose? As he said, "where is the justice?" Outside the home he was called "half-breed." As an All-American player at Providence, he was overlooked for the 1960 Olympics team, despite being MVP of the NIT and co-MVP (with Jerry West) of the East-West All-Star game and arguably the best true point guard in the country at the time and being wanted by Coach Pete Newell. Was it politics or prejudice again? Wilkens stated, "it left a hole in my heart."

In his early days as an NBA pro in St. Louis, he again repeatedly faced racial discrimination. His reaction—"I was confused. I was angry. I was embarrassed." He talked of how degraded it made you feel in America, the land of the free. He was in ROTC at Providence, served his country in the Army, yet couldn't eat or live where he had earned the right to be. He remembers being "utterly humiliated" by those searing experiences. He was determined that no one would hold him down in seeking the same opportunities as all other Americans. Yet none of his early successes seemed to matter: staying out of trouble, working one back-breaking job after another, and focusing on education and doing his best to overcome obstacles that few others faced.

PARENTS AND MENTORS

From his mother, Henrietta, he learned:
- Show gratitude to the people who care, rather than dwelling on those who don't care. Concentrate on what you have; do not moan about what is missing.
- Don't be a captive of your past with constant regrets of how you grew up and be filled with bitterness. Use your circumstances to learn what it takes to succeed in a world where things don't always go your way.
- Fight to survive and work to overcome the barriers to success.
- You can be as good as you want to be. Don't make excuses, you can accomplish whatever you set your mind to, and you're as good as the next person. Don't feel sorry for yourself. You're a human being, you're accountable for who you are. Be proud of who you are. God doesn't look at your clothes. He looks at the person inside the clothes.
- On cleanliness—"Our place was immaculate." From the time I was nine years old, that was my job.
- Working—"Working at a young age gave me confidence." He knew he could take care of himself and always had part-time jobs of all types. Lenny learned that the only way most people got anywhere was by making their own way. You had to work. As he said, "Some people act as if responsibility is a dirty word. But it was a big part of my life, and I grew to like it." Wilkens

enjoyed the independence and the satisfaction of earning money to buy what he needed. "Work gave me confidence."

From his mentor, Father Thomas Mannion, Wilkens mentions these lessons:
- He made Lenny feel special by keeping an eye on him. Father Mannion was in constant contact with him from 4th through 12th grade and throughout his life.
- Control who you choose as friends—Father Mannion guided him away from bad company whom he felt would corrupt his character development. He asked him to make new friends who would be positive forces in his life.
- Who taught him respect—that he earned for himself and gave to others? Adults need to get involved with kids and become mentors for them. As Wilkens states, "I do know I owe a lot of my success and my knowledge of what it takes to be a man to him." Father Mannion earned and demanded respect.
- Mannion taught him the fundamental skills of basketball and provided the Holy Rosary gym to practice those skills. With this guidance and Wilken's work ethic and respect for Mannion, he developed the necessary foundation for later basketball successes. "The balls, the chairs (to dribble around), the sweat, the echo of the ball bouncing in an empty gym—that became part of my life" said Wilkens. This adult

LESSONS FROM THIS LEGEND...

who mentored him, and paid attention to him developed in him a thirst for dedication and perseverance.

- Mannion got him in the CYO basketball leagues and had him coach a church girls team (he learned the game because he had to teach it).
- The impact of teachers and role models. "Never underestimate their impact", Wilkens said. "Make your students or players feel special, not by coddling, but by taking an interest in them, by pushing them the right way, by being demanding without being demeaning."

NEIGHBORHOOD

- Learning right from wrong. All the adults seemed to be watching, to help children learn the right way. Lenny felt a sense of community in the "melting-pot" ghetto where he grew up. Almost any adult demanded and received your respect.
- Sense of community—his extended family developed a family feeling and held him accountable. The neighborhood and especially Holy Rosary Church and school provided an anchor in the storm around him. The Catholic Church provided a safe haven and education in his early world.
- Parents' unconditional support of teachers. If Lenny was in trouble at school, he was also in trouble at home.

BASKETBALL AND SPORTS

- Learn the fundamentals early through your hard work and focus on having fun.
- Play a variety of sports and don't specialize too early. Kids do burn out and drop out with overemphasis and early specialization. Wilkens only played one season of high school basketball, yet became a Hall of Fame point guard. He did play a lot of CYO and playground basketball.
- Learn the game and teach the game. Father Mannion had Wilkens teach basketball to the Holy Rosary girls team, which taught him responsibility and basketball.
- Playground basketball—as opposed to today's pickup games which are more individual-based, Wilkens felt he learned a great deal from this form of the sport.
- The emphasis was on teamwork, passing, setting screens, and working for a good shot. Older players taught such team skills as moving without the ball, keeping vision on the ball and such two player plays as the give-and-go and pick-and-roll. Wilkens described the pick-and-roll as "an art form on the New York playgrounds of my youth." Then, it produced great players because it translated perfectly into organized basketball. Not so today, where it often disintegrates into a one-on-one, in-your-face, spectacular individual play game which can ruin good players.

- High School basketball team—It was about fun, a way to learn about teamwork, burn off energy, make good friends and learn character lessons. It was not about college scholarships and the NBA.
- College sports—Was always about education first for him. Basketball was just a way for him to pay for his education (an eventual degree in economics). He felt that college sports should be a ticket to a free education, not as a free ride to the NBA, but a chance to earn a degree. He believed that athletes should receive no special privileges in earning their degree, no special attention. Prepare for your whole life during the college years, not just for a pro-career.
- Basketball—Playing the team way and playing it right was important to him. Wilkens said, "I fell in love with basketball as if it were ballet—the smooth movement of all the players, and how it all came together."
- Passing —His favorite part of basketball was the assist, the pass to someone else that led to a score.
- Freshman basketball in college—Wilkens feels strongly that freshman should not play on the varsity level. The first year would be used to allow a smooth academic, physical, and emotional transition to college. This would allow time to learn humility, patience, and become connected to the team and school. Lenny took this route and said it helped him develop his life keys of hard

LESSONS FROM THIS LEGEND...

work, discipline, a strong spiritual life, and an accent on academics.

PROFESSIONAL BASKETBALL

- The early days—Coaches were former players with little coaching experience, mostly scrimmage preparation and horrible playing conditions. It was a cold, heartless business.
- Today's NBA draft—Unknown and unproven players who are over-paid before they have proven they have what it takes to play as a professional.
- Current players—Much better physically because of weight training, nutrition, but many with a selfish focus and not connected to team.
- Legends of the past:
  — Bill Russell: greatest shot blocker ever, came up with blocks in critical situation (and always tipped to a teammate, not spiked out-of-bounds), made his team much better.
  — Oscar Robertson: possibly the greatest player of all time, who averaged a triple double in 1961-62 (unheard of in any era).
  — Bob Pettit: one of the most underrated players in history, great scorer and "block-out" rebounder.
  — Elgin Baylor: would be great in any era, as athletic a player as Julius Erving or Michael Jordan.
  — Wilt Chamberlain: the strongest player Wilkens ever saw, a scoring machine.
  — Michael Jordan: one of the hardest working practice players ever.
- NBA strategy; offense — keep moving without the ball, move the ball, and know your teammates' strengths and weaknesses.

COACHING LESSONS

- Winning on the road; must be in top physical and mental shape, become familiar—make the road gym your home.
- Love the game. "I always did, always will." The games and players are the best, the competition, the challenges, and the feeling when all was good and you are in the zone.
- Learn by being quiet and listening to those around you: both players and coaches.
- Playing point guard; running the team and getting the ball to players where they can score, where they want it.
- Counseled and worked with people at the bottom of the social/economic scale in the community—serve others.
- Big problems start with the little things; they happen when coach - player communication breaks down and feelings are hurt. Don't play favorites, treat all with respect. Work differences out one-on-one.
- Gain respect of players; can't just be friends with players.
- No matter how prepared, how ready you are for your first coaching job, you are never ready.
- Keep your priorities in order; for me it is God, family, and basketball in that order.
- Teach the game to your players; assume they don't know basketball. Build on the basics and coach every player. Talk quietly and listen.
- Use veterans to show younger players how to act and win. They should be role models for the team.
- Don't let your temper get out of control so that your actions bring regrets. Don't do anything to embarrass yourself, team or family. When angry, take a timeout before making a decision.
- Use film/video carefully; limit, condense, and view in short segments. A picture is worth 1,000 words, if used properly and sparingly.
- Some of the best trades/recruits are the ones you don't make/get.
- Create a positive atmosphere where players can build confidence.
- Counsel/critique players individually and usually in private (never in the media).
- Wilkens always wanted teams that stressed quickness and defense. As a former player, he had instant credibility. Coaches who haven't played face more scrutiny and must work harder to earn respect.
- Teams who haven't won can have more desire, be on a mission to be

LESSONS FROM THIS LEGEND...

successful. It's harder to stay on top than to get there.

- Tournament or championship play requires complete commitment. Leave it all on the floor—no regrets.
- Players should learn each other's games, their tendencies. Think of your teammate first, yourself second. Learn to respect each other. Build trust between each other and sacrifice for the team. Team chemistry is players looking out for each other.
- Great players can impose their will on the game and affect it constantly, said Coach Wilkens. He believed the best measure of a player is how good he makes his team.
- "There are times when God opens up a door for us, when opportunity beckons," stated Wilkens. He believes we should all be open to change and the opportunities it brings.
- Players with drug problems have limited attention, tend to be late,

and let little things slide. They often alter their personality.
- Coaches take responsibility for losses, players get credit for wins.
- On race, Wilkens said, "One of my hopes for sports is that people learn to judge each other as people, not by race or stereotypes." This applies to players and coaches alike.
- The measure of a coach is not the final victory total but how coaches, players performed compared to their talent.
- Being successful is most about perseverance and commitment; for players, coaches and all people. It is also about controlling what you can with proper choices and not letting disappointments get you down.

LIFE LESSONS:

Former player Craig Ehlo said that "I never heard him use profanity or lose his composure in public, but he could reel off choice words and show his fiery competitiveness

behind closed doors." He always told players that what went on in the locker room never left that room.

Wilkens also clearly "walked his talk" in living the value of respect. In every speaking engagement as a coach, he always mentioned and gave credit to his wife, Marilyn.

Finally, he gave tribute to his father (who died early in his life) as a strong influence in his life, teaching him the importance of the father in child raising.

SOURCE

Wilkens, Lenny. (1974). *The Lenny Wilkens Story*. New York: Erickson Publisher.

Ehlo, Craig. Interview with Jerry Krause, 2004.

Wilkens, Lenny and Terry Pluto. (2000). *Unguarded*. New York: Simon and Schuster.

LEGACY OF
John Wooden

- Highly acclaimed philosopher-coach; creator of the "Pyramid of Success."

- Emphasized character development and taught life-enhancing skills through the game of basketball.

- Considered one of the finest teachers the game has ever seen.

- Awarded the Presidential Medal of Honor in 2003.

- Inducted into the Naismith Basketball Hall of Fame as both a player and a coach.

- Led UCLA to 10 national championships, including seven in a row.

- Directed UCLA to a record 88 consecutive victories.

JOHN WOODEN

"Success is peace of mind which is a direct result of self-satisfaction in knowing you did your best to become the best you are capable of becoming."
—John Wooden

BIOGRAPHY

Born: October 14, 1910 in Martinsville, IN

Inducted into the Naismith Memorial Basketball

Hall of Fame as a player in 1960 and as a coach in 1973

The John Wooden-coached UCLA teams reach unprecedented heights that will be difficult for any team to match. The Bruins set all-time records with four perfect 30-0 seasons, 88 consecutive victories, 38 straight NCAA tournament victories, 20 conference championships, and 10 NCAA national championships, including seven in a row. Wooden is considered one of the finest teachers in the history of the game. He is one of only three people enshrined in the Naismith Memorial Basketball Hall of Fame as both a player and a coach. Wooden was a three-time All-American at Purdue University and was selected the College Player of the Year in 1932. He played for legendary Hall of Fame coach Ward "Piggy" Lambert and helped lead the Boilermakers to the 1932 National Championship. Wooden coached at Dayton (KY) H.S., South Bend (IN) Central High School and Indiana State University prior to his arrival at UCLA. In 2003, Wooden received two special honors. He was awarded the Presidential Medal of Honor, and UCLA named the court at Pauley Pavilion the Nell and John Wooden Court. Wooden was enshrined in the Naismith Memorial Basketball Hall of Fame as a player in 1960 and as a coach in 1973.

John Wooden...

John Wooden was a philosopher-coach who believed our stature as a nation depended fundamentally on the strength and character of our people. He instructed his players with life-enhancing lessons. Wooden believed that athletics, when properly coached, provided an environment where individuals learned about themselves and about life. The skills he taught on the court are the same that are needed in the real world.

Wooden's remarkable success came primarily from his values and his consistency in living up to these values. He was selfless in example and was committed to helping others reach success and find inner peace.

It was Wooden's belief that participation in athletics should be a character-building experience. He emphasized to his players that they should be more concerned with their character than their reputation, and explained to them the difference between the two. Character is what you really are, while reputation is only what people say you are. A person of high character is trustworthy and honest.

Wooden believed that dishonesty was unacceptable. His father provided him with simple and direct rules for life. These were called "two sets of three" and served as a compass for trying to do the right thing. The first set dealt with honesty: 1) never lie; 2) never cheat; and 3) never steal. The second set dealt with how to handle adversity: 1) don't whine; 2) don't complain; and 3) don't make excuses. Everyone encounters adversity and people must discipline themselves to do the best that they can under the circumstances. An important key to success is how individuals respond to their perceived setbacks or disappointments. Unfortunately, many individuals blame others for their mistakes in an attempt to excuse themselves. Wooden acknowledged that he made many mistakes, but he had no failures because he did the best that he was capable of doing.

Winning was a word that Wooden rarely used. He preferred the word success, and success did not always mean scoring more points than your opponent. His emphasis was on doing your best. Wooden considered success a personal matter, because only you as an individual can tell if you did everything within your power to give your best effort. His focus was not on beating his opponent, but rather on developing the individuals on his team so they grew both individually and collectively. Wooden strove for his players to attain a peace of mind that came only from giving their best effort. The goal that he believed was most important was the goal of making the most of one's ability.

EIGHT SUGGESTIONS FOR SUCCEEDING

1. Fear no opponent. Respect every opponent.
2. Remember, it's the perfection of the smallest details that make the big things happen.
3. Keep in mind that hustle makes up for many mistakes.
4. Be more interested in character than reputation.
5. Be quick, but don't hurry.
6. Understand the harder you work, the more luck you will have.
7. Know that valid self-analysis is crucial for improvement.
8. Remember that there is no substitute for hard work and careful planning. Failing to prepare is preparing to fail.

It was Coach Wooden's observation that the primary cause of unhappiness was people wanting too much materially. They overemphasized money and the material things that went with it. When it didn't come quickly or when it didn't come at all, people became discontent and unhappy. Peace of mind and inner happiness should not be dependent on material things.

NINE PROMISES THAT CAN BRING HAPPINESS

1. Promise yourself that you will talk health, happiness, and prosperity as often as possible.
2. Promise yourself to make all your friends know there is something in them that is special and that you value.
3. Promise to think only of the best, to work only for the best, and to expect only the best in yourself and others.
4. Promise to be just as enthusiastic about the success of others as you are about your own.
5. Promise yourself to be strong so that nothing can disturb your peace of mind.
6. Promise to forget the mistakes of the past and press on to greater achievements in the future.

7. Promise to wear a cheerful appearance at all times and give every person you meet a smile.
8. Promise to give so much time to improving yourself that you have no time to criticize others.
9. Promise to be too large for worry, too noble for anger, too strong for fear, and too happy to permit trouble to press on you.

Wooden valued the principles of teaching and coaching as a sacred trust. The powerful influence of a teacher and coach must never be taken lightly. A coach helps mold character and instill productive principles. Wooden believed that coaches should be role models and provide positive examples to those they come in contact with. He lived and coached by his credo of industriousness and self-lessness. His teams reflected his passion for hard work and teamwork. Wooden urged his players to try their hardest to improve and to make their work on that particular day a masterpiece. He explained to players that once they came to practice, they ceased to exist as an individual. They were part of a team. Every player and team manager had a role, and there were no subordinates. Wooden said, "It is remarkable how much can be accomplished when players think beyond themselves."

Wooden utilized the pedagogical principles of the whole-part method during practice sessions. He showed the desired outcome and then divided it into teachable parts. Wooden said that he believed the laws of learning should be increased from four to eight because of the importance of repetition. His eight laws were: 1) explanation; 2) demonstration; 3) imitation; 4) repetition; 5) repetition; 6) repetition; 7) repetition; and 8) repetition. His goal was to create a correct habit that could be produced without conscious thought under great pressure. Wooden believed the best teacher was repetition of the fundamentals, performed correctly day after day, throughout the season.

When asked why he taught, Wooden responded, "There is no better place to find finer company." He warned people about taking themselves too seriously. Wooden said, "Talent is God-given, be humble; fame is man-given, be thankful; conceit is self-given, be careful."

Wooden's philosophy can be summarized in the creed given to him as he entered high school from his father:
1. Be true to yourself.
2. Help others.
3. Make each day your masterpiece.
4. Drink deeply from good books, especially the Bible.
5. Make friendship a fine art.
6. Build a shelter against a rainy day.
7. Pray for guidance and count and give thanks for your blessings every day.

In pursuing success and living every day to its fullest, Wooden identified the following as some of his favorite maxims:
1. Happiness begins where selfishness ends.
2. Big things are accomplished only through the perfection of minor details.
3. Discipline yourself and others won't need to.
4. Ability may get you to the top, but it takes character to keep you there.
5. If you do not have the time to do it right, when will you find the time to do it over?
6. Don't let yesterday take up too much of today.
7. It is what you learn after you know it all that counts.
8. Do not permit what you cannot do to interfere with what you can do.
9. Love is the greatest of all words in our language.
10. Never make excuses. Your friends don't need them, and your foes won't believe them.
11. The more concerned we become over the things we can't control, the less we will do with the things we can control.
12. Do not mistake activity for achievement.
13. Treat all people with dignity and respect.
14. You cannot live a perfect day without doing something for another without thought of something in return.
15. Acquire peace of mind by making the effort to become the best of which you are capable.

SOURCE

Hill, A. with J. Wooden. (2001). *Be Quick—But Don't Hurry*. New York: Simon & Schuster.

Krause, J. and R. Pim. (2002). *Coaching Basketball*. Chicago: Contemporary Books.

Wooden J. and S. Jamison. (1997). *Wooden: A Lifetime of Observations and Reflections On and Off the Court*. Chicago: Contemporary Books.

Wooden, John. Vertical Files, Archives. Naismith Memorial Basketball Hall of Fame. Springfield, MA.

LESSONS FROM THIS LEGEND...

THE PYRAMID OF SUCCESS

By John Wooden

SUCCESS IS PEACE OF MIND WHICH IS A DIRECT RESULT OF SELF-SATISFACTION IN KNOWING YOU DID YOUR BEST TO BECOME THE BEST THAT YOU ARE CAPABLE OF BECOMING.

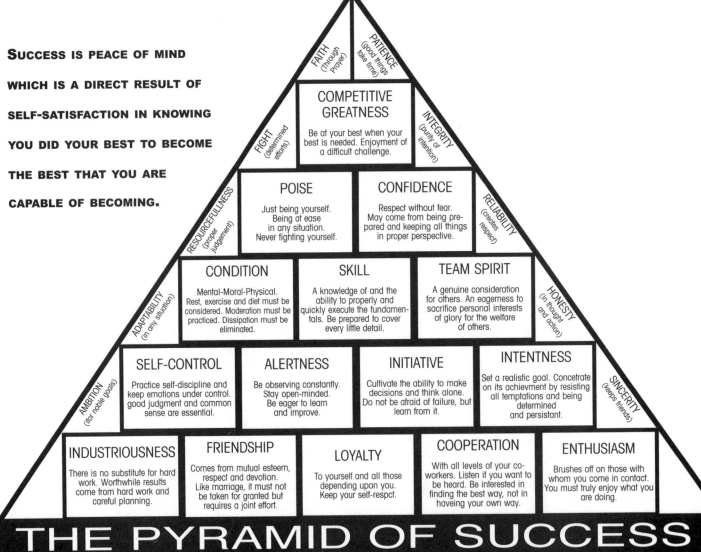

FAITH (Through Prayer)

PATIENCE (good things take time)

COMPETITIVE GREATNESS
Be at your best when your best is needed. Enjoyment of a difficult challenge.

FIGHT (determined efforts)

INTEGRITY (purity of intention)

POISE
Just being yourself. Being at ease in any situation. Never fighting yourself.

CONFIDENCE
Respect without fear. May come from being pre-pared and keeping all things in proper perspective.

RESOURCEFULLNESS (proper judgement)

RELIABILITY (creates respect)

CONDITION
Mental-Moral-Physical. Rest, exercise and diet must be considered. Moderation must be practiced. Dissipation must be eliminated.

SKILL
A knowledge of and the ability to properly and quickly execute the fundamen-tals. Be prepared to cover every little detail.

TEAM SPIRIT
A genuine consideration for others. An eagerness to sacrifice personal interests of glory for the welfare of others.

ADAPTABILITY (in any situation)

HONESTY (in thought and action)

SELF-CONTROL
Practice self-discipline and keep emotions under control. good judgment and common sense are essential.

ALERTNESS
Be observing constantly. Stay open-minded. Be eager to learn and improve.

INITIATIVE
Cultivate the ability to make decisions and think alone. Do not be afraid of failure, but learn from it.

INTENTNESS
Set a realistic goal. Concetrate on its achievment by resisting all temptations and being determined and persistant.

AMBITION (for noble goals)

SINCERITY (keeps friends)

INDUSTRIOUSNESS
There is no substitute for hard work. Worthwhile results come from hard work and careful planning.

FRIENDSHIP
Comes from mutual esteem, respect and devotion. Like marriage, it must not be taken for granted but requires a joint effort.

LOYALTY
To yourself and all those depending upon you. Keep your self-respct.

COOPERATION
With all levels of your co-workers. Listen if you want to be heard. Be interested in finding the best way, not in haveing your own way.

ENTHUSIASM
Brushes off on those with whom you come in contact. You must truly enjoy what you are doing.

THE PYRAMID OF SUCCESS

John Wooden

HEAD BASKETBALL COACH, EMERITUS, UCLA

Definitions of success vary. And everyone has a different degree of acceptance of success. My own quest for an acceptable definition began when I was in Martinsville High School. One of our teachers, Lawrence Schidler, gave the class an assignment—to define success. He tried to point out to us that success didn't necessarily mean the accumulation of material possessions or a position of power or prestige.

That started me thinking about just what a proper definition of success would be for John Wooden. Through my years in high school and college, I thought about it many times but never really had the time to delve into it deeply. While I was at South Bend Central, in the middle to late 1930's, I again became concerned over what success really was or should be.

Perhaps it was a selfish concern, I don't know. But a part of my concern was due to the fact that many parents judged teachers by the marks their children received in class. If the grades were good, the teacher was good, and if the grades were poor, it was the teacher's fault. Some parents were critical of their children if they didn't receive an A or a B and made the youngsters feel like they had failed. The good Lord didn't create all of us equal as far as intelligence is concerned, any more than a person's size or appearance. Not everyone can earn an A or a B. I had students who didn't, and I still thought they did very well.

I began to try to develop a paper that would help my students to understand how to judge success. I also believed it would help me become a better teacher. I had seen various ladders of success, so I began using blocks with key words followed by an expanded definition.

Over the next few years, and after hundreds of hour's effort, I developed what is now known as John Wooden's Pyramid of Success. My definition is at the top of the pyramid. Only one person can judge it—you. You can fool everyone else, but in the final analysis, only you know whether you goofed off or not. You know if you took the shortcut, the easy way out, or cheated. No one else does. I know that I look back with regret on some things that seemed to be success to others.

Over the years, I have given out literally thousands of copies of the pyramid. At the beginning of every season and of all my summer camps, I used to discuss the pyramid in detail and give each person a copy of it. I firmly believe it can be a base for anyone to build upon.

No building is better than its structural foundation, and no man is better than his mental foundation. Therefore, my original cornerstones are still the same—industriousness and enthusiasm. There is no substitute for work. And to really work hard at something, you must enjoy it. If you're not enthusiastic, you can't work up to your maximum ability.

The three attributes that I placed in the base between the cornerstones are friendship, cooperation, and loyalty. They are similar and help illustrate that it takes united effort to tie in the cornerstones.

The anchor blocks of the second tier of the pyramid are self-control and intentness. If you lose self-control, everything will fall. You cannot function physically or mentally or in any other way unless your emotions are under control. That's why I prefer my team to maintain a constant, slightly

increasing level of achievement, rather than hitting a number of peaks. I believe that there is a corresponding valley for every peak, just as there is a disappointment for every joy. The important thing is that we recognize the good things and not get lost in self-pity over misfortunes.

For an athlete to function properly, he must be intent. There has to be a definite purpose and goal if you are to progress. If you are not intent about what you are doing, you aren't able to resist the temptation to do something else that might be more fun at the moment.

Alertness and initiative are within the second tier. You've got to be constantly alive and alert and looking for ways to improve. This is especially true in basketball. You must be alert to take advantage of an opponent's error or weakness. Coupled with this must be the individual initiative to act alone. You must have the courage to make decisions.

Now at the heart of the pyramid is condition. I stressed this point with my players. I don't mean physical condition only. You cannot attain and maintain physical condition unless you are morally and mentally conditioned. And it is impossible to be in moral condition unless you are spiritually conditioned. I always told my players that our team condition depended on two factors—how hard they worked on the floor during practice and how well they behaved between practices. You can neither attain nor maintain proper condition without working at both.

At the very center—the heart of the structure—is skill. Skill, as it pertains to basketball, is the knowledge and the ability quickly and properly to execute the fundamentals. Being able to do them is not enough. They must be done quickly. And being able to do them quickly isn't enough either. They must be done quickly and precisely at the right time. You must learn to react properly, almost instinctively.

Team spirit is also an important block in the heart of the structure. This is an eagerness to sacrifice personal glory for the welfare of the group as a whole. It's togetherness and consideration for others. If players are not considerate of one another, there is no way we can have the proper team play that is needed. It is not necessary for everyone to particularly like each other to play well together, but they must respect each other and subordinate selfishness to the welfare of the team. The team must come first.

Poise and confidence will come from condition, skill, and team spirit. To have poise and be truly confident you must be in condition, know you are fundamentally sound, and possess the proper team attitude. You must be prepared and know that you are prepared.

Near the pinnacle must be competitive greatness. And this cannot be attained without poise and confidence. Every block is built upon the other. One will not succeed without the other, and when all are in place, you are on the road toward success. If one crumbles, it may lead to the breakdown of all.

This pyramid is tied together with a number of other qualities that are essential to the ultimate definition of success. You tie them together with ambition, which if properly focused, can be a tremendous asset, but if it is out of focus, it can be a detriment. You must be adaptable to work with others and to meet the challenge of different situations. And you must display resourcefulness because in almost every situation, good judgment is necessary.

Fight gives you the ability to do it and not be afraid of a tough battle. Faith must walk beside fight, because it is essential that you believe in your objective, and you can't have faith without prayer. Patience must be strong because the road will be rough at times and you should not expect too much too soon. Then come reliability, integrity, honesty, and sincerity.

All of these tie the blocks together into a solid structure. When all these factors are united, you can build toward a success that is based on your own personal set of goals, not those of someone else.

Some of my skeptics, and there have been a few of my players among them, question whether the pyramid really accomplished anything. I can't answer that. Each person has to answer that for himself. All I know is that I receive request after request from all types of organizations to speak about my pyramid. I do believe it can help everyone to some degree, and certainly can't hurt anyone.

A number of people have suggested that I copyright the pyramid and sell it, but I have refused. If in some small way this chart will help others, then that is enough for me. It was not created to be sold but to be used as a teaching tool, and it has been used just as much in the classroom as on the court.

SOURCE

Wooden, John. (1988). *They Call Me Coach.* Chicago: Comtemporary Books.

LESSONS FROM THIS LEGEND...

REFLECTIVE THINKING

By John Wooden

I am not going to ask you to believe everything that I say as the gospel. It's what I believe and what I have done. I won't hide anything or hold back anything. I'll give you my ideas and if they differ from yours, it doesn't mean that you are wrong, or somebody else is wrong, because there is more than one way to do things.

I believe that you should play aggressively, both offensively and defensively. I believe you should have confidence in what you are doing or else not do it. I believe in working on your team and not worry too much about the other fellow, and for that reason, I did not do a lot of scouting. If you disagree, that is fine. I'm merely going to tell you the things in which I believe and have tried to practice to the best of my ability.

The very first thing that I want to start with is that basketball is a game of balance. There are different types of balance:
1. Emotional balance
2. Mental balance
3. Physical balance
4. Rebound balance
5. Team balance
6. Offensive balance
7. Defensive balance

EMOTIONAL BALANCE

Emotional balance is controlled by the head and how well you keep your emotions under control. Self-control is most important not only from the playing point of view, but also from the coaching point of view.

PHYSICAL BALANCE

The physical balance is controlled by the extremities. The feet are the first to be considered. The feet should be just wider than the shoulders when shooting, rebounding, and defending. You play basketball on the soles of your feet and not up on your toes. If the feet are too wide, you lose maneuverability, and if too close, you lose your balance.

The hands should always be close to the body in alignment with the body. You have better control when the hands are closer to the body. On defense, you have three things to worry about: driving, passing, and shooting (depending on the floor location of your opponent). Keep the hands close to the body when blocking a shot.

The head is always directly above the midpoint between the feet. Keep all joints flexibility and relaxed.

OVER-COACHING

Over-coaching can be more harmful than under-coaching. I think the tendency is for inexperienced coaches to give too much information. They don't have enough patience. The younger coach is often going to try to impress his players with how much he knows.

Remember to teach well what you do and don't tie your players down so much that you take away all of their initiative, as long as it fits into your offensive and defensive plan of attack.

CONDITIONING

Better-conditioned teams normally prevail, provided pressure is put on early and kept on constantly throughout the game. If you are a better conditioned team than your opponent, and you are not putting pressure on all the time, it doesn't make any difference whether you are in better condition or not. I like offensive and defensive pressure. I always told my players that we would be in better condition than anyone that we played.

Conditioning is a dual responsibility between coach and player. The player's responsibilities begin when they leave the practice floor and until they return. A player can tear down between practices faster than a coach can build them up. The lack of moderation, not getting enough rest, not eating regularly, not having the proper diet, or over-eating the wrong foods can negatively affect conditioning.

On offense, most of the player's time will be without the ball. Use it and use it wisely. It's what you do without the ball that is going to determine to a great extent what you are going to be able to do when you get the ball.

A man-to-man defense that is any good is played with zone principles. Your objective in a man-to-man defense is not to keep your man from scoring, but to keep the other team from scoring. Sometimes you have to leave your man completely to keep another man from getting a real easy shot. That's defense.

ESSENTIALS FOR THE COACH

A coach must:
1. Be a teacher
2. Be industrious
3. Be enthusiastic
4. Be sympathetic, but objective
5. Have patience
6. Have self-control
7. Prepare – Failing to prepare is preparing to fail

LESSONS FROM THIS LEGEND...

8. Have discipline – Discipline is not to antagonize, but to improve, help, and correct
9. Be attentive to detail – It's the little things that make the big things happen
10. Be impartial – This means you can't treat all your players alike
11. Give players an optimistic picture – not an idealistic picture
12. Be firm, but not bull-headed

DOING YOUR BEST

A coach can only do his best, nothing more. He owes his best effort not only to himself, but also to the people who employ him and to the players under his supervision. If you truly do your best, and only you will really know, then you are successful, and the actual score is immaterial. However, when you fail to do your best, you have failed, even though the score might have been to your liking.

This does not mean that you should not coach to win. You must teach your players to play to win and do everything in your power that is ethical and honest to win. I believe that doing the best that you are capable of doing is victory in itself, and less than that is defeat.

I continually stress to my players that all I expect from them at practice and in the games is their best effort. They must be eager to become the very best that they are capable of becoming. Heads should always be held high when you have done your best, regardless of the score. There is no reason for being overly jubilant at victory or unduly depressed by defeat.

THE COACH AS A TEACHER

Since the most important responsibility of a coach in regard to the actual playing of the game is to teach his players properly and effectively to execute the various fundamentals of the game, he is, first of all, a teacher.

As a matter of fact, it is unlikely that a teacher of any subject finds it as necessary to follow the laws of learning as closely and specifically as it is for the teacher of the fundamentals of basketball. A fundamental must be explained and demonstrated, the correct demonstration must be imitated by the players, their demonstration must be constructively criticized and corrected, and then the players must repeat and repeat the execution of the proper model until the correct habit has been formed to the point where they will react instinctively in the correct manner.

THE COACH AS A LEADER

The coach must never forget that he is a leader and not merely a person with authority. The youngsters under his supervision must be able to receive proper guidance from him in all respects and not merely to the proper playing of the game of basketball.

Next to their parents, youngsters spend more time with, and are more likely to be influenced by, their teachers than anyone else. The coach is often the teacher who will provide by far the most influence.

MY FIRST SEVEN POINTS

My father was truly a gentle man, yet when he said something I knew he meant it. We had a team of mules on our farm named Jack and Kate. Kate would often get stubborn and lay down on me when I was plowing. I couldn't get her up no matter how roughly I treated her. Dad would see my predicament, walk across the field until he was close enough to say, "Kate," and she'd get up and start working again.

My father never touched Kate in anger, and it took me a long time to learn that lesson. When I graduated from the small country grade school I attended, Dad gave me a card with seven creeds or points on it that I've carried with me ever since. I've not lived up to them as well as I've wanted, but I've tried and that gives me peace. Here they are:

1. Be True to Yourself
   This covers so many areas. Be true to your faith, your wife and family, your profession, and colleagues. Shakespeare said in Hamlet, "Above all to thine ownself be true…Thou canst not then be false to any man."

2. Make Each Day Your Masterpiece
   Just do your best each day. You can't change yesterday – it's gone forever; it's door has been shut and the key thrown away. But you can work to do your best today.

3. Help Others
   Jesus said, "It is more blessed to give than to receive." We say the words but so many times don't really believe them. They're still true. You can never acquire happiness, freedom and peace, without giving of yourself to someone else.

LESSONS FROM THIS LEGEND...

4. Make Friendship a Fine Art
Work at it. Don't take friendship for granted. If you do, it may not last. And don't just work at it from one side. Friendship comes from mutual esteem, respect, and devotion. Just as in a successful marriage, both sides must work on it.

A man from the Midwest came up to me after I'd spoken at a convention in San Francisco and remarked that Californians sure weren't as friendly as the folks back home. He'd encountered a lot people while walking to the meeting room and not one had spoken to him. I asked, "Did you greet any of them?" He hadn't. If we wait for the other person to speak first, often no one speaks.

5. Build a Shelter Against a Rainy Day
This can mean material possessions, but I think it means things that are everlasting. In many ways, we've been taken in by materialism. I'm not saying possessions are unimportant, but we often put them out of proportion.

6. Drink Deeply from Good Books
Especially the book that's far outsold all the others – the Bible. We should read it every day. Make time to read Shakespeare and other great authors.

7. Pray for Guidance and Give Thanks Daily
We pray frequently for help, but how often do we give thanks for our blessings? America's imperfect, and we must constantly work to improve her, but she's the greatest nation of all, and we're blessed to be here. How much more pleasant this world would be if we magnified our blessings the way we do our disappointments.

SOURCE

Wooden, John. (1983, March / April). My First Seven Points. *Sharing the Victory*.

Wooden, John. (1984). Reflective Thinking. *MacGregor Flashback Notebook*.

LEGACY OF
Morgan Wootten

- Emphasized integrity and the development of character through participation in athletics.

- Urged players to set their priorities in the following order: God, family, school, and then basketball.

- Advocated the three D's — defense, desire, and DeMatha.

- Emphasized the importance of education and during a 30-year period, every player earned a full college scholarship.

- Compiled the all-time best record (1,274-192) among high school coaches and the highest winning percentage (.868).

- Selected as the top high school coach of the 20th century by the Naismith Foundation.

MORGAN WOOTTEN

*"Inch by inch life's a cinch.
Yard by yard it's really hard."*
—Morgan Wootten

BIOGRAPHY

Born: April 21, 1931 in Durham, NC

Inducted into the Naismith Basketball Hall of Fame in 2000

Morgan Wootten began his coaching career in 1951 at the St. Joseph's Home for Boys in Washington D.C. He then coached at St. John's High School and compiled a 60-9 record. Wootten was appointed coach at DeMatha High School (MD) in 1956 and stayed as a teacher and coach for 46 years. During that time, DeMatha won five mythical national championships (1962, 1965, 1968, 1978, and 1984). Wootten compiled the all-time best record (1,274-192) among high school coaches and the highest winning percentage (.868). With DeMatha's win on January 15, 2000, Wootten became the first basketball coach at any level (high school, college, or pro) to reach 1,200 wins. *USA Today* chose him the 1984 National Coach of the Year. Wootten's 1965 team broke the 71-game winning streak of Lew Alcindor's (now Kareem Abul-Jabbar) Power Memorial (NY) High School team. In 1991, Wootten was the first recipient of the Walt Disney Award, presented to the top sports coach in the United States. He also received the John Bunn Award in 1991 for his extraordinary contributions to the game of basketball.

Morgan Wootten...

Morgan Wootten credits his mother for his intense drive and love of competition, and his father for teaching him to tell the truth and be himself. He was strongly influenced by his parents, teachers, and coaches and this is readily observed in his philosophy. One of Wootten's favorite sayings is "I am me, and I want to be the best me that I can be."

Wootten's high school coach, Tony Creme, influenced him by stressing fundamentals, player communication, and the importance of being a gentleman and a father figure to his players. Other people who helped Wootten formulate his philosophy are: Ken Loeffler of LaSalle in the area of offensive strategy; "Red" Auerbach of the Boston Celtics in regard to having a feel for the game and developing roles for each player; and Jim Kehoe of Maryland for stressing the value of discipline, organization, and thoroughness. The heart of Wootten's philosophy seemed to come from Knute Rockne of Notre Dame who said, "We can only measure our success after 10 or 15 years, when we see how our players turn out. After all, the real game is the game of life. And it's the one that we cannot afford to lose."

Morgan intended to become a lawyer after college, but was persuaded to coach the St. Joseph's Orphanage sports' teams in 1950 at the age of 19. Something happened there that forever changed Wootten's career plans. Under his direction, the teams had mixed success., but he arranged a visit and motivational talk at the orphanage from Rocky Marciano, the new heavyweight champion of the world. One of the orphans asked Rocky if he thought he could beat Coach Wootten. Marciano said he thought he could, but it would be a terrific fight. The questioning boy countered, "I don't think you can. I think Morgan would kill you." That incident deeply affected Wootten when he saw the affect and impact a coach could have on a boy. From that time on, Morgan Wootten knew his mission in life—to teach and coach young people about life using the vehicle of sports.

And he became a master of it—starting in 1956 at DeMatha High School and carving out a legendary Hall of Fame career spanning over 46 years. It was a marriage made in heaven; the school and the coach put each other on the map.

A legendary game between DeMatha and Power Memorial Academy in New York is still talked about long after that night of January 30, 1965. Over 12,000 fans jammed Maryland University's Cole Field House to see the long-awaited high school duel between DeMatha's Stags and the Power Panthers, led by its 7' superstar, Lew Alcindor (now Hall of Famer Kareem Abdul-Jabbar). Power had carved out a 71-game winning streak of its own. The game created a local and national media frenzy. DeMatha shocked the basketball world by defeating Power Memorial by five points, holding Alcindor to 16 (he averaged 30). This came in Wootten's ninth year at DeMatha. He had his team prepare for the game by holding tennis rackets above their head to simulate shooting over Alcindor.

With all of his success, Wootten achieved his biggest win in July, 1996, when he collapsed while coaching in summer camp and was diagnosed with primary billiary cirrhosis of the liver, a rare disease that is usually fatal. With only hours left to live, a liver donor was found that was a perfect match for him, and the transplant was carried out to save his life. Wootten returned to coach the next season. During that season, he passed on to his players some of the lessons learned from the experience:

- My illness confirms the priorities needed for success: God, family, and education in that order. Anything else, including basketball can be no higher than fourth.
- Appreciate every day—sunrise and sunset, spring and autumn.
- Be thankful for families and friends.
- Enjoy each day, one day at a time.
- Inch by inch, life's a cinch. Yard by yard, it's really hard.

Morgan reminisced about his lengthy stay at DeMatha; we opened with 18 boys shortly after World War II, and now we have over 900. But we have always emphasized "character over credentials." "We stress men of integrity and character. If you don't embrace those qualities, you're out of here." We still have the coat-and-tie dress code, our students still study religion every day of their four years here, and, at the start of each day, they stand to recite the Lord's Prayer and the Pledge of Allegiance. We have won championships in every sport—more than 50 in basketball, football, and baseball alone. But we have also won national high school Blue Ribbon awards from the Department of Education for excellence in education. After my transplant and the remarkable 1996-97 season, I often asked why my life was spared. The answer was clear—God was telling me, he wants me to stay here so I can continue to do what he wants all of us to do—to touch peoples' lives.

Coach Wootten explained his defensive philosophy in these words. "The name of the game is defense. We are going to make something happen. We want to get the ball. We want to get the ball almost any way we can. We are going to trap, rotate, and not foul. We have practiced it over and over. We put our player through every imaginable situation. We score points off our opponents' mistakes."

Wootten concluded by stating, "We are very lucky to be working with young people. And the rule of thumb that we have with our coaching staff is that we feel we should be the kind of coaches that our own son or our own daughter could play for. We are lucky because players keep us young and enthusiastic. Young people today are better than ever. Obviously, they are the future of America."

Wootten has been called the "Wizard of Washington." Mike Brey, head coach at Notre Dame and former DeMatha player, said, "All great high school coaches are local heroes. Morgan is a national one. You think about him, and you think about John Wooden and Dean Smith, and you stop there."

James Brown of Fox Sports played for Wootten at DeMatha and then chose Harvard over North Carolina to further his education and basketball career. Brown had this to say about his mentor: "Morgan absolutely abides in his own life by the principles he instructs his pupils. He is the best teacher, psychologist, and motivator at any level of basketball, professional or amateur."

Wootten is often asked why he hasn't gone to the so-called "next level" of college coaching. He has turned down offers from Georgetown, University of Maryland and North Carolina State, among others. On March 8, 1980, he turned down an offer from North Caroline State for $700,000 plus free college education for his five chil-

dren. Jim Valvano took the job and those players to an NCAA National Championship. When asked why he declined a college job for that much money, he replied that "money has never been in the top three priorities in life (God, family and education) and will never be the primary factor in my definition of happiness for me and my family." He also added, as for climbing mountains, they are where you find them. Any time I help a student in one of my classes get a better start during his formative years, or touch the life of one of my basketball players, I feel I have climbed another mountain. That's the kind I prefer to keep on climbing." And so he did, for over a half century of teaching and coaching excellence.

Hall of Fame coach John Wooden said it best with the following statement. "Morgan Wootten has been called the finest high school coach in the country. I disagree. He is the finest coach, at any level, I have ever seen."

SOURCE

Wootten, Morgan. Vertical Files, Archives. Naismith Memorial Basketball Hall of Fame. Springfield, MA.

Wootten, Morgan and Bill Gilbert. (1997). *A Coach for all Seasons*. Indianapolis: Masters Press.

Wooten, Morgan. Interview with Ralph Pim. September 11, 2004.

DEVELOPING A BASKETBALL COACHING PHILOSOPHY

By Morgan Wootten

I know of no more rewarding, satisfying, and fulfilling job than working with young people on the basketball court, as I did for 46 years at DeMatha High School in Hyattsville, Maryland. In all those years, there was nothing else I would have rather been doing.

The first, and perhaps most important, step toward becoming a successful basketball coach is developing a basketball coaching philosophy. Without a philosophy, you will lack the road map and direction necessary to achieve your goals. This is true in any endeavor that you undertake in life.

A coaching philosophy is established in many ways and over many years, beginning with personal experiences as a player. Yours began forming from the first time you picked up a basketball. It grew as you observed games in person and on television. And it will continue to grow as you learn more about the game and how to work with players.

PHILOSOPHICAL FOUNDATION

To ensure that the philosophy you develop is a positive one, examine the approaches taken by successful coaches. Talk with them, read their books, and attend their clinics. Books and clinics are especially important to your growth and development as a coach.

Reading books allows you to find out what other coaches think, what they've done through the years, and what has worked for them. All types of publications are helpful, but a book – because of its depth – provides real insight into a coach's philosophical approach.

Attending clinics is an absolute necessity. Not only do you hear for yourself what respected coaches think, but you also have a chance in private sessions to talk with them, ask questions, and receive feedback about your own ideas. These gab sessions will contribute significantly to your philosophical development and growth as a coach.

The sum of your experiences as a player, the information you've gained through observing games, the lessons you've learned through reading, and the ideas you've picked up by listening and asking questions at clinics, in combination with your personality, constitutes your unique coaching philosophy. But don't be misled; simply playing, observing, reading, and listening more does not guarantee you'll have a better coaching philosophy. The quality – not just the quantity – of your experiences and how you implement your philosophy are equally important to determining your success.

Parts of your philosophy will continue to evolve through the years. These will be primarily tactical elements that change with your personnel and with the game itself.

Despite these philosophical adjustments, the core of every sound philosophy is virtually unchanging, and I call this core the philosophical foundation. Many fundamentals of basketball fall into this category, such as the proper way to shoot the ball, the proper defensive stance, the proper rebounding position, and the proper physical conditioning. Even more important, however, is a coach's value system. What do you emphasize – winning a basketball game or winning in life? What priorities do you have regarding the development of your athletes as people, not just basketball players?

THE BIG 5 IN COACHING

1. Our goal must be to provide a wholesome environment in which young men or women can develop themselves spiritually, socially, and academically.
2. As coaches, we should be the kind of coach we would want our sons or daughters to play for.
3. We must never lose sight of the fact that basketball is a game and should be fun. We should never put winning ahead of the individual.
4. Because basketball is a great teaching situation, we must use this opportunity to educate the young men or women on our teams. We must prepare them for the many decisions they will be making that will have long-range effects on the quality of their lives.
5. This is the bottom line: Are we doing all we can to make our players' sport experience as rewarding as possible?

BE YOURSELF

In determining where your philosophical foundation rests, keep in mind that you must be yourself. You can't be John Wooden, Red Auerbach, Mike Krzyzewski, or Dean Smith – you have to be you. It's all right to adopt certain ideas from other coaches, but if you try to be somebody you're not, you'll be inconsistent in your thoughts and actions, your players and assistants will question your honesty, and you will not be as successful as you could be. If you try to be someone else, the best you can do is only second best.

LESSONS FROM THIS LEGEND...

One of my favorite sayings is "I am me, and I want to be the best me that I can be." If all of us try to be the best we can be, we will be successful.

My favorite definition of success comes from John Wooden, the now-retired coaching legend from UCLA. He said, "Success is a peace of mind which comes as a direct result of knowing that you did the best you could to be the best you are capable of becoming."

BE EAGER TO LEARN

The wealth of knowledge available is immense. It is important, then, to seek as much advice and knowledge from other coaches as you possibly can. But being willing to learn is not enough – you must be eager to learn.

When I speak at clinics, coaches frequently come up to me and tell me what they are doing. I appreciate them sharing their approaches, but they don't ask me anything. When they merely tell me what they do, I may learn from them, but they won't learn from me without seeking my feedback. Remember, learning stops when you think you have all the answers.

And don't limit your learning to clinics, books, and discussions with other head coaches. Chances are you may have great resources right in your own building in the form of one or all of your assistant coaches. I have had the privilege of working with and learning from some great assistants.

TOUCH PEOPLE'S LIVES

As coaches, we are extremely fortunate to have the opportunity and ability to work with and positively influence young people. That is why I suggest following this rule of thumb: Be the kind of coach that you would want your own sons and daughters to play for. All of us should be determined to be that kind of coach.

Never lose sight of the tremendous impact you are having on young people's lives. We are with young people at their emotional heights and their emotional depths, the times when they are the most impressionable. Teachers of other subjects would love to have the classroom situation that we do, for we have a class that young people are pleading to get into and be a part of. It is our moral responsibility to use this unique opportunity in a positive manner to help prepare our young people for life.

As a coach, you must always be aware of the influence you have on your players. Because of their keen interest and emotional involvement in sports, your athletes will be hanging on every word you say. Many times, you may think you're not reaching them, but what you say to them in practice can determine how good their dinner will taste and how well they will sleep that night. An incidental cutting remark, which you forgot about as soon as you said it, can stay with that younger person and be a source of pain for a longer time than you may ever know.

PRIORITIES AND OBJECTIVES

With a solid philosophy in place, you can then establish objectives for your players, your team, and yourself. Most important of these are the objectives for your athletes. Always keep in mind that the game is for the players, and that they are the most important part of any program. The coach provides the leadership, but the athletes must be the main focus.

PLAYER OBJECTIVES

A fundamental job of a coach is to help the athletes get their priorities in order. At DeMatha, we encourage our players to devote themselves to four things.

1. God
2. Family
3. School
4. Basketball

Everything else must come after these. Show me young people who have their priorities in order, and I'll show you players who have the best chance of getting the most out of their lives, both on and off the court.

These priorities are one element of my coaching philosophy that has not changed over the years. These four cornerstones came as a result of my stepping back and taking a look at the characteristics I wanted in a player.

My primary emphasis on a strong spiritual commitment results from experience; those with such a conviction are better able to meet life's challenges than those without one. Second, I have found that young people who are loyal and devoted to their families are more capable of becoming loyal and devoted members of a team. Third, academics are the purpose of school; a student who is willing to work hard toward that purpose is more likely to work hard toward becoming a better basketball player and helping the team. And fourth, basketball is the sport the athlete is playing, so obviously a strong commitment to that is necessary as well.

Kids today want the same things as kids did when I started coaching over 50 years ago. They seek guidance, discipline, and people who are interested in them. We, as coaches, must be both teachers and guides, because kids sometimes have no one else to help them establish priorities. To reach these young people, I demonstrate to them what the proper priorities should be and give them examples of the kind of positive results such objectives can produce. I then try to attempt to put things in the proper order. Because once they've seen it work, they're convinced.

TEAM OBJECTIVES

After your athletes establish their priorities and have a good idea where they're heading, then you must establish objectives for the team. Our team objectives are very simple, and they never change: play hard; play smart; play together; and have fun.

How a team approaches the game makes all the difference in the world. A team can take the floor with one of three perspectives:

LESSONS FROM THIS LEGEND...

Team A goes out on the court feeling it must win at all costs, which places an unbelievable pressure on the athletes. This team will rarely play anywhere near its potential.

Team B comes into games with a fear of losing. Therefore, the players play the game trying not to lose rather than trying to play their best. Again, this is an unhealthy attitude that will inhibit the players on the team from playing up to their potential.

Team C enters a game with the attitude that I stress: play hard, smart, together, and have fun. This is the best approach because it promotes maximum effort from all members of the team while allowing them to enjoy the thrill of competition. In this situation, the players don't feel the pressure of winning at all costs, nor do they fear losing. Rather, they simply try to give their best effort and to have fun, and as a result, they play up to their potential.

1. Play Hard

When I tell our players to "play hard," I want them to give everything they have every second out on the basketball floor. If they give anything less than 100 percent, then they are not getting the most out of their abilities. You cannot reach your potential without putting your maximum effort into everything you do.

2. Play Smart

To encourage smart play, I try to get each player to work within the team's offense and to play within his own physical limitations. To accomplish this, players must fully understand their roles on the team, and that starts with the coach. You must identify each player's strengths; this will help you define their roles. Then you need to communicate these to each player. If the player is one of your top scorers, make sure he knows he is your "go-to" guy. If the player is your best defender, assign him the role of the defensive stopper. By focusing on their strengths, players will make the biggest contribution to the team.

If both coach and players have a good understanding of the different roles and who will fill them, you're well on your way to having your team play smart. As a general rule, I do not want inventors out there. I tell the players to just make the basic plays and let the overall flow of the play take care of itself.

3. Play Together

Simply put, your team will play together if your players are as thrilled with a teammate's accomplishments as they are with their own. No one should care who gets the credit. If the team does well, everyone does well. Every player must be as excited when another player scores a basket as when he makes one himself.

4. Have Fun

When I stress that the players have fun, I merely want them to remember that basketball is a game, and that their primary reason for participating in the sport is simply for the pleasure they experience while playing it. But they won't get any enjoyment if they play a game feeling afraid to lose, or feeling that they must win at all costs. I want my players to play with this mind-set: Basketball is just a game, it's supposed to be fun, and we can have fun while we are busy playing hard and playing smart.

5. Practice as You Play

The best way to get your athletes to enter games with the proper perspective is to help them approach each practice with a positive mindset. Stress that the players should play hard, play smart, and have fun while practicing. Conduct your practices in an upbeat manner. Your practices should move quickly and emphasize the repetition and proper execution of fundamentals.

One of the commandments of coaching is, "As you practice, so shall you play." Because my players follow this advice, our teams are as well prepared as they can be when going into a game. The players, consequently, enter the game with a feeling of confidence that inspires them to really get after the task at hand. They take the floor knowing that they will not beat themselves.

6. Put Forth a Winning Effort

I never talk to my players about a game in terms of winning it. For example, I'll never say in a pregame talk, ""Let's go out and win this game." A winning effort is more important than the actual outcome. When we can look back at a game and know we did the best we possibly could, then we know we made a winning effort. That is all any coach can ask of his players, his assistants, and himself.

A trap every coach must avoid falling into is evaluating the success of the program in terms of wins and losses. This could result in the old cycle: If you win, everything is wonderful; if you lose, everything is terrible.

LESSONS FROM THIS LEGEND...

What you should keep in mind and stress is that sometimes you can learn more from a loss than a win. The players may be more motivated to improve, and they may be more receptive to the constructive criticism that will help them do so. So maintain an even keel. Work on the mistakes you make even in a win, but also praise the successes even in the games you lose.

COACHES' OBJECTIVES

Once we've established objectives with our athletes as individuals and with the team as a whole, we must then look at ourselves. What is it that you want to accomplish through coaching?

I believe the biggest personal goal that I, as a coach, must have is to do the best I can to have my team as well prepared as possible. You owe this to your school, your assistants, your players, and their parents.

From a professional point of view, we, like our players, should work hard to become the best that we can possibly be. We need to continue to add to our knowledge of the game through reading as many books as we can get our hands on, attending as many clinics as possible, exchanging information freely with fellow coaches, and asking intelligent questions of the right people.

SIX CHALLENGES OF COACHING

When you become a basketball coach, you accept certain things that go along with the job. Through the years, I've identified six primary challenges a coach should be prepared to address.

1. All your success is dependent on the abilities of other people.

    Admiral Hyman Rickover, the father of the nuclear navy, believed that endeavors succeed or fail because of the people involved. Only by attracting the best people,

he believed, would you accomplish great things. This is also true of coaching. You've got to surround yourself with good people. To a great extent, your success is dependent on the abilities of other people and how you can mold them, direct them, guide them, work with them, and lead them.

2. Coaches are evaluated by everyone.

    In almost any other profession, few or no people see the results of the work. But if a player misses a lay-up, everyone sees it, and the coach gets blamed. The coach is always in the spotlight.

3. Everyone feels they have knowledge about coaching sports.

    Parent, fans, faculty members – pretty much everyone who attends games or has a connection to the program – will offer opinions and advice. It's easy coaching from the bleachers. Stick to your philosophy, priorities, and tactics if you are confidant in them.

4. The highs are incredibly high, and the lows are amazingly low.

    Athletes' self-images are tied to their athletic performances. And coaches are there when young men and women are most pliable. In fact, players need you most when they're really low.

5. The coach has a personal relationship with every player and has a dramatic impact on every player's life.

    This is something I don't think we ever fully appreciate. Our principal at DeMatha had every senior fill out an "exit form" when he graduated. The form included

space for the student to write about any teacher at DeMatha that had an impact on him, and these comments are then forwarded to the teacher. If you're coaching at a school, I highly recommend that you approach your principal about this practice. After looking at those comments, you remember why you're coaching. Coaches have dramatic impacts on players' lives. Be the kind of coach you always wanted to play for and treat your players the way you always wanted to be treated.

6. Success is based on the unusual paradox of getting an individual to work to develop skills and then getting him to sacrifice that for the well being of the team.

    That just about sums up coaching right there, and what a wonderful and rewarding challenge it is.

These six factors need to be taken into account as you examine your strengths and your professional objectives. Some coaches find them a burden, but I believe they are the reasons why coaching is so special.

SOURCE

Wootten, Morgan. (2003). *Coaching Basketball Successfully*. Champaign, IL: Human Kinetics.

LESSONS FROM THIS LEGEND...

MY FAVORITE COACHING CONCEPTS

By Morgan Wootten

Here are some of my favorite coaching concepts to help you enjoy every day of this wonderful profession.

1. Never lose sight of the impact you are having on young people's lives.

2. Teach your players the importance of proper priorities that allow for maximum personal, academic, and athletic development.

3. Evaluate wins and losses objectively, focusing more on effort and execution than on the outcome of the game.

4. Instruct, don't dictate.

5. Never humiliate.

6. Communicate your approach in a style that is comfortable to you and fits your personality and philosophy.

7. Learn to anticipate problems.

8. Never announce penalties for rule violations in advance.

9. Enthusiasm creates heroism.

10. If you make a mistake and fall down, you must get back up.

11. Always have a "Thought of the Day."

12. You are constantly being judged on what you are doing and not what you have done.

13. Be yourself.

14. Be eager to learn.

15. Don't play players only because they have potential if they do not hustle, work hard, and listen.

16. Never discipline to punish, discipline to teach.

17. We are, what we continually do.

LESSONS FROM THIS LEGEND...

18. Do to your opponent what you do not like done to you.

19. You play defense with your feet, eyes, and heart.

20. If you want the attention of your players, use compliments.

21. I believe that repetition of fundamentals at any level will make your players winners.

22. Play hard, play smart, play together, and have fun.

23. You must have total control of your program.

24. I will never curse my players, and they will never curse me.

25. I will never embarrass my players, and they will never embarrass me.

26. Do not assume anything.

27. Listen and learn from your players.

28. Excellence becomes a habit.

29. Don't ever tell your players to win.

30. Never write a plan for practice that takes longer than two hours.

31. Make your players sprint over to you to begin practice on a hustling, enthusiastic note.

32. Inch by inch, life's a cinch. Yard by yard, it's really hard.

33. Take time to talk individually with the players you are cutting.

34. Have your players write down their academic and athletic goals at the start of every year.

35. Building team chemistry is the most important thing you can do as a coach.

SOURCE

Wootten, Morgan. (2003). Inch by inch, life's a cinch. Notes from the Don Meyer Coaching Academy: Aberdeen, South Dakota.

Wootten, Morgan. Interview with Ralph Pim. April 20, 2005.

LESSONS FROM THE LEGENDS

trivia QUIZ

NAME THE NAISMITH HALL OF FAME COACH WHO...

1 Would light a "victory cigar" in the closing minutes of a game he knew he would win?

Hint: He directed the Boston Celtics to eight straight NBA championships.

2 Led the University of Oregon to the first NCAA championship in 1939?

Hint: He was one of the first coaches to statistically analyze the game of basketball and wrote the book Scientific Basketball.

Was the first African-American coach to win the NCAA Division I national championship? **3**

Hint: He played for the Boston Celtics and was the backup center to Bill Russell.

4 Played for Piggy Lambert at Purdue and helped lead the Boilermakers to the national championship in 1932?

Hint: He directed UCLA to 88 consecutive victories.

5 Became the first coach to win championships in both the NBA and the ABA?

Hint: His 1967 Philadelphia 76ers were selected the best team in the NBA's first 35 years.

Promoted the growth of basketball in the Southeast and is called the "Father of ACC Basketball?" **6**

Hint: He led the Frankfort (IN) H.S. Hot Dogs to four state championships.

7 Coached at Indiana, and his run-and-gun style of play earned his team the nickname the "Hurrying Hoosiers?"

Hint: He directed Indiana to the NCAA title in 1940 and 1953.

8 Played for "Phog" Allen and was a member of the 1952 University of Kansas NCAA championship team?

Hint: His North Carolina Tar Heels made 23 consecutive NCAA appearances.

9 Is called the "Mother of Women's Basketball?"

Hint: She introduced basketball to female students at Smith College at a time when a woman competing in athletics was frowned upon.

10 Became the first coach in NCAA Division I basketball history to win 500 games without athletic scholarships?

Hint: He designed a team-oriented offense that featured exceptional passing, shooting, and backdoor cuts.

12 Was the first person elected to the Hall of Fame whose entire career as both a player and coach was spent on the College Division (now called Division II) of the NCAA?

Hint: He led the Evansville "Purple Aces" to five NCAA College Division national championships.

11 Conceived the "Triangle and Two" defense while working as an assistant at Dartmouth?

Hint: He coached Marquette to the 1977 NCAA National Championship.

13 Entertained fans at halftime by wrestling a black bear?

Hint: He led Passaic (NJ) H.S. to a 159 game winning streak, longest in basketball history.

14 Coached 35 years at NYU and led teams to both the NCAA championship game and the NIT finals?

Hint: He was a three-sport star at NYU and was selected as the "greatest basketball player in the world" in 1920.

15 Was selected as the NABC Coach of the Decade for the 1990s?

Hint: He graduated from West Point and played for Bob Knight.

16 Coached the 1984 U.S. women's team to their first gold medal in Olympic competition?

Hint: She was the first woman to reach the 800-win plateau and has led the University of Tennessee to six national championships.

17 Is the namesake of the field house at the University of Kansas?

Hint: He is called the "Father of Basketball Coaching."

18 Directed Holy Cross to the NCAA championship without having a home gymnasium?

Hint: He wrote the popular basketball textbook Bread and Butter Basketball.

19 Led Delta State to three consecutive AIAW national championships?

Hint: She is the namesake of the award presented annually to the top women's collegiate player.

20 Is the all-time winningest coach in high school basketball history?

Hint: He was selected the "Outstanding High School Coach of the 20th Century" by the Naismith Club.

ANSWERS

1) Arnold "Red" Auerbach 2) Howard Hobson 3) John Thompson 4) John Wooden 5) Alex Hannum 6) Everett Case 7) Branch McCracken 8) Dean Smith 9) Senda Berenson 10) Pete Carril 11) Al McGuire 12) Arad McCutchan 13) Ernest Blood 14) Howard Cann 15) Mike Krzyzewski 16) Pat Summitt 17) Forrest "Phog" Allen 18) Alvin "Doggie" Julian 19) Margaret Wade 20) Morgan Wootten

ABOUT THE AUTHORS

JERRY KRAUSE

Jerry Krause has coached and taught basketball for over forty years and is widely recognized as a master teacher and clinician. The most prolific author in the history of basketball, he has written or edited 27 coaching books and has developed over 30 instructional videos. He is the chairman of the NABC Research Committee and former chairman of the NCAA Basketball Rules Committee.

In 1998, Krause received the prestigious NABC Cliff Wells Appreciation Award for lifetime contributions to basketball. In 2002, he was honored as NABC Guardian of the Game for Advocacy—developed a rim-testing device to equate ball rebound in every gym and from rim to rim—a 20-year research project. He has been inducted into the NAIA Basketball Coaches Hall of Fame (2000) and the National Association for Sports and Physical Education Hall of Fame as a coach and physical educator (2000). Jerry Krause currently is the Director of Basketball Operations for Gonzaga University (The Zags).

RALPH L. PIM

Ralph Pim is an associate professor in the Department of Physical Education at the United States Military Academy at West Point. He serves as the director of competitive sports.

Pim has coached and taught basketball at the secondary and collegiate levels for thirty years. As a collegiate head coach, Pim built Alma (MI) College and Limestone (SC) College into highly successful programs. His Alma teams were ranked nationally for points scored and three-point field goals, and the 1989 squad recorded the school's best overall record in forty-seven years. He also coached at Central Michigan, William and Mary, Northwestern Louisiana, and Barberton (OH) High School. Barberton won the 1976 Ohio State Championship and was selected the seventh best team in the country.

Pim spent ten years as the technical advisor for the Basketball Association of Wales. He implemented training programs to facilitate the development of basketball in the country of Wales and assisted with the training of their national teams.

Pim is the author of *Winning Basketball* and co-editor of *Coaching Basketball*. He has written numerous coaching articles and is a frequent contributor to the Naismith Basketball Hall of Fame Yearbook and Enshrinement Program.

Pim is a graduate of Springfield (MA) College. He earned his master's degree from Ohio State University and his doctorate from Northwestern Louisiana State University.

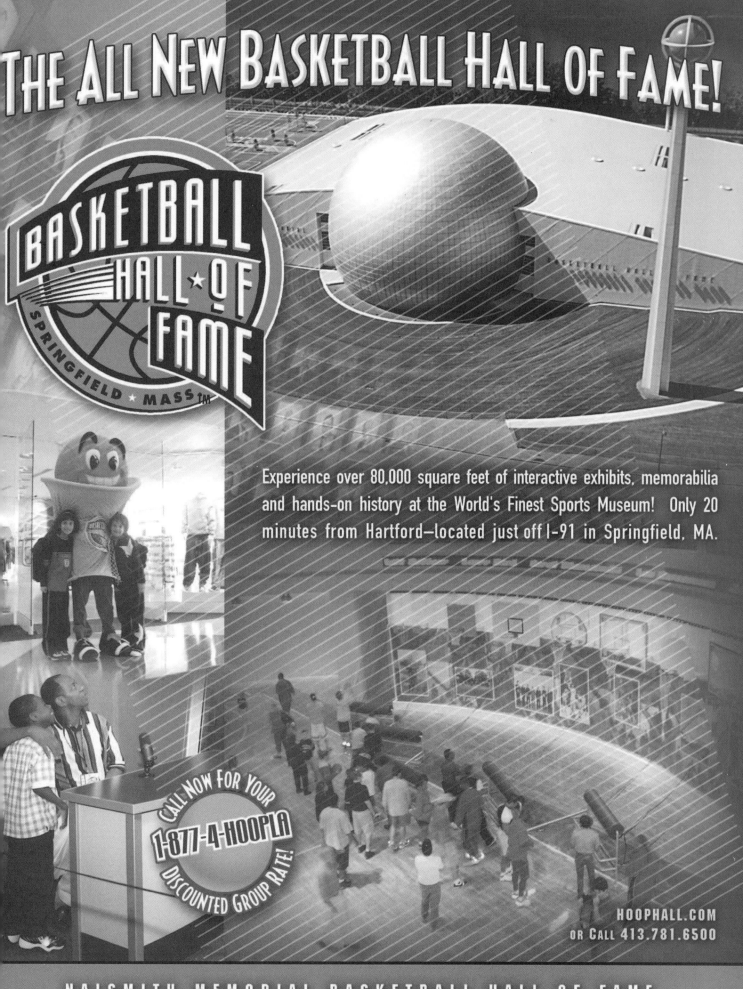